INVENTORIES

CONTROL, COSTING, AND EFFECT
UPON INCOME AND TAXES

RAYMOND A. HOFFMAN, C.P.A.
and
HENRY GUNDERS, C.P.A.

PARTNERS OF PRICE WATERHOUSE & CO.

SECOND EDITION

THE RONALD PRESS COMPANY • NEW YORK

Library of Congress Catalog Card Number: 75–128350

Preface

This book treats the entire subject of inventories and inventory accounting, with emphasis on improved methods of planning and control and effects upon income and taxes. It is a guide to the various concepts and methods applicable to inventories—covering such vital areas as forecasting and quantitative techniques, costing, the lower-of-cost-or-market rule, the retail method of computing inventories, the recognition of a flow of costs independent of the flow of goods, and various ramifications of the last-in, first-out (LIFO) principle.

Inventories represent an investment of business assets, but from the standpoint of financial liquidity, the inventory may become a dangerous burden if it is too large in relation to normal requirements. The objective of management is to achieve and maintain a proper balance between the benefits of carrying large inventories and those which result from reducing inventories to a minimum level. Various proven procedures for attaining this balance are set forth in the discussions of the subject of inventory control techniques.

During recent years there has been an increased emphasis placed upon per-share earnings, and greater attention has been given to a short-range trend. This type of financial analysis has resulted in greater importance being attached to the principles applied in allocating dollar amounts to inventories, which in turn becomes a factor in the determination of income. Consequently some of the conservative inventory practices that have long been recognized as good business are being reappraised in the light of the philosophy currently prevalent in the decisions of the issuers of securities and those trading in them.

iii

The need for adequate terminology as a prerequisite to carrying out the accounting function can hardly be overstressed. Management can grasp the significance of economic data compiled by the accountant only if the terminology used is selected with care. The concepts of "cost" and "expense" are not always applied in a meaningful manner. Adjectives and modifying phrases are usually used with both words, but the result is not completely satisfactory. With the hope that more significant terms will someday be adopted as common practice, a basis is suggested for classifying the charges entering into the determination of net income. The objective is to provide a better understanding of the computed earnings from a business activity.

Because the questions arising in assigning amounts to inventories are not restricted by geography or type of currency in use, there have been included pronouncements on the subject of inventories by The Institute of Chartered Accountants in England and Wales. The British accountants have in some ways been more painstaking than the accountants in this country in analyzing the fundamental principles involved and the alternative practices which are acceptable in income determinations.

The authors have sought and received assistance from a number of associates in Price Waterhouse & Co. Special acknowledgment is due to John B. Inglis, John G. Henderson, Michael F. Klein, Jr., Bernard Tecotzky, Jay R. Oliff, Paul Rosenfield, and Kevin G. Weis for their help in the preparation of the First Edition. Additional recognition for their contributions to the Second Edition is gratefully given to Donald R. Smith, Richard L. Forhr, and Carl H. Poedtke.

RAYMOND A. HOFFMAN
HENRY GUNDERS

October, 1970

Contents

CONTENTS

INVENTORIES

1

The Significance of Inventories in Determining Income and Taxes

Everybody does not begin his experiences in the business world selling homemade lemonade, but envisioning (or recalling) such an activity can be helpful to a discussion of the significance of inventories in the determination of income.

To the extent that the materials required for the product, that is, the lemons, sugar, and paper cups, were obtained by gift, or otherwise procured from the family kitchen without cost, no question is involved as to the amount of cash disbursed in acquiring an inventory. If the unused materials are returned and the product is all sold or consumed, there will not even be an inventory. Here the determination of the income is easy. Although a technical question could be raised about the proper accounting for the contribution from the benefactor who donated the materials, as compared with the profit realized from the sales transactions, a practical solution adequate for the purpose can usually be found for that type of problem. If materials are held overnight, however, or if some unsold product is stored in the refrigerator, an inventory question exists in even the simple situation.

1

As one goes beyond the simple venture, the question of inventories becomes increasingly important. Materials must be purchased, not just once but on a continuing basis. There will always be both materials and unsold product on hand. Furthermore, the enterprise will be managed on the assumption of an unlimited existence.

There are two distinct attributes to an inventory: the physical and the financial. The physical characteristics are factual, whereas the amount assigned to the inventory for financial reporting purposes is subjective. The inventory amount results from the exercise of judgment and the application of particular accounting procedures. An understanding of the different acceptable inventory methods is of increasing importance in dealing with the more complex business problems. However, regardless of which inventory method is used or what amount is arrived at, the true worth to the business of the articles on hand is the same.

That the physical attributes of an inventory are not affected by the dollar amount assigned to it in financial statements is not always recognized. For example, corporate executives, investment bankers, business brokers, and others have been influenced during merger negotiations by the relative "book values" of two companies, even though such book values were not comparable because of different accounting methods having been used with respect to inventories. Attempts to explain the lack of comparability have not always been successful, and *adjusted* book values have been looked upon with some misgivings because of inadequate appreciation for basic accounting concepts.

WHAT IS INVENTORY?

The word "inventory" can be used to mean several different things. It can be used to refer to the stock on hand at a particular time of raw materials, goods in process of manufacture, finished products, merchandise purchased for resale, and the like—tangible assets which can be seen, weighed, and counted. As a verb the term embraces the acts of weighing and counting the items on hand and preparing a list with appropriate descriptions. The word is also used to mean itemized lists of goods or property. In connection with financial statements and accounting records, the reference may be to the amount assigned to the stock of goods owned by an enterprise at a particular time. For present purposes, only the first and the last of these meanings need be considered.

The significance of inventories in modern business is basically attributable to the need for measuring the results of operations for a particular period, such as a month, quarter, or year. If income were being computed only for the entire existence of a business entity and there were no taxes, there would be no necessity for inventories. The income would be determined after all property had been converted into cash available for distribution to the owners.

Corporate finance has long since developed to the point of expecting a determination of periodic income for even the largest of businesses. Management needs to know the operating results on a current basis, shareholders and potential investors are interested in earnings reports from time to time, and the Internal Revenue Code provides that federal taxes on income shall be computed generally for no period longer than twelve months.

The significance of reliable inventory determinations to statements of periodic income has been emphasized by the Securities and Exchange Commission.[1] Problems have arisen particularly in situations involving the offering of securities of closely held corporations which have failed to maintain and preserve accounting records and data necessary to permit verification of financial statements.

In advance of any detailed discussion it can be observed that (a) the optimum quantity of the numerous items needed in the conduct of the business is of basic importance to the over-all profitability of the operation, (b) the amount assigned to the inventory for accounting purposes is of primary significance in the determination of income, and (c) both the quantity of the physical inventory and the amount assigned thereto can have an effect upon the assessments made against the business for property, franchise, and income taxes.

It has been found that savings equal to 15 per cent or more of the cost of excess quantities can be effected by reducing the physical volume of the inventory in some situations. If the quan-

---

[1] Accounting Series Release No. 90 (Mar. 1, 1962) reproduced as Appendix D.

tity of scrap at a foundry can be reduced 10 per cent, for example, without impairing efficiency, the business operation will be more profitable because, in addition to other factors, less storage space and a smaller amount of capital will be required.

The significance of the amount assigned to an inventory can be illustrated by the case of a retailer who purchased 1,000 novelty toys at 80¢ each and sold 950 at $1.00 before the demand slackened. A gross profit of $190 was realized from the sales. Should it be necessary to sell the remaining 50 units at 30¢ each (or for 50¢ less than cost), the gross profit realized from the entire shipment will be only $165. If a profit and loss statement is prepared when the last 50 toys are unsold, the computed profit to that date will be $190 if the amount assigned to the inventory is cost (50 at 80¢, or $40), but only $165 if the inventory amount is net realizable value (50 at 30¢, or $15). If cost is used for inventory purposes, a $25 loss will be taken into account in the period when the cut-price sales are made.

The effect upon taxes of inventory quantities and amounts has many ramifications. Ordinarily the physical volume of the inventory will have no direct effect upon taxes based upon income, and the amount assigned to the goods on hand at the end of any tax assessment period will only have the effect of accelerating or deferring the payment of taxes. Unless there is a change in the income or franchise tax rate, the aggregate tax liability will not vary because the total earnings during the life-span of a business will be the same regardless of the amount assigned to any particular inventory. Minimizing quantities on hand and assigning the proper amount to an inventory has a more direct effect upon property taxes. A property tax rate approximating 1.5 per cent is not unusual, so ownership of a $400,000 inventory rather than a $500,000 inventory may mean a direct property tax saving of approximately $1,500.

HOW MUCH INVENTORY?

Inventories enter directly in the determination of income in the sense that the amount of earnings will be less if the quantity of goods on hand and the balance among the various components are not at the most economical level. If a larger amount of capital is required to operate the business because of improper inventories, this fact will have an adverse effect on profitability, in addition to the consequence of incurring unnecessary expenses.

The expense of storing and handling materials may be substantially increased if inventories are not kept at the proper level.

Furthermore, the larger the quantity of inventory, the greater the possibility of loss as a consequence of deterioration, obsolescence, and other factors.

Income will also be indirectly affected by inventory quantities if all or some portion of certain facilities could be made available for other uses through giving more attention to the most advantageous amount of inventory to be carried.

Some of the procedures utilized to avoid inventory practices having adverse effects on income and taxes are discussed in later chapters. Decisions made by management as to when and in what quantities various required items are to be ordered will determine the number of units on hand at any particular inventory date.

A study of one company's inventories involved more than 6,000 items. With respect to a single item the annual saving from determining the most advantageous buying practice by use of a mathematical formula was approximately $1,000. The total potential savings were indeed impressive to a management which had always been conscientious about their responsibilities.

ASSIGNING AMOUNTS TO INVENTORIES

Assuming a precise enumeration of every item on hand at the inventory date is turned over to the accounting department, the next step is assigning amounts to the various inventory items.

The function of financial accounting is to reflect systematically, in terms of monetary units, the events which have occurred. This objective requires trained judgment in classifying the transactions and applying the accounting principles most appropriate under the particular circumstances. Each decision will have a bearing upon the amount to be assigned to the inventory and represent in the financial statements the aggregate of the materials, finished products, and component parts owned by the business at a particular time.

The first area of judgment pertains to the factors to be recognized as the "cost" of the units on hand. Where an item is purchased at a specific price per unit delivered at the company's plant, the question of cost is simple. If the same item is purchased f.o.b. a distant point, the question becomes somewhat more complex. After work has been performed upon the item so as to change its physical condition, there are numerous decisions involved in arriving at "cost"; and several equally acceptable answers can result from following alternative accounting procedures.

The preparation of a general statement as to what factors should be taken into account in arriving at the cost of work in process and finished goods is comparatively simple, but considerable judgment is required in applying the general statements to any particular set of circumstances. As more fully developed in Chapter 5, there is a tendency among businessmen and accountants to consider all expenditures as "costs." Although a cash expenditure or a contractual commitment is required whether an item is a "cost" or an "expense," there are comparatively few expenditures which are obviously *costs*, and it is necessary to give careful consideration to the proper categorizing of *expenses*.

After determining the number of units to be taken into account in calculating the inventory and the cost elements to be recognized, the dollar amount to be assigned to a particular inventory will still be affected by the alternative concepts as to the flow of costs. These concepts are discussed in Chapter 9, and it will be noted that the selection of the procedure to be followed need not have any relationship to the physical movement of the goods being inventoried.

AUTHORITATIVE PRONOUNCEMENTS
RELATIVE TO INVENTORIES

Before discussing the factors to be considered in determining what amounts should be used for inventory purposes in any particular type of situation, it is important to review the major authoritative statements on the subject.

Numerous articles have been published concerning various aspects of the "inventory problem," and the subject has been dealt with to some degree in books on accounting theory and practice. Few of these writings, however, specifically deal to any great extent with the matter of inventories in the determination of income. The amount assignable as "cost" to the units remaining unsold at the end of an accounting period and includable in inventories should be considered separately from a compilation of all the amounts expended in the conduct of a business which must be recovered in the proceeds of sales in order to make a profit.

Three authoritative statements on the determination of amounts to be assigned to inventories are reproduced herein as appendices and merit careful analysis:

"Inventory Pricing" by the Committee on Accounting Procedure of the American Institute of Certified Public Accountants (AICPA) published as Chapter 4 of Accounting Research Bulletin No. 43   Appendix A

"Treatment of Stock-in-Trade and Work in Progress in Financial Accounts" issued as Statement 22 by the Institute of Chartered Accountants in England and Wales   Appendix B

United States Internal Revenue Code Provisions with Respect to "Inventories" and Related Regulations   Appendix C

A comparison of these statements is helpful when applying the basic principles to a particular set of facts.

The statement by the AICPA is summarized below, with cross-references to the paragraphs in the other two statements covering the same aspect of the subject.

Paragraph in App. A		Cross-reference to related paragraphs in App. B	App. C
1	It is necessary for adequate financial accounting purposes that inventories be properly compiled periodically and recorded in the accounts.	29	1.471–1
2	Conclusions are not directed to or necessarily applicable to noncommercial businesses or to regulated utilities.	1	—
3	The term "inventory" embraces goods awaiting sale (the merchandise of a trading concern and		

*Cross-reference to
related paragraphs in
App. B   App. C*

		App. B	App. C
	the finished goods of a manufacturer), goods in the course of production (work in process), and goods to be consumed directly or indirectly in production (raw materials and supplies).	2	1.471–1
4	In accounting for the goods in the inventory at any point of time, the major objective is the matching of appropriate costs against revenues in order that there may be a proper determination of the realized income.	31	1.471–2(a)
	The inventory at any given date is the balance of costs applicable to goods on hand remaining after the matching of absorbed costs with concurrent revenues, which is appropriately carried to future periods provided it does not exceed an amount properly chargeable against the revenues expected to be obtained from ultimate disposition of the goods carried forward.	31	—
5	The primary basis of accounting for inventories is "cost," which, as applied to inventories, means in principle the sum of the applicable expenditures and charges directly or indirectly incurred in bringing an article to its existing condition and location.	4	1.471–3
	In the case of goods which have been written down below cost at the close of a fiscal period, such reduced amount is to be considered the cost for subsequent accounting purposes.	—	1.471–3(a)
	Under some circumstances, such items as idle facility expense, excessive spoilage, double freight, and rehandling costs may be so abnormal as to require treatment as current period charges rather than as a portion of the inventory cost.	9	—
	General and administrative expenses should be included as period charges, except for the portion of such expenses that may be clearly related to production.	6	1.471–3(c)
	Selling expenses constitute no part of inventory costs.	7	1.471–3(c)
	The exclusion of all overheads from inventory costs does not constitute an accepted accounting procedure.	7(a)	—
	The exercise of judgment in an individual situa-		

Para- graph in App. A		Cross-reference to related paragraphs in App. B	App. C
	tion involves a consideration of the adequacy of the procedures of the cost accounting system in use, the soundness of the principles thereof, and their consistent application.	8	1.471–2(b)
6	The cost to be matched against revenue from a sale may not be the identified cost of the specific item which is sold.	11(a)	1.471–2(d)
	Cost for inventory purposes may be determined under any one of the several assumptions as to the flow of cost factors (such as first-in, first-out; average; and last-in, first-out); the major objective in selecting a method should be to choose the one which, under the circumstances, most clearly reflects periodic income.	11, 23, and 24	1.472
	Standard costs are acceptable if adjusted at reasonable intervals to reasonably approximate costs computed under one of the recognized bases.	11(d)	—
	In some situations a reversed markup procedure of inventory pricing, such as the retail inventory method, may be both practical and appropriate.	11(e)	1.471–8
	The business operations in some cases may be such as to make it desirable to apply one of the acceptable methods of determining cost to one portion of the inventory or components thereof and another of the acceptable methods to other portions of the inventory.	11	1.471–2(d)
7	Although selection of the method should be made on the basis of the individual circumstances, financial statements will be more useful if uniform methods of inventory pricing are adopted by all companies within a given industry.	32	—
8	Cost is satisfactory only if the utility of the goods has not diminished since their acquisition; a loss of utility by damage, deterioration, obsolescence, changes in price levels, or other causes is to be reflected as a charge against the revenues of the period in which it occurs.	12	1.471–2(c)
9	As used in the phrase "lower of cost or market" the term "market" means current replacement cost (by purchase or by reproduction, as the case may be) except that (1) market should not exceed the net realizable value (i.e., esti-		

mated selling price in the ordinary course of
business less reasonably predictable costs of
completion and disposal) and (2) market
should not be less than net realizable value
reduced by an allowance for an approximately
normal profit margin.   34   1.471–4(a)

10   Because of the many variations of circumstances
encountered in inventory pricing, the statement relative to the meaning of the term
"market" is intended as a guide rather than a
literal rule and should be realistically applied,
with due regard to the form, content, and
composition of the inventory.   25(a)   —

If a business is expected to lose money for a sustained period, the inventory should not be
written down to offset a loss inherent in the
subsequent operations.   —   —

11   The most common practice is to apply the
"lower of cost or market" rule separately to
each item of the inventory; however, if there
is only one end-product category, the inventory in its entirety may have the greatest
significance.   12   1.471–4(c)

Where more than one major product or operational category exists, the application of the
rule to the total of the items included in such
major categories may result in the most useful
determination of income.   35   —

12   When no loss of income is expected to take
place as a result of a reduction of cost prices
of certain goods because others forming components of the same general categories of
finished products have a market equally in
excess of cost, such components need not be
adjusted to market to the extent that they are
in balanced quantities, provided the procedure
is applied consistently from year to year.   12   —

13   To the extent the stocks of particular materials
orc omponents are excessive in relation to
others, the procedure of applying the "lower
of cost or market" rule to the individual items
constituting the excess should be followed.   35   —

14   When substantial and unusual losses result from
the application of the "lower of cost or mar-

Para-graph in App. A		*Cross-reference to related paragraphs in*
		App. B *App. C*
	ket" rule, it will frequently be desirable to disclose the amount of the loss in the income statement.	— —
15	The basis of stating inventories must be consistently applied and should be disclosed in the financial statements; whenever a significant change is made therein, there should be disclosure of the nature of the change and, if material, the effect on income.	33 1.471–2(d)
16	It is generally recognized that income accrues only at the time of sale, and that gains may not be anticipated by reflecting assets at their current sales prices.	30 1.471–5 and 6
	Inventories of gold and silver, when there is an effective government-controlled market at a fixed monetary value, are ordinarily reflected at selling prices, and a similar treatment is not uncommon for inventories representing agricultural, mineral, and other products, units of which are interchangeable and have an immediate marketability at quoted prices and for which appropriate costs may be difficult to obtain.	20 and 21 —
	When inventories are stated at sales prices, they should be reduced by expenditures to be incurred in disposal, and the use of such basis should be fully disclosed.	20 and 21 1.471–4(b)
17	The recognition in a current period of losses arising from the decline in the utility of cost expenditures is equally applicable to similar losses which are expected to arise from firm, uncancelable, and unhedged commitments for the future purchase of inventory items.	37 —

As noted at the end of Appendix A, even the general statements on inventory pricing summarized above were not adopted unanimously and without reservation by the Committee on Accounting Procedure of the AICPA. The fact that it was not possible to obtain complete agreement among the twenty members of the committee is an indication of a lack of agreement among businessmen and accountants as a whole.

The pronouncements by the AICPA Committee are not followed literally by all members of the Institute. The authority of opinions expressed by the committee rests upon their general acceptability. The committee itself recognized that in extraordinary cases, fair presentation and justice to all parties at interest may require exceptional treatment. The philosophy of the Institute is that the burden of justifying departure from accepted procedures, to the extent that they are evidenced by committee opinions, must be assumed by those who adopt another treatment.

It is also important that the committee contemplated that its opinions would have application only to items material and significant in relative circumstances. Items of little or no consequence may be dealt with as expediency may suggest; however, freedom to deal expediently with immaterial items is not intended to extend to a group of items when its cumulative effect in any one financial statement may be material and significant.

PRINCIPAL DIFFERENCES BETWEEN
AICPA AND OTHER AUTHORITIES

The pronouncements by the Council of the Institute of Chartered Accountants and by the Treasury Department include observations commenting on several subjects which are not covered in the statement by the Committee on Accounting Procedure of the AICPA. The additional paragraphs generally pertain to details of procedure rather than principles. In general the three statements are in basic agreement. Among the conflicting observations are a few which are deemed to be particularly significant.

Statement by Institute of Chartered Accountants

1. Paragraphs 4 to 10, 26, and 34(a) permit prime costing (exclusion of all overhead expenditures from inventory costs) where appropriate.

2. Paragraph 11 does not list LIFO (last-in, first-out) among the "principal methods," and paragraph 24 refers to its use in "some overseas countries"; therefore, while the inference is that LIFO is not recognized for use in the United Kingdom, paragraph 25(b) implies that it is acceptable for use in those countries where it is a recognized practice if there is an appropriate description in the accounts.

3. Paragraphs 12 to 19 describe the conditions and methods for reducing an inventory to an amount less than cost; and paragraph 32 emphasizes that in most businesses there is a choice between writing off any excess of cost over either (*a*) the net realizable value of the stock or (*b*) the lower of net realizable value and replacement price.

4. Paragraphs 25 and 36 state that the term "market value" is not sufficiently descriptive in published reports, and recommended descriptions to use in its place are given.

Federal Income Tax Regulations

1. Section 1.471–1 provides that the rules with respect to inventories, for federal income tax purposes, shall be applied to raw materials and supplies only to the extent that they have been acquired for sale or will physically become a part of the merchandise intended for sale (e.g., kegs, bottles, and cases), if title thereto will pass to the purchaser of the product to be sold therein.

2. Section 1.471–4(c) states that where the inventory is valued upon the basis of cost or market whichever is lower, the market value of each article on hand at the inventory date shall be compared with the cost of the article, and the lower of such values shall be taken as the inventory value of the article. There is no specific recognition of the alternative of comparing the cost with the value of the inventory as a whole or the aggregate of complementary inventory items.

3. There is no provision in the income tax regulations for a deduction based upon an anticipated loss to be incurred as a consequence of outstanding purchase commitments.

4. Section 472(b) (2) of the Internal Revenue Code stipulates that goods with respect to which LIFO is used shall be inventoried "at cost," and Section 1.472–2(b) of the regulations expands the requirement by stating that the inventory "shall be taken at cost regardless of market value."

Section 1.472–2(e) of the regulations provides that the taxpayer's use of market value in lieu of LIFO cost is not considered at variance with the requirement in the Internal Revenue Code that no method other than LIFO be used in ascertaining income, profit, or loss, in statements issued for credit purposes or in reporting to owners of the business. The amount of the writedown to market, however, will not be recognized as a deduction in computing taxable income.

HOW EXACT IS AN INVENTORY?

It must be recognized that with respect to an inventory of any magnitude there is always considerable probability of error in the determination of physical quantities. Errors in counting and the compilation of basic data are reflected in the final determination; but, if the inventory taking is performed with reasonable care, the effect of these errors is generally not material. Significant errors are usually detected in the normal accounting review and auditing procedures. Undetected minor errors can be expected to cause overstatements of the inventory as well as understatements, tending to offset one another.

In view of the probability of human error and the need for judgment in the handling of numerous details, it must be readily admitted that the amount assigned to any particular inventory is not beyond question. The absence of preciseness, however, should not be overemphasized. In the determination of business income for a stated period, judgment is exercised with respect to a large number of factors. The determination of depreciation is probably the outstanding example of a factor governed by rough approximations and the selection of a particular accounting procedure. Similarly, estimates are made of liabilities under product warranties and many other obligations arising out of current transactions.

A financial statement can do no more than present fairly the results of operations for the stated period. For any particular item, including the inventory, the determination will be made through the exercise of the best judgment possible, but it is not realistic to take every item as being precisely determined.

EFFECT UPON INCOME OF
ALTERNATIVE INVENTORY AMOUNTS

An admission that mechanical errors occur in the computation of an inventory and that the amount assigned to it will depend upon the exercise of judgment in selecting from equally acceptable accounting procedures does not imply that the computed net income fails to reflect fairly the results of the business operations.

Whether the use of a different inventory amount would have a material and significant effect on income depends upon (*a*) consistency between the opening and closing inventories for the period, (*b*) the relationship between the sales proceeds and the sum of the cost of goods sold plus expenses, and (*c*) the rate of inventory turnover.

Each of the authoritative pronouncements commented upon stresses consistency. Selected sentences provide a basis for comparison, but they are not the only statements emphasizing the importance of consistency.

Comparison of Statements on Consistency

American Institute	Institute of Chartered Accountants	Federal Income Tax Regulations
While the basis of stating inventories does not affect the over-all gain or loss on the ultimate disposition of inventory items, any inconsistency in the selection or employment of a basis may improperly affect the periodic amounts of income or loss. [Par. 15.]	The basis adopted and the methods of computation should be used consistently from period to period. A change of basis or method should not normally be made unless the circumstances have changed in such a way that its continued use would prevent the accounts from showing a true and fair view of the position and results. [Par. 33.]	In order clearly to reflect income, the inventory practice of a taxpayer should be consistent from year to year, and greater weight is to be given to consistency than to any particular method of inventorying or basis of valuation . . . [§1.471–2(b).]

The importance of consistency is obvious when one realizes the net income for a stated period would be unchanged if the use of a particular inventory method, as compared with another, would merely increase both the opening and closing inventories by an identical amount.

Whether a company makes electrical appliances, cosmetics, food stuffs, or any other line of products or merely purchases merchandise for resale, the importance of consistency can be illustrated by the use of a hypothetical example in which it is assumed that the amount assigned to the inventory will be 10 per cent higher under inventory method B than it would be under method A.

	Assuming opening and closing inventory quantities are the same			
	Inventory method A		Inventory method B	
Sales.....................................		$9,000		$9,000
Cost of goods sold:				
Opening inventory....................	$1,000		$1,100	
Incurred costs.......................	6,000		6,000	
	$7,000		$7,100	
Closing inventory....................	1,000	6,000	1,100	6,000
		$3,000		$3,000
Incurred expenses......................		2,000		2,000
Net income............................		$1,000		$1,000

Had the closing inventory actually contained 20 per cent more units than the opening inventory or been assigned an amount of $1,200 for any other reason, consistent application of the two hypothetical methods would result in the following comparison:

	Assuming closing inventory is larger than opening inventory			
	Inventory method A		Inventory method B	
Sales.................................		$9,000		$9,000
Cost of goods sold:				
Opening inventory....................	$1,000		$1,100	
Incurred costs.......................	6,200		6,200	
	$7,200		$7,300	
Closing inventory....................	1,200	6,000	1,320	5,980
		$3,000		$3,020
Incurred expenses......................		2,000		2,000
Net income............................		$1,000		$1,020

This illustrates that where an inventory method is applied consistently, the effect on net income as a consequence of the use of one method compared with another will be limited to the effect of the second method on only the net increase (or decrease) in the closing inventory. The inventory under method A increased $200 because of that amount of additional costs having been incurred during the period; therefore, the net income under method B is $20 more—10 per cent of $200.

If the opening and closing inventories are not determined by the consistent application of one or the other of the methods, the distortion in the computed net income is apparent. Either of the amounts of $1,000 or $1,020 could reflect fairly the results of the business operations, but under the assumed circumstances neither $1,120 nor $900 would meet the requirements of the AICPA, the Institute of Chartered Accountants, or the United States Treasury Department.

	Assuming a change in inventory method			
	From method A to method B		From method B to method A	
Sales...............................		$9,000		$9,000
Cost of goods sold:				
Opening inventory....................	$1,000		$1,100	
Incurred costs.......................	6,200		6,200	
	$7,200		$7,300	
Closing inventory....................	1,320	5,880	1,200	6,100
		$3,120		$2,900
Incurred expenses.....................		2,000		2,000
Net income...........................		$1,120		$ 900

The fact that the relationship between the sales proceeds and the sum of the cost of goods sold plus expenses has a bearing upon whether a different inventory amount would have a material and significant effect on income can also be illustrated by continuing the simplified example. Where the goods have been sold for $9,000, the use of inventory method B has the effect of increasing the computed net income only 2 per cent, that is, the net income is $1,020 rather than $1,000. In the case of a business

	Effect of profit margin			
	Inventory method A		Inventory method B	
Sales...............................	$9,000	$8,100	$9,000	$8,100
Cost of goods sold....................	6,000	6,000	5,980	5,980
	$3,000	$2,100	$3,020	$2,120
Incurred expenses.....................	2,000	2,000	2,000	2,000
Net income...........................	$1,000	$ 100	$1,020	$ 120

selling goods acquired at a similar cost for only $8,100, the choice of inventory methods can increase net income 20 per cent, $120 compared with $100.

The greater the net income (the excess of sales proceeds over the sum of the cost of goods sold plus the expenses incurred), the less significant is the difference in the amounts which may be assigned to the inventory. This is true whether the difference results from mechanical errors or a management decision as to accounting procedures.

A simplified example is also helpful to illustrate that the rate of inventory turnover is a factor in determining whether a different inventory amount would have a material and significant effect on income. The computations of net income on page 16 assume an inventory turnover of approximately six times during the period. Had the inventory quantities been twice as large so that the rate of turnover was only three times, the choice of inventory method would be of greater significance. The fact that the choice of inventory method could affect the computed net income by 4 per cent does not preclude either of the amounts of $1,000 or $1,040 reflecting fairly the results of the business operations; however, the lower rate of inventory turnover has doubled the impact of the decision.

	Effect of inventory turnover			
	Inventory method A		Inventory method B	
Sales.................................		$9,000		$9,000
Cost of goods sold:				
Opening inventory....................	$2,000		$2,200	
Incurred costs........................	6,400		6,400	
	$8,400		$8,600	
Closing inventory.....................	2,400	6,000	2,640	5,960
		$3,000		$3,040
Incurred expenses......................		2,000		2,000
Net income............................		$1,000		$1,040

On the basis of the foregoing it can be stated that among the factors having a bearing on how inventories enter into the determination of income and taxes are:

1. Exercise of sound business judgment in the maintenance of physical inventory quantities at the proper levels.
2. Analysis of all elements of "cost" and "expense" to determine the proper amount to be recognized as expenditures to be assigned to the goods on hand and charged against future revenue to be realized upon their ultimate sale.
3. Determination of need to write down the inventory below cost because of a lower replacement price for certain items or in recognition of net realizable values.
4. Selection of alternative accounting concepts as to the flow of costs.

All these factors involve managerial decisions, and a detailed discussion of each is contained in subsequent chapters.

2

The Functions of Inventories
in the Business Enterprise

Every business carries some form of inventory. In terms of the retailer, a can of peas on a grocer's shelf is a form of finished goods inventory. In terms of the manufacturer, sheet steel in a stamping plant is a raw materials inventory. Both are examples of tangible items, requiring systems for planning and for control. Financial resources are employed to acquire and support these inventories. Ongoing expenditures are required to maintain inventories in stock.

Why do inventories exist? The primary reason for the existence of inventories is to permit an enterprise to meet the demands of the consumer, on a sufficiently timely basis to satisfy the needs of distribution and use. The competitive nature of the marketplace in which the seller operates dictates this need. Since a shopper would not be willing to wait a day or two for a can of peas from a given store (assuming that virtually the same product is available from convenient competitive sources), the grocer must have the product on hand when it is demanded, or face the consequences of a lost sale. In the same way, raw materials, purchased or manufactured parts and subassemblies must be available when required. Lack of inventories causes production shutdowns, and leads ultimately to shortages or stock-outs at subsequent levels of consumption.

Modern production methods frequently make lot-type production necessary, from an economic standpoint as well as for ease of scheduling. Inventories resulting from this type of production program, and their associated expenses of maintenance, must be balanced against the economic advantages offered from lower machine setup costs, improved efficiencies, and lower administrative expenses. In some cases, the savings offered, resulting from increased procurement quantity, (through freight rate breaks, quantity discounts, etc.) may well be greater than the expense of maintaining such higher quantities of inventories. In short, the test of effectiveness with which management controls inventories rests on its ability to plan for and maintain the most advantageous economic balance of many economic factors bearing on inventories; several of these are, by nature, opposing factors, and the most effective interaction of all of them is the goal of inventory control.

In industries where demand is not constant throughout the year, inventories are used as a means of leveling production and stabilizing the work force. Consider the case of a manufacturer whose product is consumed only six months of each year. If the company were to produce only during the period of consumption, it could be faced with numerous problems including idle facilities, the need for a facility capable of producing for peak demand, and a highly transient labor force. Through intelligent utilization of inventories, such a business can stabilize its operations and work toward optimizing its investment in inventories.

SCOPE OF INVENTORY MANAGEMENT

It is not uncommon to hear a businessman say, "Inventories are a major problem in our company." This is more likely to be a statement of effect, rather than of cause. Often the real cause of the problem is not inventories per se, but the lack of effective inventory management.

The most important concept associated with inventory management is that effective control results only from the proper *interaction* among various systems and subsystems within a company. By its nature, inventory management is the arbitrator between diametrically opposing forces. It is, therefore, important that the scope of inventory management be sufficiently comprehensive to consider all of these forces.

To attain its objectives, a business must meet the needs of the consumer. Normally the marketing or sales organization is made responsible for preparation of a short-range sales forecast. This forecasting "subsystem" triggers procurement and production subsystems, initiating activity aimed at meeting consumer needs. Changes in projected demand must also be communicated so that plans throughout the organization can be adjusted. This is a basic interaction among functional areas which must be handled effectively by any modern inventory management system.

While striving to meet corporate objectives, departments within a company may follow radically differing policies. This may come about because the particular functions performed by a department tend to shape that department's motivation. Thus, the sales area may desire large amounts of stock in reserve to meet virtually any possible sales demand, while financial management may take the stand that minimum inventory levels are desirable so as to make available additional capital for other purposes. The resolution of such conflicts can be effected best by developing rules for desired levels of service. By determining an acceptable out-of-stock rate through weighing factors such as the cost of lost sales, demand variability, and replenishment cycle variability, an optimum balance can be reached. This balance can further be tempered by executive opinion. Such a system allows management to assume an active role in controlling a vital phase of operations.

Inventory decisions have impact in most areas of an organization. A decision to purchase a year's supply of all items would minimize the number of purchase orders placed, as well as associated paperwork expense, but would result in the commitment of substantial financial resources, and would normally exceed the storage facilities available. Conversely, purchasing one day's supply at a time would result in an excessive amount of paperwork and related administrative expense. Either decision would reveal failure on the part of management to understand the interrelationship and interaction of these functions operating within most business enterprises.

In the previous example, a physical interaction was discussed. There is also an economic interaction of functions in considering various expenses associated with inventory.

Inventory carrying expenditures include a number of classes of items, e.g., the cost of capital, taxes, handling expenses in stores, and storage expenses. The expenses associated with procurement include purchasing and ordering expenses, production control expenses, machine setup costs, and receiving expenses.

There is a continuing need to find a means of balancing physical, organizational and economic factors. The objective of any inventory management system is to arrive at the most effective compromise possible among these interrelated and interacting forces.

To illustrate this point, the figure on page 25 shows a hypothetical control network in a typical manufacturing company. The interaction of physical flow, operating controls, and financial controls can be readily recognized. For example, the activities of "customers" (or the marketplace) are analyzed and translated into forecasts by the marketing function of the company. This forecast is introduced into the financial control system through the budgetary subsystem, and into the operating area by means of the inventory control system. The operation of this system activates the physical procurement and production system. As illustrated, numerous interactions of this nature occur perpetually.

The inventory management system is, thus, a modular entity composed of a number of subsystems. Each subsystem is designed to meet the needs of a specific inventory area; in turn, these subsystems are interrelated and interacting. The entire network comprising the system can be best understood if each subsystem is first isolated and examined as if it were an independent system.

The inventory management system is shown on page 24 as a network of typical subsystems with common communications terminals. Each subsystem is linked to every other subsystem. The number of subsystems is determined by the areas of service required. The subsystems selected in the illustration are for illustrative purposes only.

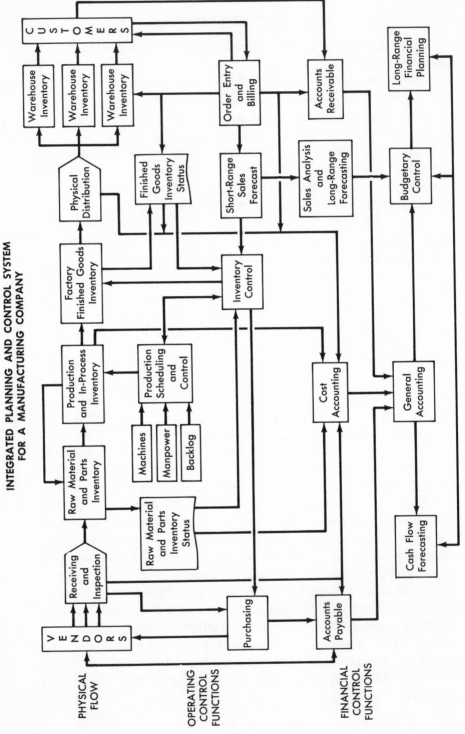

INTEGRATED PLANNING AND CONTROL SYSTEM FOR A MANUFACTURING COMPANY

24

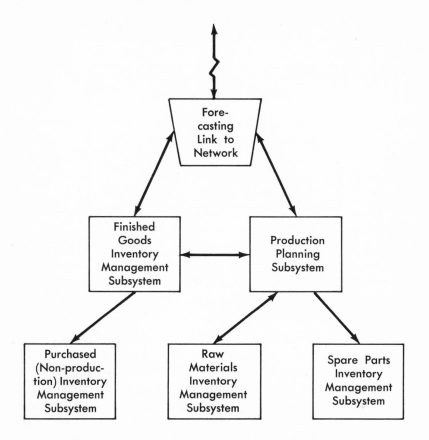

To examine the system in action, assume that a forecast is received and processed by the finished goods inventory management subsystem. If a manufacturing requirement is generated, it will be communicated to the production planning subsystem. This subsystem will determine when the item will be produced. If the decision modifies the finished goods inventory plan, it is communicated to the finished goods inventory management subsystem. The production planning subsystem then activates the spare parts, purchased goods, and raw materials inventory management subsystems. Through interaction of these subsystems, effective inventory management takes place.

By realizing that inventory control is a part of a hierarchy of systems within a company and, in turn, is composed of modular interacting subsystems, a satisfactory conceptualization of the operation and role of inventory management can be achieved.

RELATIONSHIP OF INVENTORY MANAGEMENT TO OTHER AREAS OF THE BUSINESS

In the previous section the relationships of inventory management to various broad functional areas (i.e., marketing, manufacturing, finance) was briefly discussed. Inventory management specifically affects the operations of numerous areas of a business. The purpose of this section is to discuss some of these relationships, and to highlight the departmental (or functional) goals involved in each. A complete understanding of the interaction of the various forces set in motion by such departmental objectives is a necessary prerequisite before the systems designer can establish the scope and approach that will best meet the needs of effective inventory management.

OBJECTIVES OF PRODUCT DESIGN AND ENGINEERING

There is a clear relationship between product design and inventory management. For example, if a product design change is contemplated, the lead time for its implementation should consider the inventory position of the item to be obsoleted. The "effectivity date" of an engineering change is thus of importance to the inventory management function. If an engineering change must be made immediately, the scrapping of existing inventories or the cost of modifying those inventories becomes part of the cost of the design change. Inventory policies may also have to be adjusted in the light of planned product design changes to minimize losses which might be incurred if disposal of large amounts of old models must take place after introduction of a new design.

Engineering can play a significant role in improving the management of and reducing the levels of inventories. Concerted efforts to design products with standardized parts and components have resulted in reduction in total inventories, since standardization makes it possible to draw production requirements from fewer inventoried items. In some areas, the application of value analysis techniques has led to simplifications in products or in component parts which have, in turn, contributed to standard component usage.

OBJECTIVES OF MARKETING

Marketing management is usually concerned that adequate inventories are maintained to fill customer orders and at locations that make possible a level of service at least equivalent to that of competitors. Marketing management has good reasons for pursuing a policy of high inventories. Customer relations and marketing effectiveness usually suffer when finished goods are not available to meet customer demands. Outright loss of orders, and even of customers, may be the consequence. Also, substantial clerical and distribution expenses are usually incurred as a result of back orders, which affect the profitability of the sale.

The immediate costs of customer dissatisfaction are easily measured in businesses where the customer must have immediate service and, failing to get it, goes to a competitor. The costs of that dissatisfaction are simply the profits which would have resulted from the unfilled order. The measure of an out-of-stock condition is complicated, however, when the customer becomes so dissatisfied as to never return to the company with future orders. In this case, the long-range costs become all the profits foregone from that lost customer—a difficult calculation. Dissatisfaction cost is also hard to determine in cases where the customer is willing to wait for the back order to be filled, but where repeated impositions of this nature may eventually drive him to the competition.

The costs of processing and expediting back orders are also determinable to the extent that certain employees would not have to be employed if back orders ceased to occur.

Thus, the communications link between marketing and the inventory management system is important in any business. Sales forecasting interrelationships with this system have been briefly discussed, as have the impacts of inventory management on levels of customer service. The inventory management-marketing link must also be used to communicate special needs, such as promotions, and "one-time" sales of sizeable proportions. The inventory management system also provides marketing with sales management tools in the form of reports on items moving more slowly than forecasted, developing level of service information, disclosing back-order or lost-order trends, and highlighting items for possible elimination from the line. This communication link is also used in measuring the impact of marketing decisions on existing inventories and on the production plan.

OBJECTIVES OF PRODUCTION

Manufacturing management generally prefers to have raw materials inventories at high levels. A production department can ordinarily conduct its operations most efficiently, and at lowest cost, by scheduling lengthy production runs, which build up substantial inventory levels. Long production runs reduce the amount of idle machine time used for setups between runs. For each new production run, workers must be reoriented to the manufacturing procedures; fewer changes in production will generally result in higher quality production as well as higher work rates. Tooling changes can be reduced, and associated costs minimized. If manufacturing management adheres to a policy of long production runs, however, inventories at all stages stand to be substantially increased. The utilization of labor, supervision, and physical facilities can also be increased through the elimination of idle time caused by raw material shortages. The job of production scheduling can be greatly facilitated if adequate supplies of raw materials can be assured. Both of these factors tend to create pressure in the direction of maintaining substantial levels of inventories.

The economic effects on inventories of manufacturing decisions (as related to number of setups, economic production lot sizes, etc.) can usually be ascertained from time and rate standards established by industrial engineers. From these standards, the costs of each setup can be ascertained. A major difficulty in cost determination comes in attempting to establish costs incurred by a material or in-process stockout which causes a manufacturing delay or shutdown. Such costs are substantial in situations where the labor force is assured a daily or weekly wage; in this case, the out-of-stock expenses are equal to the wages paid for such non-productive labor.

Manufacturing management has as its principal objective the manufacture of specified products for the least cost. One way in which manufacturing management can reduce its costs is to allow a substantial buildup in levels of inventory, at all stages (raw materials, in-process, and finished stocks). The costs to manufacturing of having to tolerate inventory levels which are not high enough for flexibility in scheduling can be calculated if appropriate standards are established by engineering. Without these standards, considerable analytical work is requisite for cost determination.

The operations of the manufacturing area can, in a very real sense, be predicated on the prior plans developed by the inventory management system. The planned labor requirements, and the plant and machine loading for each period, can be a direct result of the inventory plan. From these plans, various technical support areas, such as manufacturing engineering and quality control, can then develop plans for utilization of their respective resources. The activities of production scheduling and of short-term facility loading—important parts of the manufacturing function—are thus products of the short-range outputs of the inventory management system.

OBJECTIVES OF PURCHASING

Purchasing management is similar to manufacturing management in that the achievement of purchasing objectives also tends to increase inventory levels. In order to minimize the expense of the purchasing activity, a few large orders of materials and supplies are preferable to frequent orders of smaller amounts. Not only are clerical salaries in the purchasing department reduced by this policy, but substantial savings can be realized through quantity discounts.

There are three main classes of expense which will be incurred in the purchasing area if inventory levels must be maintained at less than desirable levels. Savings are foregone if quantity discounts cannot be realized; with a high number of orders for

supplies and materials, salaries for additional purchasing clerks
or agents will be incurred; and when stockouts occur in
supplies and materials inventories, high-cost transportation
methods may have to be utilized and additional employees
required for "expediting."

The costs of foregone discounts must be measured for each
individual supply or raw material according to the current purchasing schedules of the respective vendors. However, ordering
and expediting expenses are measured in terms of increased or
decreased salaries and fringe benefits for ordering and expediting
personnel.

The procurement procedures and policies of a company have
substantial impact on inventory management. Proper follow-up
by the purchasing group will contribute to better inventory management, by reducing excessive variability of replenishment cycles.
Efforts by this same group to reduce the length and variability of
replenishment cycles through development of better communications facilities, and by developing alternative sources of supply
also contribute to better inventory management. A properly designed inventory management system will also allow for optimum
utilization of quantity and/or joint procurement discounts, perhaps
utilizing a "blanket" purchase agreement supported by specific
release schedules.

Under special conditions, the procurement function may have
to initiate action to purchase materials—such as under conditions
of impending shortages, major price increases, or strikes. These
actions are properly taken in conjunction with the inventory management function to insure that good communications exist, as
well as to obtain desirable economic results.

OBJECTIVES OF WAREHOUSING AND DISTRIBUTION

There is also an interdependence between the inventory management system and an organization's system of distribution. The
number of warehouses, their geographical interrelationship, and
the level of service to be maintained at each location substantially
affect inventory levels, particularly as related to reserves or safety
stocks. Physical storage facilities can limit ordering quantities just
as special storage requirements influence inventory policy. In

cases of products being produced at more than one location, and which are to be stocked at several warehouses, the inventory management system must be designed to cope with special distribution problems. Transportation time also has a direct effect on inventory levels in some circumstances.

The expense of storing and warehousing inventories is usually proportional to inventory levels. The managements of warehouses and stockrooms, being concerned with minimizing the expense of their respective operations, would like to see general inventory levels reduced.

Generally speaking, high inventory levels increase the risk of stocks becoming obsolete—a condition where the value of inventory stocks deteriorates because of normal loss of usefulness in manufacturing, loss of saleability in the market, or by reason of physical deterioration. Because some items in inventory are more vulnerable to obsolescence than others, the assignment of an obsolescence charge should be done either individually, or according to fairly narrow categories of items. Inasmuch as obsolescence is usually not a certainty, but rather an estimate of risk of uncertain probabilities, it is necessary to estimate the length of time inventories will continue to be useful and, when obsolete, their residual dollar values. When inventories contain items which are highly perishable (either because of their physical nature or because of styling changes) the loss from obsolescence can become significant.

Inventory handling can also be expensive. Handling includes all the physical activities requisite to stockroom and warehouse operations. The expense is usually measured in terms of wages paid for personnel involved in physical handling as well as in clerical and accounting functions. To measure these expenses it is necessary to ascertain the labor actually required or saved by altering inventory levels.

The most significant warehousing cost is that for the rental of, or investment in, storage space. It is usually possible to determine what level of inventory increase would make construction or leasing of additional warehouse space necessary, thereby incurring capital investment, or a rental charge. However, storage space charges tend to change only when fairly large amounts of inventory changes are involved, with the exception of certain types of public warehousing.

OBJECTIVES OF LABOR RELATIONS

The job of labor management is eased considerably when a company's employment level does not change; however, the demand for finished products often fluctuates. The only way to maintain a uniform level of employment is to manufacture for inventory, thus creating a buffer intended to prevent major fluctuations in demand rates from directly affecting production rates and related manning levels. This of course increases inventory levels. The effect of avoiding fluctuations in production can be measured in terms of personnel expenses in the industrial relations and employment departments, and in actual outlays for severance pay, workmen's compensation, and—in severe cases—labor negotiations. It should also take into account the effect on unit labor costs of operating with fluctuating employment levels.

OBJECTIVES OF FINANCIAL MANAGEMENT

The financial management function is concerned with the creation of financial planning and control systems aimed at providing the greatest possible return on assets invested. One major element of any company's assets is usually represented by inventories. The return generated from that asset is a dual function, composed first of the amount of capital invested in inventories and its related turnover and, second, of the measure of profitability.

It may be said that financial management can serve its function best by acting to evaluate the relationships, quantify the amounts and interrelate the objectives of all business functions—as they affect and are affected by inventories—so that a "best economic balance" is created. The creation of this balance is the purpose of inventory planning and control systems.

In a sense, the financial function has an obligation to act as an arbitrator between the forces set in motion by the various departmental objectives noted earlier. The correct response of financial management is to seek to develop systems that result in the best economic balance, rather than to exert pressure to force inventories to an arbitrarily low level. Financial management must recognize that, while a low inventory level will raise the return on the investment carried, this is true only if profit levels are considered to be unaffected no matter how low the inventory level is set. This assumption tends to be incorrect, because profitability of operations is materially affected by the respective expenses of acquiring versus carrying inventories.

Financial management is also affected by inventory management in planning for and obtaining funds to meet capital requirements. The sales forecast and the related production plan, considered together with inventory plans, can be stated in financial terms to measure their influence on working capital and cash requirements. Utilization of all these provides financial management with tools to measure performance and project capital needs. The inventory management system also provides the financial manager with information for use if and when attractive opportunities for alternative uses of capital are available.

IMPACT OF DATA PROCESSING ON INVENTORY MANAGEMENT

In the past, the existence of large numbers of inventoried items, and of numerous transactions, presented formidable obstacles to the application of effective inventory management concepts and techniques. The advent of electronic data processing has made it possible to deal with these obstacles in a more effective manner. The speed, versatility, and logical powers of computers available today, coupled with effective systems design, provide the tools necessary for minimizing problems associated with managing a large number of inventory items and a substantial volume of transactions, while making it possible to consider specific individual characteristics of items that must be recognized in the inventory management system.

Lack of appropriate "exception-type" information at the proper time has been a constant managerial complaint, particularly associated with inventories. The information system supporting inventory management can be designed to provide the information required on a timely basis. This can be most effectively explained through some examples.

Inventory management is predicated upon forecasts of usage. The first advantage an automated system offers is the ability to develop and adjust forecasted usage, as required, based on the latest information available. *Adjusted* forecasts can then be employed to modify inventory management factors, employing computer techniques.

The system can also be designed to produce valuable exception reports on a timely basis. This technique can be applied to control situations involving items such as critical spare parts, to report when supplies fall below certain levels, or when past-due order conditions exist.

Use of data processing capabilities in conjunction with a properly designed inventory management system allows routine decision rules to be programmed, and subsequent decisions to be made by routinely applying these rules. Such a system insures prompt and complete review of items when they reach predetermined levels, calculation of order quantities based on given formulae, and, in some cases, direct placement of purchase orders by computer methods, all within a framework responsive to changing trends in demand rates, or in the lead time required to purchase or manufacture required items.

The use of data processing equipment not only makes possible the performance of highly integrated systems functions, which could be economically prohibitive to perform manually, but often permits reductions in existing clerical work forces through minimizing or eliminating manual records. Properly designed and controlled computer systems can also be expected to result in improved accuracy of inventory records.

Through the use of electronic data processing, management is able to evaluate potential policies—using simulation processes—and to insure that decisions are effectively implemented. The combination of the power of the computer with the integration of forecasting and inventory management techniques also makes possible the employment of the most refined management science techniques—using advanced mathematics and statistics—where and when they are required.

The basic management science techniques generally employed are not new. It is, rather, the ability to perform the required calculations at an acceptable speed that is provided by the computer.

3

Planning and Forecasting
as Related to Inventory
Management

The functions of forecasting and operational planning are two of the more important responsibilities of management. This is particularly true in connection with inventory management. Although they can be analyzed separately, the forecasting and operational planning functions are so closely interrelated that it is sometimes difficult to determine where one ends and the other one starts. In effect, every operational plan is based on a forecast of some type. Sometimes the forecast is a sophisticated analysis and prediction of future conditions; in other cases, the forecast is based on the intuitive judgment of the individuals preparing the plan, and is often not recognized as a forecast per se.

The term "forecast," in the context used here, refers to the prediction of future market demand, whereas operational planning may be defined as the means of attaining specific operating objectives established by management. Looking at planning and forecasting as two separate activities, forecasting would consider, among other factors, the external factors in the market over which the company has limited control. Operational planning, on the

other hand, would consider those factors that the internal operations and decision processes of the company can control. There
is, of course, a mix of planning and forecasting where the internal
decisions of a company affect external factors, such as future
market demand patterns. For example, the decision by a company to introduce a new product would be part of the internal
planning function; however, this decision will influence future
market demand for the new product, as well as for related and
competitive products. The conclusion to be drawn is that many
so-called external factors associated with forecasting can be influenced by internal planning decisions, especially over the longer
term.

In this chapter are reviewed the nature and types of planning,
as related to inventory management. This is followed by a review
of forecasting as it relates to these plans, and some of the forecasting techniques that can be used to improve the effectiveness of
an inventory management system.

LONG-RANGE PLANNING RELATED TO INVENTORIES

Because inventories are classified as a current asset, the importance of long-range planning relative to inventories is frequently overlooked. However, in light of the relatively large
percentage of total company assets that inventory usually represents, it becomes apparent that long-range inventory planning must
be an important aspect of any long-range corporate plan.

If the marketing patterns for a company are fairly stable, it
may be appropriate to project long-term inventory requirements
by expressing them as ratios to forecasted sales (or cost of goods
sold). These ratios can be developed from historical relationships
between inventories and sales; for example, inventory may equal
two months' sales (or costs of goods sold). The accuracy of
this method of projection can be improved by considering individual product lines, and then totaling the various product line inventory projections to determine the aggregate projected inventory.

In those situations where market conditions are more dynamic
or when the business decisions associated with the long-range plan
have a high dollar value, the use of more sophisticated methods

should be considered.   In this regard, the following factors should
be considered in developing a long-range inventory plan.

Product mix: As the product line expands, the need for additional
inventory becomes apparent.   As the number of models offered
for sale increases, the sales volume per model may well decrease.
This usually results in a higher total inventory, relative to sales results obtained.   Therefore, if the product line is being expanded
or consolidated, the impact on inventories should be considered.

Geographic distribution of sales: If sales increases are predicated
on a broader geographic market coverage, it may be necessary
to establish new regional warehouse inventories to maintain satisfactory levels of customer service.   Also, the need for increased
in-transit inventories should be considered.

Improvements of customer service: Marketing management often
tends to place great emphasis on customer service, as a means
of improving a company's competitive position.   When this form
of marketing strategy is incorporated into long-range plans, the
impact on inventory should be considered because a reduction
in delivery lead times or stock-outs can usually be generated
through higher inventory levels.

Physical distribution systems: As a company modifies its physical
distribution system, the net effect on inventories should be determined.   For example, some companies have materially reduced
inventory investment by centralizing inventories and then utilizing air transportation, allowing them to maintain a reasonable
level of service to the customer.   Other companies have consolidated warehousing locations, to take advantage of lower freight
rates and to reduce fixed warehouse overhead costs.   These are
just a few examples of the very large area relating to the analysis
of the physical distribution, or logistical systems.   In the future,
it appears that this area, which includes inventory management,
will be receiving increasing attention from management.

Data processing systems: As noted in the preceding chapter, the
increased use of data processing and related data communications
has enabled many companies to reduce inventories, as a result
of more timely reporting and improved control techniques.   This
does not mean that the anticipated installation of new data processing equipment necessarily justifies the projection of lower
inventory levels; however, such a projection may be justified
when not only have procedures been mechanized, but also an
improved control system has been developed, and when its expected effectiveness and turnover rates are compared, through
simulation, with historical operating results.

Manufacturing decisions: As a company becomes more vertically integrated from a manufacturing point of view, with a higher value-added per sales dollar, the aggregate inventory turn ratio will tend to decrease. Therefore, future make-or-buy decisions, which affect the degree of vertical integration, will have an influence on inventories and should be considered in long-range plans.

Design and engineering decisions: Meaningful inventory savings can be realized through an engineering program designed to encourage the use of common parts. The modular design of products is also very important in this respect. Through the use of modular design a large variety of end products can be assembled, using a relatively limited number of modular subassemblies. This provides marketing management with the advantages of a broad product line while retaining the advantages of mass production through the use of common modular subassemblies.

Marketing channels of distribution: Alternate channels of distribution can have a major impact on inventory. If a company decides to eliminate a step in the chain of distribution performed by another enterprise, it may be necessary to increase finished goods inventory. On the other hand, a company not using dealers or distributors may decide that the capital invested in distribution inventories can be more profitably applied in other areas, and thereby justify the establishment of "outside" channels of distribution, independent of the company.

These are some of the more important factors bearing on the long-range planning for inventory requirements of a company. In effect, they consider the basic structure of the company and the market it serves, the allocation of capital investment and many of the marketing factors which will influence the company.

INTERMEDIATE-RANGE PLANNING RELATED TO INVENTORIES

Intermediate-range planning is difficult to describe in point of time because it is frequently defined simply as falling between long- and short-range planning. In most cases, relative to inventories, it covers a period of from six months to two years in the future. It differs from long-range planning in the sense that, within its time span, the market and company structure are fairly well defined. It contrasts with short-range planning because it is not usually concerned with the type of day-to-day detail normally associated with short-range plans. For example, the intermediate-range plans normally reflect *aggregate* inventory levels for categories such as raw material, work-in-process, and finished goods, whereas a short-range plan relates to *specific* part requirements.

In most cases, intermediate-range inventory plans are concerned with inventory adjustments to compensate for: seasonal variations, demand variations resulting from anticipated changes in the business climate, large contracts, introduction of new products, special promotions, etc.

The intermediate inventory plan should be related to operating plans and financial budgets. In a sense, the planned inventory becomes the buffer between variations in forecasted market demand and the manufacturing and purchasing plan which, in turn, considers capacity restrictions, manning levels, and availability of material resources. In some cases, this balancing between the forecasted level of market demand and the manufacturing rate is fairly straightforward and tends to be handled on an intuitive basis in a quite effective manner. However, in some industries, especially those where the seasonal demand variations are large, a much more complex problem exists. Management must evaluate and determine how the marginal expenses associated with varying the production level interact with the marginal expenses of carrying seasonal inventory. This can be very difficult because the marginal expenses being considered are not readily found in the financial statement or in most cost accounting systems. They involve factors bearing on various expenses, such as laying off and rehiring employees, carrying seasonal inventories, and lost sales or poor delivery schedules. Once these expenses have been identified and quantified, mathematical models can be used to balance them so as to minimize total costs.

When a company's manufacturing activity involves expensive capital equipment, it is normally necessary to schedule production so as to maintain a high equipment utilization rate. If production were geared substantially to variations in market demand, an increased investment in capital equipment would be required so as to provide adequate machine capacity during peak demand periods.

However, in companies where the value added during the manufacturing operation is relatively low, such as in many assembly

COMPONENTS OF DEMAND

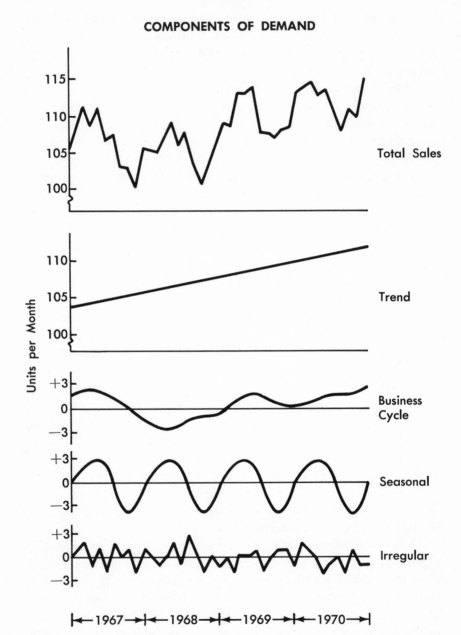

plants, the cost of carrying seasonal inventories becomes excessive in comparison with the cost of varying the production rate. Thus, in general, companies with a high value added during manufacturing tend to vary inventories, whereas companies with a low value added tend to vary the production rate.

An example of a typical operating schedule and inventory plan to cope with fluctuating demand rates is shown on page 40. In this particular case, assume that an analysis of marginal expenses, relative to changes in the production rate and the cost of carrying inventory, has indicated that the optimum strategy is to vary both the production rate and the inventory levels. The variations in the production rate in this case are limited to a plus or minus twenty-five per cent variation; the finished goods inventory levels account for the rest of the balancing process between production and demand. Variations in the production rate beyond twenty-five per cent in this particular case, resulted in expenses associated with the need to purchase additional manufacturing equipment, risks arising from possible poor union relationship (due to excessive lay-off), and training expenses and low initial employee productivity associated with employee turnover.

Operating Schedule and Inventory Plan

Millions of Dollars

Month	Forecasted cost of sales	Planned production	Beginning inventory balances			
			Finished goods	Work-in-process	Raw material	Total inventory
Jan.	2.0	5.0	2.0	5.0	4.5	11.5
Feb.	2.5	5.5	5.0	5.5	4.5	15.0
Mar.	3.5	6.0	8.0	5.5	4.0	17.5
Apr.	5.0	6.0	10.5	5.0	3.5	19.0
May	7.0	5.5	11.5	4.5	3.0	19.0
June	9.0	5.0	10.0	4.0	3.0	17.0
July	7.0	4.5	6.0	4.0	2.5	12.5
Aug.	6.0	4.5	3.5	3.5	2.5	9.5
Sept.	5.0	4.0	2.0	3.5	2.5	8.0
Oct.	4.0	4.0	1.0	3.5	2.5	7.0
Nov.	3.0	4.0	1.0	3.5	2.5	7.0
Dec.	3.5	4.0	2.0	4.0	3.0	9.0
Total	57.5	58.0	—	—	—	—

The example on page 41 begins with a column reflecting fore-casted demand for twelve months. The next column shows the production schedule which is derived from forecasted demand, and from the constraint that production should not vary more than twenty-five per cent from the annual monthly average, or more than half a million dollars, on a month-to-month basis. The third column shows the beginning finished goods inventory posi-tion which is required to balance the production schedule and the demand forecast. The beginning balances for work-in-process and raw materials are based upon material requirements derived from the production schedule. Overall, this operating schedule reflects a "cascading" type of action, beginning with the sales forecast, and ending with the raw material inventory needed to support it.

The final column in the table reflects the total inventory figure obtained by adding together finished goods, work-in-process, and raw material inventory values. This total inventory value can then be used in developing financial projections, especially for cash flow and working capital analysis.

SHORT-RANGE PLANNING RELATED TO INVENTORIES

The short-range inventory plan is actually a part of the inven-tory control system which responds to the day-to-day operating needs of the company. Although this type of plan may be sum-marized in terms of dollars, it must be primarily concerned with specific products, parts, and raw material requirements needed to meet customer orders and production plans.

When inventory requirements are associated with a fixed "build" schedule, as in the case of a job shop, or of products with relatively long manufacturing lead times, the inventory plan is normally dependent upon the bill of material of the products to be built, and on the time sequencing of the manufacturing oper-ations. There are several techniques available which can be used in this regard. In the case of discrete orders, such as in a job shop or in connection with certain types of government contracts, various network analysis systems such as PERT, Critical Path, and Line-of-Balance can be used.

These techniques establish when various events should take place, in point of time. As related to inventory management, these events can be interpreted in terms of material requirements. The purpose of these techniques is to identify the sequence of events, and to show how various events are related to and dependent upon prior events. By relating this timing manufacturing operations to the volume of finished units to be produced, and to the bill of material relative to each model, an inventory plan can be developed. Such a plan would reflect when, and in what quantity, various materials would be required to meet the overall plan set forth in the network. Although management is usually most concerned about inefficiencies and related expenses that result from lack of material which delays a job, it should not be overlooked that the receipt of materials in advance of the normal planning cycle can also result in excessive inventory carrying costs.

In the case of continuing production of longer lead time products, a bill of material "explosion" routine can be used, normally utilizing some type of data processing equipment. This routine involves multiplying the parts on the bills of material related to each particular model by the number of finished units to be produced, and analyzing these requirements in terms of purchasing and manufacturing lead times. The result of this bill of material explosion routine is the identification of specific part and material requirements, by scheduling period, which will be needed to meet a given finished goods production schedule.

In contrast to a situation where future demands and requirements are fairly well defined, there are many inventory systems which must respond to random demand patterns. These random demand patterns can usually be broken down into a forecasted demand rate, and a defined distribution of errors about that rate. When an inventory level is to be planned that pertains to a sales pattern which is random in nature, it is common to use a reorder point, or minimum balance type of control system. This type of system reacts by reordering when the physical or unassigned inventory balance drops below a predetermined inventory level, referred to as the reorder point. The reorder point is determined basically by three factors, the lead time required to replenish the inventory, the projected demand rate during the lead time period, and the additional inventory, commonly referred to as safety stock, which is required in the control of the number of stock-outs.

In addition to the decision establishing when to reorder, it is necessary to determine how much to order. This is frequently referred to as the economic order quantity; its establishment will be reviewed in detail in the next chapter, along with the method for establishing reorder points.

In effect, the combination of the determination of a reorder point and an order quantity, for each item carried in inventory or for homogeneous groupings, establishes the short-range inventory plan. In the aggregate, the inventory value under a reorder point system will equal one-half of the total order quantities for all items in inventory, plus the safety stocks associated with these items. In this context, the safety stock for a particular item can be defined as the average inventory balance when a stock replenishment order is received.

It should be pointed out that both the reorder point and the economic order quantity are dependent upon the short-range demand forecast, and the error range associated with that forecast. This again points out the close relationship of inventory planning and sales forecasting.

FORECASTING RELATED TO INVENTORY MANAGEMENT

The planning phases of inventory management are all dependent upon some type of a forecast of future demand. In some cases the forecast will be more in the nature of an assumed demand level rather than a specific analysis of the various factors that may influence future demand patterns. For example, in one company the president may simply assume a five per cent annual growth in sales, for purposes of planning. In another company, the marketing research department may prepare a detailed forecast which is based upon such factors as population age composition, average family income, patterns of consumption, etc. This points out the wide variation in the degree to which quantitative standards are used in forecasting methods.

Generally, forecasts can be broken down by time spans corresponding to the three types of planning, long-range, intermediate-range and short-range. The methodology required to develop each one of these forecasts varies, depending on the time span. The nature of the forecast itself and the techniques appropriate in each circumstance are also affected by its time span.

NATURE OF THE LONG-RANGE FORECAST

The long-range forecast, covering a period of two to ten years in the future, is normally expressed in fairly broad terms, such as dollar volume or overall physical production quantities. When the forecast is expressed in dollars, the possible effects of price inflation should be considered. The forecast may be in terms of current dollars, or it could be expressed in terms of the anticipated inflated dollars of periods being projected. When a projected price inflation is included in a forecast, it should be so identified, and it should relate to historical price trends within the industry being considered. As a general rule, forecasts stated in current dollars or physical quantities are used for long-range plans that relate to the availability of *physical* facilities and organizational requirements. On the other hand, long-range forecasts for financial planning purposes should take into consideration the anticipated influence of price levels, related to the way in which loans will be repaid.

The preparation of a long-range forecast can be very complex in some cases because of limited knowledge regarding future market conditions such as overall economic activity, actual products to be sold, and the competitive market environment. On the other hand, the long-range forecast tends to be less detailed than the shorter-range forecast and, in most cases, the degree of accuracy required is not as great. A ten per cent error in a long-range forecast may well be acceptable from a general business strategy point of view, but unacceptable for short-range decision-making.

The long-range forecast is also characterized by the relatively substantial importance and length of time period of the business decisions which depend upon it. A company may well change its overall corporate objectives, based upon expectations revealed by the long-range forecast. Capital expenditures, product research programs, basic marketing strategies and organization planning are several examples of the types of major business decisions dependent on the long-range forecast.

INTERMEDIATE-RANGE FORECASTING

The intermediate-range forecast usually relates to a period of time from six months to two years in the future. In most companies it provides the basis for developing annual budgets, operating plans, cash flow projections and sales quotas. The intermediate-range forecast may also be used in developing marketing strategy, such as the timing of new product introductions, advertising campaigns, and sales promotion programs.

The format of the intermediate-range forecast normally differs from the long-range forecasts in the time period intervals being forecast. The long-range forecast is frequently expressed in annual demand periods, whereas the intermediate-range forecast is expressed in months or quarters. The intermediate-range forecast may also provide additional detail according to product characteristics and regional sales patterns. The Operating Schedule and Inventory Plan on page 41 shows how an intermediate-range forecast can be used in developing production plans and related inventory levels. A plan of this nature may be revised monthly or quarterly so as to reflect the latest forecast.

SHORT-RANGE FORECASTING

The short-range forecast, usually covering a time period of up to six months in the future, has received a great deal of attention recently because of a growing realization of the importance of integrating production, procurement and distribution logistics with market demand, the development of new statistical forecasting techniques and the availability of computers to perform large volumes of complex calculations, at high speed and relatively economically. The primary characteristics of the short-range forecast are the amount of detail required, the frequency of updating, and the timeliness of updating.

The primary functions of most short-range forecasting systems, relative to inventory management, are to adjust dynamically the reorder points for inventoried items, and to assign priorities for production planning purposes. To accomplish these functions, the short-range forecast must be expressed in units that are meaningful in the frame of reference of the inventory and production control system. Since these systems work in terms of physical quantities, usually by product or part number, the forecast should also be expressed in these units. The time interval of the forecast will usually be weeks or months, depending largely on the production-inventory planning cycle. In some cases, the forecast may be revised for every planning cycle; however, this is not always necessary. The frequency of revising a short-range forecast is dependent upon how sensitive the forecasting system is to new data, and on the degree of variability of such data. In cases where weekly demand is known to be highly erratic, limited weight would be given to the current week's demand, and a forecast revised on a weekly basis would not vary materially from the previous forecast. In such a case, the revision of the forecast would be delayed until sufficient data had been accumulated to make it meaningful to the forecasting system.

One form of a short-range forecast, which is not always recognized as such, is the reporting of order backlogs. The size and priority of items in the backlog serves, in effect, as a short-range forecast for the inventory-production control system. Although backlogs are often thought of only in a negative sense (i.e., as out-of-stock conditions), they can be an important factor in balancing a relatively unstable inflow of orders, thus obtaining the advantage of economies available by means of stability of operating volumes in the production area. A controlled backlog can be used to reduce the size of the finished goods inventory and, at the same time, to provide an acceptable level of customer service.

Short-range forecasts may also be a very valuable tool in sales analysis. The magnitude and sequence of deviations of actual results, when associated with short-range forecasts, may provide a means of identifying changing demand patterns before they are normally recognized. The short-range forecast may also be used in revising operating plans and budgets.

DEVELOPING A FORECASTING SYSTEM

In the development of a forecasting system, the initial step is
to identify the various types of business decisions that are dependent upon or related to a forecast.   When this analysis has
been completed, the various forecast requirements should be
grouped according to long-range, intermediate-range, and short-
range forecasts, and listed accordingly.   This listing should include the units in which the forecast should be expressed, the
time span covered by the forecast, and the time unit to be used,
such as year, quarter, month, or week.

Although different types of forecasts will be based on various
forecasting techniques, there should be a consistent theoretical base
for all the forecasts (in the sense that similar concepts and factors
should be used) and there should be agreement between the forecasts; for example, the intermediate-range forecast for the second
year should relate to the initial year of the long-range forecast.

VALUE OF FORECAST ACCURACY

Having established the need for and the parameters of the various forecasting subsystems, the next step is to identify the value
of forecast accuracy relative to the related business decisions.   In
some cases, a forecasting error can result in a significant dollar
loss, while in other cases the business decision is relatively insensitive to forecast error.   The allocation of company resources to
the forecasting function should be balanced against the economic
benefits which will result from a more accurate forecast.   Although many companies do not place enough emphasis on forecasting, there are also some companies which permit the forecasting function to become more sophisticated than the related business
decisions can justify.   In effect, forecasting then becomes an end
in itself rather than a means of improving company profit.   The
likelihood of this happening is fairly great because of the intel-
lectual challenge of forecasting, from both a statistical and economic point of view.

The importance of the individual responsible for forecasting
should be mentioned at this time.   This individual must possess

technical qualifications in the areas of marketing, statistics, and economics, as well as an understanding of how business decisions at all levels interact with forecasting. In addition, and very important, he must be persuasive in communicating to management the reasonableness of the forecasts and the assumptions upon which the forecasts were developed. This frequently involves translating the technical jargon of economics and statistics into a language that can be understood both by the executives who will use the forecast in making business decisions and by operating personnel who are responsible for implementing operations contemplated by the forecasted activities, and for integrating them with operating systems, such as inventory management. It is very important that the forecasting function consider the specific requirements of all affected operating systems, and adjust forecasting formats and details accordingly.

NATURE OF FORECASTS

There is frequently some confusion regarding just what events are to be forecasted. Because of time lags and other inventory-related factors, there can be a considerable difference between the volume of orders received at the plant, plant shipments and sales to the final customer, which in many cases will, in turn, take place through an independent distributor. In selecting the event to be forecasted, the first consideration should be the sale to the final customer because, ultimately, the entire manufacturing and distribution system must respond to this demand. Unfortunately, this type of data in many cases is not available to the company, or the accuracy and timeliness of available data make it unsuitable for forecasting purposes.

Another form of demand data relates to orders received. In most cases this is a fairly accurate reflection of market demand; however, it may be distorted when customers do not send in orders because of their knowledge of extended delivery dates, or of stock-out conditions. The data which is easiest to obtain is usually related to shipments or sales. If the time lag between receipt of an order and shipment is short, sales are usually the event forecasted.

The final selection events to be forecasted will depend upon how the forecast is to be used, the accuracy of the different types of demand data, the cost of generating new types of data, the length of time lags between the various events, the distortions introduced by inventory changes in the distribution channels, and the timeliness in reporting various types of data.

COMPONENTS OF DEMAND

One of the fundamental factors relative to demand forecasting is the recognition of the four basic components which make up demand, namely: trend, business cycle, seasonal, and irregular factors. Expressed as an equation, this relationship appears as follows:

$$\text{Demand} = \text{Trend} \times \text{Cycle} \times \text{Seasonal} \times \text{Irregular}$$

In such an equation, trend can be expressed in units while the other three components reflect per cent variation from the trend. For example, the seasonal component associated with a product may increase sales by 20% for a specific month being forecast, and would therefore appear in the equation as 1.20. Exhibit II depicts how a demand pattern can be decomposed into its components, to provide a basis for developing a forecast. Before exploring the various techniques available in forecasting, an explanation of the nature of the four components of demand should prove to be helpful.

> *Trend:* The trend component is defined as long-term patterns of growth, stability and decay. "Long-term" in this case should be defined in terms of the product life cycle of the item being forecast. In projecting electrical power consumption, long-term may relate to growth patterns extending over a ten, twenty or even fifty-year period. On the other hand, a long-term trend may relate to much shorter time periods, such as weeks, for an item like a popular record which has a very short product life cycle. In some cases, like electrical power, the product life cycle is perhaps infinite; however, in the case of style goods or products susceptible to technological change, a finite product life cycle exists. Factors that typically influence trends are: size and age composition of the population, aggregate buying power of the markets being served (individuals, companies, or branches of government), social behavior as it relates to patterns of consumption,

consumer acceptance of the product or service, physical and market distribution system, changes in the company or industry productive capacity, changes in unit costs (and related price), and availability of substitute products or services.

Business cycle: The cyclical component consists of wave-like movements reflecting changes in general business activity over a period of several years. Business cycles vary from industry to industry and even within an industry. For example, a low-priced product may show a sales increase during a business recession because of buying resistance to more expensive brands of the product. Some industries are relatively insensitive to business cycles, such as certain basic food processors, while others vary widely, such as capital construction. Some of the factors which appear to influence general economic cycles are: capital expenditures, changes in business inventory, business profit margins, monetary policy, and fiscal policy as it relates to taxation and government expenditures. Cycles related to specific industries may be influenced by such factors as: mortgage rates, farm income, changes in import-export agreements, and prolonged industry-wide strikes.

Seasonal: The seasonal component reflects periodic variations having a duration of one year. The influence of seasonal factors varies greatly. In some industries it is the most important factor in predicting month-to-month changes in demand. The principal factors that are responsible for seasonality are: seasonal weather pattern which affects buying habits, holidays (particularly Christmas), annual promotions, and availability of supply, such as agricultural products.

Irregular: The irregular component reflects variations in demand which remain after discounting the trend, cycle, and seasonal components. This component can be broken down further into abnormal factors and random factors. Abnormal factors are those factors that can be identified but are not explained by the other three components of demand. Some examples of abnormal factors are: Unusual weather conditions which affect sales, price changes, introduction of new models by competition, strikes, special promotions, and advertising campaigns. The random portion of the irregular component cannot be identified with specific events but arises as a result of errors in measuring demand and the random nature of the customers' decision to buy. This random nature of buying decisions will be dependent upon the nature of consumption. If a product is consumed on a continuous basis and cannot be inventoried in sizable quantities, such as bread, it will have a relatively low random component. Conversely, an item with a discrete consumption pattern, or one that can

be inventoried, may have a relatively large random component. In this connection, durable goods can be thought of as
being inventoried during their useful life.

In addition to the four components just reviewed, there is the
need to consider calendar day adjustments. This is particularly
important in regard to short-range forecasts established for
monthly intervals, where the number of sales days per month,
which are normally directly proportional to volume, may vary
quite substantially from one month to the next. In forecasting
volumes related to retail sales, it is also important to consider such
calendar variations as the number of Saturdays in a month, or
when a variable holiday (such as Easter) will fall.

In most cases data is adjusted for calendar variations before
further analysis is performed. For example, all monthly sales data
may be adjusted for twenty-one sales days per month. In other
cases, data can be grouped into a uniform calendar period, such
as a week. A more sophisticated technique that is being used
is based upon the determination of weights for the various days
of the week. These weights reflect the historical buying habits
of the consumer with regard to the day of the week. It should
be noted that fixed holidays, such as Christmas, are not considered
a calendar variation with regard to monthly data because they
always fall in the same month and are therefore treated as a seasonal factor.

FORECASTING METHODS AND TECHNIQUES

There are two general approaches to forecasting. One relates
to subjective or intuitive methods; the other pertains to quantitative analysis involving statistical techniques. In practice, a third
type of approach evolves which is a combination of subjective
and quantitative methods. The method, or methods, that are
most appropriate for a particular forecasting situation will depend
upon the nature of the demand to be forecast, the value of the
forecast and the qualifications of personnel available to prepare
the forecast. Whatever method is used, the one indispensable
ingredient that must be present is sound business logic. The forecaster must always ask himself, "Does this forecast make sense
and are the assumptions inherent in the forecast reasonable?"

SUBJECTIVE METHODS

Forecasts based on subjective or intuitive methods can be broken down into three categories: (1) executive opinion, (2) sales force composite, and (3) customer expectation.

The *executive opinion* forecast will reflect the intuitive judgment of a single executive or the composite judgment of several executives. The advantages of this type of method are that it usually involves limited effort, can be quickly prepared, and that communicating the forecast to management is readily accomplished. An executive opinion forecast is most frequently used in smaller companies where a specialized forecasting function is not justified, and in those situations where style changes are a predominating factor. Executive opinion forecasts are also used when the forecasted events are influences by a great many variables which have a poorly defined cause-and-effect relationship with demand.

A *sales force composite* forecast involves totaling the individual forecasts of many salesmen and sales managers. The normal procedure is to have each level of sales management review and adjust the forecasts prepared by the next lower level. When this type of method is used, it is important to provide each salesman with historical sales data for his region, and also with his prior forecasts. This type of forecast can be useful in assisting the salesman in establishing his sales objectives, and in evaluating his past performance. In some cases, a sales force composite forecast can be justified on this basis alone, even if the forecast is not used for higher level planning and decision-making.

A *customer expectation* type of forecast is developed by asking customers how much they expect to order, over periods of time. It is frequently used in connection with very large customers such as chain stores and original equipment manufacturers, particularly when such customers account for a larger portion of total sales. Such large customers may also have developed long-term requirements, used as a basis for "blanket" purchase orders, with current release dates and quantities being furnished to the supplier. If these customers have done an adequate job of forecasting requirements, this type of a forecasting method can be meaningful. However, the weight given to a customer's forecast of requirements should be based on how accurately requirements have been projected in the past. In some cases, customers will forecast excessive requirements so as to insure an adequate vendor inventory of materials, thus minimizing vendor lead times, and the risk of vendor stock-out situations.

QUANTITATIVE METHODS

Recently there has been a great deal of interest in the use of quantitative methods with regard to forecasting. This interest can be related to several factors including: the reduced cost of statistical computation (by reason of the capacities of electronic data processing equipment), the development and refinement of statistical techniques applicable to forecasting, increased technical knowledge, increased availability of data regarding company operations, industry sales and economic conditions, and greater recognition by management of the importance of forecasting in planning and control.

The first step in quantitative analysis must be a consideration of the data to be analyzed. This involves determining what data is needed, the data currently available (and its form of storage), and the accuracy of data. This type of analysis should result in the development of a "data base" which will provide for the systematic accumulation and storage of data needed for forecasting and sales analysis. It should be mentioned that the functions of forecasting and sales analysis are interrelated in that analysis of historical data is a primary basis for forecasting demand. In developing a data base, it may well be necessary to establish or revise procedures relative to the reporting of historical demand data.

Concurrently with the development of a data base, the statistical techniques which will be used must be considered. These statistical techniques can be divided into two categories, time series analysis and cross-sectional analysis.

TIME SERIES ANALYSIS

A time series can be generally defined as the arrangement of measured data in chronological order. Time series analysis relates to evaluating and identifying patterns of stability and change, relative to a single variable over a period of time. The principle behind time series analysis, relative to forecasting, is that the level of demand follows identifiable patterns of change which can be projected into the future. For example, seasonal variations can be identified and expressed in quantitative terms, using time series analysis techniques.

Forecasting (relative to time series analysis) consists of identifying patterns—in terms of time—through the analysis of historical data, and then projecting these patterns into the future. The most common statistical techniques used in identifying and projecting these patterns are averages, moving averages, weighted averages, and trend fitting, using the method of least squares.

The use of averages is common to everyone in business. A straight arithmetic average (mean) can be used to identify a stable demand pattern; however, the forecaster is faced with several problems. First, he must determine the period to be covered by the average. Should it be three months, twelve months, etc.? Second, consideration must be given to the marketing factors which influenced historical demand data. The use of an average to forecast future demand implies the anticipated continuation of previous marketing conditions with regard to their effect on demand. The advantage of using an average is that it eliminates random fluctuations in demand which, in forecasting, are preferred to as the irregular factor.

More sophisticated techniques involving averages, relate to moving and weighted averages. A moving average includes adding and dropping like demand periods, and then calculating a new average. The weighted average reflects assigning varying weights to different periods included in calculating the average. The theory behind a weighted average is that the more current months will reflect future demand more accurately, and therefore should exert a greater influence on the average than the demand data that is relatively old.

One type of a weighted average is termed "exponential smoothing." "Smoothing" refers to the common characteristic of all-averaging procedures whereby period-to-period fluctuations in demand are "smoothed" by using a moving or cumulative average. "Exponential" refers to the method of weighting historical demand data. In exponential smoothing, the weights assigned to historical demand data vary according to an exponential function. This results in reducing the weight, or influence, assigned to each demand period, according to the age of the data. The primary advantage of the exponential smoothing technique is the simplicity of the calculations to update the average, and its compatibility with computer capabilities. Although the calculations are relatively simple, the rationale behind the exponential smoothing equations is rather complex. This apparent simplicity sometimes results in inexperienced individuals using the technique, but not understanding the potential problems associated with its various aspects. For example, a demand which has a seasonal component must be adjusted for the seasonal factor before the exponential smoothing calculation is performed.

The trend or line fitting technique involves the statistical calculation of a line which minimizes the sum of the squares of the deviations. In the simplest case, the fitted line is linear. More sophisticated line fitting techniques result in a curved line which is represented by an equation. The forecast is based upon an extrapolation of the fitted line. This type of technique is frequently used in conjunction with annual data to determine long-term trends which in turn relate to long-range forecasting.

A trend line can also be established directly by fitting a free-hand line to plotted data. Although this is a semi-subjective method, it can be useful because it can be done without any time-consuming statistical calculations, and does not require any special statistical know-how.

CROSS-SECTIONAL ANALYSIS

The basis of cross-sectional analysis is the determination of meaningful relationships between demand and the factors which affect demand, other than that of time. A forecast based upon cross-sectional analysis takes into consideration external factors, whereas time series analysis considers only the historical data of the demand function being forecast. The techniques associated with cross-sectional analysis are most commonly used in forecasting the trend and business cycle component of demand. The term "cross-sectional analysis" pertains to taking a cross-section of demand and other external factors during specific time periods, and then analyzing their relationships.

A long-term trend forecast can be developed by relating demand to the marketing factors which influence demand. For example, a long-term trend for car sales can be developed by relating car sales to population figures and changes in per capita personal income. In the case of forecasting business cycles, the demand for specific product lines, such as building supplies, can be forecasted based upon an external factor (or factors), such as new building permits.

In regard to cross-sectional analysis, it should be pointed out that it involves relationships between time series. The ideal situation exists when an independent external time series can be found which is related to the future demand of the product being forecast. In the case of new building permits, changes in this series usually occur prior to actual changes in the demand for building supplies. In turn, it may be possible to anticipate changes in new building permits by analyzing changes in mortgage interest rates.

There are two specific problems which arise in evaluating such cause and effect relationships, namely, how consistent are the relationships and what is the time lag between the variables.

The statistical technique used in cross-sectional analysis is correlation analysis. This technique provides a means of determining whether or not two or more variables are correlated statistically. The technique also involves consideration of the nature of the relationships if it is determined that they are correlated. Graphically, this technique can be expressed as a scatter diagram. This method is similar to the line fitting technique described in time series analysis except that the horizontal scale reflects the independent variable being tested, rather than time.

A word of caution is necessary in regard to correlation analysis as used in forecasting. Quite often two variables appear to be correlated; however, both variables are actually dependent upon a third variable. It is therefore necessary to consider the business logic of the relationship between variables, rather than simply accepting the apparent conclusion that might be drawn from the statistical calculations.

COMBINED APPROACH

So far, forecasting methods have been reviewed in terms of subjective and quantitative techniques. In actual business practice, forecasting systems are usually based upon a *mix* of subjective and quantitative techniques. In a particular forecasting system the trend and seasonal components may be projected using statistical techniques, whereas the cycle component and that part of the irregular component relating to abnormal factors may be based upon an executive opinion type of forecast.

In many cases a quantitative forecast is prepared by marketing research and then reviewed with a management committee. The use of graphs can be useful in this regard because they can convey to the committee the overall results of the statistical calculations without going into technical detail which may be confusing to individuals not trained in statistical techniques. The committee reviews the statistical forecast for reasonableness and then prepares adjustments to the forecast taking into consideration a specific list of abnormal factors which may influence demand, such as: special promotions, strikes, abnormal pricing situations, etc. The final forecast is then prepared, taking into account the statistical forecast plus adjustments prepared by the management committee.

A follow-up to this type of system is the evaluation of the forecast errors. In this analysis a determination is made as to whether or not the adjustments of the management committee have reduced the magnitude of the forecast errors. This analysis is presented to the committee so that it can evaluate the prior adjustments and improve upon future adjustments. This is a type of a "gaming situation" where the players learn both from their correct and incorrect decisions, and modify their future actions accordingly.

FORECASTING ERRORS

One of the major problems relative to demand forecasting is a general lack of understanding by businessmen of the meaning of forecast errors. Unfortunately, perfect demand forecasting systems do not exist. It should be recognized that anticipation and analysis of forecast errors are integral parts of any forecasting system.

The term "error" is probably one reason for the confusion in this area. Normally, error implies a mistake; however, as it pertains to forecasting, it also refers to deviations between actual and forecasted results which arise from the irregular components of demand. In most forecasting systems, the magnitude of the irregular components establish the forecast error range. This error range is very important as it relates to planning because it identifies the degree of uncertainty to be associated with the forecast. For example, many economic forecasts of gross national product are stated in terms of a specific amount, plus or minus a certain level. This plus or minus portion of the forecast identifies the possible error range. In effect, it states how much reliance can be placed on the specific forecasted figure.

Forecasting error is particularly important as it relates to inventory management because it is one of the principal factors considered in setting up inventory safety stocks and related reorder points. Other factors being equal, the amount of safety stock required will vary proportionately to the forecast error.

The analysis of forecasting errors can also play an important role in the selection of the type of forecasting system to be used. In this regard, the selection of a forecasting system is largely dependent upon the magnitude of the errors it generates in comparison with alternative forecasting methods. The relative effectiveness of a forecasting system can be evaluated by comparing its error range with the error range resulting from the use of a so-called "naive" statistical forecasting model. A naive model could consist of any one of the following techniques: this year's sales will equal last year's sales, a twelve-month moving average, a simple exponential smoothing equation, a linear trend line based on the last five years' sales, etc. The naive model reflects a straightforward statistical forecast, disregarding intuitive judgment and complex statistical techniques found in more sophisticated systems.

The analysis of forecast errors can also be important in identifying and correcting for deficiencies in a forecasting system. If errors can be associated with specific factors influencing demand, it may be possible to include these factors in the development of future forecasts.

4

Inventory Management Techniques

An effective inventory management system is dependent upon the development of efficient planning and control techniques and the proper implementation and administration of these techniques. In this chapter, various types of inventory management techniques will be described, along with typical operating environments in which they are frequently applied.

Prior to discussing specific techniques, a more precise definition of the respective functions of inventory *management* and inventory *control* seems appropriate.

Inventory management functions involve the development and administration of policies, systems, and procedures which will minimize total costs relative to inventory decisions and related functions such as customer service requirements, production scheduling, purchasing, traffic, etc. Viewed in that perspective, inventory management is broad in scope and affects a great number of activities in a company's organization. Because of these numerous interrelationships, inventory management stresses the need for integrated information flow and decision making, as it relates to inventory polices and overall systems.

The inventory control function, on the other hand, is frequently defined in a narrower sense than inventory management and pertains primarily to the administration of established policies, systems, and procedures. For example, inventory control activities might involve the maintenance of inventory records and reports, the initiation of material requisitions for purchased or manufactured items, and physical as well as accounting control over inventory transactions. Inventory control functions may also include special staff activities such as the development and evaluation of alternative inventory decision models, analysis of specific inventory problems, and the evaluation of existing inventory systems and procedures.

The various control techniques discussed in this chapter can be described as practical techniques which have been successfully applied in many typical business situations. Limited emphasis is placed here on certain sophisticated techniques which are normally based on complex statistical models. While these more complex techniques have been of value to a number of large companies, they are not necessarily applicable to, or economically feasible for, general inventory situations because they are frequently based upon specific assumptions and requirements which are associated with specialized operating conditions. It should also be pointed out that the use of sophisticated techniques per se does not necessarily result in an effective inventory management system. In many cases, the lack of accurate and timely data nullifies the advantages of using complex control techniques. There is also the potential problem that sophisticated control techniques may be misapplied because of a lack of understanding of their underlying rationale on the part of either management or the staff personnel directly concerned.

Finally, the benefits to be expected from the inventory control techniques described here can be said to include the major portion of those benefits available under much more sophisticated techniques which are usually also much more costly to apply.

When a company has decided to embark on an inventory management program, the first step taken should be a scoping study to establish the magnitude of such a program, the potential payback of the program, the probability of realizing the pay-back, and the resources which would be required.   Some of the factors that should be considered in such a scoping study are:

1. The objectives of the company as they relate to inventories and the level of service to be provided to customers.
2. The qualifications of staff personnel who would design and coordinate the implementation of the system.
3. The capabilities of personnel who will be responsible for managing the system on a continuing basis.
4. The nature and size of inventories and their relationship to the other functions in the company, such as manufacturing, finance, marketing, etc.
5. The capability of present and future data processing equipment.
6. The potential savings that might be anticipated from improved control of inventories.
7. The current, or potential, availability of data that can be used in controlling inventories.
8. The present method for controlling inventories, and for making inventory decisions.
9. The degree of commitment by management personnel to the development of a more effective inventory management system, and the results they anticipate from such a system.

A review of these factors should provide the framework for planning an inventory management program and should identify some of the techniques that will be incorporated into the program.

IDENTIFICATION OF INVENTORY LEVELS

Generally, the first step in recognizing inventory problems and improving management control of inventories is to identify inventory levels and associated costs and expenses, as these relate to the volume of business done.   This usually starts with a review of the financial statements of a company.   One of the most commonly used figures in this regard is the inventory turnover ratio, which is the annual cost of goods sold divided by the inventory amount.   This ratio reflects approximately how many times the physical inventory is being "turned over" per year.   The turnover ratio can be very useful; however, it is also frequently misunderstood by management when evaluating the effectiveness of the inventory management function of a company.   A high inventory turnover ratio alone does not necessarily imply effective inventory management. This ratio should be evaluated, but along with many other statistics when appraising the effectiveness of the control of inventories (e.g., level of customer service, production set-up costs, purchase price variances as related to quantity discounts, and stability of the production labor force).

Inventory turnover ratios vary widely according to industry, and, within industry, according to the nature of manufacturing and distribution. A manufacturing company that assembles purchased components will require less inventory per sales dollar than a company in the same industry with comparable sales volume that is vertically integrated from a manufacturing point of view and, as a result, must carry additional work-in-process and raw material inventories. Therefore, the degree of vertical integration will affect a company's inventory turnover ratio. This also applies to the distribution system of a company. One company may distribute goods through its own regional warehouses, whereas another company may rely upon independent wholesalers.

In summary, inventory turnover ratios may be of value to management as a means of identifying possible inventory problems. For example, a decreasing trend of the inventory turnover ratio within a company, or a ratio that is lower than comparable industry averages, may indicate the need for further analysis. This analysis should indicate the factors which have caused ratio variations, and the corrective action, as required.

Another consideration in the financial analysis of inventory has to do with the costing of inventory. If a company is on a LIFO accounting basis, any analysis relative to inventories should be based on the current cost of inventory rather than the LIFO book value. This is necessary so as to have consistent data because the cost of goods sold, other current assets, and current liabilities are stated in terms of current costs.

Another approach to analyzing inventories might be a breakdown of the balance sheet inventory amount by subsidiary, division, and/or plant. Depending upon the size and organization of a company, a further breakdown may be made by profit or cost center, warehouse, sales region, and/or product line. In a manufacturing company, management should also identify inventories according to raw material, work-in-process, finished goods, service parts, and factory supplies.

Another dimension of inventory analysis frequently used is a breakdown by material, direct labor, variable overhead, and fixed overhead. Identifying the fixed overhead content of inventory is of particular interest because a change in this category of inventory from one accounting period to another reflects the difference in reported financial operating results caused by the use of a direct cost accounting system versus an absorption cost accounting system. A direct cost accounting system does not recognize any fixed overhead in inventory, whereas an absorption cost system includes some fixed overhead as part of the inventory account. Under an absorption cost system, an increase in the fixed burden content of inventory during an accounting period represents the capitalization into inventory during an accounting period of a portion of current period fixed overhead costs, thereby reducing current period expenses. Conversely, a decrease in the fixed overhead content of inventory would reflect the expensing in the current accounting period of fixed overhead costs incurred in prior accounting periods.

Another type of analysis is the recognition of inventories which are associated with specific decisions made by management. Inventories of this nature are usually associated with specific time periods and can be referred to as "programmed" inventories. Some examples are:

Seasonal inventory: The planned buildup of inventory to meet high seasonal demand while maintaining a reasonably stable production rate.

Strike-hedge inventory: Increased finished goods inventory, based upon a management decision, in anticipation of a potential internal strike, or increased raw material stock in anticipation of possible strikes against primary suppliers.

Price-hedge inventory: The stock piling of inventory because of known or anticipated price increases in materials.

Job order inventory: Increases in raw material and work-in-process inventories related to abnormally large special orders.

Proper recognition of programmed inventories can assist management in the planning and control of inventory levels and the projected needs for additional working capital.

In addition to the classifications of inventory mentioned, there are many other detailed breakdowns that can be made such as: commodity code (e.g., sheet steel, castings, forgings, etc.), slow-moving items (e.g., no activity in the last year), excessive stock (e.g., more than two years' projected usage), obsolete parts, perishable items, salvage stock, consignment stock, in-transit stock, etc. In cases such as obsolete and surplus stock, the inventory should be carried at a value that reflects its market, scrap, or rework value. The various types of breakdown described can assist a company in identifying current and potential inventory problems so that timely management action can be taken.

The purpose of categorizing inventories is to provide management with a basis for the control of specific inventories through a continuing review of their relationship to the total inventory and of changes in specific levels from period to period. A knowledge of inventory costs also assists management in determining priorities in the development and implementation of improved inventory management techniques. There have been cases where companies directed a disproportionate amount of effort to the control of those portions of inventories which accounted for a relatively small percentage of the total. Recognition of the different types of inventory is also important in developing an integrated inventory management system. For example, different inventory control techniques are frequently required to control raw material, work-in-process, and finished goods inventories.

ABC APPROACH TO INVENTORY MANAGEMENT

One of the most widely recognized concepts of inventory management is referred to as ABC inventory control. The objective of ABC control is to vary the expense associated with maintaining appropriate control according to the potential savings associated with a proper level of such control. For example, an item having an inventory cost of $10,000, such as sheet steel, has a much greater potential for saving of expenses related to maintaining inventories than an item with a cost of $20. The ABC approach is a means of categorizing inventoried items into three classes, "A," "B," and "C," according to the potential amount to be controlled.

When items have been classified, appropriate control techniques are developed for each class of inventory. "A" items justify the use of precise control techniques, whereas "C" items should be controlled by means of general control techniques.

The primary criteria for classifying inventoried items into "A," "B," and "C" categories is the annual dollar usage of each item. This is accomplished by multiplying the annual unit usage of each inventoried item by its unit cost and then listing all items in descending order according to annual dollar usage. This listing should also include a column to show the cumulative annual dollar usage by line item. Such a listing reflects the distribution of annual dollar usage. A typical distribution in a manufacturing operation shows that the top 15% of the line items, in terms of annual dollar usage, represent 80% of the total annual dollar usage. These items are normally classified as "A" items. The next 15% of the line items, in terms of annual dollar usage, reflect an additional 15% of the annual dollar usage and are designated as "B" items. The "C" items represent the remaining 70% of the items in inventory and account for only 5% of the total annual dollar usage. In some cases the ABC classifications will be developed independently for different types of inventory such as finished goods, raw material, and service parts.

In addition to annual dollar usage, several other factors need to be considered in developing criteria for classifying items into "A," "B," and "C" categories. In this regard, a "truth table" can be used to facilitate the classification process. A typical "truth table" is shown on page 67. The questions included in such a table, and the parameters associated with the questions, will vary according to the specific inventory being analyzed.

In this table six questions are asked regarding each inventoried item. A "yes" answer is indicated by a one in the appropriate column under the part number; a "no" answer is reflected by a zero. The column next to the question provides the key to the classification by indicating the inventory class associated with a "yes" answer to each question. When there is more than one "yes" answer per item, the highest classification is used. In a typical inventory, basic raw materials, such as sheet steel, bar stock, etc., and inventoried sub-assemblies are found in the "A" cate-

"Truth" Table for ABC Classification

Questions	Yes answer	Part numbers				
		1	2	3	4	5
1. Is Annual Usage More Than $10,000?	A	①	0	0	0	0
2. Is Annual Usage Between $1,000 and $10,000?	B	0	①	0	0	0
3. Is Annual Usage Less than $1,000?	C	0	0	①	①	①
4. Is the Unit Cost Over $100?	B	①	0	0	0	0
5. Does the Physical Nature of the Item Cause Special Storage Problems?	B	0	0	0	0	①
6. Would a Stock Out Result in Excessive Costs?	B	0	0	0	①	0
Classification		A	B	C	B	B

gory. Small metal stampings with moderate usage are frequently "B" items; while "C" items are typically hardware items such as small nuts, bolts, and screws.

In summary, an ABC inventory classification provides the basis for varying the degree of control, according to the value of control, by means of establishing three inventory classifications. So far only the classification aspects of ABC inventory control have been covered; later in this chapter some of the specific techniques typically associated with the three classes of inventory will be reviewed.

INVENTORY DATA REQUIREMENTS

The effectiveness of any inventory management system is dependent upon the accuracy, timeliness, and scope of data available for input into the various control techniques and inventory reports. The importance of reviewing inventory data requirements is emphasized by the fact that in some cases elaborate decision rules, complex reports, and sophisticated equations are developed to control inventory without properly considering the nature of the data that is available or the cost of generating new forms of data.

One of the initial activities in developing a modern inventory management system is an appraisal of currently available inventory data and the development of improved reporting procedures. With the increased use of electronic data processing equipment, the development of an inventory data base should take into consideration the following unique capabilities of computers: mass storage of data, the ability to perform complex calculations, and the high degree of reliability in manipulating data. Because of these unique capabilities, the nature of a computer-based inventory management system will normally differ in terms of the size of the data base that can be accommodated from a manual or mechanical type system; however, this does not imply that manual or mechanical systems are necessarily obsolete. In many cases, the size and nature of a business organization does not justify the expense associated with electronic data processing systems. Manual or mechanical control systems can be effective, and will normally cost considerably less to install than a computer-based system.

One of the primary forms of data required in an inventory management system is a record of inventory status and the ability to locate the material. Many control systems have failed because the inventory stock status report was inaccurate or not available in sufficient time to take action. Some of the primary causes of errors in the stock status report are related to inaccuracies of input records, such as storeroom requisitions, production reports, scrap reports, returned material reports, cancellation of orders, etc. An effective inventory control system requires tight control over all basic input documents which are used to update the stock status.

Another type of data required for effective control of inventory is the projected usage of inventoried items. This relates to planning and forecasting as discussed in the previous chapter. In many cases a projection of inventory requirements is based on historical usage records which are a part of, or a by-product of, the stock status report. When production is based on fixed assembly schedules, projected material requirements are predicated on the production plan in terms of units to be assembled, multiplied by the components comprising the bill of material for each product. This method of determining requirements is referred to as a bill of material explosion routine and is frequently done on a computer. It should be stressed that the success of this method of determining material requirements is dependent upon complete and accurate bills of materials. In this regard, an accurate record of the bills of material is an essential part of the inventory management data base. When a bill of material explosion routine is used, procedures should be reviewed, or developed, to ensure that there is a systematic method of updating the bills of material so as to reflect currently all pertinent engineering change notices.

In addition to knowing projected usage, it is necessary to know the amount of time required to obtain additional stock when a requirement to replenish stock is recognized. This is normally referred to as lead time and applies to both manufactured and purchased items. Lead time can be defined as the elapsed time from the moment that an item needs to be reordered until the ordered item is physically available in inventory. The components normally associated with purchase lead time include: stock status review interval (e.g., the stock status may be reviewed daily to determine what items should be ordered), time required to issue a requisition, time required to initiate a purchase order, vendor delivery time (from mailing of the order to physical receipt of material), receiving time, inspection time, and material handling time required to place the material in the appropriate storage location. The basis for establishing manufacturing lead time is basically the same, with the exception that the components associated with vendor delivery time and receiving time are replaced by the scheduled production time. While lead times usually remain relatively constant, they require updating as a result of selecting a new vendor, material shortages, changes in quoted delivery times, and variations in the shop work load which may result in production scheduling changes.

As control techniques are refined, additional forms of data are needed, for example, the forecasted error range in connection with the projected usage of items and the anticipated variations in lead time relative to reordering items. The error range as it relates to forecasting demand was discussed in the prior chapter.

Information is also required concerning the level of service to be provided. The level of service relative to inventory control can be defined in a number of ways. Some examples are: per cent of orders shipped within two working days after receipt of the order, per cent of line items back-ordered versus line items shipped complete, per cent of stock-outs relative to inventory withdrawals, and the number of production delays per period associated with material shortages. Most inventory control systems also maintain data relative to back orders, open purchase orders, and open production orders.

The exact nature of the data base for an inventory management system will vary according to circumstances. The important point to remember is that the effectiveness of the system will be dependent in part upon the quality of the data base.

REORDER POINT SYSTEMS

The essence of an inventory management system can be defined in terms of two decisions, namely, (1) when to reorder and (2) how much to order. The first decision, when to reorder, is associated with reorder point systems which are responsible for initiating action to obtain additional material. The second decision, how much to order, is related to order quantity systems which will be discussed later in this chapter.

Reorder point systems can be divided into two basic categories; (1) those predicated on known material requirements and (2) systems which assume a degree of uncertainty in terms of future demand. A job shop type of operation schedules most materials for receipt based upon known orders in the production backlog, and is an example of the first type of system because material requirements are known with a high degree of reliability. Another example of such a system is a plant which operates according to a fixed production schedule.

The second type of system recognizes that material requirements are based upon forecasts with anticipated deviations between the forecasted and actual usage. It is assumed that these deviations or errors can be represented by known statistical distribution patterns, for example, the bell shaped (normal) distribution. Such a system is frequently referred to as a probability model because the reorder point is based in part upon the probability theory. In most cases, finished goods and service parts inventory control systems are based upon a degree of uncertainty regarding future demand.

Returning to the first category of reorder point systems, the decision to reorder is derived from an analysis of required shipping dates and production schedules. Frequently these production schedules are based upon network analysis which includes the use of such specialized techniques as Critical Path Method (CPM), Line of Balance, PERT, and Gantt charts. These techniques, in turn, utilize data such as lead times for purchased and manufactured items. The decision to reorder is based upon the materials requirements, as established in the bills of material, and the scheduling of these materials so as to meet established production and shipping dates. In most cases, materials will be scheduled into inventory prior to their immediate requirement in production. This is a form of safety stock and is used as a means of preventing production delays which might arise as a result of late receipt of purchased materials, or of production delays associated with manufactured component parts and sub-assemblies. The size of the safety stock to be carried will depend upon such factors as the potential loss from a production delay, the expense incident to carrying additional inventory for a specific period of time, and the probability of late delivery.

The second category of reorder point systems is based upon depicting the variation in stock level over a period of time. In this type of system, demand reflects a forecasted volume and an error range. The basic reorder point can be calculated as follows:

$$\text{Reorder point (ROP)} = L(D) + \text{safety stock}$$

where:

L is the anticipated lead time in weeks.
D is the forecasted demand in units per week.

When the stock level reaches the reorder point, an order is initiated for additional stock. The first portion of the equation regarding lead time multiplied by the forecasted demand is relatively easy to understand. If actual demand equals forecasted demand during the lead time period, and the delivery of materials is on time, the inventory level will reach the safety stock level at the same time as the replenishment order is received. The portion of the equation relative to safety stock is more complex and requires further explanation.

If both forecasted demand during the reordering cycle and the length of the lead time period were always known with certainty, safety stock would not be needed; however, both of these factors are normally variable and as a result represent averages rather than exact figures during a given reorder cycle. If no safety stock is carried, a stock-out condition could be anticipated fifty per cent of the time when stock is reordered. If stock were ordered twice a year, one stock-out per year would be anticipated; however, if stock were ordered weekly, twenty-six stock-outs per year would be expected. Using statistical techniques, safety stock quantities can be computed which will result in various predetermined levels of service. This relationship is expressed by the graph on page 73. As the dollar investment in safety stock increases, the level of service improves. A review of a graph of this nature, based upon inventory simulation runs using a statistical inventory control model, can provide management with the type of information needed to balance inventory levels and levels of service.

The level of service can be, and in many cases should be, varied by inventory category. For example, "C" items might have a higher level of service than "A" or "B" items because of the limited investment in safety stock required to improve the level of service. The level of service might also be varied according to the problems associated with a stock-out, as, for example, the risk of closing down an assembly line, or the profit contribution of a product line. A high-profit margin product would justify a higher level of service than a product with a very narrow profit margin.

Most computer-based inventory management systems rely on statistical calculations to determine safety stocks, while manual systems frequently depend upon decision tables, as illustrated

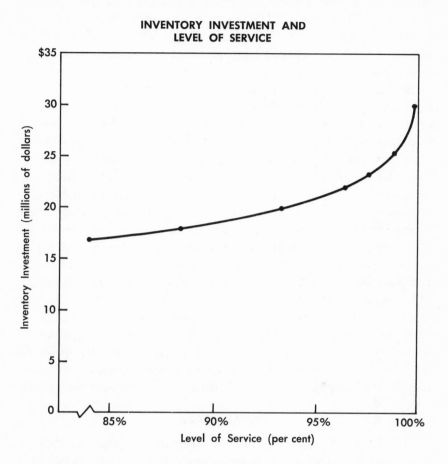

INVENTORY INVESTMENT AND
LEVEL OF SERVICE

Routine Safety Stocks Expressed in Weeks of Average Demand

Inventory class	Lead time		
	4 weeks or less	5 to 13 weeks	13 or more weeks
A	2	3	4
B	3	4	5
C	6	8	10

on the lower part of page 73.   Such a decision table may indicate
that an "A" item with a lead time of seven weeks should have a
safety stock of three weeks' average usage, while a "C" item with
the same lead time should have eight weeks' average usage as a
safety stock.

So far in the discussion of reorder points, it has been assumed
that they would be developed in an objective manner predicated
upon the data in the inventory data base and a level of service
as determined by a management policy decision.   While in most
cases this method is the most desirable, there are still many inventories which are controlled based upon reorder points which have
been developed in a subjective manner.   Although the subjective
approach, which relies upon intuitive judgment, is normally a less
time-consuming method of establishing reorder points, the resulting effectiveness of control over inventory is diminished.   The
subjective method of establishing reorder points can also make a
company overly dependent upon the judgment of one individual.
With very few exceptions, a comparison of reorder point systems
based upon both subjective and objective approaches will indicate
that the objective method results in a more effective control of
inventory as compared with the subjective approach.   Prior to
discussing the subject of how much to order, several of the more
popular techniques will be described relative to reorder points.

VISUAL REVIEW

A highly subjective method of determining when to reorder
is a visual review of stock in inventory.   For example, in the old-
time general store, the owner would inspect his inventory and determine what should be ordered.   This technique still has limited
application where the cost of the inventory is low and the cost
of control needs to be minimized, for example, a small inventory
of office supplies.   Control is based upon the judgment of the
individual ordering and a periodic review of the items being
ordered.

TWO-BIN SYSTEM

The two-bin, or reserve stock system, is a method of control
commonly used in connection with "C" type items.   Under this
type of control, it is not necessary to maintain a perpetual record

of inventory status because the need to reorder is determined as a result of physically removing material from inventory.   A two-bin system is set up by physically separating an amount of material equal to the reorder point.   This reserve stock or second bin is not used until all the stock in the primary storage bin has been used.   When the primary stock bin has been exhausted and it is necessary to issue stock from the second bin, a requisition is initiated to reorder stock.   During the reorder cycle, the reserve stock in the second bin is used.   When the reordered stock is received, a quantity of material equal to the reorder point is again placed in the second bin; the remaining material is placed in the primary storage bin.   The physical separation of the second bin, or reserve stock, can be accomplished by using partitioned bins, by placing the reserve stock in a bag within the one bin or by maintaining reserve stock quantities in an entirely separate physical storage area.

The advantages of this form of control are minimum control expense and positive physical recognition of reorder points.   The principal disadvantages are the limited information available regarding inventory status of items, lack of monthly usage data, and reliance on storeroom personnel to initiate requisitions when the reserve stock is first used.

MIN-MAX SYSTEM

The minimum-maximum (min-max) system is frequently used in connection with manual inventory control systems.   The minimum quantity is established in the same way as any reorder point. The maximum is the minimum quantity plus the optimum order lot size.   In practice, a requisition is initiated when a withdrawal reduces the inventory below the minimum level; the order quantity is the maximum minus the inventory status after the withdrawal. If the final withdrawal reduces the stock level substantially below the minimum level, the order quantity will be larger than the calculated optimum order lot quantity.

The effectiveness of a min-max system is determined by the method and precision with which the minimum and maximum parameters are established.   If these parameters are based upon arbitrary judgments with a limited factual basis, the system will be limited in its effectiveness. If the minimums are based on an objective rational basis, the system can be very effective.

REORDER POINT—EOQ SYSTEM

This system is normally based upon the use of equations and related decision tables or charts to establish objectively the reorder point and the order quantity (EOQ). These equations quantitatively balance conflicting cost objectives, based on information in the data base, so as to determine the course of action which will minimize total costs. The method of establishing the optimum order quantity will be reviewed in the next section of this chapter. When equations are used in establishing reorder points and order quantities, the set of equations used are referred to as a control model. The sophistication of the inventory control model is based upon the number of variables incorporated into the equations and the complexities of the statistical-mathematical techniques associated with the equations. In many cases, one of the principal problems associated with complex models, that of long mathematical calculations, can be resolved by developing tables and charts which reflect the result of the equations at various incremental levels. This approach has been successfully applied to the determination of reorder points as well as to that of order quantities.

A reorder point—EOQ system can be applied to all categories of inventory; however, the sophistication of the model used may be varied according to the inventory to be controlled. "A" items may justify a model which considers a large number of variables, while "C" items are controlled using a more simplified model.

RESERVATION SYSTEM

A reservation system is actually a modification of either the min-max system or the reorder point—EOQ system. Instead of simply reducing the inventory level as a result of physical disbursements, a reservation system recognizes requirements *prior to* disbursement and breaks down the stock status report in terms of available stock as well as physical stock. In effect, a reservation is made for known material requirements, such as orders received prior to physical disbursement. The available stock is normally defined as the physical stock on hand, minus open requirements, plus stock on order. The reorder point in a reservation system is based upon the available stock balance rather than the physical stock balance. The advantage of this type of system is that the need to reorder is recognized at an earlier point in time, thereby permitting action to be taken which may prevent a stock-out. Reservation systems are in common use throughout business, especially in regard to finished goods, and to materials required for manufacturing operations with long production lead times.

In the case of fixed build schedules, reservations can be determined by multiplying the items comprising the bills of material by the production forecast. In some cases this explosion routine also recognizes reservations (requirements) in terms of time periods, or time "buckets." When this is done, the bills of material must include the lead times associated with each item on the bill of material. After requirements have been identified with time periods, they are netted against available stock to determine when additional orders should be placed. A time bucketing of material requirements normally requires a great deal of data manipulation and as a result is usually confined to computer-based inventory management systems.

In summary, there are a number of techniques which can be used to determine when to order. The particular technique that should be used will depend upon a number of factors which are related to the cost of the items and the expense of maintaining the controls.

ORDER QUANTITIES

Having determined the need to reorder material, a decision must be made as to how much material should be ordered. When this decision is based upon a quantitative analysis of related costs, the quantity to be ordered is frequently referred to as the economic order quantity, or EOQ. The term "economic order quantity" implies that a specific order quantity will result in the lowest total variable expenditures to a company in terms of the variables included in the quantitative analysis and of the assumptions inherent in the equation being used.

If there were no variations in demand or replenishment lead time, the problems of inventory control would be lessened considerably. The only major problems would then center about the determination of economic production, purchasing or delivery quantities so as to balance the expenses of carrying stock against the expenses resulting from the initiation and receipt of replenishment orders, and considerations relating to price discounts for quantity purchases.

One of the earliest developments in the use of mathematical techniques in the area of inventory control was the economic lot size or economic order quantity formula. Theoretically, the economic order quantity Q corresponds to the point at which the annual carrying and ordering expenses are equal.

The so-called classical inventory control formula is illustrated by use of hypothetical data on page 79. This formula takes into account the following factors:

C = Unit cost of the item.
S = Estimated annual usage of the item.
E = Expense of handling an order.
K = Expense of carrying the inventory, stated in terms of per cent of cost of goods on hand.
E_c = Annual expense of carrying the inventory.
E_o = Annual expense of ordering in the case of purchased items, and the expense of production order and set up in the case of manufactured items.

The development of the economic order quantity formula can be shown as follows:

$$TVE = E_c + E_o = KC\frac{Q}{2} + \frac{S}{Q}E$$

where TVE is the total variable expense associated with the inventory (the annual expense of carrying the inventory plus the annual expense of ordering), and $Q/2$ is the average level of inventory over the year.

The minimum TVE occurs where $E_c = E_o$, giving:

$$Q = \sqrt{\frac{2SE}{KC}}$$

where Q is the economic order quantity.

Illustration of Use of Classical Inventory Control Formula

	Valves (High-unit value, low-usage item)	Washers (Low-unit value, high-usage item)
Original practice:		
1. Unit cost..	$10.00	$0.10
2. Quantity on hand at inventory date................	250	8,000
3. Annual usage...................................	1,200	120,000
4. Average order quantity.........................	300	5,000
5. Expense of carrying inventory, in per cent...........	15%	15%
6. Annual expense of carrying average inventory $\left(\dfrac{\text{Item } 4}{2} \times \text{Item } 1 \times \text{Item } 5\right)$ ignoring safety cushion	$225.00	$37.50
7. Expense of handling an order.....................	$8.00	$8.00
8. Expense of handling year's orders $\left(\dfrac{\text{Item } 3}{\text{Item } 4} \times \text{Item } 7\right)$.	$32.00	$192.00
9. Total expense of carrying and ordering year's requirements.....................................	$257.00	$229.50
Indicated practice:		
10. Economic order quantity* (approx.)................	115†	11,000
11. Number of orders per year (approx.)..............	10.5	11.0
12. Annual expense of carrying economic inventory $\left(\dfrac{\text{Item } 10}{2} \times \text{Item } 1 \times \text{Item } 5\right)$.................	$86.25‡	$82.50‡
13. Expense of handling year's orders (Item 11 × Item 7)..	$84.00‡	$88.00‡
14. Total expense of carrying and ordering year's requirements.....................................	$170.25	$170.50
Annual Saving:		
Amount....................................	$86.75	$59.00
Per cent...................................	34%	26%

* Formula—Economic order quantity is square root of twice annual usage times expense of handling an order, divided by unit cost times carrying expense percentage.

† The application of the formula is:

$$Q = \sqrt{\frac{2 \times 1,200 \times 8.00}{15\% \times 10.00}} = 115 \text{ (approx.)}$$

‡ Except for "rounding off" in connection with computation of square roots and number of orders to be placed, amounts on lines 12 and 13 would be equal.

While the EOQ method is frequently used in business today, the procedures for establishing the parameters used in the equation are sometimes not fully understood. In the classic EOQ there are four variables that determine the order quantity, namely: (1) the forecasted annual demand for the item expressed in units, (2) the variable expenses associated with issuing and following up an order (whether for purchase or production) in terms of dollars per order, (3) the expense of carrying inventory for one year, expressed as a percentage, and (4) the variable cost of one unit. It should be noted that all expenditures considered in an EOQ calculation are variable or marginal costs, sometimes referred to as out-of-pocket costs.

In determining whether an expenditure is variable, it is necessary to determine how a specific item would be influenced by the decision to change the number of orders issued or the amount of material carried in inventory.

The variable costs of placing an order with an outside vendor include the following: the cost of preparing a material requisition and a purchase order, the time (and related costs) required to follow up a purchase order, the time and costs of receiving and inspecting, the time and costs required to place the material in the proper inventory location, and the time and costs associated with making payment to the vendor and maintaining related accounting records. The costs associated with a material purchase order may vary from as little as one dollar to over fifteen dollars per order. Normally, "C" items have a lower ordering cost than "A" items because less order follow-up is required. If detailed analysis indicates a significant variation in ordering costs between "A," "B," and "C" items, separate ordering costs should be used in developing order quantities. The recent application of computer programs in the purchasing and accounts payable areas has tended to decrease the marginal cost of issuing an order. In many cases this lower cost of ordering has not been properly recognized in the calculation of EOQ's; thus, an analysis of the current realism of order costs used in the control model should be undertaken.

The cost of ordering a manufactured item is determined in a similar manner to that used for purchased items. The primary factors to be considered are the cost of preparing a materials requisition and a production order, the costs to set up and tear down equipment used to produce the item, material handling costs associated with movement to and from the manufacturing operation, and inspection time. The cost of ordering a manufactured item is usually comparable to the cost of ordering a purchased item, with the exception of equipment set-up and tear-down costs. This component varies widely from item to item depending upon the manufacturing processes involved. If production of an item requires a number of operations, it is necessary to add together the individual set-up and tear-down costs associated with each operation. Normally the set-up and tear-down times associated with each operation are found on the route sheet for the item.

The forecasted demand figure is the one used in determining the reorder point; however, it is expressed in terms of annual demand. The variable unit cost of an item is normally available in the standard cost records of a company.

The fourth parameter, relating to the annual cost of carrying inventory, can be controversial and requires careful review. The cost of capital is usually the largest and often also the most controversial factor included in the carrying cost. The controversy is over whether to evaluate the capital tied up in inventory in terms of current interest rates on bank loans outstanding or as long-term commitments which would require a return on investment commensurate with other capital expenditures. In the short-term, the marginal cost of capital is based primarily on bank interest rates; however, an inventory management system results in establishing levels of inventory investment on a continuing basis. As such, the capital tied up in inventory should be viewed as a long-range investment, with a cost of capital commensurate with other capital investments. If a company has an objective of returning 10% after taxes on equity investment, the cost of capital before taxes would be approximately 20%.

In some companies the cost of capital relative to inventory investment is a weighted average, which takes into consideration the debt-equity structure of the company and the relative capital costs associated with each type of financing.

In addition to the cost of capital, the inventory carrying cost calculation should consider such factors as obsolescence, spoilage, insurance, property taxes, warehousing costs, and the cost of taking physical inventories. Frequently, indications of the relative importance of these costs can be found in the accounting records. At other times, special cost studies may have to be made. Again, it should be stressed that the costs considered in establishing inventory decisions are marginal costs. If a cost is included in the inventory carrying charge, it should actually be capable of being made to vary according to the volume of the inventory being carried.

In addition to the classic EOQ, there are a number of related equations which are refinements of the classic EOQ. They take into consideration additional variables and/or operating assumptions.

One of the primary reasons for modifying the classic equation relates to the assumption in the equation that the rate of demand is constant. While this assumption may be reasonably valid a majority of the time, there are cases where demand is periodic in nature, or intrinsically highly variable. For example, a job shop operation frequently has periodic demand requirements for some types of material. When this occurs, a modified approach is required in determining order quantity that takes such variability into account. Another situation relates to equations which reflect the impact of the interrelationship between the level of safety stock associated with the reorder point and the optimum order quantity. This is accomplished by including, as variables in the order quantity calculation, the variability in lead time demand and the desired level of service.

Another very important modification in the classic EOQ equation relates to quantity discounts which are frequently available when purchasing materials. The classical EOQ formula may indicate a purchase quantity of 115 units; however, a substantial price discount may be available when 150 units are ordered, and further discounts when 200 or 500 units are ordered. Under these circumstances it is necessary to compute the EOQ quantity at each of the quantity discount levels. In evaluating quantity discounts, material cost is considered separately because it varies according to the order size.

SUMMARY

The intent of this chapter has been to explore the concept of inventory management in terms of practical techniques commonly used in business today.   In addition to discussing the techniques, considerable stress has been placed upon the importance of developing an accurate data base relative to inventory decisions.   The nature and importance of the parameters included in various inventory control equations have also been discussed. In conclusion, it should be stated that the benefits from modern inventory management control techniques are realized only when they are effectively executed by operating management.   Techniques are not an end in themselves but rather a means to an end, improved profitability.

5

Concepts of "Cost" for Purposes of Business Management

In one way or another management concerns itself with every expenditure made, and it tries to obtain from each the maximum benefits for the business. Accounting aids in the accomplishment of this objective by presenting the financial data so as to provide a means of judging the wisdom of past decisions and predicting the consequences of adopting any particular course of future action.

The decisions made by management always involve risk. Sound (or lucky) decisions help the company economically. Unsound (or unlucky) decisions hurt. Those making the decisions must be informed.

THE ACCOUNTING FUNCTION

To understand the steps taken in the determination of income, it is necessary to have an appreciation of the bases underlying the classification of expenditures for purposes of accounting for, and maintaining control over, the capital utilized in the operations. In this context "expenditures" include all transactions which result in the release of assets or the incurring of liabilities.

Controlling expenditures, with the basic and related problem of maximizing revenues, is a major factor in the success of every enterprise. At all times the best efforts of management are directed at improving efficiency, which means getting the most for every dollar spent.

Much of the information required by business management is of a nonaccounting nature, such as is provided by scientists, engineers, market researchers, industrial psychologists, and others; however, most business activities have an economic effect. The recording, classifying, analyzing, and summarizing into meaningful reports of the economic effects of these activities are all part of the accounting function.

The information provided by the accounting process must be accurate, timely, clear, and meaningful. It must be clear and meaningful to those who use it, and it cannot be judged solely from the viewpoint of specially trained accountants. Further, the information must be tailored toward the use to which it will be put and not considered as an end in itself.

MEANING OF "COST" AND "EXPENSE"

The attention given to definitions of the words "cost" and "expense" by various authoritative writers reveals the concern accountants have for their proper usage. Nevertheless, there is considerable confusion over just what the words should mean. Of particular interest is the fact that one is often used to define the other.

Set forth below are typical examples of definitions, taken from four sources:

Example A:

"Cost" is the amount, measured in money, of cash expended or other property transferred, capital stock issued, services performed or a liability incurred in consideration of goods or services received or to be received. Costs can be classified as unexpired or expired. . . . Expired costs are those which are not applicable to the production of future revenues and for that reason are treated as deductions from current revenues or are charged against retained earnings. Examples of such expired costs are costs of products or other assets sold or disposed of, and current expenses. . . . "Expense" in its broadest sense includes all expired costs which are deductible from revenues. In income statements, distinctions are often made between various types of expired costs by captions or titles including such terms as cost, expense, or loss, e.g., cost of goods or services sold, operating expenses, selling and administrative expenses, and loss on sale of property. These distinctions seem generally useful, and indicate that the narrower use of the term "expense" refers to such items as operating, selling, or administrative expenses, interest and taxes. . . .[1]

Example B:

Cost: 1. An expenditure or outlay of cash, other property, capital stock, or services, or the incurring of a liability therefor, identified with goods or services purchased or with any loss incurred, and measured in terms of the amount of cash paid or payable or the market value of other property, capital stock, or services given in exchange. . . . 2. Hence, the object of any such expenditure or outlay; as direct labor: a product cost.

Expense: 1. An item or class of cost of (or loss from carrying on) an activity; a present or past expenditure defraying a present operating cost; an item of capital expenditures written down or off. . . . 2. A class term for expenditures recognized as operating costs of a current or past period.[2]

Example C:

. . . the term "cost" is most elusive. In the income statement . . . "cost of goods sold" is the phrase that is used to describe the cost of the merchandise that was marketed during the fiscal period. However, terms like "salaries," "delivery expenses," "store supplies," "advertising," and others are not labeled costs but expenses. Such a distinction in terminology is not a happy one, but convention and euphony explain the use of the words even if they do not justify the tending to confuse. "Costs" are the fundamental data of all accounting and the term should therefore be used in its broadest sense. . . . Expenses . . . are the costs applied against revenue. . . .[3]

Example D:

The term "cost" . . . refer[s] to the amount invested in obtaining a product or a service that is expected to be useful later in a business concern, useful in obtaining sales revenue. The "investment" may be made directly by a cash payment or by a promise to pay, or by converting some kinds of assets into others. "Expense" on the other hand . . . refer[s] to expired

---

[1] Committee on Terminology, AICPA, "Cost, Expense, and Loss," *Accounting Terminology Bulletins*, No. 4 (July, 1957).

[2] Kohler, *A Dictionary for Accountants* (2d ed., 1957), pp. 140, 202.

[3] Matz, Curry & Frank, *Cost Accounting* (2d ed., 1957), p. 7.

costs, and particularly those that are charged to profit and loss for a period. . . . When the product is sold, its "cost" will be charged to profit and loss as "cost of goods sold"—an expense account. . . . The distinction is more appropriately applied to product costs than to administrative or distributive costs. The latter may be thought of as an investment in a valuable service, but it is the nature of the service to be used as fast as it is created, or as fast as the cost is recognized. Hence, as is customary, it may as well be called expense as soon as the cost of obtaining it is recorded.[4]

The word "cost" is the workhorse of accountants in discussing expenditures.

The *Accountants' Cost Handbook* lists twenty-two types of costs and states that the "word 'cost' is used in such a wide variety of ways that it is advisable to use it with an adjective or phrase which will convey the shade of meaning intended."[5] Included in this list are period costs, fixed and variable costs, controllable and noncontrollable costs, future costs, discretionary costs, and postponable costs.

These examples illustrate the tendency to consider all expenditures "costs," even when discussing the impact of the expenditures in the determination of income. In addition to the conventional term "cost of goods sold" a large variety of income charges are referred to as "costs." Even the charges which are customarily called "expenses" as soon as incurred or recognized (such as general, selling and administrative expenses) are often referred to as costs. It is not unusual to see discussions of administrative costs, distribution costs, legal costs, research and development costs, and finance costs. During the course of at least one talk on accounting procedures reference was made to "the *cost* of the president's salary."

The broad concept of "cost" as including all expenditures appears to be influenced by the fact that for almost every item of property owned by a business it is possible to establish an amount generally recognized as its cost. The cost of a trade receivable is the amount which would have been realized had the sale been made for cash rather than on credit. The cost of an insurance policy is the amount of the premium. The cost of a particular

---

[4] Vance, *Theory and Technique of Cost Accounting* (rev. ed., 1958), p. 14.
[5] Dickey, *Accountants' Cost Handbook* (2d ed., 1960), p. 1.11.

machine or automobile is the amount paid therefor. When applied to these items, this is a concept anyone can understand without a modifying adjective or explanation. There is not the same degree of clarity when the word "cost" is applied to expenditures for such items as utility bills, the janitor's salary, a salesman's airline fare or hotel bill, and interest on a loan at the bank. When used in connection with statements of income, some limitation on the concept of cost appears desirable if the accounting function is to be fully performed.

Similarly, there is no particular benefit derived from applying the single word "expense" to all amounts deductible from revenues in determining the income resulting from the business activities of a particular period. This results in classifying as one group not only the amounts paid for gas and electricity, office maintenance, travel, and interest, but also the balance of a trade receivable which must be deducted from gross income because it is uncollectible, the portion of an insurance premium which is allocated to the period, and the provision for depreciation on machinery and automobiles.

Accountants could help themselves, and the results of their work would be better understood, if more specific and limited meanings were attached to the nouns "cost" and "expense." One group of terms which has been found to be useful is suggested on page 95 for the purpose of illustrating how expenditures may be classified to better appreciate the factors having a bearing on the determination of income.

MEANING OF "FIXED" AND "VARIABLE"

The effect of changes in the level of activity on the behavior of costs and expenses is most commonly reflected by a segregation based upon each item being either "fixed" or "variable." Simply stated, this procedure makes a distinction between fixed expenses, which are not affected by changes in rate of activity, and variable expenses, which increase with increases in activity and decrease with decreases in activity.

The segregation of business expenditures as being either "fixed" or "variable" reflects tendencies which actually exist, but the segregation is not as simple as the phrase fixed-variable implies. There are many qualifications and limitations which are essential to proper understanding. The significance to management of the fixed-variable segregation may be exaggerated.

The level of activity of the various phases of a business is under the control of management. For example, management determines the products and the quantity of each to be scheduled for production in a given period; it can order decreased or increased effort by the maintenance department; and it can direct a stepped up or reduced advertising campaign. This ability to set levels of activity does not, however, provide a direct means of controlling costs and expenses. It is as though activity levels had a power of direction in themselves. Although the activity levels are subject to control, once set they take over and determine to a considerable extent the course of future expenditures. Management must, therefore, understand the ways in which activity levels affect expenses.

The fixed-variable segregation may be a valid indication of the *tendencies* of expenditures to behave in the way described, but this does not mean that they can be fitted neatly into one category or another—or even a third, middle-ground category of semifixed or semivariable.

It cannot be said that a large number of expenses are so fixed as to be completely unaffected by the level of activity. This would imply that if there were no activity, the expense would be the same as at any other level of activity. There would also be an implication that while other factors, such as inflation, might have some effect on the amount of the expense, the level of activity would have no effect. At the other extreme, few expenses are so variable that there would be no such expense if there were no activity. Changes in the amount of most variable expenses are not directly proportional to changes in activity levels. Almost every item of cost or expense is both partially fixed and partially variable.

There are many expenses which vary with volume, not in a uniform pattern but rather in stages. Expenses of this type are constant for a certain range of volume, and then a unit must be added. This unit will be adequate for the range of volume starting at the time it is first needed until, at a higher activity level, another unit is needed. Some examples are factory supervision, service department expenses as the typing pool or duplicating department, and expense of having available for use such facilities as overhead material-handling equipment. Every usage of the fixed-variable segregation must take into consideration the semivariable nature of most costs and expenses.

Another qualification in the fixed-variable segregation is the period of time involved. The shorter the period of time, the greater the number of items which tend to be fixed. The ability to carry on a particular business activity (such as the production of castings, or sales distribution in a certain territory) is not usually changed from month to month. On the other hand, management decisions as to the activity of the business can always result in changes in capacity over a longer period of time.

Additional machines are purchased, buildings are remodeled and additions are constructed, even entire new plants are built for the purpose of meeting increased needs. Conversely, excess capacity of long standing can result in leasing all or part of a facility to another user, sale of an unused plant or excess equipment, or other reductions in response to lesser requirements. For these reasons expenses are actually fixed for relatively short time periods, and all expenses tend to become variable over long periods of time.

At best the fixed-variable segregation only describes the effect of volume on expenditures. It does not describe the effect of changes in production technology, product mix, economy measures, such as deferring maintenance, or, in the opposite direction, year-end bonuses. There are numerous causes other than volume for changes in the amount of any class of expenditure.

These observations with respect to the fixed-variable segregation lead to the conclusion that it is a tool to be used with care and an understanding of the underlying patterns of the costs and expenses to be classified. Within the limitations inherent in the segregation, it is a useful device widely employed.

The National Association of Accountants has published the results of a study entitled "Separating and Using Costs as Fixed and Variable," in which it is stated that such separations "are widely performed and are put to an increasing number of uses helpful to management."[6]   The report lists, in addition to flexible budgeting, the following applications found to be in use:

1. Measurement of utilization of facilities through a fixed cost rate.
2. Understanding of the company's profit structure.
3. Adjustment of operations to market conditions.
4. Determining relative profitability of products.
5. Marginal cost information to aid in sales and purchase price decisions or utilization capacity.
6. Development of planning as a major activity.
7. Evaluation of proposed capital outlays.
8. Assistance in making other decisions among alternatives which will differ in cost effects.

It will be noted that these applications of the fixed-variable segregation practice principally represent special studies prepared for a particular management purpose.   There is no inference that this segregation is the most informative for all purposes.

FACTORS IN CLASSIFYING EXPENDITURES

The selection of a basis for classifying expenditures will depend, in part, upon the level of management for whom the classification is being prepared.   At the departmental level certain expenses must be recognized as fixed, because the decision was made at a divisional level.   Similarly, the divisional management may have no direct control over other items.   From the standpoint of general management all these items could be considered controllable and should be viewed in an entirely different light.   The rental being paid for a fleet of trucks, for example, may have been decided upon only after extensive study by top management; however, at the departmental level the rental is fixed.   Therefore, any analysis of costs and expenses must be made with a realization of the authority possessed by the user to effect changes in the operations.

The amount of detail required is another consideration in classi-

---

[6] National Association of Accountants, *Accounting Practice Report,* No. 10 (June, 1960).

fying expenditures. In general, the lower the level of management, the greater is the need for detail. A superintendent might need to know every item of expense incurred in his department. A plant manager needs reports in larger areas of responsibility, and there may be delegation of responsibility for the detailed control of expenditures. Top management will be concerned with the effect of such decisions as those involving capital asset changes, product selections, make-or-buy alternatives, and territory assignments. The reports, forecasts, and budgets designed as a basis for this class of broad decisions are normally in summary rather than in detailed form.

In some instances the behavior pattern of certain costs and expenses will depend upon the accounting procedures adopted. Accounting procedures generally have no effect on when cash is paid or other assets are exchanged to obtain goods and services. This is determined by the contract between the parties. Accounting procedures do, however, determine when and how a change in the assets owned should be recognized, and the time and manner in which assets are transformed into costs and expenses. Many areas in addition to inventories afford examples: depreciation provisions, instalment purchases under a contract which is ostensibly a lease, repairs which are so major as to actually be improvements to an asset, choice between the cash basis and accrual basis of accounting for liabilities, the designation of certain items as "period" charges because they are considered attributable to the current accounting period and should not be carried forward to be deducted from revenues of future periods.

The accounting procedures chosen govern the recognition of what has taken place, but they do not alter the facts. Accounting procedures themselves cannot affect the ultimate profitability of a company. What they can do is affect periodic income determinations. To the extent that accounting reports are relied upon, decisions are influenced by the procedures used in preparing them. Different procedures would give different results and, presumably, could lead to different decisions. For example, providing for straight-line depreciation would result in larger amounts of computed income for years of capital asset expansion than would double-declining-balance depreciation. The company is equally profitable, but the bookkeeping entries are different.

In the same way the amount assigned to a particular inventory does not have any effect upon the quantity or condition of the goods on hand. Causation flows only from the goods on hand to the amount assigned thereto. If a company has 831 units of finished goods, 2,306 units of work in process at the sixth stage in the process, and 1,097 units of raw materials, no accounting procedure will change those facts.

The influence of accounting procedures on the behavior of expenses must be considered when analyzing expenditures for the purpose of making decisions during interim periods. It must also be considered when preparing expense classifications. Expenses which appear to fit a classification by their very nature may, on closer examination, prove to fit the classification only because of the accounting procedures used. Depreciation based on the passage of time may appear to be "fixed" with respect to activity levels. Where depreciation is computed on the basis of units produced, it would become "variable" with respect to activity levels.

RECOGNIZING ALTERNATIVE COURSES OF ACTION

The practicability of alternative courses of action and the effect of the alternatives on net income must also be understood in classifying expenditures. Over a long period there are alternatives to the making of all types of expenditures, and the nature of the alternatives has a bearing on the degree of control possessed by management.

Certain types of expenses may be readily reduced or eliminated, and the important considerations are what revenues will be lost as a consequence thereof and what will be the amount of resulting substitute expenditures. In the case of a wholesale food distributor, the sales force may be reduced from ten to eight, but this action could result in a decrease in volume. In the case of a manufacturer, five production lines may be cut to four, but the per unit cost could increase because of the payment of overtime and shift premiums. A retailer can discontinue deliveries to outlying districts, but some customers may be lost.

Some expenses have ready substitutes. For example, owned automobiles may be substituted for leased cars, certain materials (such as stampings) may be manufactured or purchased, and sales can be made either from branches or through independent distributors.

Even more serious consequences may follow a decision to reduce or eliminate other types of costs or expenses, that is, those which involve heavy penalties in changing them and those which are required for the company to be prepared to carry on a vital activity.

The penalties resulting from a decision to avoid certain future expenditures involve losses on sales of assets. Special-purpose industrial properties are frequently worth the investment in them only to the initial owner, to use them for the purposes originally intended. Except for the effect of inflation or an increase in value of specific properties due to other economic forces, sales of those assets to stop the expenses involved in their ownership usually involve losses. It is seldom that a purchaser is found who can more profitably use the assets in the same location for the same purposes.

Some expenses are the result of contracts, such as interest on debentures. These expenses can often be stopped only by defaulting on the contract and incurring damages. Rent under a five-year lease on a building to be used as a gas station continues regardless of whether a new expressway takes all the traffic away from the road on which the facility is built. Without an escape clause, that rent could only be stopped by substituting a costly settlement.

Some expenses are necessary for a business to be prepared to carry on vital activities. If the company does manufacturing, it must have a plant. Even if the plant were locked up tight during a prolonged strike, if owned, the real estate taxes and similar expenses would not stop; and, if leased, the rent would continue. Merely to retain the right to be recognized as a corporation may involve yearly franchise taxes. The alternative to expenses of this kind may require abandonment of a vital activity.

Within certain contexts it is convenient to consider some expenditures as being unchangeable. This is done with a reservation similar to the limitation placed on the fixed-variable segregation. This designation does no more than reflect generally that the amount of the expenditures will not fluctuate materially within certain ranges of activity levels and for certain periods of time. Thus, certain expenses are regarded as unchangeable under conditions of "business as usual." They are not in fact unchangeable, but any change may involve considerable operating difficulty and adverse economic consequences.

SUGGESTED CLASSIFICATIONS FOR EXPENDITURES

The foregoing discussion of concepts of "cost" for purposes of business management indicates the need for development of a meaningful classification of expenditures. The same classification may not be significant for multiple purposes, and the primary consideration in preparing any compilation of economic data is to present information which will be most useful to the reader.

Although a fixed-variable segregation will be the most practical in accomplishing a stated objective in many specific cases, it has its limitations.

In considering the significance of the reported operating results for a particular period, there are instances when management will better understand the factors which have had an effect on net income if all expenditures are classified as prime costs, controllable expenses, recurring expenses, and continuing expenses. In the determination of income, if the entire amount expended for an asset consumed, lost, or disposed of is deductible from revenues of a particular period, it could be denominated a prime cost (such as cost of goods sold); but if only a portion of the cost of an asset is allocable to the period, the amount deductible would be classified into one of the three types of expenses, for example, a provision for depreciation.

Under this proposal the phrase "prime costs" would be confined to expenditures resulting in the acquisition of assets—tangible or intangible, but in any event identifiable property which can be recognized as being owned. It would include expenditures directly resulting in the addition of "form utility" or "place util-

ity" to other property in the sense that form and place utility
are "goods" from an economic standpoint.   The wages of productive labor and the transportation charges incurred in moving tangible goods to a desired location would, therefore, be classified
as *prime costs*.

In summary, the expenditures which do not represent prime
costs would be considered in a classification system under which
controllable expenses are those incurred as a result of a current
(or continuing) decision of management, *recurring expenses* are
those necessary to keep the business operating even on a minimum
basis, and *continuing expenses* are those which have resulted from
decisions of management in a prior period.

Controllable expenses include such items as the maintenance
of production equipment, gas and oil for delivery trucks, and so
forth.   Expenses of this kind can be started or stopped by current
decisions.   Although management does not consciously decide
every day whether to run certain equipment, the equipment runs
as a result of a decision by management.   This type of expense
can be most readily changed, and the consequences which follow
from the alternatives can be predicted and measured with reasonable accuracy.   As a practical matter in day-to-day operations,
assuming no major changes in internal or external conditions, the
controllable expenses occupy the major portion of the attention
of all levels of management.

Recurring expenses include such items as salaries of persons
essential to operating the business, retainer fees, insurance, and
franchise taxes and license fees required because of being organized
for business.   After a business activity has been started, recurring
expenses require the least attention from management.   They can
be changed only with the greatest difficulty, if at all, and change
may mean going out of business or into another activity.

Continuing expenses include such items as obligations under
extended term contracts, pension plan expenses, salaries of persons
not indispensable but hired on a permanent basis rather than one
involving periodic layoffs, depreciation with respect to long-lived
assets, oil exploration, and expenditures incident to specific research, and other long-term special projects.   The characteristic
of continuing expenses is that they are largely determined by single

decisions resulting in expenses which continue until other major decisions are made. Like recurring expenses, continuing expenses must be lived with for a considerable period, but they can generally be changed without the company going out of business or abandoning a major activity. Continuing expenses are in a middle ground between controllable and recurring expenses. They are subject to some control, but only with considerable difficulty. They require periodic review, but not daily attention.

The terms "controllable expense," "recurring expense," and "continuing expense" reflect the broad characteristics of expenses as to their origin and manageability. They are useful to characterize specific expenses for the use of management in its deliberations and decision making.

FACTORS IN DETERMINATIONS OF PRODUCT COSTS

In order for an enterprise to operate at a profit, it is necessary to recover through revenues all costs and expenses incurred. From this standpoint it is unimportant how the expenditures are classified. The objectives in classifying expenditures are primarily to reflect what has happened, to provide a basis for controlling both costs and expenses, and to indicate how the maximum benefits can be obtained from future expenditures. The manner in which these objectives are accomplished will depend upon the complexity of the organization, the attitude of the individuals who are compiling and using the economic data, and the availability of information.

There is no single basis for classifying expenditures which will be the most useful in all cases, and judgment is involved in applying any classification to a particular series of transactions. Consequently, with respect to a computation of the *cost* of a particular product or the *cost* of the entire production of a plant or enterprise during a stated period, no one amount can be said to be "correct" to the exclusion of all others. Cost determinations are made to be used for management purposes and are not an ultimate goal of the accounting function.

The elements represented in a computed cost for a specific product or for the production of a plant or enterprise are generally expenditures for raw materials, direct labor, and manufacturing (including extracting) overhead. No special definitions are needed for the material and direct labor cost elements, as the appropriate expenditures can usually be identified and are commonly referred to as "prime costs."

Expenditures which cannot be readily and specifically assigned to particular production are lumped into the category of overhead for disposition. It is then a question of which elements of overhead are to be included in cost.

The initial step is to ascertain which expenses will not be included because they do not aid in the productive activity. These expenses will not be included in overhead under any concept of cost. One obvious example is the group of expenses required to be incurred in connection with a closed plant at a location apart from where production is taking place.

There are several viewpoints as to the extent to which the expenses relating to production should be included in cost as a matter of principle. The alternatives with respect to the inclusion of overhead in production costs may, at a risk of oversimplification, be grouped as follows:

1. *Prime costing,* under which no overhead is included.
2. *Direct costing,* under which controllable expenses directly attributable to production are included but no fixed overhead is included.
3. *Analytical costing,* under which overhead expenses attributable to production are included, except for the portion not taken into account because of the production facilities not being fully utilized.
4. *All-inclusive costing,* under which the entire amount of overhead expense attributable to production is included.

Circumstances may be such as to make it appropriate and useful to apply procedures falling into any of these four categories in preparing statements and reports for internal management purposes; however, management should understand what procedures have been followed. If the computed costs are utilized in determining selling prices, this is particularly important. The business will show a profit only if the revenues realized are adequate to cover the aggregate of all costs and expenses regardless of how individual expenditures are classified.

Prime costing is applied most frequently where the relative magnitude of the overhead expenses makes them of little importance. It has the advantage of simplicity.

Direct costing and analytical costing procedures are premised, in part, upon a recognition of the fact that, in addition to *controllable* expenses, the items of overhead include *recurring* expenses which are necessary to provide the capacity to carry on production activities, and *continuing* expenses resulting from decisions previously made to secure the production facilities which are available for use. It is fundamental that in order to be in a position to carry on production activities, a certain level of recurring and continuing expenses must be assumed. During any period, production may be all or only a part of the total possible with the available capacity. The question is, how much of the expenses required to provide that capacity to produce should be considered as part of the cost of the actual production.

Under a direct costing procedure none of the recurring and continuing expenses is included in the computations of cost. The reasoning is that the expenses were incurred as a consequence of decisions which had nothing to do with any particular units of production, they would have been incurred whether or not any specific units had been produced, and corresponding amounts of expense will be incurred in subsequent periods regardless of the quantity of the current production. The practice of not including in overhead certain items considered to be period expenses is a partial application of the direct costing principle.

Under an analytical costing procedure the recurring and continuing expenses are included in the computations of cost on the basis of a comparison between the actual rate of activity and a predetermined norm. For example, these expenses for a particular period might be included in cost to the extent they are allocable to the portion of the available capacity which was actually utilized. To the extent that the expenses are allocable to the unused portion of available capacity, they are considered to represent a loss. This is an economic loss attributable to the level of production set by management during the period and is not part of the cost of the units actually produced.

All-inclusive costing is most frequently applied in smaller enterprises where detailed analyses of the various expense accounts are

not available.   It may also be appropriate where a plant is consistently operated at a capacity rate or where the aggregate amount
of overhead is relatively small.   It shares with prime costing the
advantage of simplicity.   In the majority of instances there will
be some elements of overhead attributable to events which are
not customarily a part of plant operations, and the all-inclusive
costing concept will not be literally applied where the amount
of expense resulting from such events can be identified.   Examples
of events which could justify special recognition in determining
the overhead expenses to be included in cost computations are
shortages of materials; receipt of defective materials; labor slow-
downs and strikes; and interruptions of production caused by a
flood, fire, or other casualty.   In a business which does not have
a regular program for model or product changes, special recognition might also be given, even under an all-inclusive costing concept, to the effect upon expenses of disruptions caused by such
factors as the introduction of a new product, the training of an
expanded labor force, and the realignment of facilities incident
to equipping a plant to manufacture a different product.

APPLYING OVERHEAD ON BASIS OF ACTIVITY

If the amount of overhead to be included in cost computations
is based upon the level of activity during a particular period, the
activity level at which all the expenses will be so included must
first be established.   Among the standards which may be used
for this purpose are the following types of levels of activity:

1. Actual
2. Expected
3. Average
4. Practical capacity
5. Theoretical capacity

Depending upon the circumstances the standard and actual level
of activity may be measured appropriately in terms of direct labor
cost, direct labor hours, machine hours, units of product, or any
other factor.   Within the same plant or business many different
measures may be used in connection with various departments
or cost centers.

The first two procedures listed, based upon actual and expected levels of activity, are similar in intent and result. They are applicable to all-inclusive costing, and the thought behind each is to apply all proper overhead expenses of the current period to production costs. The only difference between them is the timing of the application of overhead during the accounting period. As regards the period as a whole, both procedures use actual production as a standard.

To illustrate the mechanics of each of the types of measures of activity and the significance of the different results obtained, an example will be used of an operating unit of The H Company for which the basic factors are as follows:

Summary of Data Used in Illustrating Application of Overhead

| | Number of units produced | Rate of activity based upon a standard representing | | | |
		Actual production	Average production	Practical capacity	Theoretical capacity
Standard number of units per year		*	3,200	4,000	4,500
Actual number of units produced and per cent of standard:					
1st year	3,000	100%	93.75%	75.0%	66.7%
2d year	4,500	100	140.63	112.5	100.0
3d year	2,400	100	75.00	60.0	53.3
4th year	2,700	100	84.37	67.5	60.0
5th year	3,400	100	106.25	85.0	75.5
Total	16,000				

* Although a standard may be used for interim statements based upon expected production for the period, the computations for the entire period will reflect only the actual production.

In this simplified example the aggregate amount of overhead incurred during the five-year period is $360,000, or $22.50 per unit; but there are material variations from this simple average under all of the procedures illustrated.

Using actual activity as a basis for the application of overhead, the computations are made after the period in which the activity takes place. At the close of the period the total production is determined and is divided into the total amount of overhead in order to establish the overhead rate per unit of production. The computation is as follows:

Application of Overhead Based on Actual Production

	Number of units produced	Overhead incurred	Overhead per unit
1st year	3,000	$ 70,000	$23.33
2d year	4,500	84,000	18.67
3d year	2,400	65,000	27.08
4th year	2,700	67,000	24.81
5th year	3,400	74,000	21.76
Total	16,000	$360,000	

This procedure applies all overhead expenses to cost in the period incurred. The shorter the period for which the computations are made, the greater is the likelihood of fluctuations in the overhead per unit.

When the expected activity is used as a basis for the application of overhead, both the production and amount of overhead are estimated in advance for each accounting period. An overhead rate is calculated for use during the period. The expected activity method will apply all overhead expense to cost in the period incurred if the estimates are accurate. If the estimates are not accurate, there will either be an excess of expense over overhead applied (called "underabsorbed overhead") or an excess of overhead applied over expense (called "overabsorbed overhead"). These amounts are usually small, especially if the accounting period is short or the estimating good. Small excesses will be taken into account directly in computing net income, but larger differences can be applied to cost of sales and to inventory through the use of supplementary overhead rates after the close of the period.

From a theoretical viewpoint the use of an average level of activity may be justified if it is assumed the total production during the period the facility will be used in the business can be estimated with reasonable accuracy and either (*a*) the overhead amounts will be constant or (*b*) the total of the overhead amount for the entire period can also be estimated so that a constant overhead rate per unit can be applied. These are not conditions commonly found in practice. With respect to the operating unit represented by the current example, the total production of 16,000 units was probably not predictable, the overhead incurred was not constant at $72,000 per annum, and the aggregate amount of overhead for the five-year period could not have been calculated in advance. The argument advanced for the use of this type of average level of activity standard in applying overhead is that the expenses which recur or continue, period after period, have been knowingly assumed as a result of sound economic decisions by management. At the time of making the decision to acquire the production facility and assume the burden of these expenses, it was known (presumably) that the production will not be consistent because the facility will be used only to the extent the company is able to sell the product. It is further reasoned that idle time during slack periods was contemplated, and that idle time expenses are part of production costs during the periods when production is above average. Logic then leads to the conclusion that any amounts of underabsorbed or overabsorbed expenses at the end of any particular period should be carried forward to be offset in subsequent operating periods. Regardless of the logic of this approach to the application of overhead, practical considerations preclude its use. Business management is not clairvoyant, and few expenses are actually fixed in amount.

The use of a different average level of activity concept may, however, be meaningful with respect to a relatively short phase of a business cycle. Although annual production will fluctuate with sales, it may be practicable for The H Company to estimate that over a five-year period approximately 16,000 units will be produced and sold. It is known that the overhead expenses will not be constant, and it is generally impossible to estimate with a reasonable degree of accuracy what the total overhead amount will be for five years. The use of an average activity standard by the operating unit of The H Company under these conditions

Application of Overhead Based on Average Production

	Percentage of units produced to standard	Amount of overhead			
			Applied		Over- (or under-) absorbed
		Incurred	Amount	Per unit	
1st year	93.75	$ 70,000	$ 65,625	$21.87	$ (4,375)
2d year	140.63	84,000	118,129	26.25	34,129
3d year	75.00	65,000	48,750	20.31	(16,250)
4th year	84.37	67,000	56,528	20.93	(10,472)
5th year	106.25	74,000	78,625	23.12	4,625
Total		$360,000	$367,657		$ 7,657

can be illustrated by the tabulation above. Where this type of use is made of the average activity standard, the amounts of overabsorbed or underabsorbed overhead are taken into account directly in computing net income for the period. These amounts will not necessarily offset one another and require analysis from a management viewpoint. They reflect variations not only in volume but also in overhead expense. Had the overhead incurred been $72,000 each year, the per-unit amount applied would have been $22.50 in each case, and there would not have been a net overabsorbed amount of $7,657. Application of $26.25 of overhead per unit in the second year, for example, results from the fact that the overhead incurred was $84,000—an increase of 20 per cent over the previous year. An explanation for the increase should be obtained. Possibly it was partially the result of having to engage additional supervisory personnel because the production was increased from 3,000 to 4,500 units; however, it should be ascertained that the additional expense was needed. The 50 per cent increase in the number of units produced is gratifying, but inquiry should be made as to how this was achieved. There may have been inefficiencies in the operations during the first year which can be avoided in subsequent years.

The use of practical or theoretical capacity as a standard in determining the portion of incurred overhead to be included in cost involves establishing the number of units which will be considered as par for a given period of time, such as a month or a year.

Practical capacity allows for the estimated inevitable delays caused by necessary maintenance, unpredictable breakdowns, and the like. It reflects the manner in which management thought the facilities would be used during periods of normal demand at the time they were designed or acquired. Management decisions have a bearing on the capacity of a department or a plant. Management designates the number of days a week and the number of hours or shifts a day a plant is to be operated. Thus the measurement of capacity is conditioned by the regular anticipated usage, so that it is proper to speak of capacity based on a one-shift, five-days-a-week schedule. With enough sales orders to provide the demand, a plant could operate, year in and year out, at practical capacity. For limited periods the production could exceed such capacity. In the absence of engineering studies practical capacity may be established by reference to demonstrated capacity, that is, the actual production under normal operating conditions. In the present illustration The H Company produced 4,500 units during the second year and 4,000 units might be accepted as practical capacity. In this type of situation the amounts of overabsorbed and underabsorbed overhead are taken into account directly in computing net income for the period. Any overabsorbed overhead should be recognized as an indication that the computed costs reflect more than the expenses actually incurred

Application of Overhead Based on Practical Capacity

	Percentage of units produced to standard	Amount of overhead			
			Applied		Over- (or under-) absorbed
		Incurred	Amount	Per unit	
1st year	75.0	$ 70,000	$ 52,500	$17.50	$(17,500)
2d year	112.5	84,000	94,500	21.00	10,500
3d year	60.0	65,000	39,000	16.25	(26,000)
4th year	67.5	67,000	45,225	16.75	(21,775)
5th year	85.0	74,000	62,900	18.50	(11,100)
Total		$360,000	$294,125		$(65,875)

during the period and that the operating conditions have been fortuitous. An explanation for the abnormally high production should be sought. Variations in the per-unit amount of overhead applied reflect the trend of the total overhead expenses and should also be investigated.

Theoretical capacity would literally be that quantity which it is physically possible to produce with continuous uninterrupted production, assuming no shortages, no machine breakdowns, no human errors. As thus conceived, it would be impossible to maintain production at theoretical capacity, since there are inevitable interruptions in all manufacturing operations over any extended period. For the purpose of determining what portion of the overhead expenses should be applied to cost, a modified version of theoretical capacity is adopted, that is, a rate of production determined by taking into account the possibility of extra shifts but with reasonable allowances for normal interruptions. If the theoretical capacity is one which is attainable even for relatively short periods, it can be useful in some cost determinations. Continuing the example, 4,500 units might be accepted as theoretical capacity for the operating unit of The H Company. As is the case when practical capacity is used as a standard, the amounts of underabsorbed overhead are taken into account directly in computing net income for the period. There will seldom, if ever, be any overabsorbed overhead since that would indicate a level of activity in excess of theoretical capacity. Use of this type of standard

Application of Overhead Based on Theoretical Capacity

	Percentage of units produced to standard	Amount of overhead		
			Applied	
		Incurred	Amount	Per unit	Over- (or under-) absorbed
1st year	66.7	$ 70,000	$ 46,690	$15.56	$(23,310)
2d year	100.0	84,000	84,000	18.67	—
3d year	53.3	65,000	34,645	14.43	(30,355)
4th year	60.0	67,000	40,200	14.88	(26,800)
5th year	75.5	74,000	55,870	16.43	(18,130)
Total		$360,000	$261,405		$(98,595)

Per-Unit Amounts Computed in Illustration of Methods of Overhead Application

		Rate of activity based upon a standard representing		
		Actual production	Average production	Practical capacity	Theoretical capacity
1st year		$23.33	$21.87	$17.50	$15.56
2d year		18.67	26.25	21.00	18.67
3d year		27.08	20.31	16.25	14.43
4th year		24.81	20.93	16.75	14.88
5th year		21.76	23.12	18.50	16.43
	High	$27.08	$26.25	$21.00	$18.67
	Low	18.67	20.31	16.25	14.43
	Range	8.41	5.94	4.75	4.24

does not generally develop as meaningful data as do the other procedures discussed.

The amounts of overhead per unit which would be applied by The H Company under the various alternative procedures are summarized above to facilitate comparison. The effect upon income of utilizing the various procedures in assigning amounts to inventories is illustrated in Chapter 6. It is significant to observe at this point, however, that the widest range of amounts of overhead applied per unit results when actual production is used. From a management standpoint this means that the use of such a method requires more extensive analysis to determine the reasons for fluctuations in computed costs.

6

Concepts of "Cost" for Purposes of Inventory Determinations

Discussions of inventories frequently proceed on the assumption that the cost for each item is a definitely known amount. This is true only in the simplest of costing problems. Any computed cost is the result of judgment exercised in making the numerous decisions required in analyzing detailed economic data and in selecting and applying the accounting procedures deemed most appropriate to the particular situation. The concepts of "cost" for purposes of inventory determinations are fundamentally special applications of the principles underlying the establishment of cost for all other phases of business management.

FACTORS INVOLVED IN DETERMINATION OF COST GENERALLY

Highlights of the discussion of concepts of "cost" for purposes of business management in Chapter 5 merit review and may be restated in general terms.

Analyzing and summarizing the economic effects of the activities of a business are part of the accounting function. In performing this function, expenditures should be classified in such a manner as will be the most helpful in securing the maximum benefits from similar future expenditures. No one classification will necessarily best serve all management purposes. Cost determinations are made to be used and do not represent an ultimate goal.

There are no clearly established meanings for the nouns "cost" and "expense," and the significance of the adjectives "fixed" and "variable" may be exaggerated. Almost every item of cost or expense is both partially fixed and partially variable.

The fixed-variable segregation, within its inherent limitations, is a useful device and can be applied in making a variety of special-purpose studies. Any classification of expenditures should be made on a basis appropriate for the use to which it will be put. The classification and detail may have to be varied with the level of management to which it is directed and with the authority possessed to effect changes in the operations. In classifying expenditures for some purposes, available alternatives and their effect may be of primary significance.

In order to reflect the origin and manageability of charges against income, a different type of classification is suggested: prime costs, controllable expenses, recurring expenses, and continuing expenses. This suggestion is made to emphasize that the word "cost" should not be applied by habit to every income charge. Most income charges can better be denominated as some type of "expense."

Accounting procedures will not alter the facts, but they can affect the when and the how of recognizing certain types of costs and expenses.

All costs and expenses must be recovered through revenues for a business to operate at a profit, but determinations of production costs are useful if the bases thereof are understood.

Expenses which do not aid in the productive activity are not part of overhead includable in cost computations. The extent of the inclusion of other expenses depends upon such factors as the complexity of the organization, the attitude of the individuals who are compiling and using the economic data, and the availability of information. Under an analytical costing procedure, there are several possible viewpoints as to what portion of the overhead expenses related to available facilities should be considered allocable to the actual production. Costs are computed to meet best the requirements of particular situations, and no one amount can be said to be "correct" to the exclusion of all others.

FACTORS INVOLVED IN DETERMINATIONS OF COST
FOR INVENTORY PURPOSES

Assigning an amount to an inventory is but one of many determinations needed in the computation of the earnings of a business enterprise for a stated period. The acceptability of the amount so assigned is dependent upon recognized accounting procedures having been followed. Where there are alternatives, one of the principal tests of the appropriateness of the end result of the application of the procedure selected is the possible impact upon net income of applying alternative procedures.

The exact amount of the computed cost for an individual item is generally of little significance. Possible variations in such amounts seldom have a material effect on net income. The data developed in compiling the individual costs may be very important, however, from a management standpoint; and there will be a better understanding of both the income statement and the balance sheet if the aggregate inventory amount is based upon the individual costs.

There is no one prescribed procedure to be used in determinations of cost for inventory purposes. There is a wide range of procedures, and many combinations and variations, which result in a fair reflection of income if consistently applied from year to year.

From the authoritative pronouncements that are reproduced as appendices at the end of the book, the general statements concerning the elements of cost to be taken into account for inventory purposes are set forth in comparative form on the next two pages. It is particularly significant that the bulletin issued by the AICPA includes the statement that the *exclusion* of *all* overheads from inventory costs does not constitute an accepted accounting procedure, and then observes that the exercise of judgment in an

Comparison of Statements on Elements of Cost

AICPA Bulletin

The definition of cost as applied to inventories is understood to mean acquisition and production cost,* and its determination involves many problems. Although principles for the determination of inventory costs may be easily stated, their application, particularly to such inventory items as work in process and finished goods, is difficult because of the variety of problems encountered in the allocation of costs and charges. For example, under some circumstances, items such as idle facility expense, excessive spoilage, double freight, and rehandling costs may be so abnormal as to require treatment as current period charges rather than as a portion of the inventory cost. Also, general and administrative expenses should be included as period charges, except for the portion of such expenses that may be clearly related to production and thus constitute a part of inventory costs (product charges). Selling expenses constitute no part of inventory costs. It should also be recognized that the exclusion of all overheads from inventory costs does not constitute an accepted accounting procedure.

Institute of Chartered Accountants

The elements making up the cost of stock are:

(*a*) direct expenditure on the purchase of goods bought for resale, and of materials and components used in the manufacture of finished goods

(*b*) other direct expenditure which can be identified specifically as having been incurred in acquiring the stock or bringing it to its existing condition and location; examples are direct labour, transport, processing and packaging

(*c*) such part, if any, of the overhead expenditure as is properly carried forward in the circumstances of the business instead of being charged against the revenue of the period in which it was incurred. [Par. 4.]

Federal Income Tax Regulations

Cost means:

(a) In the case of merchandise on hand at the beginning of the taxable year, the inventory price of such goods.

(b) In the case of merchandise purchased since the beginning of the taxable year, the invoice price less trade or other discounts, except strictly cash discounts approximating a fair interest rate, which may be deducted or not at the option of the taxpayer, provided a consistent course is followed. To this net invoice price should be added transportation or other necessary charges incurred in acquiring possession of the goods.

(c) In the case of merchandise produced by the taxpayer since the beginning of the taxable year, (1) the cost of raw materials and supplies entering into or consumed in connection with the product, (2) expenditures for direct labor, (3) indirect expenses incident to and necessary for the production of the particular article, including in such indirect expenses a reasonable proportion of management expenses, but not including any cost of selling or return on capital, whether by way of interest or profit.

Comparison of Statements on Elements of Cost—Continued

AICPA Bulletin	Institute of Chartered Accountants	Federal Income Tax Regulations
The exercise of judgment in an individual situation involves a consideration of the adequacy of the procedures of the cost accounting system in use, the soundness of the principles thereof, and their consistent application. [Par. 5.] * In the case of goods which have been written down below cost at the close of a fiscal period, such reduced amount is to be considered the cost for subsequent accounting purposes.		(d) In any industry in which the usual rules for computation of cost of production are inapplicable, costs may be approximated upon such basis as may be reasonable and in conformity with established trade practice in the particular industry. Among such cases are: (1) Farmers and raisers of livestock (see § 1.471–6); (2) miners and manufacturers who by a single process or uniform series of processes derive a product of two or more kinds, sizes, or grades, the unit cost of which is substantially alike (see § 1.471–7); and (3) retail merchants who use what is known as the "retail method" in ascertaining approximate cost (see § 1.471–8). [§ 1.471–3.]

individual situation involves a consideration of the adequacy of the procedures of the cost accounting system in use, the soundness of the principles thereof, and their consistent application. The bulletin recognizes that there is no one standard for determining the portion of overhead to be included in cost for inventory purposes and that the extent of the inclusion will depend upon the accounting procedures and principles applied. The emphasis is again placed upon consistency.

The bulletin of the AICPA (Appendix A) relative to inventory pricing was originally issued in 1947 and contains only general statements with respect to the treatment of overhead expenditures. By contrast the pronouncement by The Institute of

Chartered Accounts in England and Wales, which was issued in 1960, discusses the subject rather extensively. Except for recognizing that there may be situations in which none of the overhead expenditures is considered part of inventory cost, the later commentary is in accord with the statements in the 1947 bulletin.

The review of various methods of dealing with overhead expenditures included in the statement by the Institute of Chartered Accountants emphasizes the diversity of current business practices, and the problems are basically the same in all parts of the Free World. The following discussion, based upon paragraphs 5 through 10 of Appendix B, should be helpful in interpreting the concise statements by the AICPA and appreciating the absence of rigid rules for the treatment of overhead in computations of cost for inventory purposes.

TREATMENT OF OVERHEAD BY INSTITUTE
OF CHARTERED ACCOUNTANTS

The Institute of Chartered Accountants includes in the expression "overhead expenditure":

  a) Production expenses such as factory rent, depreciation, insurance and supervision, and other indirect expenses of acquiring and producing goods
  b) Administration expenses not attributable directly to the acquisition or production of goods or the bringing of them to a saleable condition and location
  c) Selling expenses
  d) Finance charges

It is recognized that in total, or within each of the four divisions, expenditures might be classified so as to distinguish between "fixed overheads" which accrue or expire wholly or largely on a time basis, and "variable overheads" which vary in a greater or lesser degree with the level of activity of the enterprise or the department concerned. It is stated there is general agreement that none of the selling and finance and other expenses which do not relate to the bringing of the goods to their condition and location at the inventory date should be included in cost.

There are described three types of practices reflecting divergent opinions as to the extent to which overhead should be included in cost. There are references to the fact that in some businesses no overhead expenditure is included in determining the cost of goods in the inventory, and that in others only the "marginal" cost of the unsold production on hand at the end of the year is included. This second approach to cost determinations assigns to the inventory only that part of the cost of production which has been incurred solely because the units remaining on hand were acquired or produced. All other expenses, including depreciation, are charges against the revenue of the period during which they were incurred on the ground that they arise irrespective of the quantity of goods which remains on hand at the end of the period. Under the third recognized practice there is included in cost an "appropriate proportion" of the overhead on the ground that any expense which is related to the acquisition or production of goods ought to be included in the cost of those goods. In making this type of application of overhead, the "appropriate proportion" is determined by reference to a normal level of activity. Even under this last procedure the entire amount of overhead expenditure would not be included in cost if the level of activity was less than normal.

No one method of dealing with overhead is considered suitable for all businesses, but the method selected needs to be used consistently. A change of method would be appropriate only if there is a change in the relevant circumstances of the business.

Among the considerations which are referred to as factors affecting the selection of a method of dealing with overhead are (a) nature of the business, (b) levels of production and sales, (c) interruption or other exceptional curtailment of production, and (d) risks of loss.

In deciding whether to include a proportion of overhead in cost and also which elements of expense may properly be included, it is necessary to have regard to the nature and stage of development of the business. Among the factors to be considered are the length of the production period, the probability of fluctuations in the level of production or the volume of sales, the risk of selling campaigns by competitors at reduced prices, and the extent to which production is undertaken only to a customer's order or "for stock" in expectation of sales.

The significance of the levels of production and sales is brought out by the statements that where the production and sales levels are relatively stable, the inclusion of overhead expenditures in cost may have little impact upon the profits of any particular period. Where the levels are subject to material fluctuation and are not kept in balance, however, the overhead expenses may be excluded from cost on the ground that they would be incurred in any event. Their inclusion in inventory cost has the effect of relieving the period when they are incurred as expenses and of charging a later period to which they do not properly relate.

It is recognized that even if overhead expenditures are normally considered as part of cost, an adjustment will be necessary in the event of disruption in production by such events as a strike, a fire, an abnormal falling off in orders, or temporary difficulties in obtaining materials, with the result that the volume of production is abnormally or unexpectedly low. In such circumstances the amount included in cost with respect to overhead ought not exceed an appropriate proportion of the total overhead computed by reference to normal activity. The excess is treated as a charge against revenue in the period in which the expenditures were incurred.

In businesses which are highly competitive or have a sensitive market, the presence of risks of "realization at a loss" may justify the omission of overhead expenditures from cost determinations. The objective is to avoid carrying forward expenses which may prove irrecoverable. Examples of such businesses are those dealing in fashion goods or of a specialty character where the public taste may change quickly, with the result that the goods in the inventory can be sold only at a loss; those whose competitors may launch selling campaigns at short notice to get rid of stocks at reduced prices, sometimes at no more than the cost of material and direct manufacturing expenses; and those where new methods of production or improved designs may render existing stocks obsolete.

It is also recognized that producers of such commodities as whiskey, wine, and timber, which mature large stocks over long periods, usually exclude fixed overhead expenses from cost in order to avoid carrying forward large and increasing amounts of time-expired expenditures, the recovery of which in the ultimate selling price is uncertain.

It is specifically observed that the less the "fixed overheads" (such as rent, depreciation, insurance, and supervision) vary in amount with variations in the volume of output and the more they accrue on a purely time basis, the greater is the justification for their exclusion from cost for inventory purposes.

The reference in paragraph 10 of Appendix B to a publication by the Council of The Institute of Chartered Accountants in England and Wales entitled "Notes on the Allocation of Expense" is to a pronouncement issued in November, 1951. This discussion of the treatment of expenses refers to the fact that there may be a primary allocation of expenses under titles to indicate the kind of expense, for example, lighting, water, advertising, stationery. It is pointed out that the result of such a primary allocation gives no indication of the cost to the business of individual activities; and where such an indication is needed, a "secondary allocation" by function is appropriate, that is, an allocation to specific departments or to cost centers which may range from a single machine to a whole factory.

The secondary allocation of expense should be made in such a way that it provides an orderly framework in which expenditures can be seen in relation to each identified function. This framework should be designed to display expenses both for the purpose of controlling expenditures and ascertaining costs. In this sense the ascertainment of cost is considered from the standpoint of the cost of products and also the cost of some or all the activities of a business. It is recognized that cost determinations may be necessary for reviewing the profitability of products, to provide a guide when determining selling prices, and in determining amounts to be assigned to inventories. There are other special purposes for cost determinations, such as to meet price control regulations or the requirements of government departments, to determine whether goods can be more economically purchased than made in the business, or to measure the value or effectiveness of specific business activities.

The following paragraphs are particularly significant with reference to the determination of product costs:

If every item of expense (with the exception of certain special matters, such as finance items) is included in the allocation, the resulting framework can provide all the details normally required for the ascertainment of the expense elements of cost—whether product costs or the costs of departments or activities. All the items of expense so shown in the framework are not necessarily included when compiling product costs or departmental costs. Such costs are compiled for a number of different purposes, and it may be appropriate to include some items of expense where the cost is required for one purpose and to exclude them where the cost is required for another purpose; marginal costs (in considering costs of increased activity) and opportunity costs (in considering the alternative use of resources) are cases in point. Costs are therefore "built up" by selecting for inclusion only those items of expense which are relevant to the purpose for which the particular cost is needed. The form of the framework which secondary allocation produces must therefore be designed to enable a logical and accurate selection of expense items to be made for inclusion in costs.

. . . .

Where the capacity of a factory is not fully employed, a complete allocation of all expense, without distinction between fixed and variable items, over all the products, may be not only wasteful of effort but in fact misleading to the management. To prove that a particular product is sold at a loss, if it receives a share of all fixed expense, may be irrelevant unless it is practicable immediately to make some more profitable use of the available resources. The fixed expense of that part of the factory or plant which is unemployed is not necessarily regarded as part of the cost of the goods produced by the remainder. Where therefore fixed expense is allocated to products, it may be desirable to do so as if the inactive department had produced a normal volume of output. By so doing, the cost of the idle capacity is shown in the form of unabsorbed expense.[1]

The foregoing is consistent with the comments in paragraph 7(c) of Appendix B concerning the inclusion in cost of an "appropriate proportion" of overhead.

In connection with this entire discussion it is significant that the questions being considered pertain to the determination of *cost*. The comparison of market value with whatever amount of cost may be computed is a separate and subsequent step in ascertaining the amount to be assigned to an inventory. The practice of assigning an amount to inventories on the basis of the lower of cost or market is discussed in Chapter 7.

[1] The Council of The Institute of Chartered Accountants in England and Wales, "Notes on the Allocation of Expense," *Members' Handbook*, Pt. I, p. 9, par. 30; p. 12, par. 40.

TREATMENT OF OVERHEAD
IN FEDERAL INCOME TAX REGULATIONS

The federal income tax regulations provide for the inclusion in cost, in the case of merchandise produced by the taxpayer, of "indirect expenses incident to and necessary for the production of the particular article, including in such indirect expenses a reasonable proportion of management expense, but not including any cost of selling or return on capital, whether by way of interest or profit." The phrase "incident to and necessary for the production of the particular article" has not been specifically interpreted in any published ruling or court decision.

The Internal Revenue Code requires in section 471 that inventories shall be taken on the basis which is prescribed by regulations "as conforming as nearly as may be to the best accounting practice in the trade or business and as most clearly reflecting the income." This statutory provision is recognized in the regulations by the conclusions that (1) inventory rules cannot be uniform but must give effect to trade customs which come within the scope of the best accounting practice in the particular trade or business and (2) an inventory that can be used under the best accounting practice in a balance sheet showing the financial position of the taxpayer can, as a general rule, be regarded as clearly reflecting his income.

It is emphasized that in order clearly to reflect income, the inventory practice of a taxpayer should be consistent from year to year, and greater weight is to be given to consistency than to any particular method of inventorying or basis of valuation so long as the method or basis used is substantially in accord with the regulations.

With respect to inventories there are references in both the Internal Revenue Code and the regulations to "the best accounting practice" in the trade or business. The use of the superlative may have been the consequence of overzealousness on the part of the draftsman, who was probably a lawyer. Businessmen and accountants recognize—and lawyers should—that there is no single accounting practice which can be established as *the best* in connection with every question involved in determining the amount to be assigned to an inventory. The phraseology in the statute can be applied only in an extremely broad sense, and not literally, to such questions as the amount of overhead to be included in cost for inventory purposes. In any event precise conformity is not contemplated, as the income tax law uses the expression "conforming as nearly as may be."

USE OF SPECIFIC AND AVERAGE COSTS
FOR INVENTORY PURPOSES

In addition to the question of what expenditures are to be taken into account in computing cost, consideration must be given to the procedure to be followed in attributing to the particular units on hand at an inventory date, the cost computed for or identified with quantities produced or acquired at different times. The attribution of costs has a direct bearing on the determination of income. The costs associated with specific units of goods as they are disposed of influence not only the amount of profit for the period in which the sales occur, but also the amount to be charged against the revenues of a subsequent period when the units included in the inventory are utilized.

In Chapter 13 there is a discussion of the procedure commonly referred to as the "retail method" of computing inventories, which has been developed to meet the practical problems inherent in any attempt to assign individual costs to the variety of merchandise normally included in the inventory of department stores. Chapter 8 discusses methods of allocating costs which are based upon concepts of a "flow of costs." In the determination of income it is not necessary that the flow of costs be related to the physical movement of goods.

The most obvious procedure for attributing costs to units received, sold, and on hand is by specific identification. Regardless of the costing method applied, each unit or batch of goods has a cost which presumably could be established for it. Where it is feasible to do so, the cost of specific units is sometimes used in the accounting records when reflecting the physical movement of goods. Specific identification is an accepted procedure, but it is time consuming even where feasible. Specific identification is used most often with respect to high-value, low-quantity items, especially for unique items and for items ordered for a particular job or customer.

Inventory Record with Specific Identification of Units

| Date | Description | Receipts | | Quantity con-sumed | Inventory | | | |
		Unit cost	Quantity		Batch	Units	Cost	Amount
Jan. 12	Batch I	$300	247		I	247	$300	$ 74,100
Jan. 28	Batch II	370	316		I	247	300	$ 74,100
					II	316	370	116,920
								$191,020
Feb. 17	Batch III	280	147		I	247	300	$ 74,100
					II	316	370	116,920
					III	147	280	41,160
								$232,180
Feb. 23	Batch II			29	I	247	300	$ 74,100
	Batch III			76	II	287	370	106,190
					III	71	280	19,880
								$200,170
Mar. 13	Batch IV	320	73		I	247	300	$ 74,100
					II	287	370	106,190
					III	71	280	19,880
					IV	73	320	23,360
								$223,530
Mar. 18	Batch I			173	I	74	300	$ 22,200
	Batch IV			12	II	287	370	106,190
					III	71	280	19,880
					IV	61	320	19,520
								$167,790

Even if feasible, specific identification of costs may not be the most logical from the viewpoint of portraying periodic income. When there is a large quantity of similar units having different costs, a business is not necessarily better or worse off, depending on which of the units were extracted from the available supply. Different profit amounts should result from real economic differences, not differences which have no bearing on the financial position of the company.

The most commonly used procedures for attributing costs to similar units involve the determination of averages. Averaging practices combine reasonable accuracy with practicality. The theoretical justification for the use of average costs is that when like units acquired at different times and at different costs are commingled so as to be equally available, the units become one entity. When units are removed, a certain portion of that entity has been severed, and a proportionate share of the cost attributed to the entity should be deducted from the total cost.

There are two commonly used basic methods of computing average costs and each involves weighted averages. A weighted average gives greater recognition to the unit cost of a greater quantity than to the unit cost of a lesser quantity. For example, the weighted average cost of 10 units at $0.87, 9 units at $1.20, 13 units at $0.73, and 7 units at $1.67 is $1.04, computed as follows:

Illustration of weighted average

Units		Unit cost		Amount			Average
10	×	$0.87	=	$ 8.70			
9	×	1.20	=	10.80			
13	×	0.73	=	9.49			
7	×	1.67	=	11.69			
39				$40.68	÷	39	= $1.04

The two basic methods may be referred to as the moving-average method and the period-average method.

Under the moving-average method a new average cost is computed upon each addition to the commodity pool. The cost is the quotient of the sum of the cost of the units on hand before the receipt plus the cost of the units received, divided by the total number of units after receipt. For example, if the inventory consists of 316 units at an average cost of $1.10 each and 78 units having a cost of $1.00 each are received, the new average cost for the units on hand is $1.08, computed as follows:

Illustration of moving average

	Units	Unit cost			Amount				Average
Inventory	316				$347.60	÷	316	=	$1.10
Receipt	78	×	$1	=	78.00				
	394				$425.60	÷	394	=	1.08

The period-average method does not require the computation of a new average cost with each receipt, but only once each period, such as a month. Under this method, the new average cost is the quotient of the inventory on hand at the beginning of the period at the old average cost, plus the total cost for the units produced or otherwise acquired during the period, divided by the sum of the quantity on hand at the beginning of the period plus the quantities acquired during the period. For example, if the opening inventory consists of 1,063 units at an average cost of $2.18 each, and acquisitions during the period are 326 at $2.67, 712 at $2.14, and 186 at $2.32, the period-average for costing 1,430 units consumed is $2.25, and the same average cost will be assigned to the 857 units on hand at the beginning of the next period, tabulated as follows:

Illustration of period average

	Units	Unit cost			Amount				Average
Inventory	1,063				$2,317.34	÷	1,063	=	$2.18
Receipts	326	×	$2.67	=	870.42				
	712	×	2.14	=	1,523.68				
	186	×	2.32	=	431.52				
	2,287				$5,142.96	÷	2,287	=	2.25
Consumed	1,430	×	2.25	=	3,217.50				
Inventory	857		.		$1,925.46	÷	857	=	2.25

The period-average method is obviously more practical than the moving-average method in process cost accounting or where there is a large volume of receipts and transfers out. The cost attributed to units consumed during a period is commonly computed after the close of the period, although in some instances time requirements make it necessary to use the average cost computed for the previous period and acceptable costs result.

As with other phases of the procedure for determining amounts to be assigned to inventories, consistency from year to year is of prime importance, whether the costs of particular units are specifically identified or one of the average cost techniques is used.

EFFECT UPON INCOME OF
COST DETERMINATION PROCEDURES

In considering the effect upon income of various cost determination procedures, it is helpful to appreciate the basic attributes of inventories.

Inventories have a physical attribute. They are tangible goods which can be counted or weighed or otherwise measured and tallied at any given point in time. The taking of a physical inventory involves the determination of the number of units of the various products which are on hand, and their stage of completion if the company does manufacturing. For many employees, this is all that "inventory time" means. This physical attribute is the basis for the discussion in Chapter 4 relative to inventory management techniques. The magnitude of the inventory in this physical sense has a bearing on the amount which will be assigned to it, but the amount assigned does not have any direct effect upon the magnitude of the inventory. Further, if adequate and meaningful data are available for purposes of management decisions, the amount assigned to the inventory will have no effect upon what the inventory is worth to the business.

Inventories also have a financial attribute in the sense that an amount is assigned to them for a variety of managerial purposes. Cost determinations involve the interpretation of voluminous economic data; and so long as the procedures followed result in a fair reflection of periodic income, it is desirable not to have to make additional computations just for inventory purposes.

The determination of inventory cost is essentially an income measurement problem, a means whereby there is a rational, orderly, systematic interpretation of the effect on the economic progress of the company of expenditures involved in acquiring goods or in maintaining and operating productive facilities. The problem is primarily connected with determining in what periods expenditures are to be charged off as expenses.

Expenditures made in any accounting period are either useful in producing revenue of a subsequent period or they are not. Expenditures that are not are to be charged off as expenses or losses in the present period. Expenditures that are useful in subsequent periods are to be carried forward to the period in which the goods or services acquired are used to obtain revenue. With regard to expenditures related to the production process, those expenditures which are useful in subsequent periods are deferred as part of the cost of units to be utilized in future periods.

Overhead is the element of cost with respect to which the most widely divergent results can be obtained under various recognized procedures. The principal types of alternatives are:

1. *Prime costing*, under which no overhead is included
2. *Direct costing*, under which controllable expenses directly attributable to production are included but no fixed overhead is included
3. *Analytical costing*, under which overhead expenses attributable to production are included, except for the portion not taken into account because of the production facilities not being fully utilized, as measured by a comparison with
   a) An average expected level of activity
   b) A practical capacity level of activity
   c) A theoretical capacity level of activity
4. *All-inclusive costing*, under which the entire amount of overhead expense attributable to production is included

Each of these procedures is discussed in Chapter 5, starting on page 99; however, it cannot be overemphasized that there are many variations and combinations possible in application of the general principles to specific circumstances. The design of a costing procedure appropriate for a given situation merits the attention of accountants with broad experience in that field. Care must be taken to assure that the maximum benefits will be derived from the available information and that any additional data required to accomplish the desired objectives will be compiled in the most meaningful and economical manner.

To illustrate the effect upon periodic net income of the alternative cost procedures, the hypothetical computations made in Chapter 5 with respect to the operating unit of The H Company have been supplemented by adding the following assumed factors and making comparisons of the computed earnings:

Units sold and net realization:
   1st year—1,500 units ⎫
   2d year—3,500 units ⎪ at $200 per unit
   3d year—3,900 units ⎬
   4th year—2,700 units ⎭
   5th year—4,400 units   at $150 per unit

Direct production expenditures for:
   Material and labor.................... $ 90 per unit
   Controllable expenses.................   10 per unit
        Total........................... $100 per unit

Expenses incurred—$20,000 annually

Taking these additional factors into account the production costs and expenses, and the number of units on hand at the end of the year are as given below. The amounts assigned to the inven-

Summary of Production Costs and Expenses and Statement of Inventory Quantities for The H Company

	Direct production expenditures		Overhead incurred	Total production costs and expenses
	Material and labor	Controllable expenses		
1st year	$ 270,000	$ 30,000	$ 70,000	$ 370,000
2d year	405,000	45,000	84,000	534,000
3d year	216,000	24,000	65,000	305,000
4th year	243,000	27,000	67,000	337,000
5th year	306,000	34,000	74,000	414,000
Total	$1,440,000	$160,000	$360,000	$1,960,000

	Number of units			
	In beginning inventory	Produced	Sold	In ending inventory
1st year	—	3,000	1,500	1,500
2d year	1,500	4,500	3,500	2,500
3d year	2,500	2,400	3,900	1,000
4th year	1,000	2,700	2,700	1,000
5th year	1,000	3,400	4,400	—
Total		16,000	16,000	

tories under the several alternative procedures for determining cost
would be $90 per unit in the case of prime costing, $100 per
unit in the case of direct costing, and $100 of direct production
expenditures plus the current year's overhead applied per unit (as-

Amounts Assigned to Inventories of The H Company
Under Alternative Procedures for Determining Cost

	Prime costing	Direct costing	Average production	Practical capacity	Theoretical capacity	All-inclusive costing
			Analytical costing with rate of activity based upon a standard representing			
1st year	$135,000	$150,000	$182,805	$176,250	$173,340	$184,995
2d year	225,000	250,000	315,625	302,500	296,675	296,675
3d year	90,000	100,000	120,310	116,250	114,430	127,080
4th year	90,000	100,000	120,930	116,750	114,880	124,810
5th year	—	—	—	—	—	—

suming a first-in, first-out flow of costs) in the case of the other
illustrations. The amounts resulting from all-inclusive costing reflect the overhead applied per unit as computed on the basis of
actual production.

Income Statements Based Upon Prime Costing

	1st year	2d year	3d year	4th year	5th year
Sales.................	$300,000	$700,000	$780,000	$540,000	$660,000
Cost of goods sold:					
Beginning inventory......	$ —	$135,000	$225,000	$ 90,000	$ 90,000
Cost of production......	270,000	405,000	216,000	243,000	306,000
Total.............	$270,000	$540,000	$441,000	$333,000	$396,000
Ending inventory........	135,000	225,000	90,000	90,000	—
	$135,000	$315,000	$351,000	$243,000	$396,000
Gross profit on sales.......	$165,000	$385,000	$429,000	$297,000	$264,000
Expenses incurred.........	120,000	149,000	109,000	114,000	128,000
Net income.............	$ 45,000	$236,000	$320,000	$183,000	$136,000

Income statements reflecting inventory determinations based upon prime costing and direct costing are very similar under the assumptions adopted for the purpose of the present illustrations.

Income Statements Based Upon Direct Costing

	1st year	2d year	3d year	4th year	5th year
Sales...................	$300,000	$700,000	$780,000	$540,000	$660,000
Cost of goods sold:					
Beginning inventory......	$ —	$150,000	$250,000	$100,000	$100,000
Cost of production.......	300,000	450,000	240,000	270,000	340,000
Total.............	$300,000	$600,000	$490,000	$370,000	$440,000
Ending inventory........	150,000	250,000	100,000	100,000	—
	$150,000	$350,000	$390,000	$270,000	$440,000
Gross profit on sales.......	$150,000	$350,000	$390,000	$270,000	$220,000
Expenses incurred.........	90,000	104,000	85,000	87,000	94,000
Net income..............	$ 60,000	$246,000	$305,000	$183,000	$126,000

In the condensed income statements expenditures relating to the productive facilities which are not considered as costs for inventory purposes have been shown with other expenses incurred. In a complete operating statement the nature of the various expenses would be identified.

For purposes of external financial statements the use of prime costing would not constitute an accepted accounting procedure under the statement on inventory pricing by the AICPA. Furthermore, Carman G. Blough, while Director of Research for the American Institute, denied the general acceptance of direct costing.[2] In practice, however, there is commonly a partial application of the direct costing principle through not including certain period expenses (e.g., depreciation, taxes, and other selected items which are relatively constant in amount from year to year) in the overhead considered as part of cost. If done consistently, the treatment of particular items as period expenses may have no material effect on net income, and such treatment is not considered

[2] Blough, "Accounting and Auditing Problems," 99 *J. Accountancy* 4, 64 (Apr., 1955).

to be a deviation from the inventory methods which are acceptable in recognized accounting practice. A distortion of income could arise should a different procedure be used in assigning amounts to the beginning and ending inventories of an accounting period.

If the overhead is applied to production on the basis of an average expected level of activity for the five-year period, there would be significant differences in the amounts of net income except in the case of the fourth year. The amount of overab-

Income Statements with Overhead Applied on Basis of Average Expected Level of Activity

	1st year	2d year	3d year	4th year	5th year
Sales................	$300,000	$700,000	$780,000	$540,000	$660,000
Cost of goods sold:					
Beginning inventory...	$ —	$182,805	$315,625	$120,310	$120,930
Cost of production....	365,625	568,129	288,750	326,528	418,625
Total..........	$365,625	$750,934	$604,375	$446,838	$539,555
Ending inventory.....	182,805	315,625	120,310	120,930	—
	$182,820	$435,309	$484,065	$325,908	$539,555
Gross profit on sales....	$117,180	$264,691	$295,935	$214,092	$120,445
Overabsorbed (or under-absorbed) overhead..	(4,375)	34,129	(16,250)	(10,472)	4,625
Expenses incurred......	(20,000)	(20,000)	(20,000)	(20,000)	(20,000)
Net income...........	$ 92,805	$278,820	$259,685	$183,620	$105,070

sorbed or underabsorbed overhead would not necessarily be shown separately in published financial statements, but it would be a significant factor for management purposes.

Application of overhead by comparing the actual level of activity with practical capacity and the use of theoretical capacity would result in income determinations as illustrated on page 129. As hereinbefore stated, the use of theoretical capacity as a standard for comparison ordinarily eliminates the possibility of overabsorbed overhead, but it is not as generally acceptable as the use of practical capacity or an average expected level of activity.

The income statement would appear as on page 130 if the

Income Statements with Overhead Applied on Basis of Practical Capacity

	1st year	2d year	3d year	4th year	5th year
Sales...............	$300,000	$700,000	$780,000	$540,000	$660,000
Cost of goods sold:					
Beginning inventory...	$ —	$176,250	$302,500	$116,250	$116,750
Cost of production....	352,500	544,500	279,000	315,225	402,900
Total..........	$352,500	$720,750	$581,500	$431,475	$519,650
Ending inventory.....	176,250	302,500	116,250	116,750	—
	$176,250	$148,250	$465,250	$314,725	$519,650
Gross profit on sales....	$123,750	$281,750	$314,750	$225,275	$140,350
Overabsorbed (or underabsorbed) overhead..	(17,500)	10,500	(26,000)	(21,775)	(11,100)
Expenses incurred......	(20,000)	(20,000)	(20,000)	(20,000)	(20,000)
Net income...........	$ 86,250	$272,250	$268,750	$183,500	$109,250

Income Statements with Overhead Applied on Basis of Theoretical Capacity

	1st year	2d year	3d year	4th year	5th year
Sales...............	$300,000	$700,000	$780,000	$540,000	$660,000
Cost of goods sold:					
Beginning inventory...	$ —	$173,340	$296,675	$114,430	$114,880
Cost of production....	346,690	534,000	274,645	310,200	395,870
Total..........	$346,690	$707,340	$571,320	$424,630	$510,750
Ending inventory.....	173,340	296,675	114,430	114,880	—
	$173,350	$410,665	$456,890	$309,750	$510,750
Gross profit on sales....	$126,650	$289,335	$323,110	$230,250	$149,250
Underabsorbed overhead	(23,310)	—	(30,355)	(26,800)	(18,130)
Expenses incurred......	(20,000)	(20,000)	(20,000)	(20,000)	(20,000)
Net income...........	$ 83,340	$269,335	$272,755	$183,450	$111,120

entire overhead is applied to production by all-inclusive costing. Whether overhead is applied to production on the basis of the actual level of activity or the expected level of activity during the course of each period, with differences adjusted at the end of the period, the results would be the same.

Income Statements Based Upon All-inclusive Costing

	1st year	2d year	3d year	4th year	5th year
Sales....................	$300,000	$700,000	$780,000	$540,000	$660,000
Cost of goods sold:					
Beginning inventory......	$ —	$184,995	$296,675	$127,080	$124,810
Cost of production......	370,000	534,000	305,000	337,000	414,000
Total...............	$370,000	$718,995	$601,675	$464,080	$538,810
Ending inventory.........	184,995	296,675	127,080	124,810	—
	$185,005	$422,320	$474,595	$339,270	$538,810
Gross profit on sales....	$114,995	$277,680	$305,405	$200,730	$121,190
Expenses incurred........	20,000	20,000	20,000	20,000	20,000
Net income..............	$ 94,995	$257,680	$285,405	$180,730	$101,190

The amounts of net income for the operating unit of The H Company, as computed in each of the illustrations, have been summarized for purposes of comparison.

	Prime costing	Direct costing	Analytical costing using as standard level of activity			All-inclusive costing
			Average production	Practical capacity	Theoretical capacity	
1st year	$ 45,000	$ 60,000	$ 92,805	$ 86,250	$ 83,340	$ 94,995
2d year	236,000	246,000	278,820	272,250	269,335	257,680
3d year	320,000	305,000	259,685	268,750	272,755	285,405
4th year	183,000	183,000	183,620	183,500	183,450	180,730
5th year	136,000	126,000	105,070	109,250	111,120	101,190
Total	$920,000	$920,000	$920,000	$920,000	$920,000	$920,000

On the basis of the foregoing the following observations may be made:

1. The total net income derived from a business activity during its entire period of operation will not be affected by the procedures followed in determining cost for inventory purposes.

2. All-inclusive costing results in larger amounts being assigned to the inventory and in more net income during periods when the inventories are increasing in size.

3. The procedures followed in determining cost for inventory purposes have little effect on net income when the beginning and ending inventories are the same size—as illustrated by the fourth year in the example.

4. Excluding the first and last years of a business activity, it cannot be predetermined which of the procedures will necessarily result in either the highest or the lowest amounts of net income for any particular year.

In the condensed income statement presentation the percentage of gross profit to sales is more consistent where direct costing or prime costing is used. This would not necessarily be true in the case of published financial statements because the effect of recurring and continuing expense could be disclosed in other ways.

PRACTICAL ASPECTS OF COSTING PROCEDURES

There is a tendency to think of the costing procedures, referred to by convenient names for purposes of discussion, as being absolute. In practice it is doubtful that two applications of any of the types of procedures would be identical. There are innumerable variations and combinations of each of the general classes of procedures.

Although distortion of income as a consequence of inconsistent application of costing practices should be avoided, no procedure should be looked upon as completely unchangeable. Business management is, of necessity, dynamic; and if refinements of techniques are developed which provide a better way of accomplishing the objectives of the accounting function, they should be put into effect. Most of these refinements do not materially change net income or represent any inconsistency in the application of accounting principles.

If there is a change in the procedure for determining cost which has a material effect on income, the fact of the change and the amount involved should be disclosed in published financial statements, and it may be necessary to obtain advance permission from the Commissioner of Internal Revenue to make the new procedures operative in determining inventories for federal income tax purposes.

The federal income tax regulations provide that a change in the method of accounting includes a change in the treatment of a material item as well as a change in the over-all method of accounting for gross income or deductions. If a change in accounting method is to be made for federal income tax purposes, an application on Treasury Department Form 3115 should be filed with the Commissioner's office in Washington. The filing must be within ninety days after the beginning of the taxable year in which it is desired to make the change.

President Kennedy directed the Internal Revenue Service to give increasing attention to inventory reporting as an area of tax avoidance, and to step up emphasis on both the verification of the amounts reported as inventories and the examination of methods used in arriving at their reported valuation. In his Tax Message addressed to the Congress under date of April 20, 1961, the President referred to deviations from inventory methods which are acceptable in recognized accounting practice. The statements relating to inventories were:

> It is increasingly apparent that the manipulation of inventories has become a frequent method of avoiding taxes. Current laws and regulations generally permit the use of inventory methods which are acceptable in recognized accounting practice. Deviations from these methods, which are not always easy to detect during examination of tax returns, can often lead to complete nonpayment of taxes until the inventories are liquidated; and, for some taxpayers, this represents permanent tax reduction. The understating of the valuation of inventories is the device most frequently used.
>
> I have directed the Internal Revenue Service to give increasing attention to this area of tax avoidance, through a stepped-up emphasis on both the verification of the amounts reported as inventories and an examination of methods used in arriving at their reported valuation.[3]

The types of deviations which prompted this action are explained in a statement by the Secretary of the Treasury, Douglas Dillon, made before the Committee on Ways and Means of the House of Representatives on May 3, 1961.

After giving a simplified example of how the taxable income of a business would be understated $10,000 if an ending inventory

[3] President John F. Kennedy, *Address Before the Congress—Tax Message*, H.R. Doc. No. 140, 87th Cong. 2d Sess., p. 14 (1961).

was reported to be $50,000 rather than $60,000, Secretary Dillon observed:

To the extent that an understatement of the ending inventory continues in future years, the taxpayer will not have paid tax on the full amount of his income. At the minimum, the result is deferral of the time of paying the tax. In some cases, as the result of losses, sale of the business, or death of the taxpayer, this income may escape taxation entirely.

Understatement of the ending inventory may be accomplished by manipulation of the code provision permitting inventories to be valued at cost or market, whichever is lower. The use of very low market values, of course, reduces the amount of the ending inventory, thereby reducing taxable income. In addition, the amount of the ending inventory may be understated by not including therein a proper count of all inventory items.

In order to assist in correcting abuses in the inventory area, taxpayers might be required to report in the tax return the cost of the closing inventory before any reductions to market. The taxpayer would then separately state the amount of any inventory valuation deduction. If market values are used for any items of inventory, the taxpayer would be required to explain on what basis the market value was determined and the relationship of recent purchases and sales to that market value. In addition, taxpayers might be required to state whether and by whom a physical count of the inventory was taken, whether such inventory was taken by management alone or by a certified public accountant, and the procedures followed to insure that all items of inventory were correctly counted.

Legislation is not needed to carry out the recommendation of the President in this area, since the above reporting requirements can be effected by administrative action including changes in the data required to be included on tax returns.[4]

There is no question about there being a deviation from inventory methods acceptable in recognized accounting practice if the lower of cost or market rule is improperly applied or if the inventory is understated by not including therein a proper count of all inventory items. These areas of tax avoidance should be investigated by the Internal Revenue Service, and appropriate audit instructions are provided for the revenue agents.

The suggested procedure of requiring a statement in the tax return of the cost of the closing inventory before any reductions to market was found not practical. The procedures followed in

---

[4] Secretary of the Treasury Douglas Dillon, *Statement Before the Committee on Ways and Means*, H.R. Doc. No. 140, 87th Cong. 2d Sess., p. 87 (1961).

ascertaining that the amount assigned to an inventory does not exceed market are not uniform, and in many cases the expense involved in compiling the data needed to separately state the amount of the inventory valuation deduction would be disproportionate to the benefits derived by the Internal Revenue Service. Similarly, the suggestion that taxpayers be required to state by whom a physical count of the inventory was taken and the procedure followed to insure that all items were correctly counted had to be considered from the standpoint of practicality.

On the federal income tax return, it is reasonable to provide space for a brief description of the "Method of inventory valuations"; to specifically ask whether there was any *substantial* change in the manner of determining quantities, costs, or valuations between the opening and closing inventory; and to require the attachment of an explanation of a substantial change in the procedures for making the determinations as to quantities, costs, or valuations. In order to reflect income properly the inventory method should be consistent from year to year, and revenue agents should not propose that a taxpayer change his method of accounting where it has been consistently employed and taxable income is clearly reflected for the year under review. The consistency of method requirement should not, however, be applied in a manner which hampers the evolution of accounting techniques or the adoption of improvements in costing procedures designed to implement the method.

Without undertaking a detailed discussion of cost accounting procedures, some general observations and illustrations will be helpful as a guide to an understanding of any costing techniques. Specifically identified or acceptable allocated costs can usually be established for the material and direct labor represented in an inventory, but unless the concept of "prime costing" is appropriate, an allocation procedure for indirect manufacturing expenses is indispensable. This is true whether the basic concept being applied is "direct costing," "all-inclusive costing," or falls within the broad area of "analytical costing." It is also true that all allocation procedures are arbitrary to some degree, no matter how much *refinement* is incorporated in the mechanics of the computations.

The fundamental requirements of any cost accounting procedure are that it be practical in operation so as to provide timely
information at a reasonable expense and that it be understood by
and useful to those making management decisions. These requirements have logically led to the use of factors (commonly called
"overhead rates" or "burden rates") which are applied to a base
such as direct labor dollars, direct labor hours, or machine operating hours to establish the amount to be included in cost to represent indirect manufacturing expenses.

In a simple case a burden factor may be applied to the total
direct labor in the inventory. For example, if the material represented by the inventory is deemed to have a cost of $100,000 and
the direct labor a cost of $50,000, and a 150% overhead rate is
used, the total cost of the inventory would be $225,000, including
$75,000 (150% of $50,000) for indirect manufacturing expenses. In a more detailed cost accounting system, the various
operations involved in manufacturing a particular part might be
analyzed and several burden factors applied (some to the direct
labor dollars, others to machining time, etc.) in order to establish
a cost for that item. The various individual costs so established
for the parts or subassemblies would then be applied to the quantities on hand to determine the aggregate cost for the inventory. Detailed computations provide information which can be
useful in reaching many business decisions; however, the data
needed to make such a procedure practical in operation, so as
to provide timely information at a reasonable expense, are not
readily available in every accounting system. Depending upon
the availability of data, there is no limit to the number of factors
which might appropriately be utilized in reflecting indirect manufacturing expenses in the cost of an inventory regardless of which
of the basic costing concepts are adopted. Starting with the possibility of merely applying a single company-wide overhead rate
to the total cost of all direct labor represented in the inventory,
refinements are usually made by utilizing a separate rate for each
plant, for each department, or for each operation within a department, and by applying the rate to machining time or other standard where appropriate rather than to direct labor dollars.

The second fundamental requirement of a cost accounting

procedure (i.e., that it be understood by and useful to those making management decisions) relates primarily to the costing concept which is being applied.

Even under the all-inclusive costing concept expenses which do not relate to the goods on hand at the inventory date should not be included in cost. For example, if overtime or extra-shift premiums are paid to produce seasonal goods and to meet a particular demand of the sales department, the premiums are fully chargeable against income. Earnings for the period of shipment would be overstated if any portion of the extra expense incurred were allocated to the inventory. Similarly, the expenses of the shipping department and any other department through which the goods in the inventory would not have passed (e.g., goods may pass through a paint or inspection department or other finishing process immediately prior to and only when ready for shipment) should not be included in indirect manufacturing expenses reflected in a burden rate.

In summarizing indirect manufacturing expenses for the purpose of setting burden rates, it is also necessary to ascertain the nature of the expenditures which are charged to the various accounts. In some cases, one digit in each expense account number may be used to indicate whether the control of the expense is considered the responsibility of the sales manager, the production manager, the purchasing agent, the controller, or other particular officer or supervisor. Where an account numbering system is so used to facilitate expense control, it should not be assumed that every account with the number indicating the production manager reflects an indirect *manufacturing* expense. The salary of the security guard in the lobby of the executive suite and sales office may be charged to Plant Protection, and the expense of the entire janitorial staff and yard crew may be charged to a maintenance account identified with the production manager even though a large number of employees may be required for the cleaning of non-manufacturing space. Inventory costs would be overstated if the entire maintenance expense were included in overhead.

There are many differences in philosophies reflected in the procedures followed in the costing of inventories. The following list of a few common types of indirect manufacturing expenses indicates some of the most frequently followed practices where other than the prime costing concept is adopted.

Items usually considered as being of a controllable nature, and part of cost:

Plant superintendent
Production foremen
Production scheduling
Quality control and inspection
Power, light, and water required for production
Machinery setups
Intra-plant trucking
Clean-up time
Factory janitorial services
Payroll taxes on direct labor and includable indirect labor

Items frequently considered as being of a continuing or recurring nature, and *not* part of cost:

General superintendent
Production planning
Engineering
Purchasing department
Receiving department
Stock room
Payroll department
Employee training
Job standards
Maintenance and watchmen
Heating
Safety precautions
Property taxes
Inventory taking
Vacations and holidays
Machinery relocating

Items commonly considered as resulting from errors, inefficiencies, and other events occurring during the year, and *not* part of cost:

Waiting time
Rework labor
Spoiled material
Union grievances

Among items meriting special discussion are pension and profit-sharing payments, depreciation, and insurance.

Direct payments to retirees are commonly considered as not being part of cost because the consideration received by the employer was the aggregation of services rendered in prior years, and the services had no relationship to production of the goods in the inventory. In the case of funded pension plans the charge to income may include a past-service element, which might be considered to be excludable from cost on the same grounds as direct payments to retirees. The current-service portion of the charge for a funded plan is sometimes considered not to be part of cost for inventory purposes because, unless there is complete vesting of the benefits in the employees, there is no direct relationship to current production. Usually, however, the charges to income with respect to currently earned pensions of employees engaged in activities related to manufacturing are included in overhead for inventory costing purposes.

A literal interpretation of section 404 of the Internal Revenue Code leads to the conclusion that, for federal income tax purposes, there should not be included in overhead any amounts for contributions paid to or under a stock bonus, pension, profit-sharing, or annuity plan, or compensation paid or accrued under a plan deferring receipt. Although not specifically covered in any general rulings published to date, the National Office of the Internal Revenue Service has had occasion to consider the question and reached the conclusion that contributions by an employer to a qualified employees' trust as defined in section 404(a) of the Code are *deductible* in the year when paid (or are deemed to have been paid) and should not be included in manufacturing expense.

It is not uncommon for production employees to participate in profit-sharing bonus distributions, and these payments are commonly considered not to be part of cost for inventory purposes. Where it is concluded not to allocate a portion of these expenditures to the unsold goods on hand at the end of the accounting period, the factors taken into account may include a recognition of such facts as (1) the wages paid the production employees are comparable to the wages paid by other employers in the same locale who do not have a profit-sharing bonus plan, (2) the aggregate amount of the bonus fund is established by reference to *realized* income for the period and income is realized only from sales, not just by producing goods for inventory, and (3) the bonus is entirely discretionary and requires action annually by the Board of Directors or other officials and is recognized as being a distribution to the employee group of *realized* income, just as dividends are a distribution to the shareholder group.

Under the classification of expenses suggested in Chapter 5, depreciation would fall in the category of *continuing expenses*, i.e., it is an expense which results from previous management decisions made to secure the production facilities which are available for use. Although it can be reasoned that only *controllable expenses* should be recognized as a cost, the current provision for depreciation of machinery, factory buildings, and other production facilities is generally considered to be an element of manufacturing overhead. If a consistent practice of not including depreciation in cost has been followed, however, income can be considered to have been fairly reflected, where there would be no material differences in the computed income from year to year had depreciation been regularly included in the computation of overhead. This fact has been recognized for many years in the determination of income for federal income tax purposes. In 1953 the income tax regulations were amended to recognize the alternative acceptable accounting practices, and a revenue ruling (Rev. Rul. 141, 1953-2 CB 101) was issued to clarify the reasons for the amendment. Furthermore, as stated on pages 115 and 372, in businesses which mature large stocks over long periods (e.g., whiskey, wine, and timber) it is usual not to include fixed overhead expense items in inventoriable cost in order to avoid carrying forward large and increasing amounts which may or may not be recovered in the ultimate selling price of the goods.

Where depreciation is not included among the expenses considered in determining the amount to be assigned to an inventory, the rationale underlying the decision may be based upon a variety of factors. In some cases the cost accounting system is designed primarily to develop statements which will be of maximum utility as a management tool in controlling the expenses of departments or other operating areas for which particular individuals have responsibilities. It can be reasoned that only *controllable expenses* should be included in such statements and that there should not be included depreciation and other *continuing expenses* which are the result of previous management decisions. Some *ad volorem* property taxes are subject to a similar conception of what items should be included in cost since these taxes result from prior capital expenditures for production facilities.

A decision not to recognize depreciation as an element of cost for inventory purposes may also be influenced by a realization that it is not feasible in most cases to make the analyses which would be necessary to ascertain a "theoretically sound" amount to be allocated to the inventory. Except where the depreciation provision is determined by some type of unit-of-production method the amount is computed basically to amortize the cost of the facility, on a time basis, over the period it will remain in a usable state. The depreciation provided in any year does not reflect the extent to which the facility was actually used, and it cannot be claimed that there is any precise matching of a proper amount of depreciation against revenue derived from utilization of the facility. Further, an analysis of the basis for the depreciation provision undertaken to ascertain a "theoretically sound" amount to be allocated to the inventory would involve the compilation of data by numerous cost centers and would have to reflect the processes through which each of the units on hand at the end of the year had physically passed. This type of analysis is incorporated in only the most detailed cost accounting systems. As stated at the outset of this discussion, however, the current provision for depreciation of machinery, factory buildings, and other production facilities is generally considered to be an element of manufacturing overhead and in that way included on a "broad-brush basis" in the cost for the inventory in most businesses.

The purchase of insurance protection is not indispensable to manufacturing, and premiums paid for fire and other casualty insurance is recognized by many accountants as not representing an element of the cost of producing the articles in the inventory. Premium expense is incurred by the management of a business to shift to the insurance carrier the risk of a substantial loss. In the event a building was destroyed by fire or other casualty, or if profits were lost or extra expenses incurred, the amount of the loss sustained which might have been insured against would not be part of manufacturing cost for inventory purposes. It is appropriate to reemphasize that in establishing selling prices, all amounts expended in the conduct of a business must be taken into account in order to realize a profit, but when the *cost* of an inventory is being established for the purpose of determining the income derived from operations during a particular period, careful attention must be paid to the determination of whether an item is a "cost" or an "expense." Where the loss being insured against would not be part of the manufacturing cost for inventory purposes, it logically follows that there should not be included in cost the amount of the expenditure for insurance premiums.

Where the analytical costing concept is applied, a portion of the indirect manufacturing expenses which would be considered to be includable in cost were the production facilities being fully utilized is not taken into account during certain periods in recognition of unused capacity. In this context, facilities need not be operating at a *maximum* rate based upon a theoretical potential in order to be considered to be "fully utilized." The norm is generally a *practical capacity* rate. The most commonly used procedure for applying this concept is by establishing burden rates by reference to what the aggregate expenses would be if the facility were operated at its practical capacity. There is no necessity to classify the expenses as between "fixed" and "variable" or analyze expenses into their *fixed* and *variable* elements. Historical data for prior periods may be used to establish budgets of what the expenditures would be for individual expense accounts or groups of related expenses, and modern budgeting techniques make possible the determination of appropriate overhead rates in a variety of ways.

The application of the analytical costing concept by reference to budgeted expenses at an operating level reflecting full utilization of a facility can be simply illustrated.

	Total expense when facility is fully utilized (based upon 1000x units)
Indirect manufacturing expenses:	
Item A (e.g., salary of plant superintendent) which is fixed in amount	$ 20,000
Item B (e.g., wages of production foremen) which amounts to $15,000.00 for each 100x units or fraction thereof	150,000
Item C (e.g., power) which is based on a flat charge of $5,000.00 plus $1.00 per x unit	6,000
Item D (e.g., payroll tax) which is based on $5.00 per x unit for each of the first 600 x units	3,000
Item E (e.g., trucking) which amounts to $2.00 per x unit	2,000
	$181,000
Overhead rate per x unit	$181

Analysis of costs at various operating rates:

	Units (upon which burden absorption is based) reflected in operating rate—					
	500x		750x		1000x	
	Expense allocable to —		Expense allocable to —		Expense allocable to —	
	Production	Unused capacity	Production	Unused capacity	Production	Unused capacity
Item A	$10,000	$ 10,000	$ 15,000	$ 5,000	$ 20,000	$ —
Item B	75,000	—	112,500	7,500	150,000	—
Item C	3,000	2,500	4,500	1,250	6,000	—
Item D	1,500	1,000	2,250	750	3,000	—
Item E	1,000	—	1,500	—	2,000	—
	$90,500	$ 13,500	$135,750	$ 14,500	$181,000	$ —
Total		$104,000		$150,250		$181,000
Per x unit		$208		$200⅓		$181
Expense per x unit allocable to production	$90,500÷500=$181		$135,750÷750=$181		$181,000÷1,000=$181	

Had the units that were reflected in the operating rate exceeded 1000x in any operating period the use of an overhead rate of $181 per x unit would result in charging production with "phantom dollars" to the extent the aggregate amount so charged exceeded the total of the actual expenditures. For example, if operations were at the rate of 1200x units, the total of the actual expenditures would be $211,600 (Item A, $20,000; Item B, $180,000; Item C, $6,200; Item D, $3,000; and Item E, $2,400), whereas 1200x units multiplied by $181 equals $217,200. The excess of $5,600 is commonly referred to as "over-absorbed burden," and where this factor is sufficiently material to distort the results of operations, an adjustment will be made to the tentatively computed inventory cost for an appropriate portion of such $5,600. *Theoretically*, an adjustment should always be made for overabsorbed overhead to avoid an overstatement of income for the period in which the inventory items are produced and an artificially high charge being made against the income for the period in which the items are sold.

In this simplified example, expense Items A and E illustrate the so-called *fixed* and *variable* expense, respectively. In the actual operations of a business, however, expense categories having these characteristics are seldom found. The other three items in the illustration are examples of how expenses can be affected by many factors. Item B illustrates an expense which increases by steps as the operating rate increases. For example, if a foreman can supervise 100x volume of work and he supervises only 80x volume, 20% of his salary can be considered allocable to unused capacity, and under the analytical costing concept only 80% of his salary would be allocated to production. Item C illustrates an expense which has both fixed and variable elements. Item D illustrates an expense which behaves differently from the others because the first dollars expended are not recoverable if the production facility is not fully utilized but carry a potential "bonus," in that the expense ceases (or it could have continued at a lesser rate) when a particular operating level is reached. In this case every $6y of wages upon which the payroll tax was considered to be payable means that $4y of additional productive wages could be incurred without the payment of any additional tax, i.e., 40% of each tax payment would be allocable to unused capacity if the facility is not fully utilized. At an operating rate of 750x the expense allocable to unused capacity is 62.5% (250x/400x) of $1,200 (40% of $3,000), or $750.

The foregoing discussion of the practical aspects of costing procedures demonstrates that in inventory determinations no amount can be considered to be the *actual cost* or the *correct cost* because in every case there will be alternative amounts which are also acceptable. The word "cost" should preferably be used without an adjective. If a costing procedure meets the fundamental requirements of being practical in operation so as to provide timely information at a reasonable expense and of being understood by and useful to those making management decisions, the important factor is whether it has been consistently applied. Refinements of the costing procedure which make the accounting data more useful should be constantly encouraged, but unless there has been a substantial change in the costing concept adopted, these can be made without distorting income.

7

Lower of Cost
or Market

A reference to inventories being stated at the lower of cost or market is so common that the significance of the phrase is not always fully appreciated. Further, it may not be recognized that this is an area where substantial disagreement among accountants exists. There are differences both on basic issues and on details.

To determine whether the practice of stating inventories at the lower of cost or market is merely an expedient rule of conservatism or reflects a fundamental accounting principle justifies a review of its ancestry. As indicated by the following references to accounting literature and specific historical economic events, practical factors have prompted development of the rule as well as the general philosophy that, while potential losses should be provided for, no profit should be anticipated in preparing financial statements.

In the twentieth century the word "valuation" is more commonly used in connection with inventories than with any other balance sheet item. This practice tends to obscure the fact that the amount assigned to a particular inventory is generally the cost considered to be applicable thereto with appropriate adjustments to reflect a lower market value.

EARLY REFERENCES TO VALUATION OF INVENTORIES

It is not claimed that the available information discloses the rule's real origin, but the material at hand indicates that it is a result of the mingling of two bloodlines: expediency and convenience. Medieval trading practices, banking and credit requirements, the aftermath of war, and inequitable taxation have profoundly influenced the development of this valuation rule. This mixed ancestry may partially account for the notion that taking an inventory is a process of evaluation.

As early as the beginning of the fifteenth century, goods in inventory were priced below their purchase cost. Dr. Baulduin Penndorf did considerable research work on bookkeeping practices (including a translation of Paciolo's writings) when he was professor of business administration and director of the College of Business Administration of Leipzig in the 1930's. This German scholar, writing of the manuscript records of an Italian businessman, Francesco di Marco, pointed out that certain stock bought for trade in 1406 at a cost of 60 florins, appeared still unsold in a later inventory at 50 florins. Beneath the item was this notation: "We have entered the 10 fl. in the debit of goods profit account as damage (loss) because we no longer value them (the goods) as above since they have fallen in price." It is doubtful that this change was made in the inventory merely for the satisfaction of producing an accurate profit calculation and a conservative statement of assets. It appears there may have been present some motive other than a high resolve to record the facts.[1]

This writer provides a clue to the reason for recognizing declines in inventory values when he points out[2] that the tax burden in Italian cities early in the fifteenth century was very heavy. The taxes were calculated on the amount of a citizen's land, investments, and business capital less certain deductions. Since the amounts of lands and investments could be determined by tax officials with considerable exactness, "endeavors to pay the lowest

---

[1] Littleton, "A Genealogy for 'Cost or Market,'" 16 *Accounting Rev.* 161 (June, 1941).
[2] Penndorf, "The Relation of Taxation to the History of the Balance Sheet," 5 *Accounting Rev.* 247 (Sept., 1930).

possible amount of taxes could only be made with reference to business capital." Penndorf does not give the details of the methods used in stating business capital at a minimum.

In 1494 Paciolo published the first printed text on bookkeeping. In discussing what would now be called an opening entry, he advised the merchant who desired to begin keeping systematic accounts to prepare a statement (*bilancio*) "of whatever he has in this world, personal property or real estate." Precious stones should be included "according to current prices"; for silver articles he mentions, "give each thing its customary price." The reader is left in doubt as to what prices are meant. Until systematic business records came into use, *valuing* the inventory was no doubt the usual practice and a proper base for the inventory rules which Paciolo mentions.

One of Paciolo's followers, Don Angelo Pietra, a monk of Genoa, offered the advice that a value should be given to things harvested and things manufactured, but this value should be lower than current prices "so that the proceeds will not fall below this value in case of sale." His book published in 1586 showed a thorough knowledge of mercantile accounting adapted to the requirements of monasteries and is chiefly remarkable for the completeness of the stocktaking which he introduces. Pietra, incidentally, was cellarer of his monastery and took charge of its business affairs.

In France, under an ordinance promulgated by Louis XIV in 1673, merchants and bankers were required to keep a journal of their transactions for reference in case of dispute. They were also to have the book authenticated by the signature of a public official. Furthermore, as one author points out, they were required to make a statement (*inventaire*) of all their fixed and movable properties and their debts receivable and payable every two years.[3] The French law at this point used words that are almost identical with those used by Paciolo in writing about the opening entry. That early writer's instructions about opening entries were thus reflected in European law regarding periodic financial reports.

[3] Howard, "Public Rules for Private Accounting in France, 1673 and 1807," 7 *Accounting Rev.* 92 (June, 1932).

Jacques Savary, the principal author of the ordinance of 1673 published a book in 1675 entitled *Le Parfait Mégociant* (*The Complete Tradesman*). In this he explained the statute and described current business practices. Among other things, he made some observations on the treatment of merchandise for inventory purposes. The reader is vaguely advised to take care not to estimate merchandise at more than it is worth. If the merchandise is newly purchased, he goes on to say, "and if one judges that it has not decreased in price at the factory . . . it should be put in at the current price." If the merchandise has begun to deteriorate or go out of style, he says to "reduce the price considerably." In 1712, he suggested that merchandise which could be replaced at 5 per cent less should be reduced to the replacement price.[4]

It appears that questions of business solvency prompted the inventory practices fostered by the French law. The ordinance of 1673 served as the basis for a part of the Napoleonic Code of 1807. In the section dealing with books of account, four items dealt with bookkeeping rules, such as authentication, making an inventory of all property, and the like, and six items dealt with the use of the records in case of litigation. French legal commentators have explained the relation of these rules to bankruptcy. A merchant's records would contribute a factual basis for a fair settlement with the creditors. If a merchant did not keep authenticated records, his bankruptcy was fraudulent under several conditions, namely, if the merchant kept no records, if he concealed records, or if the records did not correctly show his financial position. Legal regulations affecting inventories in France seem to be related to frauds suffered by creditors at the hands of a bankrupt.

In 1797 John Harries Wickes, of Egham, England, published his *Bookkeeping Reformed* which suggested inventory valuation "at prime cost."

At about the same time, a Bristol accountant, Edward Thomas Jones, subscribed to the prime cost rule in his *English System of Bookkeeping*. This book, incidentally, was introduced to the English public with great promotional fanfare and thus proved to be a great financial success for Jones. The full title of the

---

[4] Littleton, *Accounting Evolution to 1900* (1933), p. 152.

work is indicative of the claims made by the author for his new system: "Jones English System of Bookkeeping by Single or Double Entry, in which it is impossible for an error of the most trifling amount to be passed unnoticed. Calculated effectually to prevent the evils attendant on the methods so long established and adopted to every species of trade. Secured to the Inventor by the King's Letters Patent, Bristol, 1796." Launched as a death-blow to the Italian method (Paciolo *et al.*), the book met with considerable ridicule and derision in England. His fame, how-ever, spread abroad. The book undoubtedly was the first English work on accounting to achieve international renown, and even at the turn of the twentieth century, it was possibly the most widely known book on the subject of accounting in the English language.

James Morrison, a Glasgow accountant, in his *Elements of Book-keeping by Single and Double Entry* (1813), suggested esti-mating inventory "at prime cost, or at the current prices." This statement is, of course, ambiguous. It may mean that the inven-tory should be valued either at prime cost or at current prices, or at the lower of cost or market. In any event, Morrison's book marks one of the earliest disagreements with the straightforward prime cost rule.

In 1819 another English writer, Clerk Morrison, endorsed the market-price view in his *Introduction to Bookkeeping and Busi-ness*, in which he stated that it was fallacious to value at cost if the present price of an article is less than cost. He suggested that "the gain is in reality obtained as soon as the prices rise, or the loss suffered as soon as they fall."

Seventeen years later, in 1836, an English publication, entitled *New Check Journal upon the Principle of Double Entry*, written by George Jackson, strongly advocated valuation at cost. He insisted that at inventory time price increases or price decreases should not be taken into account since the gain or the loss is not realized or "has not actually yet been suffered."

Thus in the first half of the nineteenth century, British writers were noting the conflict between the balance sheet viewpoint as expressed by Clerk Morrison and the profit and loss viewpoint expressed by George Jackson.

In 1857 a conference was called for the purpose of drafting

a uniform commercial code for the German independent states. This draft, which specified valuation at the lower of cost or market, was not approved in that form. In 1861 the statute was made to read that goods and materials should be shown at the "value which ought to be ascribed at the date as of which the inventory and balance sheet are being drawn up."

A wave of promotion and stock speculation in Germany, which began in 1870, came to an abrupt and disastrous climax in 1873. The resulting depression prompted a legislative investigation. It was found that promoters and their attorneys, who were supported by a German court decision in 1873, had interpreted a phrase of the law of 1861 as permitting the use of probable sales price in stating balance sheet assets. This enabled them to publish very attractive balance sheets and to sell vast quantities of stock on the surpluses shown. A new corporation law was developed in 1884 which approved the rule of cost or market. Section 261 of the German Commercial Code of 1897 provided: "Securities and merchandise that have an exchange or market quotation may not be valued higher than at the price at which they were carried at the date of the balance sheet. Or if such price exceeds the price at which they were acquired or produced, then at the last mentioned price."

In 1885, C. R. Trevor, addressing the Manchester Accountants Students' Society, endorsed the cost or market rule. His paper is of slight significance except for the discussion which followed its delivery. One member of the Society commented that it was so thoroughly orthodox from beginning to end that it was very difficult to find any fault with the views expressed. This remark leaves little room for doubt that the cost or market rule had been generally accepted for a considerable period of time.

RECOGNITION OF COST OR MARKET IN THE UNITED STATES

The concept of valuing inventory at lower than its cost was alluded to in an opinion of the Supreme Court of Massachusetts in 1871. The court decided that loss in value of inventory due to a fire should be deducted in computing the profits of the business. In his opinion the judge said: "The profit and loss of trade in merchandise is not confined to that which results from sales.

Depreciation or advance in value of the stock unsold must also be taken into account. Depreciation may come from fluctuation of prices in the market, from deterioration in quality, or diminution in quantity, occasioned by the numerous causes incident to the business."[5] Although this statement suggests that market should be used even where cost is the lower figure, the facts before the court involved a lower market figure. The reference by the court to a situation involving a lower cost is of doubtful significance.

In 1897 two American authors, Broaker and Chapman,[6] insisted that it was "a sound principle to carry the stock at its actual cost, and let the profits or losses be determined upon final sale or disposition." These authors qualify this instruction somewhat, but it is interesting to notice their insistence upon the profit and loss viewpoint. Incidentally, Frank Broaker and Richard Chapman became rather famous in accounting circles through their prodigious efforts pressing for public accounting legislation in New York State. In 1896 the legislature passed the first law in the United States creating the professional designation Certified Public Accountant, and Broaker and Chapman received certificates Nos. 1 and 2.

At the St. Louis World's Fair in 1904 a Congress of Accountants was held under the auspices of the Federation of Societies of Public Accountants. Arthur Lowes Dickinson, then senior partner of an American public accounting firm and an outstanding Cambridge-educated accounting authority well acquainted with British and American practices, presented a paper in which he stated, "The general rule for valuation of stocks on hand, namely, 'cost or market, whichever is the lower,' has been evolved and is adopted by the most conservative commercial institutions."[7] The significance of this is threefold. First, Dickinson was an undoubted authority; second, he refers to the rule as a "general rule"; and third, by inference, he justifies the rule by the doctrine of conservatism.

[5] *Meserve v. Andrews*, 106 Mass. 419, 422 (1871).
[6] Broaker and Chapman, *The American Accountants Manual* (1897), p. 60.
[7] Dichinson, *Congress of Accountants Official Record 1904 World's Fair, St. Louis,* under the auspices of the Federation of Societies of Public Accountants in the United States of America, p. 182.

In 1909 W. R. MacKenzie endorsed the rule's consistent application when he affirmed that once adopted, the cost or market rule
"should be strictly adhered to, as one year at cost and another
at market, regardless of market being lower, will never produce
any degree of dependability. Like depreciation, it is only the
regular pursuit of the principle adopted that will give satisfactory
comparative results."[8]

In 1910 Leo Greendlinger, an Austrian-born accounting writer
who later became a director, treasurer, and secretary of the Alex-
ander Hamilton Institute in New York, attacked the cost or
market rule when he stated,

> It is wrong in principle to value it (inventory) at market price as
> it interferes with the correct showing of the profit and loss account. If
> we take the inventory for any reason, not for the purpose of rendering
> a correct profit and loss account for any given period, we are at liberty
> to use either form, cost or market value, but when we take inventory
> for the purpose of ascertaining the cost of sales, for the purpose of showing
> a correct profit and loss account, we must figure it at cost price only.[9]

This statement seems to mark the beginning of modern expressions
of accounting thought which question the soundness of the cost
or market rule because of the effect upon income determinations.

From an income tax viewpoint 1917 marked a most important
year in the history of the cost or market rule. The British Board
of Inland Revenue, based upon recommendations of a committee
of accountants, affirmed the general correctness of using cost or
market. In this same year the United States Treasury Department
took similar action. United States taxpayers were given an option
to adopt the basis of either (1) cost or (2) cost or market, whichever is lower, for their 1920 inventories. The basis adopted for that
year or for any subsequent year when inventories are first a factor
in the determination of income must be used consistently, and
can be changed only after permission is secured from the Commissioner of Internal Revenue.

During the period commencing with the 1929 stock market
crash and concomitant depression, there was a marked change from

---

[8] MacKenzie, "The Verification and Treatment of Inventories in Audits and
Examinations of Manufacturing and Trading Concerns," 9 *J. Accountancy* 115
(Dec., 1909).
[9] Greendlinger, *Accountancy Problems with Solutions*, Vol. I (1910), pp. 192,
193.

the former balance sheet viewpoint toward financial accounting. At least equal attention has since been given to the income statement.

A letter dated September 22, 1932, was written to the Committee on Stock List of the New York Stock Exchange by the American Institute of Accountants' Special Committee on Co-operation with Stock Exchanges, officially emphasizing that "the income account is usually far more important than the balance sheet" and referring to the cost or market rule as the principal exception to the primary accounting objective of securing "a proper charge or credit to the income account for the year."[10]

George D. Bailey[11] pointed out, in 1940, that the theory of the lower of cost or market need not be discarded in favor of a cost theory for income determination if the former results in provision for *anticipated loss*, rather than being used as an artificial rule applied regardless of the probability of loss.

Theoretical discussions of the cost or market rule were interrupted around 1942 by the exigencies of accounting in wartime, and since the war the questions have been of lesser immediate concern because of the effects of the inflationary trend.

From this brief history of the cost or market rule it is interesting to observe the relationship of some of the dates in its development to wars, panics, and taxes. The German depression of 1873 was accompanied by legal approval of the cost or market rule. The year 1917, when the cost or market rule was approved by the British Board of Inland Revenue and the United States Treasury Department, was a year of war and high taxes. The year 1932, which may be identified as the beginning of a period when the arbitrary application of the rule was questioned because of a new emphasis upon the income statement, represented a low point in the depression which had started in the fall of 1929. During the past two decades the subject has received comparatively little attention as a consequence of inflation. In recent years, however,

[10] Quoted in May, *Twenty-five Years of Accounting Responsibility, 1911–1936* (1936), p. 112.

[11] Bailey, "Some Thoughts on the Theory of Inventory Pricing," *Experiences with Extensions of Auditing Procedure and Papers on Other Accounting Subjects Presented at the Fifty-third Annual Meeting, American Institute of Accountants* (1940), p. 60.

instances where market values for inventory items are below their costs have been found with increasing frequency.

CONCEPTS OF "MARKET" IN INVENTORY DETERMINATIONS

Just as there is no single concept of "cost" which will be the most meaningful in all situations, there is no universally accepted basis for determining "market." The statement by the Institute of Chartered Accountants recommends that the use of the term "market value" be discontinued, but in the present context the word is used to embrace all the amounts with which a computed cost may be compared in inventory determinations. The most commonly used comparatives are "replacement price," "net realizable value," and "net realizable value less normal profit."

"Replacement price," or "replacement cost," represents the amount for which, in the ordinary course of business, the inventory items could have been acquired or produced either at the inventory date or during the last operating period. For this purpose recognition is given to the volume in which the company usually purchases the various inventory items and the normal sources of supply.

"Net realizable value" represents the amount at which the inventory items are offered for sale in the regular course of business less any direct expenses of disposition. This determination requires giving recognition to all available information, including changes in selling prices subsequent to the inventory date. Consideration is given to the prospects for disposing of the inventory, having regard to the quantity and condition of the goods on hand.

"Net realizable value less normal profit" represents the amount remaining after allowing for the profit which the business can be expected to realize from the sale of the items included in its inventory.

The bulletin of the AICPA (paragraph 9 of Appendix A) states that the term "market" is to be interpreted as indicating utility on the inventory date and may be thought of in terms of the equivalent expenditure which would have to be made in the ordinary course at that date to procure corresponding utility. The AICPA position is that the cost for an inventory will generally be compared with current replacement cost (by purchase or re-production), but replacement cost should not be used if it exceeds net realizable value (the estimated selling price in the ordinary course of business less reasonably predictable costs of completion and expenses of disposal) or is less than the latter reduced by an approximately normal profit margin.

The statement by the Institute of Chartered Accountants (paragraph 12 of Appendix B) asserts that a provision for a loss should be made at the inventory date if any portion of the cost is not recoverable. It is stated that this irrecoverable portion of cost is normally determined by a comparison with net realizable value (paragraph 13), but that in some circumstances the replacement price may be considered the best available guide to the net realizable value (paragraph 15). Where the replacement price basis is adopted the inventory is stated at the lowest of cost, net realizable value, and replacement price.

Where the lower of cost or market basis has been adopted for federal income tax purposes, the regulations provide (section 1.471–4 of Appendix C) that under ordinary circumstances and for normal goods in an inventory, cost is to be compared generally with replacement price. An interpretation of this and related provisions in the regulations was the subject of litigation in the case of *D. Loveman & Son Export Corporation.* The decision by the Tax Court (34 T.C. 776) was filed August 5, 1960; the decision in favor of the taxpayer was affirmed by the Court of Appeals for the Sixth Circuit on December 16, 1961, without any detailed discussion; and on April 23, 1962, the Supreme Court denied a petition to review the decision.

In the *D. Loveman & Son Export Corporation* case, a warehouser had purchased steel from a premium mill, because during a period of steel shortage the major producing mills sold their production to other customers. The inventory of steel on hand was valued at the posted prices of the major producing mills which were lower than the taxpayer's cost. Where the steel was ultimately sold at a price in excess of the price paid to the premium mill, it was held that the posted prices of the major steel producers did not represent "market." The following paragraphs are quoted from the opinion of the Tax Court:

The parties are in basic disagreement as to what petitioners' "market" was during the years involved herein. Petitioners argue that the "combination of unusual circumstances" which "temporarily prevented (them) from buying their steel requirements from their usual sources did not effect any change in (their) market for inventory valuation purposes, nor require them to change their customary method of inventory valuation." In support of this contention, they point out that the major mills produced "close to 100 per cent" of all the carbon steel plate rolled in the United States, and that the determination of market value by reference to the published prices of those mills was not only "consistent with petitioners' prior practice, but * * * customary in the steel warehouse business."

Respondent, on the other hand, maintains that the term "particular merchandise," as used in the above-quoted regulation, refers only to the steel which was available to the petitioners during the taxable years in question and, therefore, that petitioners' market did not include steel produced by the major mills. The record, viewed in the light of applicable precedent, compellingly supports respondent's position on this issue.

This case also considers the appropriate treatment of "freight-in" expenditures. It was held that the transportation expense had to be added to the cost of the steel in order to reflect income clearly. The inventory volume had not been at all constant, so the decision is not applicable to a situation involving an established accounting practice of consistently considering "freight-in" as a current expense where there are only normal fluctuations in the annual inventories.

The income tax regulations specifically recognize situations in which net realizable value may be the appropriate amount to be assigned to an inventory item. Replacement cost of work in process and finished goods (or articles bought for resale) would not constitute market if it exceeds what could be realized upon sale in the ordinary course of business. For example, paper stock may have a definite market value, but if it is converted into a printed book which no one wants to buy, its market value has become nil.

The federal income tax regulations also provide in section 1.471–2(c) that, whether cost or the lower of cost or market basis of stating inventories is used, the amount assigned to goods which are "unsalable at normal prices or unusable in the normal way because of damage, imperfections, shop wear, changes of style, odd or broken lots, or other similar causes, including second-hand goods taken in exchange" should not exceed net realizable value.

Further, it is stated that if the inventory items unusable in the normal way "consist of raw materials or partly finished goods held for use or consumption, they shall be valued upon a reasonable basis, taking into consideration the usability and the condition of the goods, but in no case shall such value be less than the scrap value." Under the regulations these adjustments, made under a procedure for stating inventories at cost as well as under a lower of cost or market election, represent redeterminations of the cost allocable to the units on hand rather than writedowns to market. When a shipment of merchandise is received or a production order is completed, it is normally expected that some units will be unsalable at normal prices or unusable in the normal way. It cannot be predicted precisely which or how many units will reach this status so for convenience all units may be considered tentatively as though they have the same cost. After the major portion of the shipment has been disposed of in the normal manner, hindsight is applied to adjust the cost allocated to the remaining units. The correct cost for these units is net realizable value, and the excessive amount tentatively allocated is an addition to the cost of the units sold. Similarly, if secondhand goods taken in an exchange cannot be sold for an amount equal to the credit allowed on the trade-in transaction, there is no writedown to market when the cost of the secondhand goods is reduced to net realizable value. The cost revision represents an adjustment of the originally computed profit on the prior sale.

Application of the various concepts of "market" can be illustrated by assuming situations involving an inventory item as to which the profit factors would normally be as follows:

	Amount	%
Sales value	$3.00	100
Expense incurred in disposing of inventory	.30	10
Net realizable value	$2.70	90
Cost of inventory item	2.10	70
Gross profit	$ .60	20

The amounts assigned to the item for inventory purposes under each of six different assumed conditions, in accordance with the

AICPA bulletin, the statement by the Institute of Chartered Accountants, and the United States income tax regulations, are shown on page 160.

In the first of these assumed situations, there would be justification for assigning to the inventory an amount less than cost if the explanation for the 10 per cent smaller selling price was that the goods on hand were damaged or otherwise not in their normal condition. On the same basis, an amount less than $1.95 might be justified for the inventory in the second situation.

A smaller amount than has been stated as being in accordance with the AICPA bulletin would be assigned to the inventory under the sixth situation if the normal profit of 60¢ had been deducted from the net realizable value of $2.43 rather than the 54¢ determined by applying the same *rate* of profit. Whether the amount or rate of profit should be used for this purpose must be determined by the circumstance of each individual case. The controlling consideration is which procedure will make the financial statements more useful to the reader.

The objective of the AICPA bulletin is to assign to the goods in the inventory an amount reflecting their usefulness. The reasons for the recommended procedure are stated as follows:

. . . As a general guide, utility is indicated primarily by the current cost of replacement of the goods as they would be obtained by purchase or reproduction. In applying the rule, however, judgment must always be exercised and no less should be recognized unless the evidence indicates clearly that a loss has been sustained. There are therefore exceptions to such a standard. Replacement or reproduction prices would not be appropriate as a measure of utility when the estimated sales value, reduced by the costs of completion and disposal, is lower, in which case the realizable value so determined more appropriately measures utility. Furthermore, where the evidence indicates that cost will be recovered with an approximately normal profit upon sale in the ordinary course of business, no loss should be recognized even though replacement or reproduction costs are lower. [Par. 9, Appendix A.]

Hence, the AICPA bulletin supports the replacement cost interpretation of market on the grounds that a decline in replacement price below cost indicates that the usefulness of the inventory as a revenue-producing potential declined and that this loss should be charged against revenues of the period in which it occurs. Fundamentally, this interpretation assumes that a decrease in purchase or reproduction cost will be followed by a decrease in selling price.

The Institute of Chartered Accountants prefers to use net realizable value in place of "market," but the use of the alternative of the lower of net realizable value or replacement price is recognized as appropriate in some situations. Reference to replacement price is considered to be appropriate principally where net realizable value is unobtainable or deemed irrelevant in the light of all the circumstances, where the ultimate sales price is problematical, or where experience has shown that selling prices usually tend in time to reflect replacement cost. A writedown to replacement cost is also considered appropriate where the excess of actual cost over replacement cost is due to poor purchasing or inefficient manufacturing. In these circumstances the replacement price may be considered to be the best available guide to an inventory's net realizable value.

APPLICATION OF LOWER OF COST OR MARKET RULE

Publications of both the AICPA and the Institute of Chartered Accountants provide that the lower of cost or market rule may be applied to aggregate values of inventories, to different categories, or to individual items. The reasons for the alternative bases of comparison are summarized below:

1. If there is only one end-product category, the utility of the total stock—the inventory in its entirety—may have the greatest significance.
2. When no loss of income is expected to take place as a result of reduced replacement prices for certain goods because others forming components of the same general categories of finished products have a market equally in excess of cost, such components need not be adjusted to market to the extent that they are in balanced quantities.
3. To the extent that the stocks of particular materials or components are excessive in relation to others, the procedure of applying the lower of cost or market to the individual items constituting the excess should be followed. This would also apply in cases in which the items enter into the production of unrelated products or products having a material variation in the rate of turnover.

Application of Different Lower-of-Cost-or-Market Rules Under Varying Circumstances

	Replacement price exceeds cost, but		Cost exceeds replacement price and			
					Net realizable value declines	
	Normal profit will not be obtained (1)	Cost exceeds net realizable value (2)	Sales value is unchanged (3)	In proportion to decline in cost (4)	More than cost (5)	Less than cost (6)
Cost............................	$2.10	$2.10	$2.10	$2.10	$2.10	$2.10
Replacement price.............	2.20	2.20	1.89	1.89	1.89	1.68
Net realizable value..........	2.40	1.95	2.70	2.43	2.16	2.43
Net realizable value less normal profit (7/9 of net realizable value).....	1.86⅔	1.51⅔	2.10	1.89	1.68	1.89
Amount assigned to inventory in accordance with:						
AICPA..........................	2.10	1.95	2.10	1.89	1.89	1.89
Institute of Chartered Accountants:						
Normal practice..............	2.10	1.95	2.10	2.10	2.10	2.10
Alternative practice.........	2.10	1.95	1.89	1.89	1.89	1.68
Income tax regulations........	2.10	1.95	1.89	1.89	1.89	1.68

Assumed situations with respect to inventory item:

(1) Sales value is down 10 per cent, i.e., $2.70.
(2) Sales value is down 25 per cent, i.e., $2.25.
(3) Replacement price is 10 per cent below cost and net realizable value is unchanged.
(4) Replacement price is 10 per cent below cost and net realizable value is down 10 per cent.
(5) Replacement price is 10 per cent below cost and net realizable value is down 20 per cent.
(6) Replacement price is 20 per cent below cost and net realizable value is down 10 per cent.

Unless an effective method of classifying categories is practicable, the cost or market rule should be applied to each item in the inventory. This is the basis for comparison contemplated by section 1.471–4(c) of the federal income tax regulations.

Obviously the amount assigned to the inventory in its entirety may differ substantially, depending upon the procedure followed in making comparisons between cost and market. The most appropriate procedure will depend upon the character and composition of the inventory, and the selection should be that which most clearly reflects periodic income. Whatever procedure is adopted should be applied consistently from year to year.

INVENTORY WRITEDOWNS AND THE INCOME STATEMENT

The evaluation of inventories is significant from the standpoint of both the balance sheet and the income statement. In the former the inventory evaluation influences the current asset total, the grand total of all the assets, the ratio between current assets and current liabilities, and the retained earnings figure. In the latter the inventory evaluation may materially influence the cost of goods sold and the net profit.

From an accounting standpoint the cost or market rule was originally justified on the basis of balance sheet conservatism. In general it is wise to anticipate no profits and to provide for all possible losses. As the historical review has demonstrated, the cost or market rule was developed during the long period when bankers and other creditors were primarily concerned with the balance sheet and when relatively little consideration was given to the income statement. By those who thought in terms of realizable value, inventory was considered in relation to possible cash proceeds from selling that inventory. Inventories were valued under the same general theory as receivables by reasoning that all assets ultimately will be converted into cash and should not be stated at an amount greater than their cash equivalent.

Since the 1930s the income statement has become more generally recognized as a significant measure of debt-paying ability and investment desirability. As a consequence, bankers, other creditors, business management, and stockholders are becoming increasingly concerned with the reported earnings—not only with the income statement for a single period, but with the trend of earnings over a series of years.

There is an inconsistency in absorbing against current profits an unrealized loss on unsold merchandise while ignoring an unrealized potential increase in gross profit which may result from a rising market. This is justified on the grounds of conservatism; however, unless there is adequate disclosure, the cost or market rule may not be as conservative as it appears to be. This is particularly true when giving consideration to the income statements for a series of periods. If, at the close of one period, the market value of the inventory is less than its cost, the reduction of the inventory valuation to market undoubtedly produces a conservative balance sheet valuation and a conservative computation of income in the statements for that period. Nevertheless, the amount of earnings reported by periods may be altered materially by the shifting of income from one period to another.

For the purpose of illustration it is assumed that at the beginning of January merchandise was purchased at a cost of $100,000; that half of the goods were sold in January for $75,000; that the remaining half were sold in February for $73,000; and that the inventory at the end of January, which cost $50,000, had a market value of $40,000. The following statement shows the computation of gross profit for the two months, both under the cost or market rule and with the inventory valued at cost.

	With inventory valued at	
	Cost or market	Cost
January:		
Sales..	$75,000	$75,000
Cost of goods sold ($100,000 of purchases minus the inventory).	60,000	50,000
Gross profit..	$15,000	$25,000
February:		
Sales..	$73,000	$73,000
Cost of goods sold (consisting of the opening inventory).......	40,000	50,000
Gross profit..	$33,000	$23,000

The $40,000 balance sheet valuation for the inventory at the end of January and the statement of $15,000 of gross profit for the month may be accepted as conservative. But some explanation is required for showing $33,000 of gross profit for February even though the selling prices had to be reduced so that $2,000 less was actually realized from the second half of the merchandise. The reader of the income statements must be made to realize that the increase in February's profit was caused by the $10,000 writedown of the inventory at the end of January.

In the illustration it was assumed that the anticipated market decline did not fully materialize in February. The next statement assumes that the sales proceeds decreased $10,000—an amount equal to the decrease in inventory valuation—during the second month:

	With inventory valued at	
	Cost or market	Cost
January:		
Sales..................	$75,000	$75,000
Cost of goods sold........	60,000	50,000
Gross profit............	$15,000	$25,000
February:		
Sales..................	$65,000	$65,000
Cost of goods sold........	40,000	50,000
Gross profit............	$25,000	$15,000

The figures in the "Cost" column reflect what actually happened. The company made less profit in February than in January because of the decrease in selling prices. The "Cost or Market" column tells a very strange story. The company made more profit in February than in January, despite the decrease in selling prices. Where there has been an inventory writedown from cost to market, the gross profit margin may bear no relation to the volume of sales.

The cost or market inventory-pricing basis is founded on the assumption that a decrease in market purchase costs will be followed by a decrease in selling prices before the disposal of the inventory. In the long run there is a tendency for cost and selling prices to move together, but a lower market value at the close of one fiscal period need not always mean a loss of profit in the following period. Selling prices are not always adjusted downward to accord with a decline in current buying cost. Furthermore, not all declines in market value are permanent. A counter market movement often restores the price prior to the sale of the inventory. It should also be noted that the loss which is feared is not always a loss of cost, but rather a loss of potential profit. Hence, there is a trend toward the opinion that it is not necessary or desirable to reduce the inventory valuation to market if there is no probability that sales prices will also decrease.

From the standpoint of measurement of net income, consideration must be given to the procedures associated with the assignment or "matching" of costs against related revenues. The emphasis should not be one of inventory "valuation," but of cost assignment, the aim being to carry forward the amount of unabsorbed costs (residue) properly chargeable against future sales. As stressed by George O. May,

> . . . The primary objective in accounting for those items which are subject to inventory accounting is to assure a proper charge against revenue in the determination of periodic income in accordance with the concept of income by which the accounting is governed. This involves (a) a proper matching of costs against the revenues that are attributed to the period and (b) the elimination of such part, if any, of the remaining costs as is found to be in excess of the useful costs properly chargeable against future periods.[12]

Thus, an inventory writedown because of a price level decline is predicated on loss of utility.

When a diminution in the revenue-producing potential of an inventory is recognized, it may be desirable in detailed income statements prepared for management purposes to disclose any material amount of loss as a charge separately identified from the consumed costs described as "cost of goods sold." Such disclosure allows comparisons to be made between operating results of different periods without the abnormal loss arising from the ownership of inventory when the market value declined. In shareholders' reports and other published financial statements, this type of loss

[12] May, "Inventory Pricing and Contingency Reserves: Comment on New Accounting Research Bulletins," 84 *J. Accountancy* 366 (Nov., 1947).

is seldom specifically identified because it is not generally material in amount, and, further, the treatment of the loss as a separate item may be interpreted as implying that management should not be held accountable for the fact that there are goods held in the inventory with respect to which the market value has declined below cost.

8

Flow of Costs vs. Flow of Goods

Mrs. Smith is asked to serve coffee at her church for a group of visiting ministers. There is a pound can of coffee on her pantry shelf imprinted "10¢ off regular price," and the rubber stamped cost of 69¢ is still legible. Her kitchen cannister is almost empty and Mrs. Smith stops at her favorite supermarket on the way to the church. Another pound can of the same brand is purchased for 74¢. When she arrives at the church, Mrs. Smith uses the 69¢ coffee for the ministers, leaving the 74¢ can in the car to take home for her family's use, and later in the day she starts wondering whether she did the right thing. The vacuum pack assured the freshness of the coffee served the ministers and many complimentary remarks had been made during the social hour, but would it have been a more generous act to have used the pound for which 74¢ had been paid?

The discussion at the Smith family dinner table that evening started with considering whether the contribution to the church had been 69¢, 74¢, or 79¢. Mrs. Smith made a plea for the 79¢ figure (after all, the fact of a 10¢ saving was printed in large letters and she should get credit for an advantageous purchase), but her husband pointed out that their family accounts and those of business generally reflect only the actual amounts expended. In concluding that the contribution was 74¢ rather than 69¢, the Smiths were basically applying a concept of the flow of costs independent of the flow of goods.

Under normal circumstances financial statements reflecting the results of the operation of a business enterprise during a particular period are prepared on a going-concern basis. Consistent with this concept of continuing operations, there will always be goods on hand available for sale. The goods owned at the end of an accounting period will seldom be exactly comparable to the goods in the opening inventory, but the purpose of the inventory will be the same: to make possible uninterrupted realization of income through sales.

ALTERNATIVES TO USE OF SPECIFIC COSTS

The appropriateness of using average costs rather than specifically identified costs has been discussed in Chapter 6, beginning on page 119. The averaging process is in one sense a concept of a flow of costs, but it can also be viewed as merely a compilation of the actual cost for a group of similar items under circumstances where the amount paid for each item has no significance. The entire group of items is considered as a single entity; and when particular items are separated, they are treated as merely a proportionate part of the whole.

The retail method discussed in Chapter 13 is another example of a procedure not dependent upon identifying the actual cost of particular items. This inventory method, like the others, was developed to summarize in a significant manner the voluminous transactions of an enterprise. The assumptions upon which it is based are sound, and the determinations of amounts to be assigned to inventories permit a fair reflection of the results of business operations.

Other inventory methods not dependent upon the actual cost for the specific items on hand have been developed for use in particular industries. Products of agriculture and mining are sometimes inventoried at sales prices less expenditures to be incurred in marketing.[1] By-products may be inventoried at current selling prices less any expenses to be incurred before disposal where separate costs are not ascertainable.[2] A portion of the profit expected to be earned when a long-term contract is completed may be added to the expenditures incurred to the inventory date.[3] A dealer in securities may inventory unsold securities at market value.[4] Livestock raisers may use the unit-livestock-price method, which provides for the valuation of the different classes of animals in the inventory at a standard unit price for each animal within a class.[5] These inventory methods are of special-purpose design, and there may be other procedures appropriate for particular circumstances; but there are three important inventory procedures based upon assumptions as to the flow of costs which will be considered in some detail: *first-in, first-out; base stock;* and *last-in, first-out.*

Computations of income which attempt to reflect the actual flow of goods are not necessarily the most meaningful to business management, investors, or creditors. Each of these groups is normally more concerned with what the future earnings of the business enterprise will be than with the amount which could be realized from the inventory if it were liquidated completely and the activity discontinued.

FIRST-IN, FIRST-OUT (FIFO) INVENTORY METHOD

Under the first-in, first-out (FIFO) inventory method cost is computed on the assumption that goods sold or consumed are those which have been longest on hand and that those remaining in stock represent the latest purchases or production.

The federal income tax regulations (section 1.471-2(d) of Appendix C) imply that the FIFO method should be used only where the goods in the inventory have been so intermingled that they cannot be identified with specific invoices. On the other

---

[1] Paragraph 16, Appendix A; paragraph 20, Appendix B; and section 1.471-6(d), Appendix C.
[2] Paragraph 21, Appendix B.
[3] Paragraph 22, Appendix B.
[4] Section 1.471-5, Appendix C.
[5] Section 1.471-6(e), Appendix C.

hand, it is recognized by the American Institute of Certified Public Accountants (paragraph 6 of Appendix A) that if the materials purchased in various lots are identical and interchangeable, the use of identified cost for the various lots may not produce the most useful financial statements. Regardless of the restrictions implied in the wording of the federal income tax regulations, there is no actual conflict between the procedures used for financial statement and federal income tax purposes. Both the Internal Revenue Code and the income tax regulations provide that inventories are to be taken on such basis as will conform as nearly as may be to the best accounting practice in the trade or business and most clearly reflect the income.

In practice some form of FIFO method is used in the majority of inventory computations. The principle can be applied to individual items, such as particular parts, or to the entire production of a plant or department (particularly in the application of overhead). A FIFO assumption was made for the purpose of the illustrations in Chapter 6.

BASE STOCK INVENTORY METHOD

Under the base stock inventory method the minimum quantity of raw materials or other goods without which management considers the operation cannot be continued, except for limited periods, is treated as being a fixed asset subject to constant renewal. The base quantity is carried forward at the cost of the original stock.

If a quantity of goods larger than the base stock is owned at the end of any period, the excess will be carrried at its identified cost or at the cost determined under a FIFO method. This is considered a temporary condition.

If a quantity of goods less than the base stock is owned at the end of any period, this condition is similarly considered temporary. In order not to inflate the income of the period during which the base stock was depleted a reserve is set up equal to the excess of the replacement cost over the amount at which the goods would have been included in the base stock inventory. Even if the reserve for replacement is not provided for out of income of the year in which the base stock is depleted, the originally established cost is assigned to the replacement goods in the subsequent inventories when the base stock quantities are actually on hand.

Use of the base stock method is not allowed for federal income tax purposes. Among the methods which are specifically stated as not being in accord with the regulations is, "Using a constant price or nominal value for so-called normal quantity of materials or goods in stock."[6]

A special adaptation of the base stock method was considered by The Supreme Court of the United States in the *Kansas City Structural Steel Co.* case,[7] and was held to be unacceptable for federal income tax purposes. The factual situation involved in that case and some of the comments by the Court are of interest.

Kansas City Structural Steel Company was engaged in the fabrication and erection of steel plates for buildings, bridges, and other structures. It did not carry finished products in stock, but fabricated the plates for specified structures or contracts. It ordered material from the mills for each structure or contract, but it also kept a supply on hand to avoid delay in performing its contracts. Material was taken from this supply as needed, and the stock was subsequently replenished with approximately the same quantities.

On December 31, 1916, the quantity in stock was 5,554 tons. The company then inventoried it at cost—$1.70 per hundredweight f.o.b. Pittsburgh. At the close of each year thereafter until 1921, the company inventoried its stock on hand up to 5,554 tons at that price, regardless of its actual cost or the market value, and the excess, if any, at the lower of cost or market.

In the tax years in question the market price was higher than $1.70. The actual cost of the stock was not shown, and the Commissioner revalued the entire stock at current market prices. The changes resulted in increasing the December 31, 1918, inventory by $165,849.46 and the December 31, 1920, inventory by $117,113.61.

The company did not contest the question that the use of inventories was necessary for the determination of income. Nor did

[6] Section 1.471–2(f) (4), Appendix C.
[7] *Lucas v. Kansas City Structural Steel Co.*, 281 U.S. 264 (1930).

it contest the disapproval of the base stock method of valuing inventory. It did urge, however, that the inventory requirement was not applicable to the company's stock to the extent of 5,554 tons. The taxpayer contended that its income resulted from the performance of its construction contracts and that the material in its stand-by stock had no relation to those contracts, the contract prices, or the company's profits. It reasoned that the material was merely borrowed from this stock for specific jobs and since it was promptly replaced in kind, it was not an income-producing factor but was like machinery and equipment; that is, any accretion to the value of this material was of no consequence until a final liquidation.

The Supreme Court, in reversing the Circuit Court of Appeals, held that the taxpayer's contention was inconsistent with its practice and unsound. The Court held that the purchase and production of steel plates was an income-producing factor and observed, "The value of the particular material used, at the time of use, plainly affects its profits. That the material is replaced in kind and its amount kept within some limits is not exceptional and is of no significance. Most concerns strive ordinarily to carry no more stock than is required for the safe and profitable conduct of the business. They plan neither to run short nor to overstock. They replace supplies as they are consumed. And the cost or value of the new material is properly reflected in the later inventories and returns."

The 5,554 tons were not set aside and earmarked as stand-by stock; the material was commingled and indiscriminately used in production. The Court concluded, "To draw an artificial line at that amount would distort the computation of income in the accounting periods, although the errors might be equalized in a series of years. Since inventories are properly deemed necessary, the exception of that or any amount is nothing but the use of the discarded 'base stock' method."

It appears that the Court was not correctly informed when is applied the adjective "discarded" to the base stock method.

Although no exhaustive review of published financial statements has been made to ascertain how many corporations have used the base stock principle in reporting to shareholders, a number have adopted the method independent of federal income tax considerations and use it because it results in a better reflection of income. Reports of publicly owned corporations indicate that use of the base stock method was started by at least one company in each of the years 1906 and 1913, by at least four companies during the following four years, by at least five companies during the 1920's, and by at least 15 companies during the period 1932 through 1937. An investigation of prevailing inventory practices made in 1938 by the National Industrial Conference Board showed that of 826 widely scattered enterprises selected for the study, 4 per cent used a base stock method. Acceptance of the base stock method in annual accounts, with an appropriate description, is implied in the statement by the Institute of Chartered Accountants.[8]

After the last-in, first-out (LIFO) inventory method was accepted for federal income tax purposes, most of the companies using the base stock method adopted LIFO. This was done in view of the practical tax considerations involved and not because it was felt that the change was to a better method.

The early users of the base stock method were mostly engaged in processing basic raw materials. Smelting and refining companies were the first industry group, and they were followed by tanners and representatives of the oil industry. Wherever management seeks to derive a continuing profit from processing and to avoid the effect of fluctuations in the market price for the material involved, there is a natural desire to obtain commitments for the future purchase of their production, similar to a hedge. The magnitude of the investment in the basic material and the potential effect of market value declines are disproportionate to the earnings which will result from processing.

The quantity of material included in the base stock is actually a somewhat flexible minimum amount necessary to permit orderly operations. Within reasonable limits, the processor must be able to accept goods tendered by the suppliers with whom he has continuing relations, and similarly his customers' demands must be met—not only the anticipated demands for which the customer gives an order for future delivery but also the orders for immediate delivery resulting from unforeseen circumstances.

[8] Paragraphs 23 and 25(b), Appendix B.

The base stock requirement in the case of a metal or leather processor is paralleled in the case of an oil company which must at all time have its supply lines filled. Again, the supply lines are not only those from the source of the crude oil to the refinery but also the pipelines, storage tanks, and delivery trucks essential to making sure that the finished product will be at the place, in the form, and in the quantities the customer will want. Similarly, a manufacturer of agricultural machinery, electrical appliances, and most other items, must maintain a minimum of stock from year to year to unify his production forces and be in a position to meet customer demands.

If the base stock quantity is properly established, this method should result in income being fairly reflected. The cost of acquiring an equal volume of goods will be charged against revenues derived from sales. Earnings will not be affected by increases or decreases in the cost or market value of the base stock.

Income is not realized from merely replacing inventory quantities, and it can be argued that there should be deducted from the revenue derived from selling the goods previously owned whatever expenditures are necessary to restore the company to a position of being able to continue operations. However, among the inventory procedures presently acceptable for federal income tax purposes, LIFO is the only one which permits taking this economic factor into account. This situation is regretted because the base stock method does not have the shortcomings inherent in the LIFO method.

Conceivably, an appropriate adaptation of the base stock principle may at some future date be developed which will become generally accepted for use by both processors and manufacturers in computing taxable income as well as for financial reporting.

LAST-IN, FIRST-OUT (LIFO) INVENTORY METHOD

The third of the important inventory procedures to be discussed in detail is the last-in, first-out (LIFO) method. Under LIFO it is assumed that the stocks sold or consumed in any period are those most recently acquired or made. As a consequence of this assumption the stocks to be carried forward as the inventory are considered as if they were those earliest acquired or made.

The result of the LIFO method is to charge current revenues with amounts approximating current replacement costs. To the goods owned at the end of any period are assigned costs applicable to items purchased or made in earlier periods.

It is more obvious with respect to LIFO than FIFO—although true under both inventory methods—that the concepts are as to the flow of costs independent of the flow of goods. A company roasting, grinding, and selling coffee, or one dealing in meats or produce, will not physically have in its closing inventory the same units that were on hand at the beginning of the year. Similarly, it must be emphasized that the dollar amount assigned to an inventory has no effect upon its actual value to the company. The revenue-producing potential of the property owned is not changed by the inventory method adopted.

The federal income tax regulations (section 1.472-1(b) of Appendix C) recognize that the LIFO flow of cost concept can be extended to transactions involving goods which cannot be physically identified, and may not even be in existence. In the case of a business which regularly and consistently matches purchases with sales in a manner similar to hedging on a futures market, contracts not legally subject to cancellation by either party, entered into at fixed prices on or before the date of an inventory, may be included in purchases or sales, as the case may be, in determining the cost of goods sold. The only requirements are that the practice be regularly and consistently adhered to and that it results in income being clearly reflected.

Many types of business risks can be shifted to others by the purchase of insurance, but no general insurance is available specifically against price fluctuations. A large part of the risk of price declines and advances can be shifted to others, however, for goods traded on organized commodity exchanges. These exchanges make hedging possible, and some businesses strive similarly to avoid the risk of price changes by matching purchases with sales and entering into firm contracts for future delivery whenever a purchase or sale is made. The objective is to permit the manufacturer or processor to concentrate on performing his own conversion function efficiently and to minimize the extent to which income is affected by fluctuations in the market value of the material involved.

The development of the LIFO principle, its acceptance for financial statement and federal income tax purposes, and the procedures followed in its application under varying circumstances are discussed in subsequent chapters. The fact that LIFO is fundamentally a principle for determining income is evidenced by the name "last-in, first-out." The phrase itself connotes a flow of costs. It is easier to compute a cost for the items in an inventory than to compute a cost for each sales transaction; consequently, the inventory approach is adopted to accomplish as simply as possible the desired objective of properly stating income under this flow of cost concept.

REFLECTING THE LIFO CONCEPT IN INTERIM STATEMENTS

Theoretically the LIFO concept can be applied to any accounting period—a month, a calendar quarter, or a fiscal year. Because of the federal income tax requirement that it be applied to the period for which the tax is being computed, however, the most common application of the principle is to the taxable year, which is normally a full twelve-months period.

One of the principal functions of an accounting department is the preparation of periodic financial and operating reports for the many purposes for which such reports are required. With the possible exception of those where the owners are personally familiar with all transactions, corporations generally prepare, in addition to the annual income account and balance sheet, detailed operating statements at one or more interim dates.

Reporting on profits by application of the LIFO principle under ideal conditions is simple. As here used, conditions are "ideal" when closing inventories equal opening inventories and the goods sold are equivalent to the purchases for each accounting period throughout the year. Since such conditions are rarely found in practice, an accounting system must be sufficiently flexible to reflect the facts, whatever they may be.

If at the end of an interim accounting period the inventory of any LIFO group is below the opening inventory for the year, an estimate should be made of the amount of the closing inventory for the year.

Assuming that at the interim date no reduction is expected for the year, cost of sales for the interim period should be charged with the cost of goods purchased plus an estimated amount to cover the cost to be incurred in making good the temporary decrease in inventory, and an account should be established (ordinarily shown among current liabilities) for the difference between the estimated replacement cost and the LIFO inventory cost of the quantities liquidated to the interim date.

If, on the other hand, a reduction is expected in the closing inventory as compared with what was on hand at the beginning of the year, the problem must be met as to the treatment of the LIFO cost of the goods liquidated. Should a substantial difference exist between LIFO cost and replacement cost and should the major part of the liquidation occur in one month, that month's charge to cost of sales for the goods liquidated may be abnormally low (or high) and result in a distortion of monthly profits. In some cases this difference has been spread over the months remaining from the time such decrease became apparent until the year end. In other cases cost of sales has been charged with amounts computed by reference to current replacement costs and a special credit (or charge) has been shown for the period as being attributable to the liquidation of a portion of the beginning LIFO inventory. This latter disclosure procedure is generally considered preferable.

Problems also exist when there is an increase in inventory at an interim date. A satisfactory solution may not be as difficult as when there are liquidations, but again estimates must be made of the year-end position. If a decrease or at least no substantial increase is expected for the year as a whole, the temporary increase should be priced at the most easily identified acquisition cost. If an increase is expected for the year, such increase will be reflected in the closing inventory at prices determined under the method specified in the original election made by the company for federal income tax purposes—generally first-purchase costs for the year, last-purchase costs, or average cost.[9]

The difference between the actual acquisition costs at an interim date and the cost at which the increased quantity will be included in the closing LIFO inventory must be taken into cost of sales during some part of the year. If the amount of such difference

[9] Sections 1.472–2(d) and 1.472–8(e)(2), Appendix C.

is large, care should be exercised not to reflect it in one period so as to distort profits. If it can be predetermined with reasonable accuracy, this type of difference can appropriately be spread over the remainder of the year because the existence of an inventory volume at the year end in excess of the opening inventory is a consequence of the purchasing or production policy followed throughout the year rather than during any particular period.

The manner in which inventory conditions are recognized in interim statements is governed by the facts that (1) for federal income tax purposes there is usually but one significant LIFO computation each year, based upon a comparison of volume at the beginning and end of the year, and (2) the cost to be assigned to any year's increment in the LIFO inventory is determined by a procedure which the company elected to follow consistently rather than by specific business transactions.

Although a variety of methods can be used to cost sales by individual products or product lines, many companies have found it desirable to continue using, in the preparation of internal financial statements for management, the method of costing goods sold which they used prior to adoption of LIFO. Under these circumstances the difference between the amount of income computed under the prior inventory method and the result under LIFO is set forth in one amount on the over-all statement of profit and loss, and not allocated to the profit results of individual products or product lines.

ILLUSTRATION OF LIFO IN MONTHLY STATEMENTS

The mechanics of compiling the information needed for monthly income statements may be illustrated by the case of a company using a commodity measured in terms of tons, such as steel scrap, where the purchases or production during the year is as shown in the Summary of Monthly Acquisitions on page 178. If this company has elected to assign an amount equal to the average cost of acquisitions during the year to quantities in a closing inventory in excess of the quantities in the opening inventory, the cost of the month-end inventories could be determined by the year-to-date averages computed in the summary of monthly acquisitions. It may be noted that the month-end quantities drop below the January 1 inventory in March, and the liquidations are not replaced until August. At year end there has been a net increment of 4,000 tons.

Summary of Monthly Acquisitions

| | Tons | Cost | |
		Total	Per ton
January................	10,000	$ 300,000	$30.00
February...............	10,000	310,000	31.00
To date..........	20,000	$ 610,000	30.50
March.................	8,000	264,000	33.00
To date..........	28,000	$ 874,000	31.21
April.................	5,000	150,000	30.00
To date..........	33,000	$1,024,000	31.03
May..................	7,000	224,000	32.00
To date..........	40,000	$1,248,000	31.20
June..................	13,000	377,000	29.00
To date..........	53,000	$1,625,000	30.66
July..................	15,000	450,000	30.00
To date..........	68,000	$2,075,000	30.52
August................	10,000	330,000	33.00
To date..........	78,000	$2,405,000	30.83
September.............	12,000	408,000	34.00
To date..........	90,000	$2,813,000	31.26
October...............	10,000	360,000	36.00
To date..........	100,000	$3,173,000	31.73
November..............	10,000	375,000	37.50
To date..........	110,000	$3,548,000	32.25
December..............	8,000	288,000	36.00
To date..........	118,000	$3,836,000	32.51

If it was anticipated the liquidations were only temporary, a replacement reserve could be provided so as to adjust the monthly charges for materials consumed. Unless the reserve is established, the charge will be artificially low during the liquidation months March through May, and artificially high in the replacement months June through August. The amount added to or deducted from the reserve each month is the difference between the LIFO

Summary of Monthly Inventories

| | Quantities (Tons) | | Inventory | | |
| | | | | Cost | |
	Acquired	Consumed	Tons	Per ton	Total
Opening inventory:					
Initial layer.............			15,000	$24.00	$360,000
1st increment...........			1,000	40.00	40,000
2d increment...........			5,000	28.00	140,000
			21,000		$540,000
January.................	10,000	9,000			
Opening inventory.......			21,000		$540,000
Current increment........			1,000	30.00	30,000
			22,000		$570,000
February................	10,000	6,000			
Opening inventory.......			21,000		$540,000
Current increment........			5,000	30.50	152,500
			26,000		$692,500
March..................	8,000	13,500			
Initial layer.............			15,000	24.00	$360,000
1st increment...........			1,000	40.00	40,000
2d increment...........			4,500	28.00	126,000
			20,500		$526,000
April...................	5,000	15,500			
Initial layer.............			10,000	24.00	$240,000
May....................	7,000	13,000			
Initial layer.............			4,000	24.00	$ 96,000
June....................	13,000	6,000			
Initial layer.............			11,000	24.00	$264,000
July....................	15,000	6,000			
Initial layer.............			15,000	24.00	$360,000
1st increment...........			1,000	40.00	40,000
2d increment...........			4,000	28.00	112,000
			20,000		$512,000
August..................	10,000	8,000			
Opening inventory.......			21,000		$540,000
Current increment........			1,000	30.83	30,830
			22,000		$570,830
September...............	12,000	7,000			
Opening inventory.......			21,000		$540,000
Current increment........			6,000	31.26	187,560
			27,000		$727,560
October.................	10,000	10,000			
Opening inventory.......			21,000		$540,000
Current increment........			6,000	31.73	190,380
			27,000		$730,380
November................	10,000	10,000			
Opening inventory.......			21,000		$540,000
Current increment........			6,000	32.25	193,500
			27,000		$733,500
December................	8,000	10,000			
Opening inventory.......			21,000		$540,000
Current increment........			4,000	32.51	130,040
			25,000		$670,040
Total quantities............	118,000	114,000			

cost and the average current-year cost to date for the tonnage liquidated or replaced. After all the temporary liquidations are replaced at the end of August, the balance in the reserve is assumed to be material and is applied equally to the remaining four months of the year rather than being absorbed in one month. The net difference of $8,490 at August 31 is attributable to monthly fluctuations in the year-to-date average cost (see below).

The tonnage costs consumed, before and after adjustment for charges and credits to the reserve, are summarized on page 181. Establishment of a replacement reserve may be advisable even if it is not certain that the lower inventory quantity at an interim date represents a temporary liquidation. Any balance in the reserve at the end of the year can be closed to profit and loss and will measure the effect upon income of costs carried forward from prior years. Other charges against income will be the aggregate of expenditures attributable to purchases and production of the current year.

Replacement Reserve Adjustments for Monthly Statements

Month	Tons liquidated (or replaced)	LIFO cost Per ton	LIFO cost Total	Average current-year cost Per ton	Average current-year cost Total	Reserve adjustment
March.......	500	$28	$ 14,000	$31.21	$ 15,605	$ 1,605
April........	4,500	28	126,000			
	1,000	40	40,000	31.03	325,815	39,815
	5,000	24	120,000			
To date....	11,000		$ 300,000		$ 341,420	$ 41,420
May.........	6,000	24	144,000	31.20	187,200	43,200
To date....	17,000		$ 444,000		$ 528,620	$ 84,620
June.........	(7,000)	24	(168,000)	30.66	(214,620)	(46,620)
To date....	10,000		$ 276,000		$ 314,000	$ 38,000
July.........	(4,000)	24	(96,000)			
	(1,000)	40	(40,000)	30.52	(274,680)	(26,680)
	(4,000)	28	(112,000)			
To date....	1,000		$ 28,000		$ 39,320	$ 11,320
August.......	(1,000)	28	(28,000)	30.83	(30,830)	(2,830)
To date....	—		$ —		$ 8,490	$ 8,490

Summary of Cost of Tonnage Consumed

| | Opening inventory | Cost of acquisitions | Closing inventory | Cost of tonnage consumed | | |
				Unadjusted	Reserve adjustment	Adjusted
January	$540,000	$ 300,000	$570,000	$ 270,000	$ —	$ 270,000
February	570,000	310,000	692,500	187,500	—	187,500
March	692,500	264,000	526,000	430,500	1,605	432,105
April	526,000	150,000	240,000	436,000	39,815	475,815
May	240,000	224,000	96,000	368,000	43,200	411,200
June	96,000	377,000	264,000	209,000	(46,620)	162,380
July	264,000	450,000	512,000	202,000	(26,680)	175,320
August	512,000	330,000	570,830	271,170	(2,830)	268,340
September	570,830	408,000	727,560	251,270	(2,122)	249,148
October	727,560	360,000	730,380	357,180	(2,123)	355,057
November	730,380	375,000	733,500	371,880	(2,122)	369,758
December	733,500	288,000	670,040	351,460	(2,123)	349,337
		$3,836,000		$3,705,960		$3,705,960

The reasonableness of the adjusted computed costs and the need for the reserve adjustments in preparing interim statements are evident from the following comparisons:

Comparison of Per-Ton Costs

| | Per-ton cost of acquisitions | | Per-ton cost of tonnage consumed | |
	Monthly	Year-to-date	Unadjusted	Adjusted
January..........	$30.00	$30.00	$30.00	$30.00
February.........	31.00	30.50	31.25	31.25
March...........	33.00	31.21	31.89	32.01
April............	30.00	31.03	28.13	30.70
May............	32.00	31.20	28.31	31.63
June............	29.00	30.66	34.83	27.06
July............	30.00	30.52	33.67	29.22
August..........	33.00	30.83	33.90	33.54
September.......	34.00	31.26	35.89	35.59
October..........	36.00	31.73	35.72	35.51
November........	37.50	32.25	37.19	36.98
December........	36.00	32.51	35.15	34.93

ANALYZING LIFO INVENTORIES FOR BALANCE SHEET PURPOSES

An indication of the extent to which an inventory is composed of raw materials, work in process, and finished goods may be significant to readers of financial statements. In certain cases other or more detailed breakdowns may be considered desirable. This information is important to the extent that it permits the reader to ascertain whether the inventory is reasonably balanced. For example, a larger portion of the inventory being in the form of finished goods at the end of the year than at the beginning of the year may indicate the consumers' demand for the product is diminishing. Under other circumstances the accumulation of a finished goods inventory may reflect management decisions made in anticipation of difficulties incident to renewal of an agreement with a labor union.

Where inventories are determined under a LIFO method and pools are established on a natural business unit or other broad basis, no amounts can be specifically identified with the various types of goods within a pool. In some instances, however, significant information will be provided if the total LIFO cost is allocated to whatever classifications of goods are deemed appropriate by reference to the relative current values for each classification. Alternatively, this allocation might be made by considering the relative amounts of base-year costs for the various types of goods in the inventory. The amount assigned to the inventory as a whole will reflect a last-in, first-out flow of costs, but the flow of goods will govern the allocation of the total to the items owned on the balance sheet date.

9

Development of LIFO

The significance of the income statement and the necessity for matching costs with revenue is generally acknowledged by bankers, management, and others interested in financial statements. It is not always appreciated, however, that in periods of rapid price change a part of the increase in earnings during the upward cycle is attributable to the rise in prices of raw materials, labor, and overhead items. Among the factors upon which businessmen base selling prices are the anticipated costs which will be incurred in replacing the units sold.

During an inflationary period the goods on hand at the beginning of the year will generally be sold at a higher price than contemplated at the time they were acquired. This increase in sales proceeds will be reflected in the income for the year; but if the inventory is maintained at the same level in terms of physical quantities, the additional dollars received from the sales transactions will have been expended to a substantial extent in acquiring the replacement units.

Dollars of earnings needed to maintain the inventory so that the business operations may continue are not available for plant expansion, the payment of dividends, or any of the other purposes to which funds derived from sales at a profit are applied.

LIFO has been developed as a modification of other accepted inventory cost theories to give a more meaningful income statement.

DEVELOPMENT OF LIFO BY THE
PETROLEUM INDUSTRY

In August, 1934, the chairman of the Committee on Uniform Methods of Oil Accounting of the American Petroleum Institute notified the board of directors of that Institute that, after several years' study, his committee had voted unanimously the previous May to recommend for approval the determination of inventories of petroleum companies on a LIFO basis. This recommendation was considered by the board of directors of the Petroleum Institute at a meeting in Dallas, and the following resolution was passed on November 12, 1934:

> RESOLVED: That the uniform method of valuing petroleum inventories called the "last-in, first-out" system, as presented by the committee on uniform methods of oil accounting, is hereby accepted and recommended for adoption for the calendar year 1934 or as soon thereafter as practicable, as a method of valuing petroleum inventories, to be used in conjunction with the general form of balance-sheet and text as approved December 9, 1926, as a system for keeping books and accounts and for making the report for all those engaged in the oil industry, it being understood this uniform method of valuing petroleum inventories, as well as the balance-sheet and text, is subject to such changes and improvements from time to time as the committee may deem necessary after approval by the board of directors.

Use of the phrase "last-in, first-out" appears to have started with committees representing the petroleum industry. As commented upon in Chapter 8, however, LIFO is similar in many respects to the base stock method and that method has been used to a limited extent at least since the turn of the century.

The basic LIFO principles for petroleum inventories approved in 1934 and an illustration of its application, as included in the 1936 edition of "Uniform System of Accounts for the Oil Industry" published by the American Petroleum Institute, are reproduced as pages 185–88.

PARTICIPATION BY ACCOUNTING PROFESSION
IN THE DEVELOPMENT OF LIFO

The Special Committee on Inventories of the American Institute of Accountants (now the American Institute of Certified Public Accountants) collaborated with the American Petroleum Insti-

Basic Principles of

"LAST IN, FIRST OUT"

Uniform Method of Valuing Petroleum Inventories[1]

Recommended by the Committee on Uniform Methods of Oil Accounting and approved by the Board of Directors of the American Petroleum Institute, Dallas, Texas, November 12, 1934.

Current Costs Against Current Sales: Current costs of crude oil and products should be charged against current sales as long as inventory quantities remain approximately unchanged, or sales are about equivalent to new acquisitions (production and purchases).

Crude Oil: In the costing of crude oil stock (inventory), current production and current purchases should be the first applied to current cost of sales and current operations. Wherever practicable, the various grades of crude oil handled by the company may be classified or grouped into a minimum number of "Grades." "Grades" of crude oil mean a major grouping of crude oils such as used in reporting to the Bureau of Mines. This method should be applied to stocks in the field, storage, transit, at refineries, and all other points, as far as it is practicable for the company to do so.

Products: In the costing of product inventories, current purchases and current production should be the first applied to current cost of sales and current operations. This method should be applied to stocks at refineries, bulk terminals, in transit, and at all other points, as far as it is practicable for the company to do so.

The various kinds or brands of oil products handled by the company may be classified or grouped into a minimum number of "Products." The term "Products" means a combination of a number of individual brands or kinds of finished or unfinished oils. Examples of "Products" are: Kerosene (Refined Oil), Gasoline (Naphthas), Lubricating Oils, Motor Oils, Gas Oils, Fuel Oils, Waxes, Asphalts, Coke, etc. No definite recommendation is made as to the number of products each company should carry as a separate item on the inventory. However, it is suggested that it be the smallest number feasible to obtain full advantage of the equalizing effect of the "Last In, First Out" inventory plan.

Valuation: In starting the "Last In, First Out" inventory plan, the prices should be set at a conservative or reasonable figure. In the future, inventory prices should not be reduced to market prices, when lower than the regular inventory value. Where the market value of the inventory is less than that carried in the Balance Sheet, such condition should be shown in parenthesis or as a footnote in such manner that the approximate difference can be ascertained, either in dollars or percentage.

Transportation: In ascertaining the inventory value, all transportation should be taken at full tariff or market rates. Obviously, where a company has had a Reserve for the Elimination of Inter-Company Profits in Inven-

[1] Quoted by permission of the American Petroleum Institute.

Example of the "Last In, First out"

Uniform Method of Valuing Petroleum Inventories
(When applied on a year-to-date basis)

Approved by the American Petroleum Institute, Nov. 12, 1934

1936.	Opening Inventory	Production or Purchases	Cost of Sales	Closing Inventory
1. January	100 @ 10c	200 @ 9c	150 @ 9c	100 @ 10c / 50 @ 9c
2. February	100 @ 10c / 50 @ 9c	200 @ 8c	175 @ 8.07c	100 @ 10c / 75 @ 8.5c
3. 2 Months		400 @ 8.5c	325 @ 8.5c	100 @ 10c / 75 @ 8.5c
4. March	100 @ 10c / 75 @ 8.5c	175 @ 7c	275 @ 7.681c / 575 @ 8.043c Avg.	75 @ 10c
5. 3 Months		575 @ 8.043c	25 @ 10c } 8.125c	75 @ 10c
6. April	75 @ 10c	225 @ 7.5c	175 @ 7.086c	100 @ 10c / 25 @ 7.890c
7. 4 months		800 @ 7.890c	775 @ 7.890c	100 @ 10c / 25 @ 7.890c
8. May	100 @ 10c / 25 @ 7.890c	220 @ 9c	240 @ 8.904c	100 @ 10c / 5 @ 8.130c
9. 5 Months		1,020 @ 8.130c	1,015 @ 8.130c	100 @ 10c / 5 @ 8.130c
10. June	100 @ 10c / 5 @ 8.130c	215 @ 10.5c	230 @ 10.426c	

11. 6 Months		1,235 @ 8.543c	10 @ 10c } 8.554c	90 @ 10c
12. July	90 @ 10c	205 @ 11.5c	225 @ 11.369c	
13. 7 Months		1,440 @ 8.964c	1,440 @ 8.964c, 30 @ 10c } Avg. 8.985c	70 @ 10c
14. August	70 @ 10c	210 @ 12.5c	200 @ 12.625c	
15. 8 Months		1,650 @ 9.414c	1,650 @ 9.414c, 20 @ 10c } Avg. 9.412c	80 @ 10c
16. September	80 @ 10c	230 @ 13.5c	215 @ 13.744c	
17. 9 Months		1,880 @ 9.914c	1,880 @ 9.914c, 5 @ 10c } Avg. 9.914c	95 @ 10c
18. October	95 @ 10c	235 @ 13c	230 @ 13.065c	
19. 10 Months		2,115 @ 10.257c	2,115 @ 10.257c	100 @ 10c
20. November	100 @ 10c	240 @ 12.5c	235 @ 12.545c	
21. 11 Months		2,355 @ 10.485c	2,350 @ 10.485c	100 @ 10c, 5 @ 10.485c
22. December	100 @ 10c, 5 @ 10.485c	250 @ 11.5c	240 @ 11.533c	
23. 12 Months		2,605 @ 10.583c	2,590 @ 10.583c	100 @ 10c, 15 @ 10.583e } Avg. 10.076c

1937 (New Opening Inventory)
January 115 @ 10.076c

tory, such reserve will remain practically constant under this method of valuing inventory, so long as the quantity of inventory on hand remains about the same.

COMMENTS ON EXAMPLE

1. To illustrate the principles of the inventory plan, an example has been prepared showing the various effects, month by month, on the inventory at the beginning and end of each month, as well as the cost of sales.

Assuming the accounting period is the fiscal year of the company, the calculations are made at the end of each month on a "year to date basis."

2. *January:* Since 200 units were acquired (produced or purchased), and only 150 units disposed of, obviously, under the "Last In, First Out" plan the 150 units would take a cost of 9c, or the average of the units produced or purchased. Accordingly, the 150 units on hand January 31st would be inventoried as follows:

100 at 10c
50 at 9c

3. *Two Months Ended February 28th (Line 3):* For the year to date, 400 units have been produced or purchased at an average price of 8.5c each. Since there have been only 325 units disposed of, being all acquired in the current year, the price is 8.5c each. Therefore, the original 100 units are still on hand at 10c each, plus 75 units of this year's acquisition at 8.5c each. The single month of February (Line 2) is simply the difference between Lines 1 and 3.

4. *Three Months Ended March 31st (Line 5):* At the end of the first quarter of the accounting period, 575 units have been acquired at an average price of 8.043c each. However, 600 units have been disposed of. Since more units have been disposed of than acquired, it becomes necessary to charge cost of sales with 25 units at 10c each, being the average price at the beginning of the year. As set forth in the preceding paragraph, the month of March (Line 4) is the difference between Lines 3 and 5.

5. From the above, it will be seen that so long as the quantity on hand is not in excess of the opening inventory, the closing inventory price will be the same as the opening inventory price.

At the end of any month, if the quantity on hand exceeds the opening inventory, such excess will be priced at the average production or purchase cost.

---

tute's committee and in May, 1936, submitted a report to the Council of the American Institute in which the activity was discussed in detail. The conclusion of the Special Committee, as stated in its report, was:

The "last-in, first-out" method for the valuation of oil company inventories, as recommended by the American Petroleum Institute, constitutes an acceptable accounting principle for those companies, which, finding it adaptable to their needs and views as correctly reflecting their income, apply it consistently from year to year; it is important, however, that full and clear disclosure, in their published financial statements, be made by the companies adopting it, both as to the fact of its adoption and the manner of its application, including information as to the period adopted for the unit of time within which the goods "last-in" are deemed to be the "first-out," that is, whether the fiscal year or a shorter or longer period.

Since the method as outlined by the committee of the American Petroleum Institute requires that the valuation to be placed upon the inventory be "conservative or reasonable," without, however, providing for a uniform standard or common basis in the determination of such valuations, it must be understood by readers of the financial statements of companies adopting the method that the inventory valuation of one such company is not to be regarded as comparable with that of another, except only in so far as the current replacement valuation, required to be disclosed when less than the valuations arrived at under the method, afford such a comparison.

The foregoing conclusion of our committee, however, does not preclude our viewing other methods as being either equally acceptable or preferable in the case of other companies where different conditions may prevail.

Briefly, this conception of LIFO is that current costs of crude oil and products should be charged against current sales. Where an increase in the inventory quantity occurs during the year, the increase is to be reflected at the average cost of purchases or production for the year. Where a decrease in inventory quantity occurs, the entire inventory is to be stated at the same unit price as was used at the beginning of the year.[2]

The January, 1938, issue of *The Journal of Accountancy* contains the text of a report to the Council of the American Institute by another special committee on inventories. The first paragraph of the report reads:

In connection with the appointment of this committee, the president, at the beginning of the current fiscal year, expressed the desire that the

[2] For a more current and detailed description of oil inventory practices, see *Outline of Petroleum-Industry Accounting* (1954 ed.), pp. 133–43, published by the Financial and Accounting Committee, American Petroleum Institute; see also Irving and Draper, *Accounting Practices in the Petroleum Industry* (1958).

committee, having previously concerned itself with the discussion of methods of valuation of oil inventories, now turn its attention to inventory problems in other industries. The current activities of the committee in this respect have not followed the form or scope of its deliberations with the representatives of the American Petroleum Institute, in the prior years; it has, however, during the year participated in discussions on the subject of the "last-in, first-out" method, through the attendance of its chairman at informal conferences held by unofficial groups representative of the non-ferrous metals and leather industries interested, not only in the adoption of the method under discussion for corporate reporting purposes, but also in efforts to have the Internal Revenue Bureau approve such method for the computation of taxable income. There is, however, nothing for final reporting by the committee in this connection at the present time.

Another example of the activity of representatives of the accounting profession in furthering the development of a practical procedure for applying LIFO in particular industries is found in a report by the Institute's Committee on Cooperation with Controllers' Congress of the National Retail Dry Goods Association (now the National Retail Merchants Association) published in the February, 1942, issue of *The Journal of Accountancy*. In this report the Committee analyzes the advantages claimed for the use of the LIFO method by retailers, and the report concludes with the following summary:

> The LIFO inventory basis, being one of three inventory bases in general use, is an acceptable basis for the purpose of preparing financial statements for management, security holders, and creditors, provided it is adequately disclosed and consistently applied and provided a representative price index is prepared and maintained currently which is sufficiently departmentalized to embrace the inventories of the stores.
> For federal income-tax purposes the LIFO basis is specifically allowed under section 22(d) of the Internal Revenue Code. The Treasury Department should not object to its use by retailers by the application of a price index, although considerable discussion may be necessary. . . .

A practical method of applying LIFO by retailers has been accepted for federal income tax purposes since the decision of the Tax Court in the *Hutzler Bros. Co.* case in 1947.[3]

The acceptance by the American Institute of Certified Public Accountants of the LIFO inventory method is officially reported in paragraph 6 of Appendix A.

[3] *Hutzler Bros. Co. v. Commissioner*, 8 T.C. 14 (1947).

STATUTORY AUTHORIZATION OF LIFO
FOR FEDERAL INCOME TAX PURPOSES

At the insistence of taxpayers the Congress of the United States in the Revenue Act of 1938 authorized the use of LIFO, but only for specified raw materials used by tanners, and the producers and processors of certain non-ferrous metals. The designation of these particular businesses appears to have been the result of their use of the base stock method for financial statement purposes as noted in Chapter 8, and the fact that representatives of those industries had been unsuccessful in efforts to develop with the Bureau of Internal Revenue a satisfactory procedure for recognizing sales commitments for future delivery as being in the nature of hedges against fluctuations in the market value of inventories.

Representatives of the tanning and non-ferrous metals industries had asserted for several years prior to 1938 that they needed special consideration from the standpoint of determining income for federal tax purposes. The base stock inventory method some were using for financial statement purposes was disapproved by the Treasury Department. Processors of certain materials were able to protect themselves against price fluctuations by transactions on well-established commodity futures markets—particularly cotton and wheat—but the same opportunities for hedging were not available to these other processors. The Bureau of Internal Revenue had been unable to establish an administrative procedure for recognizing the economics of their position. There were a number of industries in the same position as the tanners and producers and processors of non-ferrous metals, and equitable treatment could not be accorded taxpayers by merely adding to the list of industries for which LIFO would be available.

In 1939 Congress expanded the provisions for the elective use of LIFO and removed the restrictions in the 1938 Act. Under the Revenue Act of 1939 any taxpayer could elect the LIFO method for any of the goods in his inventory. The general LIFO provision has been continued in the Internal Revenue Code without material change.[4]

[4] The section in the current statute is set forth in section 1.472, Appendix C.

After the outbreak of World War II, shortages developed in some commodities and manufactured products, which had the effect of depleting inventories in many industries. Under the general LIFO procedures depletions having a LIFO cost below then current costs directly affected income and produced high profits subject to normal tax, surtax, and excess profits tax rates. It was foreseen that when conditions again became normal the replacement of these depletions would have to be inventoried at the prevailing costs in the year of replacement. This would have the effect of subjecting to extremely high tax rates the difference between LIFO costs (at 1939, 1940, or 1941 prices, depending on the year a taxpayer adopted LIFO) and the costs prevailing when replacements became available.

To meet this situation, Congress amended the Internal Revenue Code in the Revenue Act of 1942 by adding a provision commonly referred to as the "Involuntary Liquidation and Replacement Section." Under this section a taxpayer having a liquidation due to wartime conditions in any goods subject to LIFO pricing had the privilege at that time of electing to replace such liquidation at a future date. It is significant that the statutory definition of an "involuntary liquidation" emphasizes the taxpayer's *inability to replace* the goods because of war conditions.

The election to replace had the effect of carrying back to the year of liquidation the difference between the LIFO cost for the goods involuntarily liquidated and the cost of the replacement. If the cost of replacement exceeded the cost of the quantities liquidated, the taxpayer was entitled to a tax refund (without interest) for the year of liquidation. If the cost of replacement was less than the cost of the quantities liquidated, the taxpayer was assessed an additional tax for the year of liquidation. In either case taxes for years other than the year of liquidation might also require adjustments, due to the carryback and carryover provisions for losses and unused excess profits credits.

The summary of the 1947 inventory of A Packing Company, on pages 194–95, reflects a replacement that year of involuntary inventory liquidations which occurred in each of the three previous years. Although the replacement quantities are inventoried at the original LIFO cost, the purchases taken into account in computing the cost of sales for 1947 will be reduced by the amount of $134,250, representing the aggregate excess replacement cost. A recomputation of taxable income for the prior years will be made with increases in cost of sales of $12,750 for 1944, $65,000 for 1945, and $56,500 for 1946.

The 1942 Act provided that an involuntary liquidation had to occur before the termination of World War II as proclaimed by the President, and the replacement had to occur within three years after that date. Congress later specified that the liquidation had to take place before January 1, 1948, and the replacement had to occur before January 1, 1953. Although the law required the taxpayer to show that the liquidation was involuntary, which meant that it was due to a condition arising out of the war, no special proof was required of taxpayers in some of the cases because the conditions causing the material shortage were a matter of common knowledge.

Replacements in years after an involuntary liquidation are considered as replacements of the most recent liquidations whether or not involuntary. Thus in the case of a taxpayer with a liquidation in 1942 which he elected to replace and also a liquidation in 1943 for which he made no election, a replacement in 1944 was deemed to apply first to the 1943 liquidation (includable in inventory at current 1944 costs) and then to the 1942 liquidation (includable in inventory at the cost of the goods liquidated in that year).

Material shortages similar to those in World War II were again experienced in 1950 when hostilities began in Korea. Congress provided relief by giving taxpayers the same elections as in World War II with respect to involuntary liquidations occurring between June 30, 1950, and December 31, 1954. Replacements of liquidations during this period were required to be made by January 1, 1956.

As a consequence of the general rule concerning the order in which replacements were applied to liquidations, a taxpayer could have replaced a liquidation incurred after June 30, 1950, without having replaced World War II liquidations for which no relief would be afforded unless a replacement could be made by the end of 1952. To avoid hardship in such a situation, Congress

**A Packing Company: Summary of
and Computation of Excess Over LIFO
Inventories Involuntarily**

	LIFO inventory			Non-LIFO inventory at lower of cost or market
	Green weight	Unit cost	Amount	
Group I:				
1940 base....................	600,000 lbs.	$0.10	$ 60,000	
Increments—1941..............	300,000	.11	33,000	
1942.............	350,000	.15	52,500	
1943.............	100,000	.25	25,000	
1947.............	150,000	.40	60,000	
	1,500,000			
Group II:				
1940 base....................	150,000	.08	12,000	
Increments—1941..............	30,000	.10	3,000	
1942.............	320,000	.15	48,000	
	500,000			
Group III:				
1940 base....................	100,000	.04	4,000	
Increments—1942..............	50,000	.07	3,500	
1947.............	100,000	.18	18,000	
	250,000			
Group IV:				
1940 base....................	300,000	.02	6,000	
Increments—1941..............	25,000	.05	1,250	
1943.............	50,000	.05	2,500	
1945.............	25,000	.06	1,500	
	400,000			
Processing expense.............				$ 75,000
Other pork sausage, and canned meats.....................				200,000
Cattle and beef................				175,000
Supplies......................				350,000
Ice plant.....................				10,000
Power plant..................				15,000
			$330,250	$ 825,000
Total inventory.........				$1,155,250

nventories at December 31, 1947,
nventory Cost of Cost of Replacing
quidated in Prior Years

	Replacements in 1947 of inventories involuntarily liquidated in prior years					
				Excess replacement cost		
Quantity replaced	Replacement cost	LIFO inventory cost	1944 liqui-dation	1945 liqui-dation	1946 liqui-dation	Total
00,000 lbs.	$ 40,000	$11,000			$29,000	$ 29,000
50,000	140,000	52,500		$60,000	27,500	87,000
00,000	40,000	25,000	$10,000	5,000		15,000
25,000	4,500	1,750	2,750			2,750
			$12,750	$65,000	$56,500	

Reduction in purchases for purpose of cost of sales
computation, attributable to inventorying at original LIFO cost the quantities involuntarily liquidated in prior years and replaced in 1947 $134,250

provided that the liquidations after June 30, 1950, should be deemed to have occurred before World War II liquidations for the purpose of the replacement section. Generally replacements were applied to the most recent liquidations, but the statutory amendment[5] providing that involutary liquidations during 1950 and 1951 should be treated as having occurred prior to unreplaced 1941–1947 liquidations gave effect to the extended replacement period.

No substantive changes in the general provisions governing the use of LIFO were made at the time of enactment of the Internal Revenue Code of 1954. There was added, however, a new provision[6] which may have an effect upon corporations using LIFO or contemplating adoption of the method. As a general rule a corporation does not realize taxable income on the distribution of its property with respect to its stock, but this section provides for the recognition of taxable income when inventory which has been costed on the LIFO method is distributed. The amount of income, which is treated as if arising from the sale of inventory assets, is equal to the amount by which the aggregate cost at which the LIFO inventory is carried, is below the amount which would be assigned to the inventory at the time of distribution, if LIFO had not been used.

This section is not applicable to a distribution of property pursuant to a plan for complete liquidation of a subsidiary corporation. In the case of other corporations contemplating complete liquidation, consideration should be given to making a sale of substantially all the inventory to one person in a single transaction. If the inventory is disposed of in this manner and the other conditions are met,[7] no gain or loss is recognized to the corporation from the disposition of its property.

SHORTCOMINGS IN LIFO PROVISIONS OF INTERNAL REVENUE CODE

From the business viewpoint, two major deficiencies exist in the LIFO method as it has developed for federal income tax purposes at the present time. For tax purposes no writedown to market

[5] Rev. Act of 1951, § 306.
[6] Int. Rev. Code of 1954, § 311(b).
[7] Int. Rev. Code of 1954, § 337.

is permitted when market is lower than LIFO cost, while for accounting purposes it is recognized that inventories should be priced at market when lower than cost, irrespective of the method employed in determining cost. Further, there is no current procedure for a replacement of temporary liquidations being priced at the cost of the goods temporarily liquidated.

ARGUMENTS FOR THE LOWER OF LIFO COST OR MARKET

One of the principal reasons why a larger number of businesses have not adopted LIFO is the fear of declines in prices below the costs prevailing on the basic LIFO date. From time to time proposals have been submitted to amend the Internal Revenue Code to provide for a deduction, in computing taxable income, equal to the amount by which the LIFO inventory cost exceeds the market value of the goods on hand.[8] Representatives of the Treasury Department have opposed this legislation on the ground that it would result in a loss of revenue. The question of loss of revenue may have been overemphasized. There would be no effect unless or until prices should fall, and the same aggregate business income would be reported so long as the alternative is for business to defer the adoption of LIFO until there has actually been a price decline.

As regards businesses which adopted LIFO on the basis of comparatively high cost levels, a statutory amendment is one way of placing them in substantially the same position as competitors using LIFO with a lower price level as a starting point. This result is desirable from an economic standpoint, and part of the justification for the statutory amendment is the time taken by the Internal Revenue Service in the development of administrative rulings.

For several years after the Internal Revenue Code permitted the use of LIFO regardless of industry, interpretations by Treasury Department representatives were so restrictive that many

[8] In 1952 the Senate Finance Committee requested the staff of the Joint Committee of Congress on Internal Revenue to make a study and report on the matter. A bill was introduced in the House of Representatives (H.R. 7447) which would have permitted a taxpayer to use the lower of LIFO cost or market in valuing inventories. Generally any writedown to market would have been reversed if at the end of a subsequent year there was a smaller excess of LIFO cost over market value.

companies were led to believe the method could not be applied
in their case. Narrow limitations upon acceptable LIFO groups
rendered the method impracticable except for such industries as
oil, steel, and meat packing, where the character of the inventories
does not vary substantially year to year. A somewhat broader
view as to groupings was adopted by the Treasury Department
in 1944 with the issuance of Treasury Decision 5407; but the
Hutzler Bros. Co. case (8 T.C. 14), which approved the application of LIFO to taxpayers using the retail inventory method, was
not decided until 1947, and the Tax Court decision approving
the use of the dollar-value principle was more than a year later.

It was, therefore, not until almost ten years after the LIFO
provision was included in the law that even the broad principles
of procedure were established. The general trend of prices in
this country at that time was quite uncertain. Not until 1950
was there a renewed interest in LIFO occasioned by further price
increases and the national preparedness program, indicating the
probability of another extended period of inflation. Companies
not adopting LIFO until 1950 because of the critical position taken
by the Treasury Department during the preceding decade have
not enjoyed advantages comparable to those derived by taxpayers
who applied LIFO as of an earlier date and have a lower basic
inventory cost.

It is also significant that it was not until January, 1961—after
more than another ten years had elapsed—that any explanation
of the dollar-value method of pricing LIFO inventories was added
to the regulations.[9]

The practical justification for a statutory amendment to permit a writedown to market where lower than the LIFO cost is
that such a provision would tend to equalize the position of all
taxpayers.

The theoretical justification for an amendment to permit a
writedown to market is based upon the fact that in the view of
most businessmen, economists, and accountants, no inventory carried on financial statements at an amount in excess of market is
realistic. Over fifty years ago it was recognized that for tax
purposes inventories need not be stated at costs which are in excess

[9] Section 1.472–8, Appendix C.

of current market value, and this change in earlier procedures was effected by an amendment to the income tax regulations.

Consistent with the accounting practice of providing for measurable expected future losses, the amount of accumulated earnings to the date of a financial statement will be overstated if market declines are not taken into account.

The Sixteenth Amendment to the Constitution says simply, "The Congress shall have power to lay and collect taxes on incomes, from whatever source derived, without apportionment among the several States, and without regard to any census or enumeration." Congress has had to provide for all the details as to how incomes are to be taxed. As developed over the years, the underlying principle of the Internal Revenue Code is to tax the income for each accounting period irrespective of the happenings of prior or subsequent years. It can be argued that if events occur during any particular year (including a decline in the market value of inventories) which have an effect on the measurement of the accumulated amount of the earnings retained in the business, such events should be recognized as part of the basis for computing taxes on income.

Although the most fundamental of the justifications for the LIFO method is that income for any particular period is more clearly reflected thereby, as presently provided for in the Internal Revenue Code, this is true only for completed transactions. The increase in the amount of accumulated earnings between two dates, with appropriate recognition of distributions to shareholders and other special factors, can be a measure of the income during the elapsed period; and if a decline in value of an inventory occurs during any year, this event should also be recognized to reflect properly the accumulated earnings for the business.

ARGUMENTS FOR PERMITTING THE REPLACEMENT OF TEMPORARY LIQUIDATIONS

The factors which prompted enactment of the temporary provisions of the Internal Revenue Code permitting a retroactive adjustment of income after the replacement of LIFO inventory quantities involuntarily liquidated as a result of war conditions or economic causes attributable to the national preparedness program are equally significant in demonstrating the need for a relief provision applicable to liquidations of inventory quantities attributable to other causes.

For example, if the inventory quantities at the end of a particular year should be reduced below the quantities as of the beginning of the year because of labor difficulties in the taxpayer's plant or the plant of one or more suppliers of its materials, the entire excess of the proceeds of sale over the LIFO inventory cost would be included in income. Such cost might represent the price paid for that type of goods many years before. Even if the quantities are replaced in the following year, under the present provisions of the Internal Revenue Code, no correction could be made of the income for the year of liquidation. The inventory replacement would be treated as any other increment and would be carried at the cost incurred in making the replacement. This type of "involuntary liquidation" should be recognized in the Internal Revenue Code to make the LIFO provisions complete.

In cases where the inventory quantities are diminished as a consequence of a fire, it might be possible to apply the involuntary conversion provision of the Internal Revenue Code if the inventory is fully covered by insurance. This section[10] provides that if property is converted into cash as a consequence of fire, theft, and the like, and then into similar property, no gain is to be recognized for federal income tax purposes, and the replacement property is deemed to have the same cost as that destroyed. But if the insurance proceeds do not cover the entire cost of replacing the inventory, the involuntary conversion provision would not provide a satisfactory solution to the problem.

The possible causes of an inventory liquidation as a result of accident are innumerable. Conceivably, it could be the result of delays in shipping, a flood, or even inclement weather; consequently, it is not possible to prepare a completely satisfactory definition of an involuntary liquidation which might be replaced and restored to the inventory at the original LIFO cost. Because of the basic need for protection against such liquidations, it has

[10] Int. Rev. Code of 1954, § 1033.

been suggested that the statute be amended to permit taxpayers to file an election to consider any decrease in LIFO inventory quantities subject to replacement within a reasonable period, such as five years. The decision of the taxpayer would, of course, be made at the time of filing the income tax return for the year of liquidation or shortly thereafter. It should not be possible for the company to await the actual incurrence of the replacement cost before deciding whether or not income should be adjusted retroactively.

An automatic right of election to effect replacement of liquidations of LIFO inventory quantities would largely remove the disturbing economic conditions in some markets when the principal members of an industry are attempting at the same time to make abnormal purchases to build up inventory quantities which were temporarily diminished. In certain industries prices have risen merely because concerns using LIFO were making purchases to avoid closing inventory quantities being below those at the beginning of the year. The statute should be amended to eliminate the cause of purchases made to avoid the tax consequences of a liquidation in the LIFO inventory quantities rather than because of existing market conditions.

The making of abnormal purchases is but one of the ways of increasing LIFO inventory quantities at the end of any particular year. Businesses using the LIFO method have also, on occasion, deferred making shipments. Wherever normal shipments are being deferred because of tax considerations, management is not exercising normal business judgment. The impact of taxes upon the company's profitability can be greater than was intended by the lawmakers.

In considering statutory amendments involving a recomputation of tax on a previous year's income, a procedure might be incorporated whereby the net decrease or increase in previous years' taxes could be deducted from or added to the tax computed on the income for the year of replacement. From an administrative standpoint this might be preferable to a specific refund of, or assessment of a deficiency in, tax for a prior year. Another suggested procedure would provide that the income for the year of involuntary liquidation be reduced initially in the return by the difference between the inventory cost and the current replacement cost of the liquidated items. The difference between such current cost and the replacement cost as determined in the year of actual replacement could be adjusted in such year. If replacement is not made, the interim adjustment could be reversed in the last year in which a replacement would have been recognized.[11]

INTERPRETATIONS OF THE INTERNAL REVENUE CODE BY LITIGATION AND REGULATIONS

A review of the legislative history of LIFO does not disclose the many differences that arose between taxpayers and the Commissioner of Internal Revenue in practice. After the enactment of the Revenue Act of 1939 the general opinion seemed to be that LIFO was applicable to industries with relatively few basic commodities that could be accounted for readily in terms of units of quantity, for example, oil, rubber, textiles, leather, chemicals, lead, copper, and other metal industries. The application of LIFO to commodities that could be accounted for in terms of barrels, yards, gallons, or tons was accepted by the Treasury Department. Members of other industries carrying inventories composed of heterogeneous goods, such as retail department stores and wholesale and retail grocery stores, used the LIFO method but were challenged by the Treasury on the grounds that separate LIFO computations had to be made for each item. Some of these companies submitted to the Commissioner's interpretation by either applying LIFO to individual items or going back to the lower-of-cost-or-market method. Others took up the challenge and subsequently received favorable decisions from the Tax Court.

The Commissioner of Internal Revenue acquiesced in vital decisions rendered by the Tax Court and amended his regulations,

---

[11] Enactment of an amendment to the Internal Revenue Code to permit replacements of temporary LIFO inventory liquidations has been recommended to Congress by the American Institute of Certified Public Accountants, the American Bar Association, and other groups. A dissertation entitled "Involuntary Liquidation of Inventories Priced by LIFO" summarized an intensive review of this subject, concluded in 1961 by James M. Fremgen as part of the requirements for a degree of Doctor of Business Administration from the School of Business of Indiana University.

so that since 1949 taxpayers have been officially permitted to use any method of LIFO computation established to the Commissioner's satisfaction as being reasonably adaptable to the purpose and intent of the statute. The first amendment dealt with taxpayers which had, as a matter of past practice, determined inventories under the retail method of accounting. As explained in Chapter 14, the application of LIFO to the retail method is accomplished by reducing the retail sales value of an inventory at the close of the year to the price level existing at the beginning of the year when LIFO was first adopted. This conversion from current sales prices to the level when LIFO was first adopted is done by means of an index especially developed for this purpose by the Bureau of Labor Statistics.

The second major amendment to the regulations was made after the decision of the Tax Court in the *Basse* case.[12] That case dealt with the application of LIFO to the inventories of a wholesale grocer. As in the case of department stores it is not practicable for wholesale grocers to compare quantities of inventories by items at the beginning and end of each year. This wholesaler utilized a procedure referred to as the "dollar-value method" which in essence compares the investment in inventory by groups at the beginning of the year when LIFO was adopted with the investment at the end of the year stated in terms of dollars at the same price level.

The dollar-value method is similar to the procedure followed by department stores in that in both cases there is no comparison of quantities of individual items, and the relative inventory quantities are determined only by aggregate dollar amounts allocated to the inventories. The application of the department store procedure is generally limited to stores using the retail method of inventory valuation, and it is to be noted that the price index is computed by reference to sales value rather than cost levels.

The dollar-value method can be applied by any business, including retail stores which compute the cost or lower-of-cost-or-market for their merchandise directly rather than by the retail method. Under the dollar-value method the extent of change

---

[12] *Edgar A. Basse v. Commissioner*, 10 T.C. 328 (1948).

in cost levels is generally determined by a dual extension of the quantities in the closing inventories. The quantities on hand at the end of the year may be priced first at the costs prevailing at the beginning of the year when LIFO was adopted and again at the costs prevailing at the end of the current year. The ratio of the total dollars produced in the first computation to the total dollars produced in the second computation reflects the rise or decline in prices for the period since the beginning of the year in which LIFO was first adopted. Manufacturers and others unable as a practical matter to make dual pricings have developed indexes of price changes of materials, labor, and overhead during each year reflecting their particular circumstances.

Some of the early LIFO applications grouped items of inventory on the basis of being raw material, goods in process, or finished stock. It soon became apparent that a substantial part of the inflationary profit in inventories, which Congress recognized need not be subjected to tax, was being included in the taxable income stream where there were no material changes in the total inventories. Violent fluctuations in quantities occurred from year to year between the categories of raw materials, goods in process, and finished stock.

In 1944 the regulations were amended so as to permit the application of LIFO to raw materials and the raw-material content of in-process and finished stock. In the example illustrating this procedure, labor and overhead are priced at current rather than LIFO cost.[13] Application of the LIFO principle to only a portion of the costs attributable to the goods included in the inventory was not a completely logical procedure, and efforts were continued to have the Treasury Department approve the techniques essential to applying dollar-value methods to inventories generally.

The amendment to the regulations in 1949 provided merely that if a taxpayer uses consistently the so-called dollar-value method of pricing inventories, or any other method of computation established to the satisfaction of the Commissioner as reasonably adaptable to the "purpose and intent" of the LIFO provisions of the Internal Revenue Code, and if an appropriate election is

[13] Section 1.472–1(c), Appendix C.

made, the inventory shall be determined by the use of the "appropriate adaptation."[14]

Internal Revenue Service representatives started as early as 1954 working on a revenue ruling or amendment to the regulations to describe the procedures to be followed in applying the dollar-value principle. Such an amendment to the regulations was finally published as T.D. 6539 on January 20, 1961.[15]

The major change in the recently amended regulations is the addition of a specific section (Section 1.472–8 of Appendix C) pertaining to the dollar-value method. The position of the Treasury Department and the questions encountered in the application of the regulations are discussed in Chapter 12.

PRACTICAL IMPETUS FOR USE OF LIFO

The artificiality of paper profits resulting from assigning a larger amount to a closing inventory merely because market prices have increased—when from the standpoint of physical attributes the opening and closing inventories are comparable—has particular practical significance when tax rates are high. Only the income remaining after paying taxes can be used to replace inventories, expand the plant, pay dividends, and so forth. The higher the taxes, the lower is the rate of earnings, and the greater is the proportion of the year's earnings needed to maintain inventories during a period of rising prices.

Assuming no additional capital is invested for this purpose, the portion of the net earnings of a business needed to maintain the inventory required for continuing operations during a period of rising costs can be expressed as a formula. If—

I = Cost of the inventory at the beginning of the year

t = Turnover rate for the inventory investment

r = Rate of earnings stated as the percentage which the net income after tax is of the total cost of goods sold for the year

[14] Section 1.472–1(1), Appendix C.
[15] See McAnly, "The Current Status of LIFO," 105 *J. Accountancy* 5, 55 (May, 1958), and Barker, "Dollar-Value LIFO and the Klein Chocolate Case," 112 *J. Accountancy* 3, 41 (Sept., 1961).

then the product of the three factors Itr equals the net earnings. If i represents the percentage of increase during the year in the replacement cost for the inventory and e represents the fraction of the year's earnings neded to maintain the same physical volume of inventory, then

$$iI = eItr, \quad \text{and } e = \frac{i}{tr}$$

In most situations the percentage of increase during the year in the replacement cost for the inventory i and the other factors t and r can be computed with reasonable accuracy. After these three factors are established, the computation of the fraction of the year's earnings needed to maintain the same physical volume of inventory e is automatic.

Use of the formula developed above can be illustrated by an example.

Given:

The cost of goods sold for the year is six times the inventory $(t = 6)$.

The net income after tax is 5 per cent of the cost of goods sold $(r = 5\%)$.

The replacement cost for the inventory has increased 2 per cent during the year $(i = 2\%)$.

Computation:

$$e = \frac{i}{tr} = \frac{0.02}{6 \times 0.05} = \frac{1}{15} = 6\tfrac{2}{3}\%$$

Under these circumstances $6\tfrac{2}{3}$ per cent of the net earnings for the year is needed to maintain the same physical volume of inventory.

The results produced by this formula are illustrated on page 207.

Use of the table can be demonstrated by a situation in which there is an increase in inventory cost of 5 per cent, the rate of net earnings to cost of sales is 3 per cent, and the inventory is turned over 4 times each year. Approximately 41.7 per cent of the earnings is needed to maintain the same physical volume of inventory.

Income tax rates are significant in this analysis of the consequences of increases in inventory replacement cost because of their effect on the amount of net earnings. Every increase in income tax rate causes a reduction in the rate of earnings and results in a larger portion of the net earnings being required to maintain the inventory during a period of rising costs.

Portion of Earnings Needed to Maintain Inventory

Increase in cost of inventory	% of net earnings to cost of sales	Approximate % of net earnings needed to maintain inventory, if annual turnover is					
		2 times	3 times	4 times	6 times	10 times	12 times
1%	3	16.7	11.1	8.3	5.6	3.3	2.8
	5	10.0	6.7	5.0	3.3	2.0	1.7
	10	5.0	3.3	2.5	1.7	1.0	0.8
	15	3.3	2.2	1.7	1.1	0.7	0.6
	20	2.5	1.7	1.3	0.8	0.5	0.4
2%	3	33.3	22.2	16.7	11.1	6.7	5.6
	5	20.0	13.3	10.0	6.7	4.0	3.3
	10	10.0	6.7	5.0	3.3	2.0	1.7
	15	6.7	4.4	3.3	2.2	1.3	1.1
	20	5.0	3.3	2.5	1.7	1.0	0.8
5%	3	83.3	55.5	41.7	27.8	16.7	13.9
	5	50.0	33.3	25.0	16.7	10.0	8.3
	10	25.0	16.7	12.5	8.3	5.0	4.2
	15	16.7	11.1	8.3	5.6	3.3	2.8
	20	12.5	8.3	6.3	4.2	2.5	2.1

Effect of Increases in Income Tax Rates on Net Earnings

If income tax rates are increased		Net earnings (income after tax) will be reduced
From	To	
13¾%	25%	13.04%
25%	38%	17.33%
38%	52%	22.58%
52%	80%	58.33%

Costing an inventory by reference to the LIFO assumption as to the flow of costs will not alter the amount required to maintain, or the intrinsic value of, the inventory, but its use will tend to keep the increase in cost (i.e., paper profits) out of the computed income from operations. Also, any reduction in the amount of income taxes payable by a business will result in more dollars being available to maintain the inventory and for other needs of the enterprise.

COMPARISON OF EFFECT OF LIFO AND FIFO

The effects upon income of using either LIFO or FIFO in the costing of inventories are generally compared on page 209. The Internal Revenue Code requires (section 1.472 of Appendix C), as a condition to electing and continuing to use LIFO, that no other procedure be used in inventorying the goods covered by the LIFO election to ascertain the income, profit, or loss for the purpose of an annual report or statement to shareholders or other owners of the business or for credit purposes. The regulations (section 1.472–2(e) of Appendix C) state that the use of market value in lieu of cost, or the issuance of reports or credit statements covering a period of operations less than the whole of a taxable year, is not considered at variance with the statutory requirement.

The generalizations as to the effects upon income of using LIFO are illustrated on pages 210–12.

DISCLOSURE OF REPLACEMENT COST FOR LIFO INVENTORIES

Some companies using LIFO disclose in their financial statements the amount which would be assigned to the inventory had the FIFO method been used. This is most frequently done by a parenthetical observation on the balance sheet, a footnote, or comment in the text of the annual report. Such disclosure is not contrary to the requirements of the Internal Revenue Code, but its significance is questionable.

Robert Morris Associates, the national association of bank loan officers and credit men, published a booklet in December, 1951,

Generalizations as to Effect upon Income of
Alternative Inventory Methods

| | Effect upon income with flow of costs assumed to be | |
	First-in, first-out	Last-in, first-out
If the closing inventory volume is equal to or greater than that of the opening inventory, and		
Costs increase	—	Increase in cost of replacing opening inventory is charged against income.
Costs decrease but not below LIFO cost .	Excess cost for opening inventory is charged against income.	—
Costs decrease below LIFO cost	Excess cost for opening inventory is charged against income.	Reserve is provided to reduce LIFO cost to market value.*
If the closing inventory volume is less than that of the opening inventory, and		
Costs increase	—	Increase in cost of replacing opening inventory is charged against income; and excess of current cost over LIFO cost for liquidated quantity is credited to income.
Costs decrease but not below LIFO cost	Excess cost for opening inventory is charged against income.	Excess of current cost over LIFO cost for liquidated quantity is credited to income.
Costs decrease below LIFO cost	Excess cost for opening inventory is charged against income.	Excess of LIFO cost over current cost for liquidated quantity is charged against income; and reserve is provided to reduce LIFO cost to market value.*

* Where operations are normally profitable, the reserve to reduce the LIFO cost of the inventory to market value may be provided on a net-of-tax basis, that is, the writedown is not taken into account in computing current income taxes, but the reserve will be only 48% of the excess over market value if based upon a 52% tax rate.

Illustrations of Effect of LIFO upon Income

	Quantity (barrels)	First-in, first-out Per barrel	First-in, first-out Amount	Last-in, first-out Per barrel	Last-in, first-out Amount	Effect of LIFO upon income I—Increase D—Decrease
Assuming both inventory volume and costs increase:						
Opening inventory......	300	$3.00	$ 900	$2.40	$ 720	
Purchases.............	1,500	3.50	5,250	3.50	5,250	
Total.............	1,800		$6,150		$5,970	
Closing inventory:						
Opening volume.....	300	3.50	$1,050	2.40	$ 720	
Increase...........	200	3.50	700	3.50	700	
Total.............	500		$1,750		$1,420	
Cost of sales..........	1,300		$4,400		$4,550	
Difference—300 bbl. at $0.50..........						D $(150)
Assuming inventory volume increases and costs decrease but not below LIFO cost:						
Opening inventory......	300	$3.00	$ 900	$2.40	$ 720	
Purchases.............	1,500	2.75	4,125	2.75	4,125	
Total..............	1,800		$5,025		$4,845	
Closing inventory:						
Opening volume.......	300	2.75	825	2.40	720	
Increase..............	200	2.75	550	2.75	550	
Total..............	500		$1,375		$1,270	
Cost of sales...........	1,300		$3,650		$3,575	
Difference—300 bbl. at $0.25..........						I $ 75
Assuming inventory volume increases and costs decrease below LIFO cost:						
Opening inventory......	300	$3.00	$ 900	$2.40	$ 720	
Purchases.............	1,500	2.25	3,375	2.25	3,375	
Total.............	1,800		$4,275		$4,095	

Closing inventory:						
Opening volume.....	300	2.25	675	2.40	720	
Increase...........	200	2.25	450	2.25	450	
Total.............	500		$1,125		$1,170	
Market reserve....			—		(45)	
Net..............			$1,125		$1,125	
Cost of sales.........	1,300		$3,150		$2,970	
Difference—						
300 bbl. at $0.75..						I $ 225
Market reserve....						D (45)
Net..............						I $ 180
Assuming inventory volume decreases and costs increase:						
Opening inventory......	500	$3.00	$1,500	$2.40	$1,200	
Purchases............	1,500	3.50	5,250	3.50	5,250	
Total.............	2,000		$6,750		$6,450	
Closing inventory.......	300	3.50	1,050	2.40	720	
Cost of sales.........	1,700		$5,700		$5,730	
Difference—						
500 bbl. at $0.50...						D $(250)
200 bbl. at $1.10...						I 220
Net............						D $ (30)
Assuming inventory volume decreases and costs decrease but not below LIFO cost:						
Opening inventory......	500	$3.00	$1,500	$2.40	$1,200	
Purchases............	1,500	2.75	4,125	2.75	4,125	
Total.............	2,000		$5,625		$5,325	
Closing inventory.......	300	2.75	825	2.40	720	
Cost of sales.........	1,700		$4,800		$4,605	
Difference—						
500 bbl. at $0.25...						I $ 125
200 bbl. at $0.35...						I 70
Total............						I $ 195
Assuming inventory volume decreases and costs decrease below LIFO cost:						
Opening inventory......	500	$3.00	$1,500	$2.40	$1,200	
Purchases............	1,500	2.25	3,375	2.25	3,375	
Total............	2,000		$4,875		$4,575	

Illustrations of Effect of LIFO upon Income—Continued

| | Quantity (barrels) | Cost of sales with flow of costs assumed to be | | | | Effect of LIFO upon income |
| | | First-in, first-out | | Last-in, first-out | | |
		Per barrel	Amount	Per barrel	Amount	I—Increase D—Decrease
Closing inventory.......	300	2.25	675	2.40	720	
Market reserve......			—		(45)	
Net...............			$ 675		$ 675	
Cost of sales..........	1,700		$4,200		$3,900	
Difference—						
500 bbl. at $0.75...						I $ 375
200 bbl. at $0.15...						D (30)
Market reserve......						D (45)
Net...............						I $ 300

entitled "Financial Statements for Bank Credit Purposes." The paragraph pertaining to the inventory is quoted below:

> Where appropriate and practical, the inventory total should be broken down by stage of manufacture (supplies, raw materials, goods in process, finished goods), and the various forms of inventories should be further classified by location, divisions, branches, departments, or products. Merchandise shipped to others on consignment and pledged inventories should be segregated. The basis of valuation should be clearly explained and mention made of how "cost" and "market" were determined for valuation purposes. If the "LIFO" basis is used, the year of its adoption should be indicated. Where material inventory valuation adjustments have been made in the period covered, the amount should be stated and the adjustments explained. The amount and character of slow-moving inventory, if material, should be indicated.

Although it seems natural that a banker or other lender might be interested in knowing the current value of the inventory, it is not expressly requested. Presumably the association's committe which prepared the study concluded the banker could obtain adequate information from available statistics of price trends in various industries if the year of adoption of LIFO is indicated. It is doubtful that the original LIFO year is of much significance to the average shareholder or prospective investor, and for any complete analysis it would be necessary to know each of the years in which there has been inventory increments and the relative amounts of each increment. Stating only the year LIFO was first adopted might in some cases provide a basis for computing the amount of what would otherwise be unrealized inventory profits, but could lead to inaccurate conclusions being drawn in other circumstances.

The Securities and Exchange Commission requires a statement of the principles applied in valuing inventories, and in its preliminary draft (issued in 1949) of a proposal to amend Regulation S–X provided, "If inventories are priced on the last-in, first-out basis, state, if practicable, the replacement value thereof, and the date when the last-in, first-out basis was first adopted." This paragraph was not, however, included in the amendments to the regulation as finally published.

Mere disclosure of the replacement cost of a LIFO inventory is susceptible of misinterpretation by readers of financial statements. Consistent with the going-concern concept the inventories will continue to be replaced, and the market value is not an amount available for the payment of debt or dividends. If the inventory were liquidated completely and the proceeds were greater than the LIFO cost, a substantial income tax might be payable. However, the investment in inventory will be converted into cash only should the company discontinue operations, and the amount that might be realized in such event may have no relationship to the current replacement cost.

If it is desired to indicate the approximate net earnings and financial position had FIFO been consistently used in place of LIFO, a sentence similar to the following might be appropriate after disclosing the replacement cost of the LIFO inventory:

> . . . Had the company not adopted the LIFO inventory method in 1950, the aggregate reported income after taxes for subsequent years and the stated amount of retained earnings at December 31, 1971, would have been approximately $———— greater, but the effect upon net income for the calendar year 1971 would not have been material.

Where appropriate, the conclusion of the foregoing sentence might be: ". . . and the effect upon net income for the calendar year 1971 would have been an increase (or decrease) of approxi-

mately — per cent." This type of observation has not been found
in published statements, but it would give the reader some indication of the effect upon the financial statements of the action taken
by management in electing to use the LIFO principle in assigning
dollar amounts to the inventories.

Not infrequently a business operation is started by purchasing
all the assets of a predecessor. Where the predecessor's operations
have not been profitable, the cost to the new corporation for the
inventory may be substantially below the aggregate of the replacement cost of the individual items on hand. In financing the new
company, it may be advantageous to go further than merely showing the replacement cost of the inventory in a parenthetical expression or footnote, and actually incorporate the excess of the replacement cost over the LIFO cost in the financial statements. One
procedure occasionally used for including the information in the
financial statements is to carry the difference between market value
and the LIFO cost of the inventory in an appropriately captioned
reserve account inserted between the liability and capital account
sections on the balance sheet. The Washington office of the
Internal Revenue Service has ruled, in response to a taxpayer's
specific inquiry, that where the LIFO method is used for purposes
of determining income, reflection of the market value for the inventories in the balance sheet prepared for credit purposes and
for reports to shareholders will not be considered in violation of
the provisions of the Internal Revenue Code, provided a cross-reference to the LIFO reserve is also shown in the inventory section
of the balance sheet.

Rather than showing a reserve account in the balance sheet
between the liability and capital account sections for the excess
of the replacement cost for the inventory over the LIFO cost,
it would be preferable from an accounting standpoint to incorporate the fair market value in the inventory section in the following manner:

Inventories:
  Fair market value as determined by reference to re-
    placement (first-in, first-out) cost $***
  Excess over last-in, first-out cost   ***
                                                            ─────
  Cost computed in accordance with last-in, first-out
    principle $***

This manner of disclosing the market value for LIFO inventories is held in Revenue Ruling 60–244 (1960–2 C.B. 167) to be consistent with the provisions of and the principles underlying the Internal Revenue Code.[16]

Both procedures for reflecting replacement costs are, however, inconsistent with complete acceptance of the LIFO concept as to the flow of costs for purposes of income determinations, and neither is considered desirable as a regular practice.

[16] Section 1.472(c) and (e), Appendix C.

10

Timing of LIFO Election, The Significance of Volume, and Special Factors

"Brawny" Brown, who had been a star athlete during his college days and was voted by his fraternity as the one "most likely to succeed," was tramping through the Northwoods with his guide. "Silent" Joe had been highly recommended as a guide who knew the steep climbs of the trails and the density of the underbrush and also the dangers of rocks, rapids, and waterfalls in the streams. From time to time Brown looked toward the stream and wondered when the portable canoe would be used to continue their journey. The trail was rough in many spots, and the going had not been easy.

In front of the campfire that night Brown raised the question as to *when* it would be advantageous to change from the trail to the stream. In some respects "Silent" Joe was in the same position as a business adviser who is asked whether a business should elect to use LIFO or continue with FIFO or some other inventory method. Many factors must be considered and judgment must be exercised.[1]

Adoption of the LIFO inventory method does not guarantee that the effects upon income and taxes will be beneficial. LIFO will be helpful only if its adoption—with respect to all or part of the inventory—is timed in a judicious manner. If this is not done, not only can the potential benefits of the method be dissipated but, due to those shortcomings in the provisions of the Internal Revenue Code discussed in the preceding chapter, detrimental income tax consequences may result.

Before deciding to use LIFO, management must make realistic appraisals of future trends in the following areas:

> Price levels, specifically production or purchase costs for the company's products
>
> Inventory quantities, particularly with respect to volume increases or possible uncontrollable liquidations of significant items
>
> Technological changes, including new products, materials, and production processes

Only after a company has considered possible future trends in each of these areas with respect to the major components of its inventory investment can it make informed decisions as to whether LIFO should be adopted at all and, if so, when the election should be made, with respect to which products, and what pooling methods should be used.

PRICE LEVEL CONSIDERATIONS

Where the quantity of goods in an inventory remains constant or increases during a period of rising costs, LIFO will result in charging larger amounts against current income rather than reflecting the full effect of higher costs in inventory as paper profits. For example, assume that at the beginning of a particular year Company A has 500 units in its inventory at a current cost of $1 per unit, or a total inventory investment of $500. During the next ten years the per-unit cost increases at the rate of 10¢

---

[1] For a report on a study directed specifically to an appraisal of the force of the income tax factor, see Butters, *Effects of Taxation: Inventory Accounting and Policies* (1949).

per year, so that at the end of the decade the then current replacement cost for each unit is $2.

If Company A has used FIFO, its inventory investment in 500 comparable units at the end of the period will be $1,000. Included in its reported (and taxable) income will have been an amount of $500 reinvested in maintaining a constant volume of inventory. On the other hand, had Company A adopted LIFO at the beginning of the period, its reported income would have been $500 less, and its income taxes would have been reduced $250. At the end of the period its inventory investment would remain at the base-year cost of $500, and $250 more cash would have been available for use in the business.

Consider next what the effect would be had LIFO been adopted in the eighth year, at which time the FIFO cost per unit was $1.70. At the end of the tenth year the reduction in reported earnings, as opposed to remaining on FIFO during the entire period, would have been 30¢ per unit, or $150 before income tax and approximately $72 after tax. Delaying the LIFO election until the price spiral has reached an advanced stage diminishes the extent to which the reporting of unrealized inventory appreciation could be avoided. Nevertheless, it may be that adopting LIFO is still a favorable move.

The danger, however, lies in the possibility of subsequent cost decreases. Assume that in the eleventh year the current (FIFO) cost drops to $1.60 per unit. Since Company A adopted LIFO with a base cost of $1.00 per unit, the election continues to be advantageous despite the price decline. Had LIFO not been adopted until the eighth year, however, the LIFO cost of $1.70 would be greater than the $1.60 current FIFO cost. For federal income tax purposes, no writedowns from LIFO cost to market (replacement cost) are recognized. Moreover, a company may not switch from LIFO to another inventory method without the consent of the Commissioner of Internal Revenue. For tax purposes, a company may have to carry its inventory at a LIFO cost in excess of market value, and report a greater amount of income than if LIFO had not been adopted at all.

It is obvious that LIFO yields the greatest benefits, in terms of reduced taxes, if adopted at or near the bottom of a price spiral. If LIFO is elected after a period of rising prices has elapsed, it may still prove beneficial, but the predicted trend of future costs must be carefully considered.

Since LIFO first became a permissible inventory method for federal income tax purposes (1938), a dramatic rise in the general price level has taken place in the United States. Whether price levels will continue to rise is a question on which even trained economists do not agree. It is frequently said that some further gradual increases in costs are to be expected.

It is not, however, the general price level which determines whether a particular company should elect LIFO. The future cost prospects for its specific products are all that need be considered. After appropriate study management may conclude that during the next three to five years the cost of its principal products will rise, although there may be temporary or isolated decreases in certain areas. In this case the company might consider placing its entire inventory on LIFO in a single dollar-value pool as described in Chapter 12. Under this method minor price decreases for certain products will tend to average out, and the pool as a whole should show satisfactory cost stability.

If, on the other hand, it is foreseen that for one or more significant products, the immediate outlook is for decreased costs, such products may be omitted from the immediate LIFO election. LIFO may be elected for only part of the goods in the inventory. If at some future date it appears the cost of other products is likely to rise, an additional election can be made.

VOLUME CONSIDERATIONS

While the expected trend of future costs is the keystone to deliberations involving the adopting of LIFO, physical volume of the inventories must also receive consideration.

To the extent possible, LIFO will generally be adopted at a time when inventory quantities are at or near normal levels. This is to guard against a twofold danger:

1. If the election is made when quantities are low, increments during years of inflated prices may have to be carried in the LIFO inventory at high costs indefinitely.

2. If the election is made at a time when inventory quantities are in excess of normal requirements, subsequent quantity reductions during periods of high prices can result in charging relatively low LIFO costs against inflated income and should higher income tax rates be applicable to the year of inventory liquidation more of the cash resources of the company may be required to discharge the tax liability.

In some cases the inventory volume is an important consideration in selecting a fiscal year-end for seasonal businesses. The larger the volume at the end of the year, the greater the impact of price-level changes and of the difference in results from using FIFO or LIFO.

Assume that Company X normally carries 40,000 tons of material A in inventory. During 1971 the price falls to a low point of $3 per ton, and an election is made to place material A on LIFO, although the quantity in inventory at the end of 1971 is only 10,000 tons. During succeeding years inventory quantities are built up to normal levels, but at higher prices. At the end of 1973 the situation is as follows:

Additions to LIFO Inventory at Increasing Costs
Followed by Decline in Market Value

	Tons	Unit cost	LIFO cost
1971 base	10,000	$3	$ 30,000
1972 increment	25,000	5	125,000
1973 increment	5,000	6	30,000
Total inventory	40,000		$185,000
Average LIFO cost—$4.625			

Although LIFO was originally elected when the price for material A was low, subsequent quantity increments have raised the average LIFO cost to the relatively high level of $4.625 per ton. Company X may be in a vulnerable position in view of the volatile price structure for the material. If in 1974 the cost should fall to $4 while the inventory quantity is held at 40,000 tons, the replacement (FIFO) cost of the inventory ($160,000) will be lower than the LIFO cost. Under these circumstances, Company

X would be required to carry its inventory at an amount in excess of market value for federal income tax purposes; however, if the year-end inventory quantity could be reduced to 20,000 tons, the average LIFO cost would be equal to the market value, and the $25,000 excess cost could be charged against income as part of the cost of sales.

The observation concerning vulnerability is inapplicable where the price trend is predominately upward rather than cyclical. Under such circumstances the LIFO election can advantageously be made as soon as an upward price trend is discernible with reasonable assurance, whether inventory quantities are at or below normal levels. This is particularly pertinent for an expanding business operation where inventory quantities may be expected to show normal increases from year to year. Assume LIFO has been adopted by Company Y with inventory increments as follows over three succeeding years:

Additions to LIFO Inventory at Increasing Costs Where Market Value Continues Upward

	Tons	Unit cost	LIFO cost
1971 base	10,000	$2	$ 20,000
1972 increment	5,000	3	15,000
1973 increment	20,000	4	80,000
1974 increment	10,000	5	50,000
Total inventory	45,000		$165,000

Had Company Y waited until 1973 to elect LIFO, its inventory at the end of 1974 would have been $10,000 higher. To general-

Effect of Delaying LIFO Election Where Market Value Continues Upward

	Tons	Unit cost	LIFO cost
1972 base	15,000	$3	$ 45,000
1973 increment	20,000	4	80,000
1974 increment	10,000	5	50,000
Total inventory	45,000		$175,000

ize, it may be concluded that when dealing with a material subject to cyclical cost variations, the correlation of normal inventory quantities with a bottoming-out of the price cycle presents the optimum point at which to make the LIFO election; and if prices are expected to show a steady rise, the earlier the election, irrespective of volume, the lower will be the LIFO inventory cost.

If the LIFO election is made at a time when inventory quantities are in excess of normal requirements, a subsequent reduction in quantity can have the effect of offsetting base-year LIFO costs against inflated sales income. Assuming no increase in tax rates, an election by Company Z would still be beneficial, as in the following example:

Partial Liquidation of LIFO Inventory
Where Market Value Continues Upward

	Tons	Unit cost	LIFO cost
1972 base	30,000	$3	$ 90,000
1973—No change	—		—
1974 liquidation	(10,000)		(30,000)
Total inventory	20,000	3	$ 60,000

Company Z is better off having elected LIFO, despite the subsequent liquidation, since the inventory cost on a FIFO basis at the end of 1974 would be $100,000, that is, 20,000 tons at $5 per ton.

As discussed on page 199, the Internal Revenue Code at present contains no relief provisions applicable to a current involuntary liquidation of a LIFO inventory quantity. Thus the consequences of volume reductions must be considered. This does not mean, however, that a potential involuntary liquidation is necessarily a reason for not adopting LIFO. From an income tax viewpoint the disadvantage of an involuntary liquidation is merely that previously deferred income becomes taxable. Even if the LIFO base is completely liquidated, the company is no worse off than if it had not elected LIFO in the first place, *assuming* no increase in the effective tax rate. If the amounts of paper profits in the inventory and the taxable income are sufficiently small so that the former would be taxed at 22 per cent, a LIFO election would normally not be advisable. A subsequent liquidation of the inventory could result in the income deferred as a consequence of the LIFO election being subjected to tax at 48 per cent even if there is no change in the federal income tax law.

The projection of anticipated inventory volume is at least as significant in selecting from the pooling methods discussed in Chapters 11 and 12 as in deciding upon the adoption of LIFO in the first instance. Some businesses use separate LIFO pools for their inventories of raw materials, work in process, and finished goods; but this method is not normally recommended if significant relative differences in the volume of goods in each of the three groups from year to year or gradual changes over an extended period are expected. If, for example, the bulk of the inventory investment would be concentrated in finished goods one year and raw materials the next, the result during a period of rising prices would be the liquidation of the finished goods LIFO base and the accumulation of a high-cost layer in the raw materials pool. Under such circumstances it would be advantageous to employ a single pool for the entire inventory of a natural business unit. Similarly, where at any year end the quantity of one or more significant material components of a company's inventory might be temporarily cut back below normal levels, a broad pooling arrangement would be preferable.

The volume of the inventory is also significant in selecting an accounting period. To illustrate, the following assumptions have been made as to acquisition costs for a material regularly stocked at October 31 in a volume equivalent to 140 per cent of the quantity owned at the end of the calendar year.

The costs charged against income for the units consumed on the basis of accounting periods ending on either October 31 or December 31 are tabulated on page 225. If the accounting period is changed during 1973 from the calendar year to a fiscal period ending October 31, costs would be absorbed in a different manner.

The following examples of the effect of the accounting period used upon the manner in which costs are allocated to units consumed are summarized in comparative form on page 227.

As discussed on page 175, a reserve to provide for the excess

Hypothetical Inventory of Seasonal Goods

| | Acqui-sition cost per unit | Quantities | | LIFO inventory cost if accounting periods end on | | | | | |
| | | | | Oct. 31 | | | Dec. 31 | | |
		Ac-quired	Con-sumed	Units	Per unit	LIFO cost	Units	Per unit	LIFO cost
1971:									
Closing inventory.				100	$10	$1,000	100	$10	$1,000
1972:									
Jan.–Oct........	$10	700	660	140	10	$1,400	140	10	$1,400
Nov.–Dec.......	15	200	240	100	10	$1,000	100	10	$1,000
1973:									
Jan.–Oct........	15	700	660	140	10	$1,400	100	10	$1,000
							40	15	600
							140		$1,600
Nov.–Dec.......	20	200	240	100	10	$1,000	100	10	$1,000
1974:									
Jan.–Oct........	20	700	660	140	10	$1,400	100	10	$1,000
							40	20	800
							140		$1,800
Nov.–Dec.......	20	200	240	100	10	$1,000	100	10	$1,000

cost of replacing the 40 units temporarily liquidated at December 31, 1974, would under these circumstances be provided where the accounting period was a fiscal year ending October 31. For accounting purposes the cost of the units consumed during the months of November and December, 1974, would be recognized as being $4,800 in all three situations.

From the illustrations it can be concluded that during a period of rising prices, the increase in costs will be absorbed sooner, and the amount of income will be less, if the accounting period ends when the inventory volume is at its maximum. Also, if the replacement cost for an inventory item is less than the LIFO cost, changing the accounting period to one ending when the inventory volume is at a minimum will have the effect of a partial liquidation, and a portion of the excess cost will be charged against income.

The volume of the inventory and recurring seasonal fluctuations

Costs for Units Consumed During Alternative Accounting Periods

| | Cost of acquisitions | | | LIFO inventory cost and cost of units consumed if accounting periods end on | | | |
| | | | | October 31 | | December 31 | |
	Per unit	Units	Total cost	Inventory	Costs absorbed	Inventory	Costs absorbed
1971:							
Closing inventory..				$1,000		$1,000	
1972:							
Jan.–Oct.........	$10	700	$ 7,000	1,400	$ 6,600		
Nov.–Dec........	15	200	3,000			1,000	$10,000
1973:							
Jan.–Oct.........	15	700	10,500	1,400	13,500		
Nov.–Dec........	20	200	4,000			1,000	14,500
1974:							
Jan.–Oct.........	20	700	14,000	1,400	18,000		
Nov.–Dec........	20	200	4,000			1,000	18,000
			$42,500				
Total costs absorbed for completed accounting periods					$38,100		$42,500
Costs absorbed during interim period, Nov.–Dec. 1974.					4,400		
					$42,500		

are factors in selecting an accounting period. This is particularly
true in the case of canners of fruits and vegetables, meat packers,
and manufacturers of products purchased to an appreciable extent
for Christmas and graduation gifts, for example; toys, watches,
fountain pens, and small electrical appliances.

The practical significance of the accounting period can be
dramatically illustrated by assuming an energetic businessman sells
ice cream bars by the swimming pool during the summer and
wool mittens by the toboggan slide during the winter. The ice-
cream bar business presents no inventory problem because whatever has been expended to acquire the merchandise will be deducted from sales proceeds in determining profit. In computing
income on a calendar year basis, however, an inventory will be
required of the wool mittens. Assume the normal practice is to
purchase one gross (144 pairs) during October as the season's

Costs for Units Consumed if Accounting Period Is Changed During 1973

	Cost of acquisitions			LIFO inventory cost and cost of units consumed if accounting period is changed	
	Per unit	Units	Total cost	Inventory	Costs absorbed
1971:					
Closing inventory.....				$1,000	
1972:					
Jan.–Oct.............	$10	700	$ 7,000		
Nov.–Dec...........	15	200	3,000	1,000	$10,000
1973:					
Jan.–Oct.............	15	700	10,500	1,600	9,900
Nov.–Dec............	20	200	4,000		
1974:					
Jan.-Oct.............	20	700	14,000	1,600	18,000
Nov.–Dec............	20	200	4,000		
			$42,500		
Total costs absorbed for completed accounting periods					$37,900
Costs absorbed during interim period, Nov.–Dec. 1974					4,600
					$42,500

stock, and there are 100 pairs on hand at both the beginning and end of the year. The quantity sold is equal to the quantity purchased, and under the LIFO inventory method the same dollar amount assigned to the 100 pairs in the opening inventory will be assigned to the 100 pairs in the closing inventory. The amount expended during October to maintain the inventory and continue the business will be deducted from the sales proceeds for the closing months of the prior season and the beginning of the current season, even though in fact 100 pairs were sold before the purchase and only 44 pairs afterward. LIFO is a theory of a "flow of cost" and is not dependent upon the physical movement of goods.

If the hypothetical vendor of mittens had 110 pairs on hand at the end of the year, the closing inventory cost would be the amount assigned to the 100 pairs in the opening inventory plus an amount considered as the cost of 10 of the pairs purchased during the year. If at the end of the year following the 110-pair

Different Allocations of Costs Resulting from Election of Accounting Period

	Units consumed	Cost of units consumed if accounting period					
		Ends on October 31		Ends on December 31		Is changed	
		Per unit	Costs absorbed	Per unit	Costs absorbed	Per unit	Costs absorbed
1972:							
Jan.–Oct....	660	$10	$ 6,600	$10	$ 6,600	$10	$ 6,600
Nov.–Dec....	200	15	3,000	15	3,000	15	3,000
	40	15	600	10	400	10	400
			$10,200		$10,000		$10,000
1973:							
Jan.–Oct....	660	15	9,900	15	9,900	15	9,900
			$20,100		$19,900		$19,900
Nov.–Dec....	200	20	4,000	20	4,000	20	4,000
	40	20	800	15	600	20	800
			$24,900		$24,500		$24,700
1974:							
Jan.–Oct.....	660	20	13,200	20	13,200	20	13,200
			$38,100		$37,700		$37,900
Nov.–Dec....	200	20	4,000	20	4,000	20	4,000
	40	10*	400	20	800	15*	600
			$42,500		$42,500		$42,500

* LIFO cost for units temporarily liquidated.

inventory there are only 95 pairs on hand, the closing inventory cost would be such portion of the amount assigned to the original 100 pairs as is applicable to 95 of them. The cost of sales for the year would be the sum of (a) the total purchases made during the year, (b) the cost established in the preceding year for the 10 pairs considered to have been purchased in that year and on hand at the year end, and (c) such portion of the amount assigned to the original 100 pairs as is deemed applicable to 5 pairs.

A computation of the income of the hypothetical mitten vendor for a fiscal year ended September 30 or October 31 could show results substantially different from those for the calendar year. There would be no inventory at all on September 30. On October 31 the entire season's stock of 144 pairs would be on hand, so that the investment in unsold goods would be greater than on December 31, and there could be a larger amount of inventory profit to be eliminated from income by the LIFO method.

The possibility of income being distorted by unrealized inventory profits necessarily increases with the size of the inventory, but few businesses have inventory fluctuations to the extent of the hypothetical vendor.

SIGNIFICANCE OF FORESEEABLE TECHNOLOGICAL CHANGES

In the case of a retail or other commercial trading operation "cost" is usually a single amount—the purchase price. For a manufacturer there are various elements of cost, for example, the cost of raw material used and conversion costs (labor and overhead). In LIFO as well as in FIFO determinations, each element should be considered separately.

Because business is constantly striving to be more efficient, it is not uncommon to encounter situations in which the material cost per unit shows an upward trend, but the conversion cost element either remains constant or decreases. This conversion cost trend may result from automation, decreased labor hours per unit produced, increased volume, or numerous other factors. The conversion cost per unit can decrease even though there have been increases in labor rates and in the individual items of overhead expense. If LIFO is applied to the aggregate of the cost elements as a unit, the cost reductions made possible by increased production efficiency would be offset against the increases attributable to the materials. This can be seen in an example which reflects what can happen through an interplay of cost factors. The material cost element per unit has increased from $5.00 to $6.00, whereas conversion costs have decreased from $6.00 to $4.62. If the aggregate of the material and conversion costs is treated as a single amount, the LIFO cost will continue to be $11.00 per unit, 38¢ in excess of replacement cost. If, however, LIFO is applied only to the material cost, the inventory will be carried at $9.62 per unit, i.e., a LIFO cost of $5.00 for the material content plus a FIFO cost of $4.62 for labor and overhead.

The material-content pooling method combines in one LIFO

pool both the cost of raw materials on hand and the material cost element of work in process and finished goods. Conversion costs may be inventoried on a FIFO basis. Material cost increases are charged off to current earnings, while the benefits of technological improvements in production efficiency are reflected in lower per unit inventory amounts for conversion costs. Where conversion costs are relatively small, this procedure is satisfactory because it minimizes the liquidation problem caused by shifts in volume in the raw materials, work in process, and finished goods components of the inventory from year to year.

First year:
Material cost	$ 5.00
Labor cost—2 hr. at $2	4.00
Overhead cost—50% of labor	2.00
	$11.00

Second year:
Material cost	$ 6.00
Labor cost—1.5 hr. at $2.20	3.30
Overhead cost—40% of labor	1.32
	$10.62

Where the details of cost elements can be established from the accounting records, the benefits of lower per-unit conversion costs resulting from increased efficiency may be maintained by inventorying conversion costs on the basis of direct labor hours. Labor is purchased in a manufacturing business in terms of hours, just as steel is purchased in terms of tons, and the inventory analysis may disclose that at the beginning of a period there was on hand the product of 1,500 direct labor hours and at the end of the period the inventory represents the fruits of 1,800 direct labor hours. The number of hours will, in many situations, be a better measure of the "form utility" element of the goods on hand than the number of units of particular articles.

In contemplating an election to use LIFO, consideration should be given to possible effects of future changes in production methods and product lines. These changes may result in the substitution of new types of raw materials for materials presently used, the purchase of materials presently manufactured or vice versa, or even distinct changes in the type of finished product.

For example, a member of the woolen industry which adopted

LIFO thirty years ago would have faced the problem of integrating into its inventory computations certain synthetic fibers substituted for natural wool previously used. A business originally engaged in the manufacture of railroad locomotives or equipment may now be subcontracting for the automobile or aircraft industry. An appliance manufacturer which ten years ago used principally metal parts may now be using plastic components. A pharmaceutical producer which formerly purchased fine bulk chemicals may begin manufacturing them. Industry is constantly substituting new products, materials, and production methods for the outmoded and obsolete. With the passage of time almost any business may expect some changes of this nature. In every case the question is whether the substitution of new materials or products will cause a liquidation of the LIFO base for a superseded inventory item.

In the case of the woolen company, if the natural fibers no longer in use had been carried in separate, specifically identified quantity pools, a liquidation of those pools would have occurred, with a consequent recognition of inventory profits deferred by LIFO. If on the other hand the company had carried all fibers in a single generic pool under the dollar-value method, the new synthetic fibers could be included in that pool without recognizing any significant loss of LIFO base. To facilitate the integration of new products and materials into existing pools, careful consideration should be given at the time of making the LIFO election to the description of the inventory goods—a general description by basic function may be preferable to specific names. A single dollar-value pool for the entire inventory investment of a natural business unit or a few pools grouped by broad product classifications, presently offers the best means of avoiding substantial liquidations upon the substitution of new materials for old in the inventory.

In the case of a company which switches to manufacturing a material or group of materials previously purchased, the problem of recognition of previously deferred income arises if the company has been using a material-content pool, with conversion costs included in separate pools or inventoried on a FIFO basis. Here the effect is partial liquidation of the material pool. At best only the raw-material element of the product's cost could now be included in the original material pool, whereas the LIFO principle would previously have been applied to the entire purchase cost. The conversion cost element would be treated as a current increment in another pool, or would be part of the FIFO inventory.

If the change in operating practice from purchasing to producing could have been foreseen and the expectation was for rising prices, the LIFO election could have been so phrased as not to cover this particular item. Alternatively, it might be feasible for the company to organize the new production facility as a separate operating subsidiary which would then sell the finished item to the parent company. The parent would continue to treat the product as a purchased material, and no change in its inventory pooling would be necessary.

All potential consequences of LIFO under changed future conditions cannot be foreseen, but management must weigh carefully the various possibilities in making the original LIFO election.

ILLUSTRATION OF ALTERNATIVES IN TIMING A LIFO ELECTION

The observations concerning the timing and extent of a LIFO election may be illustrated by a hypothetical case. The Panacea Corporation, a maufacturer of cosmetics, is considering the adoption of LIFO in 1972. Panacea's finished product line is in a constant state of flux, with new items and packaging being introduced continuously, and faded products dropped as soon as practicable. Essentially, however, its products are compounded from groups of the same basic materials termed, with a confessed lack of grace, the "musk," "wax," "lavender," and "gum" groups. As of the end of 1971, Panacea's inventory on a FIFO basis is as follows:

```
Raw materials:
    Musk—50,000 lb. at $2.00............ $  100,000
    Wax—160,000 lb. at $3.50............     560,000
    Lavender—80,000 lb. at $4.00.........     320,000
    Gum—30,000 lb. at $2.00.............      60,000
    Others—.........................      40,000
                                      $1,080,000
Packaging materials...................   2,000,000
Work in process......................     200,000
Finished goods.......................   3,000,000
                                      $6,280,000
```

An analysis of the cost elements of a typical Panacea product discloses the following:

Raw materials....................	25%
Packaging materials...............	60
Conversion costs..................	15
	100%

Packaging materials constitute the largest product cost element, but this category of inventory is composed of a multitude of individual items which are constantly being added to, dropped, or otherwise changed.   Although no single individual item dominates this inventory category, the prices which the company must pay for its packaging materials have been constantly increasing in recent years, and there is every expectation that they will continue to rise in the foreseeable future.

With respect to the various groups of raw materials, the outlook is as follows:

Musk—This group has a volatile price history.   Current average price of $2.00 per pound is expected to rise sharply to between $3.00 and $3.50 within the year.   These prices, however, are believed to result from unusual shortages at the present time.   It is expected that within a few years the price will fall below $2.00.   Two years ago it was $1.25.

Wax—Price has shown a slow but steady increase in recent years. It was $3.00 a pound five years ago, and it is believed that the price will continue to rise at a similar rate in future years.

Lavender—Price has been fairly stable in recent years averaging $4.00 per pound, with only minor variations.   This trend is expected to continue.

Gum—It is expected that the price of this material will increase within the next few years; however, the company is presently investigating a substitute material which can be obtained at a lower cost.

Labor costs per man-hour are expected to remain stable within the immediate future, although a moderate increase in future years is foreseen.   Gradual but constant increases in the cost of overhead items such as payroll benefits, maintenance, depreciation, and taxes are also foreseen.   In total, however, conversion costs per unit of product will probably decline slightly or at least hold steady over the next several years, due to production efficiencies and increased volume.

Based on this analysis of cost and other trends, unless the management of The Panacea Corporation wishes to adopt LIFO with a natural business unit pool so that in the future less attention will need to be given to the inventory position for the various materials, LIFO should be adopted at the present time for only a portion of the inventory investment. Because the future outlook for conversion costs does not indicate substantial increases on a per-unit basis and significant direct labor hour statistics are unavailable, these costs could be continued on FIFO. Material-content pools (raw materials plus the material-cost element of work in process and finished goods) could be established advantageously for only two broad groupings of materials: packaging materials and waxes.

All packaging materials should be grouped within a single pool, and the dollar-value principle of measurement applied. The dollar-value method is essential in this situation so that cost increases can be eliminated from the amount assigned to future inventories without distortions caused by changes and liquidations of individual items. Applying LIFO by comparing quantities of individual packages would be impractical.

Because of the upward price trend for waxes, a LIFO pool should also be established for this group of materials.

There would be no present advantage in electing LIFO for lavender. If the price trend should turn upward, an election can be made to include this material at some future date. Gum should also be omitted from the initial LIFO election, since a new, lower-priced material may be substituted for this item in the near future. Because of its volatile price tendencies, musk is the type of material which should be on LIFO, but only if the election is made when the price has touched bottom and materials are on hand in at least normal quantities. Because the present price of musk is expected to dip sharply within a few years, the election of LIFO for this item should be deferred.

If the election is to use a single pool for the entire inventory in recognition of the fact that the business of The Panacea Corporation constitutes one natural business unit, the pool will consist of all items—raw materials, packaging materials, work in process, and finished goods.

TRANSFERS OF LIFO INVENTORIES IN NONTAXABLE EXCHANGES

In general any sale or exchange of an asset can give rise to a taxable gain under the provisions of the Internal Revenue Code. The statute provides, however, that no gain (or loss) shall be recognized as a consequence of certain types of exchanges. Although such exchanges are currently nontaxable, it is more accurate to think of merely a deferment of recognition of the gain or loss. The previously established federal income tax basis for the asset is usually not changed when its ownership is transferred from one person to another in a nontaxable exchange; however, unless the transaction is considered as a "pooling of interests" for financial accounting purposes the inventories may have to be restated.

One question encountered in a nontaxable exchange involving a LIFO inventory concerned the necessity for making a new election in order to continue using that method for federal income tax purposes.[2] A corporation was organized in 1946 and acquired the assets of three proprietorships in exchange for shares of its capital stock. The proprietorships had used LIFO. For income tax purposes the cost of the inventory to the corporation was the same as the cost in the hands of the prior owners, and the corporation continued the LIFO basis in its first tax return. It did not, however, file an election as required by the Internal Revenue Code and regulations.[3] The Internal Revenue Service was upheld by the Tax Court in its contention that Textile Apron Company could not use LIFO. The closing inventories for the corporation were determined on a FIFO basis, and the inventory profits deferred by the proprietorships were included in taxable income.

Many companies which acquired LIFO inventories in nontaxable exchanges made appropriate elections and had to decide whether a new average cost for the entire opening inventory

[2] *Textile Apron Co. v. Commissioner*, 21 T.C. 147 (1953).
[3] Sections 1.472 and 1.472–2, Appendix C.

should be computed or the cost previously established for each LIFO inventory layer should be carried over. The common practice approved by representatives of the Internal Revenue Service was for the transferee of the inventory to continue the same layer stratification for the inventory whether the LIFO inventory was acquired in a statutory merger, a consolidation, or other type of nontaxable transaction. This conclusion is justified by considering each inventory layer as a separate item of property, which is consistent with the fact that each layer is computed to represent a definite quantity of inventory with a specifically identified cost.

Since 1954 the Internal Revenue Code has provided that continuation of a predecessor's inventory method is required after certain types of nontaxable exchange, that is, a distribution by a subsidiary corporation of all its assets in exchange for the stock held by the parent company where the cost of the stock is not to be assigned to the assets, and a corporate acquisition of assets in exchange for voting stock, whether or not the exchange is incidental to a statutory merger or consolidation, or a reorganization involving only a change in identity, form, or place of organization. The continuation of the inventory method is not mandatory in cases of nontaxable exchanges representing transfers of assets to controlled corporations, so the current statutory provision would not have eliminated the necessity for an affirmative election by Textile Apron Company.

The wording of the Internal Revenue Code is as follows:

> In any case in which inventories are received by the acquiring corporation, such inventories shall be taken by such corporation (in determining its income) on the same basis on which such inventories were taken by the distributor or transferor corporation, unless different methods were used by several distributor or transferor corporations or by a distributor or transferor corporation and the acquiring corporation. If different methods were used, the acquiring corporation shall use the method or combination of methods of taking inventory adopted pursuant to regulations prescribed by the Secretary or his delegate. [Int. Rev. Code of 1954, §381(c)(5).]

Although this provision has been part of the Internal Revenue Code since 1954, the regulations referred to have not yet been prescribed, and even proposed regulations were not published until December 29, 1960.

Under the proposed regulations the inventory basis depends upon whether the operation of an acquired business is continued as a separate business. If so, the general rule is that the same inventory method is required. This does not preclude an election to use LIFO where FIFO has been previously used, however, because the Code specifically permits adoption of LIFO commencing with any taxable year.

If the acquired business is combined with another, the proposed regulations require that the "principal" inventory method in use prior to the nontaxable exchange be followed in resolving any variations. "The fair market value of the particular types of goods, for a representative period for each group of trades or businesses with respect to which one method of taking inventories common to all was employed, shall be compared," say the proposed regulations, "with the fair market value of comparable goods for such period for other groups of trades or businesses with respect to which another method of taking inventory common to all was employed. The method of taking inventories with respect to a particular type of goods for the group of trades or businesses having the largest fair market value of such goods for a representative period shall be the principal method of taking inventories for that particular type of goods."

The proposed regulations also provide that where the acquiring corporation is required or permitted to use LIFO the base-year inventories and any layers of increment must be retained and all segments attributable to the same year should be combined. The situation in which the previous owners of the combined businesses used different accounting periods for federal income tax purposes is not specifically covered. The general practice is to sandwich a LIFO inventory layer attributable to a fiscal year between layers attributable to the calendar year in which the fiscal year began and that in which it ended. The sequence of accounting periods has been maintained by reference to the date upon which each period ended.

The procedures set forth in the proposed regulations are generally reasonable interpretations of the statute, but since they have not been adopted in final form and there may be significant changes in wording, further analysis is not presently justified.

Where a nontaxable exchange has involved a transfer of a LIFO inventory, the general practice for many years has been to consider that the cost basis carries over in the hands of the new owner as though each layer of the LIFO inventory was a separate item of property. In the hands of a corporation which had previously used the LIFO method for comparable goods, the transferred inventories would be integrated with those of the new owner, layer by layer. If previously owned inventories of the acquiring taxpayer were similar to the LIFO inventories being acquired, it might be necessary to combine all inventories of similar goods. Generally, the Treasury Department has refused to permit the segregation of inventories by location or by the treating of the goods on hand at the various plants as part on LIFO and part on the lower-of-cost-or-market basis, or even as a separate LIFO pool. In one case of a manufacturing concern with a large inventory of finished products at the factory and small inventories at sales branches scattered over a wide area, Treasury Department representatives refused to approve the adoption of LIFO at the factory while excluding from LIFO similar goods at branches. Exception was permitted as to goods at foreign branches.

In the event of a merger at the beginning of or at any time during a taxable year, the general rule has been that the LIFO inventory quantities at the end of the year are determined by combining, on a layer-by-layer basis, the inventories of the two companies, and the opening inventory of the merged company is assumed to be the quantity on hand at the beginning of the taxable year provided it is at least as great as the quantity owned by that company at the date of the merger.

For example, assume Company A is a continuing corporation and has 10 units in its opening inventory, and Company B was merged into Company A as of June 30, 1972. At December 31, 1972, Company A's plants had 15 units of inventory, and the plants acquired from Company B had 25 units of inventory. The closing inventory quantities of Company A would be 40 units, and to determine whether or not there had been an increment in the LIFO inventories during 1972, a comparison would be made with the 10 units of Company A's opening inventory and the units in Company B's inventory at December 31, 1971, or June 30,

1972, whichever is less. If the inventory of Company B at December 31, 1971, and June 30, 1972, had been 20 and 25 units, respectively, the 1972 increment for Company A would be considered as 10 units. The LIFO cost for the 1972 layer would be determined in accordance with the practice followed by Company A. If Company A inventoried its increments by reference to first purchase costs, the 10 units in the 1972 increment would be costed on the basis of the first purchases by Company A even though the period taken into account preceded the date of merger.

In computing the income of Company B for the period from January 1 to June 30, 1972, it would be recognized that there was an increment of 5 units, and the inventory at June 30 would be determined by stating the 5-unit increase under Company B's LIFO procedure with respect to annual increments. The cost for the June 30, 1972 inventory of Company B would be charged to Company A's 1972 purchases for June. Under this procedure the cost assigned to the 5-unit increment of Company B to determine its income for the six months would be entirely different from the cost used in determining the amount to be assigned the increment in the merged inventory of Company A at the end of the year, but the cost of Company B's opening inventory of 20 units would carry over into the closing inventory of Company A.

One case in which the generally accepted practice of retaining the status of LIFO inventory layers, after a transfer in a nontaxable exchange, was questioned in federal income tax litigation is *J. E. Seagram & Sons, Inc.* (394 F 2d 738, April 23, 1968) and the Court of Appeals for the Second Circuit reversed the decision of the Tax Court. Seagram had, for good business reasons, transferred substantially all of its assets in Kentucky as a capital contribution to one of its subsidiaries which was engaged in business in that state. Both corporations had used and continued to use the LIFO principle in determining their inventories. As indicated by the following excerpts from the opinion of the Court of Appeals, the decision did not turn upon a technical interpretation of the wording of the Internal Revenue Code but rather upon the underlying purpose of the LIFO principle.

The issue in this case has been somewhat blurred by the emphasis placed by the parties on specific sections of the Code. Seagram contends that Section 472, which authorizes the application of the LIFO method, mandates the use of Kessler's acquisition date. That section states in subdivision (b) that in inventorying goods specified, the taxpayer shall treat the inventory on hand at the close of the taxable year as being: First, the inventory included in the opening inventory of the taxable year; and second, "those acquired in the taxable year." The Commissioner asserts that Section 362 (a) of the Code, which, by cross-reference to Section 118, provides that when property is acquired by a corporation through a tax-free contribution to capital, the basis of the property "shall be the same as it would be in the hands of the transferor," requires Seagram's acquisition dates. He argues that since the date of the cost basis in the hands of Seagram is earlier than the date of the transfer in 1957 to Kessler, the date basis of Seagram follows its cost basis under Section 362 (a) and that accordingly Seagram's acquisition dates are the only dates which may be used; otherwise, he claims, inventory accounting would lack consistency from year to year and Kessler's income would be distorted.

Neither of these sections, in our opinion, is controlling because they do not specifically or impliedly cover a tax-free capital contribution of inventory from a parent to its subsidiary. The legislative history seems to be silent upon the issue and the controversy cannot be determined by an extension of the definition of the word "basis" in Section 362(a) or a restriction of the definition of the word "acquired" in Section 472(b)(1). In the absence of something more specific, these sections must be read in the light of the policy underlying the Internal Revenue Code that income must be determined in the final analysis in accordance with good accounting practice. Therefore, the above sections must be read together with Section 471 and 472(a) and Regulations §§1.471-2(b) and 1.472-4 requiring that the taking of inventory must accord with the best accounting practice for the purpose of clearly and consistently reflecting income.

It is the underlying purpose of the LIFO method of inventory accounting to match current income against current costs, which in turn includes the cost of that inventory most recently purchased or produced. The inventory received through a tax-free contribution to capital does not represent current cost to Kessler and its use as of the date of Kessler's acquisition seems to undercut the underlying assumption of the LIFO method. . . .

Seagram argues that the Commissioner has no authority to impose upon the taxpayer an accounting method or procedure preferred by him where the method used by the taxpayer does not violate any tax or accounting rules or regulations . . . The Commissioner in this case is not seeking to substitute one accounting method for an accepted accounting method heretofore used by the taxpayer. His determination is not an expression of preference, but the application to a particular and non-recurring transaction of what he claims is the proper accounting principle as opposed to the taxpayer's procedure which he asserts violates proper accounting procedure.

The Commissioner has determined that in treating this particular transaction the best accounting practice requires Kessler to retain the identity
of Seagram's LIFO layers and to integrate them into its own corresponding
monthly layers of inventory in order to consistently and properly reflect
Kessler's income. If the taxpayer's method of accounting for inventory
does not reflect income as clearly as the method proposed by the Commissioner, it is within the Comissioner's discretion to insist upon his method
and he need not predicate his determination upon a showing of bad faith
on the part of the taxpayer . . . When the Commissioner has made such
a determination, the taxpayer faces a heavy burden of proof to establish
that it was arbitrary or an abuse of discretion . . . Seagram has failed to
satisfy this burden. . . .

This decision suggests that, rather than following a general rule
with respect to the retention of the status of LIFO inventory
layers after a transfer in a nontaxable exchange, the circumstances
of each case and the effect upon income—determined upon the
LIFO principle—must be specifically appraised. The Court of
Appeals placed particular emphasis upon the observation that the
underlying purpose of LIFO is to match *current* income against
current costs.

INVENTORY PROBLEMS IN CONSOLIDATED TAX RETURNS

Property transfers between members of an affiliated group have
resulted in some differences in method of computing inventory
costs for financial-statement and tax purposes. Where consolidated federal income tax returns are filed, the income is first determined for each of the corporate entities, and, except for various
types of intercompany transactions, the consolidated income
merely represents the combination of the amounts of net income
as computed for the several members of the affiliated group. For
the purpose of consolidated financial statements, however, the inventory may be determined as though one LIFO computation
was made for the inventories of all the companies. This practice
has the effect of offsetting increments in a LIFO group for one
company against liquidations in the corresponding group of other
companies. The computation of LIFO inventories on this basis
is consistent with the theory of consolidated accounts, but raises
problems as to the amount of intercompany profit in the inventory
and the recognition to be given federal income taxes paid on the
intercompany profit.

Under the commonly followed practice of making separate LIFO computations for each member of an affiliated group individual companies may have inventory increments at a current intercompany transfer price for the year. In eliminating intercompany profit in the inventory, the comparison is made with an amount determined by reference to the LIFO computation for the supplying company. If it happens to have a liquidation for the year in the same LIFO pool, the cost will be that applicable to a prior year's increment or to the basic LIFO inventory rather than the cost incurred in the current year. This measurement of intercompany profit should be acceptable for federal income tax purposes where consolidated returns are to be filed.

Quoted below are the principal paragraphs specifically referring to inventories in the consolidated federal income tax regulations applicable to years beginning before January 1, 1966.

§ 1.1502-39 Inventories.

(a) *Consolidated return for first year of affiliation.* If the income of an affiliated corporation is included in a consolidated return for the period immediately following the date upon which such corporation became a member of the affiliated group, the value of its opening inventory to be used in computing the consolidated taxable income shall be the proper value of the closing inventory used in computing its taxable income for the preceding taxable year.

(b) *Consolidated return after separate return by affiliates.* If—

(1) A corporation which is a member of the affiliated group for the first consolidated return period was a member of the group in the preceding taxable year, or

(2) A corporation which filed a separate return for its previous taxable year was not a member of the affiliated group within the meaning of section 141 of the Internal Revenue Code of 1939, at any time during the last taxable year of the group not subject to section 1502, but which would have been a member of the group during such period if section 1504 had been applicable and is a member of the affiliated group filing a consolidated return for the first taxable year to which section 1502 is applicable,

the value of its opening inventory to be used in computing the consolidated taxable income for the first consolidated return period shall be the proper value of the closing inventory used in computing its taxable income for the preceding taxable year, decreased in the amount of profits or increased in the amount of losses reflected in such inventories which arose in transactions between members of the affiliated group and which have not been realized by the group through final transactions with persons other than members of the group.

(c) *Separate returns made after consolidated returns.* If a corporation which was a member of an affiliated group in a consolidated return period makes or is required to make a separate return for the succeeding taxable year, the value of its opening inventory to be used in computing its taxable income for such succeeding taxable year shall be the proper value of its closing inventory used in computing consolidated taxable income for the last consolidated return period increased in the amount of profits or decreased in the amount of losses eliminated in the computation of such inventory as profits or losses arising in transactions between members of the affiliated group, but in an amount not exceeding, in the case of profits, either the amount of profits arising from such intercompany transactions reflected in the closing inventory of such corporation for such succeeding taxable year or the amount of such intercompany profits eliminated from its opening inventory for its first consolidated return period pursuant to the provisions of paragraph (b) of this section, and not exceeding, in the case of losses, either the amount of losses arising from intercompany transactions reflected in the closing inventory for such corporation for such succeeding taxable year or the amount of such intercompany losses eliminated from its opening inventory for its first consolidated return period pursuant to the provisions of paragraph (b) of this section.

These rules may be illustrated by simplified examples.

Assume Corporation P and its subsidiary Corporation S adopted LIFO as of the beginning of 1962, many years after becoming affiliated, and filed consolidated federal income tax returns for the calendar years 1962 and 1963. Separate returns were filed for 1961 and prior years. Corporation S was completely liquidated on June 30, 1963, so that the consolidated 1963 return included the income of Corporation P for the entire year and the income of Corporation S for the first six months. The December 31, 1961, inventory of Corporation P consisted of goods purchased from Corporation S for $1 million, including $100,000 of intercompany profit. The same inventory quantities were owned by Corporation P at December 31, 1962, and 1963. The net income of Corporation P would be computed by considering the closing inventory for 1961 at $1 million, the opening and closing inventory for 1962 and 1963 at $900,000, and the opening inventory for 1964 again at $1 million. The calendar year 1964 would be the first separate return year, and the opening inventory would be shown at cost without any adjustment for intercompany profit.

Assume, on the other hand, the facts in the foregoing example were changed so that the goods were purchased by Corporation S from Corporation P. The net income of Corporation S would

be computed by considering the closing inventory for 1961 at
$1 million and the inventories at January 1, 1962, December 31,
1962, and June 30, 1963, at $900,000. The inventory at Decem-
ber 31, 1963, would likewise be valued at $900,000 in the hands
of Corporation P. Since Corporation S would not file a separate
return after liquidation, it would not receive a compensating benefit for the $100,000 downward adjustment made to its opening
inventory for 1962. As the LIFO cost basis of the inventory
transferred by Corporation S would carry over to Corporation
P in the tax-free liquidation, the ending inventory for 1963 would
be $1 million. Under the regulations a question arises as to
whether there would be a double tax on the $100,000 of inter-
company profit. A literal reading of the regulations might lead
to the conclusion that the adjustment to the opening inventory
in 1964 is limited to the profit eliminated from the parent company's inventory on filing the 1962 consolidated return. Under
the stated facts there was no intercompany profit in the 1962 opening inventory of Corporation P, so that the opening 1964 inventory might have to be $900,000 although the closing inventory
for 1963 was $1 million.

Quoted below are the principal paragraphs specifically referring
to inventories in the consolidated federal income tax regulations
applicable to years beginning after December 31, 1965.

§ 1.1502-18   Inventory adjustment

(a) *Definition of intercompany profit amount.* For purposes of this
section, the term "intercompany profit amount" for a taxable year means
an amount equal to the profits of a corporation (other than those profits
which such corporation has elected not to defer pursuant to §1.1502–
13(c)(3)) arising in transactions with other members of the group with
respect to goods which are, at the close of such corporation's taxable year,
included in the inventories of other members of the group. See §1.1502–
13(c)(2) with respect to the determination of profits. See the last sentence
of §1.1502–13(f)(1)(i) for rules for determining which goods are considered to be disposed of outside the group and therefore not included in
inventories of other members.

(b) *Addition of initial inventory amount to taxable income.* If a
corporation—

(1) Is a member of a group filing a consolidated return for the taxable
year,

(2) Was a member of such group for its immediately preceding taxable
year, and

(3) Filed a separate return for such preceding year,
then the intercompany profit amount of such corporation for such separate
return year (hereinafter referred to as the "initial inventory amount")
shall be added to the income of such corporation for the consolidated
return year (or years) in which the goods to which the initial inventory
amount is attributable are disposed of outside the group or such corporation
becomes a nonmember. Such amount shall be treated as gain from the
sale or exchange of property which is neither a capital asset nor property
described in section 1231.

(c) *Recovery of initial inventory amount*—(1) *Unrecovered inventory
amount.* The term "unrecovered inventory amount" for any consolidated
return year means the lesser of—

(i) The intercompany profit amount for such year, or

(ii) The initial inventory amount.

However, if a corporation ceases to be a member of the group during
a consolidated return year, its unrecovered inventory amount for such
year shall be considered to be zero.

(2) *Recovery during consolidated return years.* (i) To the extent that
the unrecovered inventory amount of a corporation for a consolidated
return year is less than such amount for its immediately preceding year,
such decrease shall be treated for such year by such corporation as a
loss from the sale or exchange of property which is neither a capital
asset nor property described in section 1231.

(ii) To the extent that the unrecovered inventory amount for a consolidated return year exceeds such amount for the preceding year, such
increase shall be treated as gain from the sale or exchange of property
which is neither a capital asset nor property described in section 1231.

(3) *Recovery during first separate return year.* For the first separate
return year of a member following a consolidated return year, the unrecovered inventory amount for such consolidated return year (minus any
part of the initial inventory amount which has not been added to income
pursuant to paragraph (b) of this section) shall be treated as a loss from
the sale or exchange of property which is neither a capital asset nor property described in section 1231.

(d) *Examples.* The provisions of paragraphs (a), (b), and (c) of this
section may be illustrated by the following examples:

Example (1). Corporations P, S, and T report income on the basis
of a calendar year. Such corporations file separate returns for 1965. P
manufactures widgets which it sells to both S and T, who act as distributors. The inventories of S and T at the close of 1965 are comprised
of widgets which they purchased from P and with respect to which P
derived profits of $5,000 and $8,000, respectively. P, S, and T file a consolidated return for 1966. During 1966, P sells widgets to S and T with
respect to which it derives profits of $7,000 and $10,000, respectively. The
inventories of S and T as of December 31, 1966, are comprised of widgets
on which P derived net profits of $4,000 and $8,000, respectively. P's
initial inventory amount is $13,000, P's intercompany profit amount for
1965 (such $13,000 amount is the profits of P with respect to goods sold
to S and T and included in their inventories at the close of 1965). Assum-

ing that S and T identify their goods on a first-in, first-out basis, the entire opening inventory amount of $13,000 is added to P's income for 1966 as gain from the sale or exchange of property which is neither a capital asset nor property described in section 1231, since the goods to which the initial inventory amount is attributable were disposed of in 1966 outside the group. However, since P's unrecovered inventory amount for 1966, $12,000 (the intercompany profit amount for the year, which is less than the initial inventory amount), is less than the unrecovered inventory amount for 1965, $13,000, this decrease of $1,000 is treated by P for 1966 as a loss from the sale or exchange of property which is neither a capital asset nor property described in section 1231.

Example (2). Assume the same facts as in example (1) and that at the close of 1967, a consolidated return year, the inventories of S and T are comprised of widgets on which P derived profits of $5,000 and $3,000, respectively. Since P's unrecovered inventory amount for 1967, $8,000, is less than $12,000, the unrecovered inventory amount for 1966, this decrease of $4,000 is treated by P for 1967 as a loss from the sale or exchange of property which is neither a capital asset nor property described in section 1231.

Example (3). Assume the same facts as in examples (1) and (2) and that in 1968, a consolidated return year, P's intercompany profit amount is $11,000. P will report $3,000 (the excess of $11,000, P's unrecovered inventory amount for 1968, over $8,000, P's unrecovered inventory amount for 1967) for 1968 as a gain from the sale or exchange of property which is neither a capital asset nor property described in section 1231.

Example (4). Assume the same facts as in examples (1), (2), and (3) and that in 1969 P, S, and T file separate returns. P will report $11,000 (its unrecovered inventory amount for 1968, $11,000, minus the portion of the initial inventory amount which has not been added to income during 1966, 1967, and 1968, zero) as a loss from the sale or exchange of property which is neither a capital asset nor property described in section 1231.

Example (5). Corporations P and S file a consolidated return for the first time for the calendar year 1966. P manufactures machines and sells them to S, which sells them to users throughout the country. At the close of 1965, S had on hand 20 machines which it purchased from P and with respect to which P derived profits of $3,500. During 1966, P sells 6 machines to S on which it derives profits of $1,300, and S sells 5 machines which it had on hand at the beginning of the year (S specifically identifies the machines which it sells) and on which P had derived profits of $900. P's initial inventory amount is $3,500, of which $900 is added to P's income in 1966 as gain from the sale or exchange of property which is neither a capital asset nor property described in section 1231, since such $900 amount is attributable to goods disposed of in 1966 outside the group, which goods were included in S's inventory at the close of 1965. If P and S continue to file consolidated returns, the remaining $2,600 of the initial inventory amount will be added to P's income as the machines on which such profits were derived are disposed of outside the group.

Example (6). Assume that in example (5) S had elected to inventory its goods under section 472 (relating to last-in, first-out inventories). None of P's initial inventory amount of $3,500 would be added to P's income in 1966, since none of the goods to which such amount is attributable would be considered to be disposed of during such year under the last-in, first-out method of identifying inventories.

(e) *Section 381 transfer.* If a member of the group is a transferor or distributor of assets to another member of the group within the meaning of section 381(a), then the acquiring corporation shall be treated as succeeding to the initial inventory amount of the transferor or distributor corporation to the extent that as of the date of distribution or transfer such amount has not yet been added to income. Such amount shall then be added to the acquiring corporation's income under the provisions of paragraph (b) of this section. For purposes of applying paragraph (c) of this section—

(1) The initial inventory amount of the transferor or distributor corporation shall be added to such amount of the acquiring corporation as of the close of the acquiring corporation's taxable year in which the date of distribution or transfer occurs, and

(2) The unrecovered inventory amount of the transferor or distributor corporation for its taxable year preceding the taxable year of the group in which the date of distribution or transfer occurs shall be added to such amount of the acquiring corporation.

(f) *Transitional rules—(1) In general.* If—

(i) A group filed a consolidated return for the taxable year immediately preceding the first taxable year to which this section applies,

(ii) Any member of such group made an opening adjustment to its inventory pursuant to paragraph (b) of § 1.1502–39A, and

(iii) Paragraph (c) of § 1.1502–39A has not been applicable for any taxable year subsequent to the taxable year for which such adjustment was made,

then subparagraphs (2) and (3) of this paragraph shall apply.

(2) *Closing adjustment to inventory.* (i) For the first consolidated return year to which this section applies, the increase in inventory prescribed in paragraph (c) of § 1.1502–39A shall be made as if such year were a separate return year.

(ii) For the first separate return year of a member to which this section applies, the adjustment to inventory (whether an increase or a decrease) prescribed in paragraph (c) of § 1.1502–39A, minus any adjustment already made pursuant to subdivision (i) of this subparagraph, shall be made to the inventory of such member.

(3) *Addition and recovery of initial inventory amount.* Each selling member shall treat as an initial inventory amount its share of the net amount by which the inventories of all members are increased pursuant to subparagraph (2) (i) of this paragraph for the first taxable year to which this section applies. A member's share shall be such net amount multiplied by a fraction, the numerator of which is its initial inventory amount (computed under paragraph (b) as if such taxable year were its first consolidated return year), and the denominator of which is the

sum of such initial inventory amounts of all members. Such initial inventory amount shall be added to the income of such selling member and shall be recovered at the time and in the manner prescribed in paragraphs (b) and (c) of this section.

(4) *Example.* The provisions of this paragraph may be illustrated by the following example:

Example. (i) Corporations P, S, and T file consolidated returns for calendar 1966, having filed consolidated returns continuously since 1962. P is a wholesale distributor of groceries selling to chains of supermarkets, including those owned by S and T. The opening inventories of S and T for 1962 were reduced by $40,000 and $80,000, respectively, pursuant to paragraph (b) of § 1.1502–39A. At the close of 1965, S and T have on hand in their inventories goods on which P derived profits of $80,000 and $90,000, respectively. The inventories of S and T at the close of 1966 include goods which they purchased from P during the year on which P derived profits of $85,000 and $105,000, respectively.

(ii) The opening inventories of S and T for 1966, the first year to which this section applies, are increased by $40,000 and $80,000, respectively, pursuant to the provisions of subparagraph (2)(i) of this paragraph. P will take into account (as provided in paragraphs (b) and (c) of this section) an initial inventory amount of $120,000 as of the beginning of 1966, the net amount by which the inventories of S and T were increased in such year. Since the increases in the inventories of S and T are the maximum allowable under paragraph (c) of § 1.1502–39A (i.e., the amount by which such inventories were originally decreased), no further adjustments will be made pursuant to subparagraph (2)(ii) of this paragraph to such inventories in the event that separate returns are subsequently filed.

(5) *Election not to eliminate.* If a group filed a consolidated return for the taxable year immediately preceding the first taxable year to which this section applies, and for such preceding year the members of the group did not eliminate gain or loss on intercompany inventory transactions pursuant to the adoption under § 1.1502–31A(b)(1) of a consistent accounting practice taking into account such gain or loss, then for purposes of this section each member shall be treated as if it had filed a separate return for such immediately preceding year.

Section 1.1502–13(c)(2), to which reference is made with respect to the determination of profits, reads: "In determining the amount of deferred gain or loss, the cost of property, services, or any other expenditure shall include both direct costs and indirect costs which are properly includible in the cost of goods sold or cost of the services or other expenditures. See §1.471–3 for costs properly includible in cost of goods sold." The last sentence of Section 1.1502–13(f)(1)(i), to which reference is made for rules to determine which goods are considered to have been disposed of outside the group, provides that the determination is to be made by reference to the "method of inventory identification (e.g., first-in, first-out, last-in, first-out, or specific identification)" of the member of the affiliated group which made the transfer outside the group.   The reference to Section 1.1502–39A is merely a new designation for the section quoted on pages 241 and 242.

Section 1.1502–13 of the consolidated federal income tax regulations applicable to years beginning after December 31, 1965, contains the general provisions relating to the treatment of intercompany transactions.   Under this section the gain from intercompany sales of inventory items, unless an election is made by the affiliated group not to defer recognition of such gains, is taken into account by the selling member as of the date the goods are disposed of outside the group.

Two principal changes were effected in the regulations applicable to years beginning after December 31, 1965.

Under the revised regulations, as and when gain is realized by a disposition outside the group or when income is subjected to tax because of a company's terminating its affiliation, the income is attributed to the corporation which made the intercompany sale rather than to the corporation which made the sale to the unrelated party or which owned the goods at the time the affiliation is terminated.   Identifying the corporation to which income is attributed is particularly significant in determining the accumulated earnings and profits of the various corporations or where the income of one of the corporations is the basis for measuring a special tax-computation factor, such as the income of a Western Hemisphere trade corporation.

The second major change effected by the revised regulations is elimination of the possibility of the inequitable tax result discussed on page 243.   Adding the intercompany profit in the opening inventory for the first consolidated return year (i.e., the "initial inventory amount") to income as the goods are disposed of outside the affiliated group is duplication because the same income was included in the return for the year in which the sale was made, when separate returns were filed by each corporation rather than a consolidated return.   A deduction will ultimately be allowed, however, to offset this duplication, and as long as the amount of intercompany profit in subsequent inventories is at least as large as the initial amount, the realized income for the affiliated group will be appropriately stated on a consolidated basis. This can be illustrated by a simplified example based upon the following assumptions:

Corporation P produces goods for sale only to its subsidiary, Corporation S

Corporation S sells only the goods purchased from Corporation P

Corporation S determines its inventories on a first-in, first-out basis

Corporation S had in its inventory at the end of each of the years 1970–1973 and 1975–1976 all of the goods produced by and purchased from Corporation P during the year

Corporation S had no inventory at the end of either of the years 1974 or 1977

Consolidated income tax returns are filed for years subsequent to 1970.

	Sales	Costs	Expenses	Income
Corporation P—				
1970	$ 300,000	$ 200,000	$ 10,000	$ 90,000
1971	360,000	240,000	10,000	110,000
1972	300,000	200,000	10,000	90,000
1973	240,000	160,000	10,000	70,000
1974	300,000	200,000	10,000	90,000
1975	270,000	180,000	10,000	80,000
1976	330,000	220,000	10,000	100,000
1977	300,000	200,000	10,000	90,000
Total 1971–77	$2,100,000	$1,400,000	$ 70,000	$630,000
Corporation S—				
1970	$ —	$ —	$ —	$ —
1971	350,000	300,000	20,000	30,000
1972	420,000	360,000	20,000	40,000
1973	350,000	300,000	20,000	30,000
1974	630,000	540,000	20,000	70,000
1975	—	—	20,000	(20,000)
1976	315,000	270,000	20,000	25,000
1977	735,000	630,000	20,000	85,000
Total 1971–77	$2,800,000	$2,400,000	$140,000	$260,000

From this example, it can be observed that (a) the aggregate amount of consolidated income for the period 1971–77 equals the sum of the income of the corporations separately computed (i.e., the addition of the intercompany profit in the opening inventory for the first consolidated return year has been offset by deductions

| | Inter-company profit in year-end inventory | Unrecovered inventory amount | Adjustments for consolidated return | | |
			Net change in deferred gain	Initial inventory adjustment	Net increase or (decrease)
1970	$100,000	$100,000*			
1971	120,000	100,000	$(120,000)	$ 100,000*	$(20,000)
1972	100,000	100,000	20,000	—	20,000
1973	80,000	80,000	20,000	(20,000)	—
1974	—	—	80,000	(80,000)	—
1975	90,000	90,000	(90,000)	90,000	—
1976	110,000	100,000	(20,000)	10,000	(10,000)
1977	—	—	110,000	(100,000)	10,000

* Initial inventory amount

| | Corporation P | | | Corporation S | Consolidated income |
	Per books	Adjustments	Adjusted		
1970	$ 90,000			$ —	**
1971	110,000	$(20,000)	$ 90,000	30,000	$120,000
1972	90,000	20,000	110,000	40,000	150,000
1973	70,000	—	70,000	30,000	100,000
1974	90,000	—	90,000	70,000	160,000
1975	80,000	—	80,000	(20,000)	60,000
1976	100,000	(10,000)	90,000	25,000	115,000
1977	90,000	10,000	100,000	85,000	185,000
Total 1971–77	$630,000	—	$630,000	$260,000	$890,000

** Returns not filed on consolidated basis

allowed as inventory adjustments) and (b) the realized income for the affiliated group has been appropriately stated on a consolidated basis in each year in which the amount of intercompany profit in the inventory is at least as large as the initial amount. The goods sold by Corporation S in 1971 for $350,000 cost Corporation P $200,000 to produce in 1970, and after deducting the expenses incurred by both corporations in 1971 aggregating $30,000, the net consolidated income is $120,000. The goods sold by Corporation S in 1972 for $420,000 cost Corporation P $240,000 to produce in 1971, and after deducting the $30,000 of 1972 expenses, the net consolidated income is $150,000. The net consolidated income for 1976 of $115,000 includes a $10,000 gain required to be recognized under Section 1.1502–18(c) (2) (ii) of the regulations. The total net consolidated income for the seven year period of $890,000 can be accounted for by the factors of sales by Corporation S ($2,800,000), costs of production incurred by Corporation P ($1,600,000, including $200,000 for the 1970 production), expenses of both corporations ($210,000), and the elimination of the $100,000 of intercompany profit in the January 1, 1971 inventory of Corporation S which was recognized in the 1970 separate return filed by Corporation P.

INVENTORY DETERMINATIONS FOR STATE TAX PURPOSES

For purposes of computing taxable income, the general policy of the states is to accept inventories as reported in federal returns. Therefore, where LIFO is used for federal tax purposes, generally its use is also accepted for state tax purposes.

More than 75% of the states and the District of Columbia impose corporate taxes on income or measured by income. Only a few of these states have specific statutes, rulings, or regulations pertaining to LIFO. Some states have incorporated the federal inventory and accounting procedures in their law and regulations by reference. Other states have their own inventory and accounting provisions which are sufficiently broad to encompass the use of LIFO, or have no specific provisions but do not take exception to LIFO. Particularly in the case of these states, it would be advisable to make specific inquiries as to local practice at the time LIFO is being adopted. In general, however, state tax authorities are primarily concerned with the allocation and apportionment of income to their respective states rather than the computation of total income or inventory determinations.

Notice and permission requirements for the use of LIFO vary among the several states, but generally follow a pattern based upon the type of provision under which the use of LIFO is authorized. States with specific provisions relating to LIFO generally require a copy of the federal election form or a similar statement. Some states which do not have specific LIFO provisions but have provisions pertaining to inventory and accounting methods treat the adoption of LIFO as a change in accounting method for which permission must be obtained from the tax authorities. Where the states have merely incorporated the federal provisions by reference, usually no notice or permission is required.

In many cases costing of inventories on a LIFO basis for federal purposes is a prerequisite to reporting on that basis in the state return. In others, if the LIFO basis is used for federal purposes, it is a mandatory basis in the state return, and in still other cases the LIFO basis is allowed for state purposes even though such method is not used in reporting income to the federal government.

The principal factors in state practices relating to LIFO are summarized in tabular form on page 429 and are discussed generally in the notes on pages 430–35.

USE OF LIFO FOR FOREIGN INCOME TAX PURPOSES

LIFO is not recognized for use in the United Kingdom, either for financial statement or income tax purposes. The tax laws of a few foreign countries permit the use of LIFO, and one enumeration includes Canada, Nationalist China, Italy, Japan, and The Netherlands in this group.[4]

The acceptability of LIFO for Canadian income tax purposes is questionable. The leading case dealing with the use of LIFO in Canada involved Anaconda American Brass Limited.[5] The case was first heard in the Exchequer Court of Canada, and a decision favorable to the taxpayer was issued on June 7, 1952. This decision was upheld on November 1, 1954, by the Supreme Court of Canada; but on further appeal to the Privy Council in London, in one of the last cases taken before that body from Canada, the decision was reversed. The Privy Council decision issued on December 13, 1955, held that LIFO was not acceptable for Canadian tax purposes.

Although the present Canadian Income Tax Act differs to some extent from the Income War Tax Act applicable to the years considered in the *Anaconda* decision, there has been no litigation under the current act and the reasoning of their Lordships is probably still applicable.

[4] MacNeill, "Accounting for Inflation Abroad," 112 *J. Accountancy* 2, 67 (Aug., 1961), where it is also observed that the base stock method is widely used in Sweden, recommended by professional accountants in Japan (although not permitted there for tax purposes), and permitted in modified form in France and Italy.
[5] *Minister of National Revenue v. Anaconda Brass, Ltd.*, 1 All E.R. 20 (P.C.), (1956).

11

Use of LIFO for
Federal Tax Purposes

A person having and exercising a right to approximately half the earnings of an enterprise is usually thought of as a *principal partner* even though he has no authority to direct the operations or even vote whether the business is to continue. The interest of such a principal partner is in the determination of income, and when a definite stand is taken as to procedural details, his authority must be respected. This is the position of the federal government. For this reason the tax laws and regulations must be considered in establishing procedures for determining the amount to be assigned to any particular inventory.

Inventory determinations for tax purposes do not have to be used for financial statements, but they usually are—primarily because the taxing statutes recognize generally accepted accounting methods, but also to avoid nonessential computations.

OUTLINE OF INVENTORY PROVISIONS OF INTERNAL REVENUE CODE

The provisions of the Internal Revenue Code relating to amounts assigned to inventories are outlined beginning on page 254.

Appendix C:

§ 1.471. The general rule is inventories are to be taken:
   A. Whenever necessary in order clearly to determine income.
   B. On such basis as is prescribed—
      1. As conforming as nearly as may be to the best accounting practice in the trade or business, and
      2. As most clearly reflecting income.

§ 1.472. Whether or not the method is prescribed under the general rule, LIFO may be used in inventorying goods provided:
   A. An application specifying the goods has been filed at such time and in such manner as prescribed by regulations.
   B. Taxpayer establishes no procedure other than LIFO has been used in inventorying the goods to ascertain the income, profit, or loss of the first LIFO taxable year for purposes of a report or statement to shareholders or other owners, or for credit purposes.
   C. In determining income for the year preceding the first LIFO year, the closing inventory of the goods is at cost.
   D. Taxpayer shall—
      1. Treat the goods remaining on hand as being: *First*, those included in the opening inventory of the year (in the order of acquisition) to the extent thereof; and *second*, those acquired in the year;
      2. Inventory the goods at cost; and
      3. Treat the goods included in the opening inventory of the first LIFO year as having been acquired at the same time and determine their cost by the average cost method.
   E. The change to, and the use of, the method is in accordance with such regulations as may be prescribed in order that income may be clearly reflected.
   F. The change to, and the use of, a *different* method for a subsequent inventory shall be in accordance with such regulations as may be prescribed in order that income may be clearly reflected, where—
      1. A change to the different method is authorized by the Secretary of the Treasury or his delegate; or
      2. The Secretary of the Treasury or his delegate:
         a) Determines that the taxpayer has used for a year subsequent to the first LIFO year some other procedure in inventorying the goods to ascertain the income, profit, or loss of such sub-

sequent year for the purpose of a report or
statement to shareholders or other owners, or
for credit purposes; and

b) Requires a change to a different method beginning with such subsequent year or any taxable
year thereafter.

The statutory provisions are not complex, but do not state how
to determine amounts to be assigned to inventories.

REQUIREMENTS OF ELECTION TO USE LIFO
FOR FEDERAL INCOME TAX PURPOSES

Reproduced on page 257 is Treasury Department Form
970. This form is technically an application for adoption and
use of LIFO, and its principal features are stipulations by the taxpayer as to:

1. The specific goods to be inventoried under LIFO.
2. The goods for which LIFO will not be used.
3. Whether any of the LIFO goods on hand at the beginning of
   the year were taken into the closing inventory of the preceding
   taxable year at values other than cost.
4. The inventory method used in ascertaining income, profit, or
   loss for the purpose of credit statements, or reports to shareholders or other owners, covering the first LIFO year.
5. Method selected to determine the cost of goods in a closing inventory in excess of the quantity in the opening inventory.
6. An agreement "to such adjustments incident to the change to
   or from the LIFO method, or to the use of such method, in
   the inventories of prior taxable years or otherwise, as the District
   Director of Internal Revenue upon the examination of the taxpayer's returns for the years involved may deem necessary in
   order to clearly reflect income."

The instructions printed on the reverse side of the application
form are as follows:

1. Attach this form, in duplicate, to your income tax return for
   the year as of the close of which the LIFO inventory method
   is first to be used.
2. State the taxable year as of the close of which the LIFO method
   is first to be used, and specify in detail the goods to which

it is to be applied. Attach an analysis of all inventories as of
the beginning and as of the end of the taxable year for which
the LIFO method is proposed first to be used, and also as of
the beginning of the preceding taxable year. Prepare this analysis in detail in accordance with sections 1.472–2 and 1.472–3 of
the regulations.

3. The taxpayer may not change to the LIFO method unless he
agrees to and makes such adjustments incident to the change
to or from such method, or incident to the use of such method,
in the inventories of prior taxable years or otherwise, as the
District Director of Internal Revenue may deem necessary to
clearly reflect income for the years involved.

4. The LIFO inventory method, once adopted, is irrevocable and
must be used in all subsequent years unless the Commissioner
requires or permits a change to another method.

5. Any taxpayer may elect to determine the cost of his LIFO inventories under the so-called "dollar-value" LIFO method, provided
that method is used consistently and clearly reflects income in
accordance with section 1.472–8 of the regulations.

Section 1.472–8(b) of the regulations sets forth the principles
for establishing the dollar-value LIFO pools of manufacturers
and processors. Subject to the provisions of that section, they
may use natural business unit pools, multiple pools, or raw materials content pools.

Section 1.472–8(c) of the regulations sets forth the principles
for establishing dollar-value LIFO pools for wholesalers, retailers,
jobbers, and distributors.

Section 1.472–8(e) of the regulations sets forth the methods of
computation of the LIFO value of a dollar-value pool. If the
"double-extension" method as described in section 1.472–8(e)(2)
of the regulations is not used for computing the value of the
dollar-value pool, a statement describing the method used must
be furnished in sufficient detail to facilitate the determination
as to whether the method used meets the standards set forth
in section 1.472–8(e)(1) of the regulations.

6. If the taxpayer is a corporation, the application must be signed
by either the president, vice-president, treasurer, assistant treasurer or chief accounting officer, or by any corporate officer
(such as tax officer) authorized to sign.

7. Identifying number.—Individuals enter their social security number; all others enter their employer identification number.

The formal application to use LIFO for federal tax purposes
is made with the *completed* income tax return and not when an

Form **970**	**Application to Use LIFO Inventory Method**
(Rev. Apr. 1969) Department of the Treasury Internal Revenue Service	(To be filed in duplicate)

Name	Identifying Number (See instruction 7)

Address (Number, street, city, State and ZIP code)

The taxpayer named above hereby applies to adopt and use the LIFO inventory method provided by section 472 of the Code. This method is first to apply as of the close of the taxable year ending .... with respect to the following specified goods (see instruction 2 and use additional sheets if necessary):

The taxpayer hereby agrees to such adjustments incident to the change to or from the LIFO method, or to the use of such method, in the inventories of prior taxable years or otherwise, as the District Director of Internal Revenue upon the examination of the taxpayer's returns for the years involved may deem necessary in order to clearly reflect income.

1. Nature of business

2. Inventory method used up to this time

3. Was the closing inventory of the specified goods at the end of the immediately preceding taxable year valued at cost as required by section 472(d) of the Code? . . . . ☐ Yes   ☐ No

4. Goods subject to inventory not to be inventoried pursuant to the LIFO method

5. (a) Did you issue credit statements, or reports to shareholders, partners, or other proprietors, or to beneficiaries, covering the first taxable year to which this application refers? . . . . ☐ Yes   ☐ No

  (b) If "Yes," to whom, and on what dates

  (c) Inventory method used in ascertaining income, profit, or loss for the purpose of such statements

6. Method used to determine the cost of the goods in the closing inventory in excess of those in the opening inventory. (See Section 1.472–2, Income Tax Regulations.)

☐ Most recent purchases   ☐ Earliest acquisitions during the year   ☐ Average cost of purchases during the year   ☐ Other—Attach explanation

7. Method used in valuing LIFO inventories—
☐ Unit method   ☐ Dollar value method

8. (a) If pools are used, list and describe contents of each pool

  (b) Describe briefly the cost system used

  (c) Method used in computing LIFO value of dollar-value pools—
     ☐ Double extension method   ☐ Other method (If other, describe and justify—see last paragraph of instruction 5.)

Signature

Under penalties of perjury, I declare that I have examined this application, including any accompanying schedules and statements, and to the best of my knowledge and belief it is true, correct, and complete.

CORPORATE SEAL		
	Date	Signature of taxpayer

Date	Signature of officer	Title

Form **970** (Rev. 4–69)

extension of time for filling is requested. It is important that the return be timely filed, because a LIFO election with a delinquent return may not be effective. Since the LIFO election need not be made until after the end of the year for which the method is first used and since it is not unusual to secure as long as a six-month extension of time for filing the "completed" return, a taxpayer can actually have the benefit of 20½ months of hindsight as regards the initial price rise to be eliminated from inventories by LIFO.

Instruction 2 on Form 970 calls for an analysis of all inventories at the beginning and end of the first LIFO year and also at the beginning of the preceding taxable year. This request is generally complied with by furnishing summaries of each of the three inventories in whatever detail is readily available. In the case of a manufacturer, however, the regulations state the analysis shall show in detail the manner in which costs are computed for raw materials, goods in process, and finished goods, segregating the products (whether in process or finished goods) into natural groups on the basis of (1) similarity in factory processes through which they pass, (2) similarity of raw materials used, or (3) similarity in style, shape, or use of finished products. Details of the manner in which costs are computed could presumably be supplied by attaching a copy of the cost accounting manual or manuals or a concise description of the procedures followed in establishing costs. In practice, however, it is customary to give only a limited description of the manner of costing.

The analysis should show each of the categories of inventories for which LIFO is elected and also each of those for which LIFO is not elected. The sum of all categories should agree with the total inventory shown in the tax return of the previous year. Where there was a writedown from cost to market at the close of the preceding year, the writedown must be added back as required by the Code and regulations.

The goods to which LIFO is being applied included in the opening inventory of the first LIFO year are to be stated at the average of their cost, and the total cost for those goods is to be used as the closing inventory in determining income for the preceding year. ". . . The actual cost of the aggregate," according to section 1.472-2(c) of Appendix C, "shall be determined pursuant to the inventory method employed by the taxpayer under the regulations applicable to the prior taxable year with the exception that restoration shall be made with respect to any writedown to market values resulting from the pricing of former inventories."

The Commissioner cannot deny the use of LIFO to any taxpayer. The manner in which it is used and the extent to which it is used (if elected for only part of the inventory by the taxpayer) are, however, subject to the Commissioner's approval. Thus the Commissioner may require LIFO to be used for other goods if in his opinion it is necessary to clearly reflect income. As an example, a taxpayer having two raw material commodities that can be used interchangeably in the process of manufacture could elect LIFO for but one. In such a situation it might be held that income can be clearly reflected only if neither or both of the commodities are on LIFO.

The general rule is that only goods which are the property of the taxpayer should be included in inventory. It is also a general rule that the LIFO method of pricing must be applied to all the goods, wherever located, which fall into the LIFO group and are the property of the taxpayer. Although this will usually be sound, situations may arise where it is undesirable or impractical and logic may justify separate pools by locations, or using LIFO for some locations and FIFO for others. For example, a retailer using LIFO for its principal operating units in New York acquired a department store in a city 500 miles away. Operations of this store were continued without interruption and for valid management reasons it was determined that LIFO should not be applied to the additional inventories. Similarly, where a manufacturer acquired a plant producing a somewhat comparable but distinct product line, and continued to operate the newly acquired business as an independent unit, continuing the use of LIFO for one plant and FIFO for the other was justified although both were in the same metropolitan area.

When, in the examination of the return for the first LIFO year, a conflict arises between the Commissioner's representatives and the taxpayer as to categories of inventories or method of application, it has been the practice of the Internal Revenue Service to permit taxpayers to return to FIFO or other prior method. This usually arises where the LIFO categories or details of application acceptable to the Service are not satisfactory to the taxpayer.

ALTERNATIVE METHODS FOR COSTING INVENTORY INCREMENTS

Form 970 requires that the taxpayer select a method for determining the cost of increases in inventories, and a method should be selected even where there are no increases in the first year for any of the goods subject to LIFO. Any proper method which in the opinion of the Commisssioner clearly reflects income is acceptable; but whatever method is adopted, it must be consistently followed in all subsequent years. A change in the method can be made only with the approval of the Commissioner.

The rules in the regulations for costing increases in inventory quantities are more specific for taxpayers engaged in the purchase and sale of merchandise (such as a retail grocer or druggist) or in the initial production and sale of goods (such as a miner selling his ore output without smelting or refining) than for those engaged in manufacturing or processing. In the case of the former group it is provided that costs of additions to inventories shall be determined as follows:

1. By reference to the actual cost of the goods most recently purchased or produced
2. By reference to the actual cost of the goods purchased or produced during the taxable year in the order of acquisition
3. By application of an average unit cost equal to the aggregate cost of all of the goods purchased or produced throughout the taxable year divided by the total number of units so purchased or produced, the goods reflected in such inventory increase being considered as having been acquired all at the same time
4. By any other proper method which, in the opinion of the Commissioner, clearly reflects income[1]

In the case of taxpayers engaged in manufacturing, fabricating, processing, or otherwise producing merchandise, it is provided that costs shall be determined for raw materials by one of the methods described above. For finished goods and for goods in

[1] Section 1.472-2 (d) (1) (i), Appendix C.

process, regardless of the stage to which manufacturing, fabricating, or processing may have advanced, costs may be determined "pursuant to any proper method which, in the opinion of the Commissioner, clearly reflects income."

The opening inventory for the year of adoption is the basic LIFO "layer." At the close of the year the quantity of goods on hand is compared with the quantity at the beginning. If there is no increase, the average cost of the basic layer is applied to the quantity at the end of the year to obtain the inventory cost. If there is an increase in quantity, such increase is treated as having been acquired during the taxable year and must be reflected at costs for the year as determined under the various methods available.

Many companies that elect to price quantity increments by reference to the actual cost of goods most recently acquired, or by reference to the actual cost of goods acquired during the taxable year in the order of acquisition, determine an average cost of acquisition for each month during which acquisitions are made, the aggregate of which equals or exceeds the increase in inventory, and then treat the quantity acquired and average cost as a single "layer" for inventory purposes.

A simple example illustrates the costing of acquisitions under the commonly used methods.

Assume purchases and average costs as follows:

	Quantities	Average cost	Amount
January............	5,000	$0.80	$ 4,000
February..........	7,500	.90	6,750
March.............	9,500	.90	8,550
April..............	4,000	.80	3,200
May..............	6,000	.90	5,400
June..............	9,000	1.00	9,000
July..............	4,500	1.00	4,500
August...........	5,500	.90	4,950
September........	6,000	1.00	6,000
October..........	6,500	1.10	7,150
November........	7,000	1.00	7,000
December.........	7,500	1.20	9,000
	78,000	.9679	$75,500

Assume an increase of 21,000 units during the first LIFO year.

I. Acquisitions stated at cost of most recent purchases or production. Months necessary to include all of increase:

	Quantities	Average cost	Amount
December.........	7,500	$1.20	$ 9,000
November........	7,000	1.00	7,000
October..........	6,500	1.10	7,150
	21,000	1.10238	$23,150

The inventory cost for the increment would be $23,150.00, that is, 21,000 times $1.10238.

Another taxpayer electing to use most recent costs might contend that his closing inventory consisted of the basic layer plus three layers representing the additions for the taxable year, which three layers would be as follows:

	Quantities	Average cost	Amount
December..........	7,500	$1.20	$ 9,000
November.........	7,000	1.00	7,000
October...........	6,500	1.10	7,150
	21,000		$23,150

Theoretically, it would be proper to price additions by individual items instead of averaging costs for even a period of a month or more. In practice, however, one average cost is frequently used (i.e., $1.10238) in preference to even separately computed monthly averages although the example in the regulations supports the use of monthly averages.

II. Acquisitions stated at cost of earliest purchases or production. Months necessary to include all of increase:

	Quantities	Average cost	Amount
January...........	5,000	$0.80	$ 4,000
February..........	7,500	.90	6,750
March.............	9,500	.90	8,550
	22,000	.8773	$19,300

The inventory cost for the increment would be $18,423.30, that is, 21,000 times $0.8773, if one average cost is used.

III. Average unit cost of all acquisitions during the taxable year.

Increase in inventory	Average cost	Amount
21,000	$0.9679	$20,325.90

Of the three methods the second is frequently advantageous from a practical standpoint, not only because it results in a lower inventory cost in case of a rising market, but also because it permits a determination early in the year of the cost at which any increment will be carried. Under the first and third alternatives this determination cannot be made until the end of the year, and this may delay the closing of the accounts.

Decreases in quantities during a taxable year are taken from the most recent acquisitions. Using the figures in the preceding illustration, if the basic layer were 100,000 units at 80 cents (that is the opening inventory when LIFO was adopted) and the quantity increase for the year of adoption was 21,000 units, and assuming at the end of the second year an inventory of 110,000 units, the closing inventory under the various methods would be as follows:

I. Acquisitions stated at cost of most recent purchases or production. Basis of costing layers by months:

	Quantities	Cost	Amount
Basic layer..............	100,000	$0.80	$80,000
First-year additions:			
December.............	7,500	1.20	9,000
November...........	2,500	1.00	2,500
	110,000		$91,500

Basis of costing which treats additions for year as one layer:

	Quantities	Cost	Amount
Basic layer..............	100,000	$0.80	$80,000
First-year increment.......	10,000	1.10238	11,024
	110,0C0		$91,024

II. Acquistions stated at cost of earliest purchases or production. Basis of costing layers by months:

	Quantities	Cost	Amount
Basic layer.............	100,000	$0.80	$80,000
First-year additions:			
January.............	5,000	.80	4,000
February............	5,000	.90	4,500
	110,000		$88,500

Basis of costing which treats additions for year as one layer:

	Quantities	Cost	Amount
Basic layer.............	100,000	$0.80	$80,000
First-year increment.......	10,000	.8773	8,773
	110,000		$88,773

III. Average unit cost of all acquistions during the taxable year.

	Quantities	Cost	Amount
Basic layer.............	100,000	$0.80	$80,000
First-year increment.......	10,000	.9679	9,679
	110,000		$89,679

Care should be used in selecting a method of costing inventory increments, and separate methods may be followed for each of the LIFO pools. In a business having consistently higher prices or costs in a particular month or months in the year than in others, the months in which costs are high should generally be avoided. A discussion of the use of the alternative procedures for costing increments where the dollar-value principle of measuring inventory quantities is applied commences on page 289.

DISCONTINUING THE USE OF LIFO

Having made the election to adopt LIFO, a taxpayer must continue its use unless prior approval to change to another method is obtained from the Commissioner. The Commissioner, however, may determine that the taxpayer has used for any taxable year subsequent to the year of adoption a method other than LIFO in ascertaining income, profit, or loss for credit purposes or for the purpose of reports to shareholders, partners or other proprietors, or to beneficiaries, and he may require the taxpayer to change to a different method for such subsequent taxable year or any taxable year thereafter. The significance of this provision where companies wish to state in their annual reports the current replacement cost of LIFO inventories is discussed on page 208; however, merely stating the replacement cost can be misleading.

If LIFO becomes disadvantageous from a practical income tax standpoint, a change to another inventory method for accounting purposes will not necessarily cause the Commissioner to insist on a change for tax purposes. Under the terms of the Code the use of a method other than LIFO gives the Secretary of the Treasury (or his delegate) the *right* to require a change to a non-LIFO method beginning with the year in which the taxpayer used an inconsistent method *or* in any taxable year thereafter. Reading the statute literally, the Internal Revenue Service appears to have unlimited discretion in picking the year when the right to use LIFO must be forfeited because of the treatment of inventories in financial statements. If this discretion were exercised in an arbitrary manner, with unreasonable hardship resulting to the taxpayer, it is doubtful the courts would sustain the action. There has been no litigation on this point.

Although a change *to* the LIFO method does not require the prior approval of the Commissioner of Internal Revenue, a change *from* LIFO to another method can be made only with prior approval. An application to change from LIFO must be filed within ninety days after the beginning of the taxable year in which the change is to be made on Treasury Department Form 3115. A discussion of changes in accounting methods begins on page 131. Permission to change will not be granted unless the taxpayer and the Commissioner agree to the terms and conditions under which the change will be effected.

Where companies have obtained permission to discontinue the use of LIFO, generally the only terms imposed by the Commissioner have been (1) that the LIFO cost of the closing inventory for the preceding year will be used as the opening inventory for the year of change and (2) that the company will again apply for permission to make a change in its method of accounting for inventories should a further change be desired, and it cannot re-elect LIFO in a subsequent year by merely filing Treasury Department Form 970 with its tax return.

Accepting, as a condition to the discontinuance of the use of LIFO, that the LIFO cost of the closing inventory for the preceding year will be used as the opening inventory for the year of change has the effect of including in the income for the year in which the change is made the entire difference between the LIFO cost and the amount at which the opening inventory would have been stated under the newly adopted method. Where the recognition of a substantial amount of income had been deferred as a consequence of using LIFO, many companies which might otherwise have changed to another method for valid business reasons were reluctant to make the change because of the immediacy of the abnormal income tax payment. To alleviate this situation Revenue Procedure 69-11 (I.R.B. 1969–9, 49) was issued by the Commissioner of Internal Revenue under which taxpayers may request that a positive adjustment resulting from the discontinuance of LIFO be spread ratably over a period of ten years. The request for permission to defer recognition of the income should be made at the same time as the Form 3115 is filed, by a statement attached to the form. This taxpayer option was effective for taxable years beginning after December 31, 1968.

SELECTING LIFO GROUPS OR POOLS

Any taxpayer owning inventories may use LIFO for federal income tax purposes, and the regulations recognize that the LIFO method is not dependent upon the character of the business in which the taxpayer is engaged, or upon the identity or want of identity through commingling of any of the goods on hand. The most important decision to be made in any specific case, however, is how the inventory is to be analyzed into LIFO "groups" or "pools" for the purpose of comparing the relative quantity of goods on hand at the end of each year.

The principal general provisions of the regulations referring to LIFO "pools"—which is the more frequently used of the two terms—may be summarized as follows:

Appendix C
§1.472–

Where a taxpayer is engaged in more than one trade or business, the Commissioner may require that if LIFO is used for goods in one business it shall also be applied to similar goods in the other, where uniform treatment is essential to a clear reflection of income.   2(i)

LIFO may be applied to types of materials, depending upon the character, quality, or price, and each type of material in the opening inventory must be compared with a similar type in the closing inventory.   1(d)

In the *cotton textile industry* there may be different raw materials depending upon marked differences in length of staple or in color or grade of the cotton. But where different staple lengths or grades are being used from time to time in the same mill to produce the same class of goods, the differences would not necessarily require classifications of raw materials.   1(e)

In the *pork packing industry* a live hog is considered as being composed of various raw materials, different cuts of a hog varying markedly in price and use. Generally a hog is processed into approximately 10 primal cuts and several miscellaneous articles; however, due to similarity in price and use, these may be grouped into fewer classifications, each group being classed as one raw material.[2]   1(f)

A *manufacturer or processor* may elect to apply LIFO to one or more types of materials and include the material in goods in process and in finished goods—commonly referred to as a material-content pool.   1(c)

A material-content pool may be limited to that phase in the manufacturing process where a product recognized generally as salable is produced. For example, in the textile industry one phase of the process is the production of yarn. In the case of copper and brass processors, the material-content pool may be limited to the material identified with the production of bars, plates, sheets, etc., although these may be further processed into other products.   1(i)

When the finished product contains two or more different materials, as in the case of cotton and rayon mixtures, each material is treated separately.   1(g)

---

[2] Pork cuts are commonly classified in four LIFO pools: (1) hams, loins, bellies, butts, and picnics; (2) spareribs, regular trimmings, and squares; (3) fat backs, plates, lard, and jowls; and (4) tails, hearts, livers, snouts, skins, bones, and hocks.

For a *manufacturer or processor* who has elected to use the dollar-value method—

A pool shall consist of all items entering into the entire inventory for a "natural business unit" unless the taxpayer elects to use "multiple pools." 8(b) (1)

Multiple pools may be established for inventory items which are not within a natural business unit pool. Each pool shall ordinarily consist of a group of items which are substantially similar. 8(b) (3) (i) (a)

Where similar goods are inventoried in both natural business unit and multiple pools, the Commissioner may apportion or allocate the goods among the pools, if necessary to clearly reflect income. 8(b) (3) (i) (a)

Materials of an unlike nature may not be pooled even though they become part of otherwise identical finished products. 8(b) (3) (i) (b)

The same class or type of finished goods and goods in process shall ordinarily be included in the same pool. Where the material used has changed (e.g., to conform with industry trends) a new pool will not ordinarily be required unless the result is a substantial change in the finished product. 8(b) (3) (i) (c)

A miscellaneous pool may be used, but it shall consist only of items which are relatively insignificant by comparison with other inventory items and are not properly includable in another pool. 8(b) (3) (i) (d)

Material-content pools may be used, but materials of an unlike nature may not be pooled even though they become part of otherwise identical finished products. 8(b) (3) (ii)

For a *wholesaler, retailer, jobber or distributor* who has elected to use the dollar-value method inventory items shall be pooled by major lines, types, or classes of goods, and for this purpose customary classifications of the particular business is *an* important consideration. In appropriate cases, however, the natural business unit pooling principles may be used. 8(c)

The section specifically describing the dollar-value method of applying LIFO, discussed in Chapter 11, was not added to the regulations until January 20, 1961. In recognition of the fact that many unsatisfactory pooling practices had developed over the years because of this deficiency, paragraph 1.472-8(h) of Appendix C provides that for the first taxable year ending after April 15, 1961, a taxpayer using the dollar-value method might change from one authorized pooling practice to another without following the general rules for effecting a change. Also for this year, a natural business unit pool could be established if a taxpayer had been using the dollar-value principle with an authorized pooling method, or a method of pooling which would be authorized if additional items were included, and could otherwise change to the use of a natural business unit pool. Except for these special situations, the pools established for the first LIFO year must be used for subsequent years unless a change is required by the Commissioner to clearly reflect income or unless permission to change is secured in advance.

Taxpayers using LIFO pools for which inventory quantities are measured in terms of pounds, gallons, yards, and so forth, may not commence the use of the dollar-value principle unless (a) steps are taken as prescribed for obtaining the consent of the Commissioner to a change in accounting method, (b) the same pools are continued, or (c) a new election is being filed to use LIFO for a portion of the inventory not covered by a prior election, and no change is contemplated for the existing LIFO inventories, by inclusion in a natural business unit pool or otherwise.

A revenue ruling (Rev. Rul. 62-77, I.R.B. 1962–21, 9) has been issued with respect to (a) changes to dollar-value LIFO inventory procedures and (b) the use of a "natural business unit" pool by a wholesaler, retailer, jobber, or distributor. The complete text of this ruling is quoted below:

> Advice has been requested as to the various circumstances under which taxpayers, particularly wholesalers, retailers, jobbers and distributors, are required to obtain the permission of the Commissioner of Internal Revenue to change to the dollar-value last-in, first-out (LIFO) inventory method, using a natural business unit pool or pools, of valuing inventories, particularly in view of the respective provisions of section 1.472–8(c), 1.472–8(f)(1), and 1.472–8(h)(1) of the Income Tax Regulations.
>
> Section 1.472–8(a) of the regulations provides, in part, that any taxpayer may elect to determine the cost of his LIFO inventories under the so-called "dollar-value" LIFO method, provided such method is used consistently and clearly reflects the income of the taxpayer in accordance with the rules of that section. The dollar-value method of valuing LIFO inventories is a method of determining cost by using "base-year" cost expressed in terms of total dollars rather than the quantity and price of specific goods as the unit of measurement. Under such method the goods contained in the inventory are grouped in a pool or pools as described in

paragraphs (b) and (c) of section 1.472-8 of the regulations with reference
to manufacturers or processors and in paragraph (c) of that section with
reference to wholesalers, retailers, etc.

Under section 1.472-8(c) of the regulations, items of inventory in the
hands of wholesalers, retailers, jobbers, and distributors, shall be placed
into pools by major lines, types, or classes of goods. In determining such
groupings, it is provided that customary business classifications of the
particular trade in which the taxpayer is engaged is an important consideration. An example of such customary business classification is the department in the department store. In such cases, practices are relatively uniform throughout the trade, and departmental grouping is peculiarly adapted
to the customs and needs of the business. However, in appropriate cases,
the principles set forth in paragraphs (b) (1) and (2) of section 1.472-8
of the regulations, relating to pooling by natural business units, may be
used by wholesalers, retailers, jobbers, or distributors with the permission
of the Commissioner.

Section 1.472-8(f)(1) of the regulations provides that, except as provided
in section 1.472-3 of the regulations, in the case of a taxpayer electing
to use a LIFO inventory method for the first time, or in the case of
a taxpayer changing to the dollar-value method and continuing to use
the same pools as were used under another LIFO method, a taxpayer
using another LIFO method of pricing inventories may not change to
the dollar-value method of pricing such inventories unless he first secures
the consent of the Commissioner in accordance with paragraph (e) of
section 1.446-1 of the regulations.

Section 1.472-8(g)(1) of the regulations provides that any method of
pooling authorized by section 1.472-8 and used by the taxpayer in computing his LIFO inventories under the dollar-value method shall be treated
as a method of accounting. Any method of pooling which is authorized
by that section shall be used for the year of adoption and for all subsequent
taxable years unless a change is required by the Commissioner in order
to clearly reflect income, or unless permission to change is granted by
the Commissioner as provided in paragraph (e) of section 1.446-1 of the
regulations. Where the taxpayer changes from one method of pooling
to another method of pooling permitted by that section, the ending LIFO
inventory for the taxable year preceding the year of change shall be restated under the new method of pooling.

Under section 1.472-8(h)(1) of the regulations, it is provided, in part,
that notwithstanding the provisions of paragraph (g) of section 1.472-8,
a taxpayer, for his first taxable year ending after April 15, 1961, may
change from one method of pooling authorized by section 1.472-8 to any
other method of pooling authorized by that section, provided the requirements of subparagraph (2) of paragraph (h) are met. Also, it is provided
that, for such year if a taxpayer is currently using only a method of
pooling which would be authorized by that section if additional items
were included in the pool, and could change to the natural business unit
method except for the fact that he has not inventoried all items entering
into the inventory investment for such natural business unit on the LIFO
method, he may change to the natural business unit method if he elects,

under the provisions of section 1.472–3, to extend the LIFO election to all items entering into the entire inventory investment for such natural business unit, provided the requirements of subparagraph (2) of that paragraph are met.

Since the natural business unit method of pooling is not an authorized method for wholesalers, retailers, jobbers and distributors without the Commissioner's prior permission under section 1.472–8(c) of the regulations, and since section 1.472–8(h) is applicable only to taxpayers changing from one authorized method of pooling to another authorized method of pooling under section 1.472–8, it is held that wholesalers, retailers, jobbers and distributors may not change from any other method of pooling to the natural business unit method without the Commissioner's prior permission.

A change from the unit or specific goods LIFO method using separate LIFO pools, to the dollar-value LIFO method, using the same LIFO pools as used under the unit or specific goods LIFO method, may be made by such a taxpayer without the Commissioner's permission under the exception provided in section 1.472–8(f)(1) of the regulations.

With respect to all taxpayers using the unit or specific goods LIFO method, nothing in sections 1.472–8(f)(1) and 1.472–8(h)(1) of the regulations permits the change from such unit or specific goods LIFO method to the dollar-value LIFO method, using a natural business pool or pools, without the Commissioner's permission for the first taxable year ending after April 15, 1961.

However, wholesalers, retailers, jobbers and distributors electing to use the dollar-value LIFO method for the first time, utilizing a method of pooling by major lines, types or classes of goods, shall do so by filing an application, Form 970, Application for the Adoption and Use of the Elective Inventory Method, and by otherwise complying with the provisions of sections 1.472–3 of the regulations. In such case the appropriateness of the method of pooling used, as well as the propriety of all computations incidental to the use of such pools, will be determined by the Commissioner through the appropriate District Director in connection with the examination of the returns of such taxpayers. See sections 1.472–3(d) and 1.472–8(d) of the regulations.

Where wholesalers, retailers, jobbers and distributors wish to use the natural business unit method of pooling in connection with a change to the dollar-value LIFO method from a method of valuation other than the LIFO method, the prior permission of the Commissioner to do so is required for any taxable year. See section 1.472–8(c) of the regulations. Such permission must be secured in accordance with section 1.446–1(e) of the regulations.

In each case where a wholesaler, retailer, jobber or distributor applies to the Commissioner for permission to change to the dollar-value LIFO method, using a natural business unit pool or pools, for valuing his inventories, he must clearly demonstrate that such natural business unit method of pooling is appropriate and clearly reflects income.

Particular attention is directed to the penultimate above-quoted paragraph holding that wholesalers, retailers, jobbers, and distribu-

X Clothing Company
Summary of Inventories at December 31, 19—

	Yards			
	Piece goods*	Stock goods	Total	Amount
Cotton goods on LIFO:				
Group I—Heavy weight	1,700,000 yds.	875,000 yds.	2,575,000 yds.	$ 417,500
II—Medium weight	1,800,000	950,000	2,750,000	305,000
III—Light weight	3,400,000	800,000	4,200,000	392,000
IV—Corduroys	5,250	5,000	10,250	4,940
	6,905,250 yds.	2,630,000 yds.	9,535,250 yds.	$1,119,440
Other yard goods on lower of FIFO cost or market:				
Wools and part wools	150,000 yds.			$ 180,000
Part rayon	100,000			65,000
Rayon	1,000,000			600,000
	1,250,000 yds.			$ 845,000†
Finished goods:				
Containing cotton piece goods:				
Total cost		2,630,000 yds.	$1,500,000	700,000
Less: Cost of material content			800,000	
				750,000†
Containing wool and rayon				700,000
Other inventory factors:				
Trim				1,000,000†
Packing				100,000†
Labor and overhead on piece goods in process				155,000
Total inventory				$4,669,440

*Yardage shown as "Piece goods" includes material in process at end of year.
† Stated on lower-of-cost-or-market basis.

Inventories on LIFO

	Group I—Heavy weight			Group II—Medium weight			Group III—Light weight			Group IV—Corduroys		
	Yards	Unit cost	Amount	Yards	Unit cost	Amount	Yards	Unit cost	Amount	Yards	Unit cost	Amount
Closing inventory layers:												
Base	2,500,000	$0.16	$400,000	1,500,000	$0.10	$150,000	3,950,000	$0.09	$355,500	9,500	$0.47	$4,465
1941	50,000	.20	10,000	1,000,000	.105	105,000	100,000	.11	11,000	250	.50	125
1942	—		—	—		—	—		—	—		—
1943	—		—	—		—	—		—	—		—
1944	25,000	.30	7,500	250,000	.20	50,000	150,000	.17	25,500	500	.70	350
	2,575,000		$417,500	2,750,000		$305,000	4,200,000		$392,000	10,250		$4,940

tors wishing to use a "natural business unit" pool cannot do so merely be stating their position in an original LIFO election, and must follow the procedure of applying in advance for permission to change an accounting method. This position of the Internal Revenue Service is based upon the statement in section 1.472-8(c) of Appendix C that, in appropriate cases, the principles relating to pooling by natural business units may be used, "with permission of the Commissioner," by wholesalers, retailers, jobbers, or distributors. Prior to the issuance of this ruling it was assumed that the required permission would be obtained if the use of a "natural business unit" pool was found to be appropriate when the LIFO procedures were reviewed in connection with an examination of the federal income tax return for the first year the method is used. There is no apparent justification for requiring wholesalers, retailers, jobbers, and distributors to anticipate a decision to elect to use LIFO and file Treasury Department Form 3115 during the first ninety days of the year.

APPLICATION OF LIFO WITH POOLING BY SPECIFIC GOODS

Where the relative volume of an inventory is not determined by application of the dollar-value principle, the procedure is commonly designated as pooling by specific goods.

In using specific goods pools, the possible combinations of items includable in a category of inventory are limited. In general only items of a homogeneous nature can be combined. It is not necessary, however, that the units of quantity represent the physical weight, measurement, or count. For many types of goods there can be combinations of items within a category by adjusting for differences of grade, so as to bring all items to common standard. This is particularly applicable where the goods are bought or sold at prices based on physical measurement but adjusted for variations in quality or chemical content.

One illustration of this principle of specific goods pooling is afforded by a manufacturer of gelatin. Gelatin is made principally from by-products of slaughterhouses and leather tanners, for example, skins, hides, and bones. By processing these materials, the manufacturer produces a salable gelatin product used in the making of photographic film, food products, pharmaceuticals, and other items. Measuring quantities in terms of pounds on hand in the various categories of raw materials, work in process, and finished stock would not produce satisfactory results. A pound of one type of raw material may yield considerably more or less gelatin than a pound of another type and have a different cost. It is practical, however, to measure the jelling consistency of the raw materials, referred to in the trade as *bloompoints*. All raw materials can thus be reduced to bloompoints, and the bloompoints contained in the in-process and finished goods can be added to those in raw materials for a material-content pool.

On page 272 is a summary analysis of the LIFO inventory of X Clothing Company, a manufacturer of shirts, work clothes, dresses, and sports attire. The company used material-content pools and classified the various types of cotton goods required in its business as heavy weight, medium weight, light weight, and corduroys. In addition to illustrating how specific goods pools may take into account similarity of character, quality, or price of each type of material, this is an example of LIFO being applied to only a portion of the total inventory. It is to be noted that the manufacturing costs for the finished goods containing cotton piece goods is stated at cost rather than the lower of cost or market. No market writedowns can be recognized as to the material content of the product, and it cannot be determined whether a writedown of finished products would be attributable to the material content or the manufacturing costs.

The principle disadvantage to pooling by specific goods is the inability to continue to avoid recognition of inflationary profits when a particular commodity for which LIFO has been elected is being displaced by another commodity either temporarily or permanently. Such displacement may occur for competitive reasons because of changes in manufacturing processes or requirements of customers, or merely because of a shortage of the raw material previously used. In many cases it is not practical to treat the new commodity as part of the old LIFO pool; so the profit previously deferred is reflected in income as the quantities of the old commodity are reduced.

12

Measuring LIFO Inventories
By Dollar-Value Principle

The possible uses of the dollar-value principle in measuring
LIFO inventories are practically unlimited, but may be illustrated
by the following descriptions of procedures, approved by representatives of the Internal Revenue Service, developed by three
machinery manufacturers prior to the 1961 additions to the regulations which favor a single inventory pool for a natural business
unit of a manufacturer or processor.[1] As emphasized in the regulations,[2] where inventories are measured by the dollar-value principle, the primary determination is an aggregate for the goods
on hand at any particular time in terms of cost levels prevailing
as of a specified base date.

Company A, a large manufacturer of heavy equipment, was
able to analyze its inventory records so as to classify the raw material on hand and the material content of the in-process and finished
goods into six pools. The materials had sufficiently common basic
characteristics to justify the assumption that price fluctuations
would be approximately the same for the items in the respective
pools. Direct labor was considered the seventh LIFO pool, and

[1] Section 1.472–8(b), Appendix C (discussed on p. 282 et seq.)
[2] Section 1.472–8(a), Appendix C.

the overhead applicable to the inventory constituted the eighth pool. In this instance the company maintained its regular accounting records on a standard cost basis, and continued to use the same standards as were in effect at the beginning of the first LIFO year. Where necessary, these standards were adjusted at that time to the then current costs for the items in the opening inventory. By use of these fixed standards and standards computed on a comparable base for new items added to the inventory, the regular accounting records provided an extension of the inventory on hand at the cost level prevailing at the basic LIFO date. A comparison of the aggregate amounts of the standard costs provided a direct measure of the relative inventory quantities at each year end. If there was an increase in any pool, the basic LIFO cost was converted to the current cost for the year of the increment by reference to the percentage of variances from standard for the current year as reflected by the variance amounts compiled under the general accounting procedures.

Company B decided to reflect current costs rather than fixed standards in the detailed accounting records and merely supplement inventory determinations at current prices to establish LIFO cost.

Physical inventories at Company B's manufacturing plants are taken annually one month prior to the end of the year, and the book inventory balances at that date are adjusted to the amounts of the physical inventories. The inventories of the manufacturing plants at the year end are book figures based upon the amount of the physical inventories adjusted for purchases, usage, and the like, during the last month. Inventories at the various sales branches are taken annually as at the year end, and the book inventory balances at that date are adjusted to the amounts of the physical inventories. The procedures followed in determining the LIFO cost for the inventories were set up to minimize special computations.

Raw materials inventories at each plant as of one month prior to the year end, based on physical inventories taken as at that date, were extended at either (a) the unit cost used for the same material in the 1950 inventory or (b) a substitute cost. In the determination of substitute costs two principal methods were used:

1. Unit costs as at the 1950 inventory date, as shown by stock records, price lists, or other information available in the purchasing department.

2. Another item of the same general type of material purchased from the same supplier was selected from the 1950 inventory and a substitute cost was computed, based on the assumption that different items of the same general type of material purchased from the same supplier would increase in cost in the same ratio.

In certain instances a general ratio between prices as at the 1950 and current inventory dates was computed for each inventory

Company B's Dollar-Value LIFO Pools

Pool	Description
I	Steel bars, shapes, and plates
	Sheet steel
	Steel pipe, pipe fittings, and tubing
	Forgings—purchased rough
II	Lumber
	Paint
	Belting
	Other direct materials
III	Tires, tubes, valve cores, and caps
IV	Bolts, nuts, screws, and other hardware
	Bearings and bushings
	Gears—purchased rough
V	Hydraulic units and parts
	Electrical equipment
	Engines and parts
VI	Foundry materials
VII	Product line A
	Material
	Labor
	Burden
VIII	Product line B
	Material
	Labor
	Burden
IX	Product line C
	Material
	Labor
	Burden
X	Domestic freight applicable to products

account and applied, by accounts, to the items which had not been included in the 1950 inventory.

A percentage was computed for each raw material pool by calculating the relationship between the total current costs as at the inventory date (book values after adjustments to reflect physical inventories) and the total dollar amount computed on the basis of 1950 or substitute costs. These percentages were applied to the total dollar amounts of the respective pools as shown by the book inventory accounts at year end to state the inventories on a 1950 cost basis.

Finished and unfinished products, represented by work in process, finished goods at plants and branches, and repair parts at plants and branches, were classified into three major product lines. The material, labor, and burden content of the inventories were established as follows:

a) *Work in process:* The regular analyses of inventories showed the material, labor, and burden content of the work in process inventories.

b) *Finished goods:* The physical inventories of finished goods at the plants were split as between material, labor, and burden on the basis of computed costs at the inventory dates. The percentage of each of the three to the total amount of finished goods was determined and the year-end book inventories were split into material, labor, and burden by use of these percentages.

c) *Repair parts:* The percentages of material, labor, and burden to total cost of repair parts produced during the year were determined, and these percentages were applied to the cost of such parts to establish the material, labor, and burden content of the repair parts inventories.

Inventories at the branches at the year end are based on physical inventories as at that date. The physical inventories of finished goods at the branches were split as between material, labor, and burden on the basis of computed costs. Repair parts at the branches were combined with the repair parts at the plants for the purposes of determining material, labor, and burden content.

A material index was computed for each plant on the basis of the relationship between the aggregate raw materials inventories at physical inventory date extended at current costs and at 1950 costs. For purposes of this computation all raw materials inventories at each plant were considered together. The indexes were used to reduce the material content of the inventories of finished and unfinished products at each plant from current costs to 1950 costs. The material-content amounts by plants were then combined to arrive at a total for each of the three major product lines.

The average labor rates per hour were determined for each plant on the basis of the number of employees in each labor grade multiplied by the timing rate for each grade. A labor index was then computed for each plant on the basis of the relationship between the average rates per hour. The indexes were used to re-

Computation of Labor Rate Index

Labor grade	Number of employees in labor grade at end of current year	Beginning of first LIFO year		End of current year	
		Timing rate per hour	Timing rate multiplied by number of employees	Timing rate per hour	Timing rate multiplied by number of employees
10	25	$1.25	$ 31.25	$1.30	$ 32.50
9	150	1.30	195.00	1.40	210.00
8	100	1.40	140.00	1.50	150.00
	275		$366.25		$392.50
Average rate per employee per hour			$ 1.33		$ 1.43
Percentage of current average rate to 1950 average rate					107.5%

duce the labor content of the inventories of finished and unfinished products at each plant from current costs to 1950 costs. The labor content amounts by plants were then combined to arrive at a total for each of the three major product lines.

The average burden rate applicable to the labor content of finished and unfinished product inventories for 1950 was determined by summarizing the labor and burden for each of the major product lines. These percentages were applied to the total labor, expressed on the basis of 1950 costs, included in the current inventories.

Domestic freight applicable to current finished product inventories (including repair parts) at the sales branches was computed by multiplying the total weight of the products by the average freight rates from the respective plants to the branches. Base-year cost was computed by multiplying the weight by the respective 1950 freight rates.

In applying the dollar-value principle, Company C, another machinery manufacturer, classified all raw materials in one pool and classified the in-process and finished goods into pools according to broad categories of end products. Since the various types of end products were manufactured in different plants, the end product classification was in general by plants. Its physical inventories were taken two months in advance of the end of the year. By pricing a substantial portion of a physical inventory at current costs and also at base-year costs, a percentage of change was secured. It was assumed that the composition of the year-end inventory was proportionately the same as at the date of the physical inventory, and that the percentage of cost change to the current year was fairly reflected by the percentage of change to the date of the physical inventory. For these computations a dual extension was made of approximately 60 per cent of the total inventory and after making this representative sampling an additional 5 per cent was extended to confirm the validity of the original computation. The fact that the percentage of cost change was not modified materially by adding the additional 5 per cent was considered an indication of the fairness of the original sampling.

Although machinery manufacturers constitute a large proportion of the users of the dollar-value principle, there are many other instances in which the method has proved helpful. Enumeration of a few will indicate the possibilities in almost any type of inventory:

Breweries: The dollar-value method has been applied in inventorying returnable bottles where for federal income tax purposes they are considered as having been sold to and repurchased from customers.

Fertilizer manufacturers: The dollar-value method has been applied in inventorying material costs and processing expenses.

Newspapers: The dollar-value method has been applied in inventorying newsprint.

Paper manufacturers: The dollar-value method has been applied in inventorying pulpwood and the pulpwood content of in-process and finished goods.

Steel manufacturers: The dollar-value method has been applied in inventorying ores, coal, and other materials as well as products.

Textile manufacturers: The dollar-value method has been applied to the material content in all stages of production and in some cases to all elements of cost.

Wholesalers of hardware and industrial and farm supplies: The dollar-value method has been applied to inventories held for resale.

Wire rope manufacturers: The dollar-value method has been applied to finished goods and in-process inventories.

A ruling by the Internal Revenue Service[3] holds that a securities "specialist" may elect to use LIFO for his inventory of unsold securities in which he is a specialist. The term "specialist" refers to a stock exchange member who accepts orders in selected securities from other members for execution.

The fact that this revenue ruling is limited to a "specialist" does not preclude the use of LIFO by other dealers who inventory unsold securities. Possibly the dealer to whom the ruling was addressed carried an inventory of only one issue of stock so that the LIFO principle could be effectively applied on the basis of the number of shares owned at the end of each taxable year, but the dollar-value principle might be used to apply LIFO to a diversified portfolio.

The income tax regulations contain a special section pertaining to inventories by dealers in securities, and its scope is indicated by the following excerpt:

. . . For the purpose of this section, a dealer in securities is a merchant of securities, whether an individual, partnership, or corporation, with an established place of business, regularly engaged in the purchase of securities and their resale to customers; that is, one who as a merchant buys securities and sells them to customers with a view to the gains and profits that may be derived therefrom. If such business is simply a branch of the activities carried on by such person, the securities inventoried as provided in this section may include only those held for purposes of resale and not for investment. Taxpayers who buy and sell or hold securities for investment or speculation, irrespective of whether such buying or selling constitutes the carrying on of a trade or business, and officers of corpora-

[3] Rev. Rul. 60–321, 1960–2 C.B. 166.

tions and members of partnerships who in their individual capacities buy and sell securities, are not dealers in securities within the meaning of this section. [Section 1.471–5, Appendix C.]

In the case of a large diversified business organization, a dealer in securities using the dollar-value principle of applying LIFO would presumably have pools by major lines, types, or classes of securities. For example, the operations of the business might be so departmentalized that three separate dollar-value pools would be appropriate for corporate stocks and stock rights, corporate bonds, and state and municipal bonds.

LIFO POOL FOR NATURAL BUSINESS UNIT

With regard to establishing dollar-value pools for inventories of manufacturers and processors, the following statements are made in the income tax regulations:

A pool shall consist of all items entering into the entire inventory investment for a natural business unit of a business enterprise, unless the taxpayer elects to use the multiple pooling method . . . Thus, if a business enterprise is composed of only one natural business unit, one pool shall be used for all of its inventories, including raw materials, goods in process, and finished goods . . . [Section 1.472–8(b)(1), Appendix C.]

The regulations wisely avoid an exact definition of "natural business unit." Certain observations are made and several examples are given, but it is stated that whether an enterprise is composed of more than one natural business unit is a matter of fact to be determined from all the circumstances. As important considerations entering into the determination are mentioned, the "natural business divisions adopted by the taxpayer for internal management purposes, the existence of separate and distinct production facilities and processes, and the maintenance of separate profit and loss records"—unless such divisions, facilities, or accounting records are set up merely because of differences in geographical location.

Comments by interested parties on the regulations as published in proposed form, directed attention to the position of a producer of a basic material marketed in part at that stage and also transferred to manufacturing plants which individually constituted a natural business unit. A question was raised as to whether all the material owned by the corporation could be included in a LIFO pool separate from those established for the business units. The answer of the Internal Revenue Service is indicated by the addition of a specific sentence in the final regulations to the effect that where similar types of goods are inventoried in two or more natural business units, the Commissioner may apportion or allocate the goods among the various units, *if he determines* that such apportionment or allocation is necessary in order to clearly reflect income. The Service appears to favor establishing inventories along the lines of natural business units but is reserving the right to reallocate inventories between business units if it is determined that some artificial allocations have been made for the purpose of minimizing reported income.

Another sentence added in the final regulations specifically provides that where a manufacturer or producer is also engaged in the wholesaling or retailing of goods purchased from others, any pooling of such purchased goods shall be determined in accordance with the stated principles relative to pools for wholesalers and retailers. This provision may have been added to cover such goods as miscellaneous accessories handled by an oil company in connection with service station operations. The inventory considered as a single pool on the basis of a natural business unit might exclude the purchased accessories. There could be a separate LIFO pool for the miscellaneous items acquired for resale or, alternatively, the miscellaneous items could be inventoried on a lower-of-cost-or-market basis. The language in the regulations should not be extended to apply to parts which may be purchased by a manufacturer for inclusion in a finished product and carried in inventory for the purpose of effecting incidental sales for replacement purposes. Replacement parts under these circumstances would be part of the total LIFO pool for the business unit.

The fact that a natural business unit pool is to include all items entering into the entire inventory investment requires careful consideration of the scope of the term "inventory" for federal income tax purposes.

. . . The inventory should include all finished or partly finished goods and, in the case of raw materials and supplies, only those which have been acquired for sale or which will physically become a part of merchandise intended for sale, in which class fall containers, such as kegs, bottles, and cases, whether returnable or not, if title thereto will pass to the purchaser of the product to be sold therein. [Section 1.471–1, Appendix C.]

On the basis of this concept it has been contended by some Treasury Department representatives that materials and supplies consumed in manufacturing operations, but which do not physically go into the articles to be sold, are not to be inventoried. If taken literally, a question could be raised as to why expenditures made for the acquisition of such items should not be written off as they are incurred; however, the common practice is to consider the cost of supplies on hand either as a deferred charge comparable to prepaid insurance or as inventory. Since it has been the custom for business generally to inventory many types of operating supplies and apply the lower-of-cost-or-market rule to them, there should be no serious question concerning the application of LIFO to those items.

The statement by the Committee on Accounting Procedure of the American Institute of Certified Public Accountants (paragraph 3 of Appendix A) specifies that the term "inventory" embraces supplies to be *consumed* directly or indirectly in production of goods or services to be available for sale.[4]

There are several industries having goods which are sometimes thought of as supplies but which can be properly treated only under the provisions for inventories. One illustration is the cement industry. Coal is used in substantial quantities by that industry for firing the kiln during the burning operation. Although a large part of the coal may be discharged through the smokestack in the form of gas, all the solid residue (the ash) becomes part of the cement. Another illustration is the steel industry, which consumes refractories in its operations. A third is the electric power industry, where huge quantities of coal are consumed for the purpose of generating steam to turn the turbines. The burning of the coal is a step in providing the energy which produces the revenue, but it could be argued that the coal does not become part of the electric energy which is sold.

---

[4] Prior to 1933 the income tax regulations provided for including in inventories "raw material and supplies on hand that have been acquired for sale, consumption or use in productive processes, together with all finished or partly finished goods." The earlier regulations were construed to permit the statement of inventories of supplies at the lower of cost or market in the case of *Aluminum Company of America v. United States* (24 F. Supp. 811 (1938)) involving the determination of tax for the calendar year 1920.

Some doubt has also been expressed as to whether or not LIFO can be applied to spare parts and supplies used for repair or construction purposes. To the extent that spare parts or supplies are capitalized, the use of LIFO would not have a material effect on the income account, as the current cost would rest in a fixed asset account and the LIFO cost would be retained in the supply account. Through depreciation income would gradually be charged with the current cost for the year of replacement. The method of accounting for parts used for maintenance purposes does, however, directly affect income, and the parts represent an essential segment of the necessary investment for the business and, from an accounting standpoint, should be included in the natural business unit pool.

Inclusion of containers, crating materials, cartons, spools, and so forth in a natural business unit pool may require the compilation of additional accounting detail. The adequacy of the procedures used for these items must be judged, however, from the standpoint of the relative significance of their possible effect upon the LIFO cost for the total inventory pool.

A somewhat unique question arises in applying the natural business unit concept to articles which are to be given away or sold at a nominal price to further the sale of the major product. Examples might include safety razors sold with a set of blades for but slightly more than the price of the blades themselves, novelties and toys sold at bargain prices at gasoline stations or with coupons packed in boxes of breakfast foods or detergents, magazines containing sewing patterns, and so forth. These items are being held for *sale* and are part of the inventory within the meaning of the federal income tax regulations.[5] Although they do have advertising value, it is doubtful that they should be considered in the same category as advertising brochures. Advertising supplies are generally accounted for as prepaid expenses or deferred charges,

---

[5] If the business is expected to operate at a profit, it is doubtful that the inventory of these items should be written down below cost; however, in the case of magazines and pamphlets containing certain sales stimuli, the cost properly allocable to the quantities on hand should be determined on a marginal basis rather than a per-unit basis after the principal portion of a particular issue has been disposed of.

but any item being offered for sale would be part of the inventory investment.

PERMISSIVE USE OF MORE THAN ONE DOLLAR-VALUE POOL

The regulations specifically state that the formulation of detailed rules for selection of pools applicable to all taxpayers is not feasible, and cover in general terms the situation in which a taxpayer elects to establish multiple pools for items not within a business unit LIFO pool. A change in language was made in the final regulations because the regulations as originally proposed were susceptible of being interpreted in such manner as to preclude the establishment of a pool for a type of goods which would be common to more than one business unit.

With respect to multiple pools as an alternative to pooling based upon business units, the following significant statements are made:

> . . . Each such pool shall ordinarily consist of a group of inventory items which are substantially similar. In determining whether such similarity exists, consideration shall be given to all the facts and circumstances. The formulation of detailed rules for selection of pools applicable to all taxpayers is not feasible. Important considerations to be taken into account include, for example, whether there is substantial similarity in the types of raw materials used or in the processing operations applied; whether the raw materials used are readily interchangeable; whether there is similarity in the use of the products; whether the groupings are consistently followed for purposes of internal accounting and management; and whether the groupings follow customary business practice in the taxpayer's industry. The selection of pools in each case must also take into consideration such factors as the nature of the inventory items subject to the dollar-value LIFO method and the significance of such items to the taxpayer's business operations. [Section 1.472–8(b)(3)(i)(a), Appendix C.]

In the regulations as issued in final form a sentence was added to the effect that where similar goods are inventoried in "natural business unit" pools and in "multiple" pools, the Commissioner may apportion or allocate such goods *if he determines* such apportionment or allocation is necessary in order to clearly reflect income. Although there is adequate basis for the Commissioner's reservation of the authority to reallocate inventories among LIFO pools,[6] such authority will presumably be used only in extreme cases, for example, where the taxpayer's computations are artificial and do not reflect an allocation of goods consistent with sound business management or are inconsistent with appropriations actually made by operating personnel.

Where the taxpayer elects not to use a single LIFO pool for a business unit, raw or unprocessed materials which are substantially similar may be pooled together, but materials of an unlike nature may not be placed in one pool merely because they become part of otherwise identical finished products.

Finished goods and goods in process in the inventory should be pooled by major classes or types of goods, and ordinarily the finished goods and goods in process will be included in the same pool. Where the material content of a class of products has been changed, for example, to confrom with current trends in an industry, a separate pool will not ordinarily be required unless the change in material content results in a substantial change in the finished product.

The practical necessity of having a miscellaneous pool is recognized in the regulations, but such a miscellaneous pool should consist only of items which are relatively insignificant in dollar value by comparison with other inventory items, and which are not properly includable as part of another pool.

The dollar-value principle may be used in conjunction with the material-content method to which specific reference has been made in the regulations since 1944. The general intent of the section added to the regulations in January, 1961, appears to be to permit continuation of LIFO dollar-value pooling methods where the company does not elect to use a single pool for the inventory investment of a natural business unit.

---

[6] Section 1.472(a) of Appendix C provides that the use of LIFO "shall be in accordance with such regulations as the Secretary or his delegate may prescribe as necessary in order that the use of such method may clearly reflect income." Further, the LIFO election (Form 970) contains an agreement by the taxpayer to adjustments incident to the use of such method "as the District Director of Internal Revenue upon the examination of the taxpayer's returns . . . may deem necessary in order to clearly reflect income."

MEASURING COST-LEVEL CHANGES

Except for taxpayers entitled to use retail price indexes prepared by the Bureau of Labor Statistics the regulations state that only the so-called double-extension method may ordinarily be used in measuring cost-level changes for the purpose of applying the dollar-value principle to a LIFO inventory pool.

Where the total base-year cost of a LIFO inventory pool at the end of a year does not exceed the corresponding total for the pool at the beginning of the year, there is no need for the total current-year cost. The LIFO cost for the ending inventory is merely a carryforward of all or some portion of the LIFO cost for the beginning inventory. If the total base-year cost of the ending inventory is greater than the corresponding total for the beginning inventory an additional cost figure must be computed. The general rule is that the LIFO cost for an inventory increment is determined by multiplying the amount of the increment measured in terms of base-year cost by the ratio of the total current-year cost of the pool to the total base-year cost of the pool.

In each case, therefore, it is necessary to determine the feasibility of extending inventories at *base-year costs* and *current-year costs* if needed because of increments.

Although considerable emphasis is placed upon the double-extension method, it is clear there is a need for an index or for more than one extension of even a portion of an inventory only if (*a*) there is an increment in the inventory pool during the year or (*b*) the complete extension of the inventory is at current-year costs rather than at base-year costs. Consequently, there are advantages from adopting accounting procedures under which extensions at base-year costs are the initial determinations. In such cases Treasury Department representatives are interested in the indexes used only to the extent they enter into the computation of the LIFO cost for the portion of the inventory representing an increment for the year. Indexes used to estimate the current cost for internal management purposes would not be significant for tax purposes.

The *base-year cost* for an inventory item is generally its cost as determined at the beginning of the taxable year for which LIFO was first adopted. For an item entering a pool for the first time subsequent to the beginning of the base year, the base-year cost may be established in any number of ways:

1. The taxpayer using reasonable means may determine what the cost of the item would have been had it been in existence in the base year.
2. The taxpayer using available data or records may determine what the cost of an item in existence on the base date would have been had he stocked the item.
3. If the taxpayer does not reconstruct or establish a base-year cost, but does reconstruct or establish the cost for some subsequent year, the earliest cost which is reconstructed or established may be used as the base-year cost for the item. [Section 1.472–8(e)(2)(iii), Appendix C.]

The examples of acceptable procedures set forth in the regulations do not preclude the use of other procedures appropriate in particular cases. The exercise of judgment is clearly contemplated.

The *current-year cost* of the items making up a pool may be determined under the specific provisions of the regulations as follows:

1. By reference to the actual cost of the goods most recently purchased or produced;
2. By reference to the actual cost of the goods purchased or produced during the taxable year in the order of acquisition;
3. By application of an average unit cost equal to the aggregate cost of all of the goods purchased or produced throughout the taxable year divided by the total number of units so purchased or produced; or
4. Pursuant to any other proper method which, in the opinion of the Commissioner, clearly reflects income. [Section 1.472–8(e)(2)(ii), Appendix C.]

The full meaning of the alternative of "any other proper method" is not readily apparent, but it does permit accounting procedures which involve some variation from the general statements of how current-year cost is to be computed. These procedures for establishing current-year costs represent one approach to adapting the dollar-value principle to the methods for costing inventory increments discussed in the section starting on page 260.

Complete double extensions are frequent in the case of relatively small inventories and sometimes in the case of large companies; however, complete double extension of an inventory is not practical in the majority of instances.

Businesses using the dollar-value principle are generally those having on hand at all times a wide variety of materials and a large number of items, parts, subassemblies and products. Further, the items required are constantly changing. Among the characteristics of a competitive economy is the constant endeavor to provide customers with a better product at a lower price. The materials used may be changed because of variations in public taste (e.g., heavy work clothing has been replaced to a large extent by garments made of lighter-weight materials and sports-type garments), because of improved manufacturing techniques (e.g., machines are constantly being developed which can process a lighter or less expensive metal), or because of limitless other factors. End products and individual component parts are being changed all the time, and most business units maintain market research and engineering specialists to further these changes.

Where the "double extension" method is not used in applying the dollar-value principle to LIFO inventories, the more frequently encountered alternative procedures for measuring the relative quantity of goods included in an inventory and the current cost for an increment are as follows:

1. Measuring the relative quantity of goods on hand by applying to the total current cost of the inventory:
    a) An index developed by double-extending less than all of the items
    b) An index developed from published statistics
    c) An index developed by double-extending all or a portion of each inventory at current-year costs and at costs for a year subsequent to the base year
    d) A link-chain index developed by double-extending all or a portion of each inventory at beginning-of-year and end-of-year costs and computing a cumulative index
2. Establishing the current cost for an inventory increment by applying to the amount of the increase measured in terms of base-year cost:
    a) A ratio developed by comparing current-year acquisition costs with extensions at base-year costs for quantities ac-

quired during the year rather than for quantities in the year-end inventory

b) A ratio developed by comparing the amount of the total current-year cost as computed for the closing inventory of the preceding year with the amount of the total base-year cost for that inventory

c) A ratio developed by comparing the amount of the total current-year cost as computed for the physical inventory taken in advance of the end of the year with the amount of the total base-year cost for that inventory.

All the foregoing procedures will result in income being clearly reflected under appropriate circumstances and others not referred to may be equally acceptable. The primary test which has been stated in the regulations since 1949 is that the method of computation be established to the satisfaction of the Commissioner as "reasonably adaptable to the purpose and intent" of LIFO.[7] The general rules added to the regulations in 1961 are not absolute, and accounting procedures must take into consideration the practicability of compiling basic data.

Because LIFO determinations are dependent upon a comparison of inventories at the beginning and end of the year without regard to interim fluctuations, many businesses electing LIFO continue to maintain their accounting records on a FIFO basis. This means that the starting point for year-end LIFO computations is the total current cost for the goods on hand. The relative quantity of goods represented by the inventory can be established under these circumstances by applying to the total current cost an index developed by double-extending less than all the items. The mechanics of this type of computation can be illustrated by assuming an inventory for which the total current cost is $1 million. The quantities on hand of items having an aggregate current cost of $600,000 are extended at base-year costs and found to have an aggregate base-year cost of $500,000. This produces an index of 120 per cent, that is $600,000/$500,000. The total base-year

[7] A discussion of the purpose and intent of LIFO is included in a memorandum entitled "Pooling of LIFO Inventories by Use of Dollar-Value Method" prepared by Carman G. Blough, Samuel J. Broad, and Robert M. Trueblood, and submitted to the Treasury Department under date of Feb. 23, 1960. See 110 *J. Accountancy* 1, 77 (July 1960).

cost for the inventory is then established at $833,333 by dividing $1,000,000 by 120 per cent.

Generally, it is not difficult to establish the extent to which double extensions need to be made to construct a valid index to be applied to the total of any particular inventory. Depending upon the types of goods included in the inventory, a valid index can frequently be determined by extending quantities which represent just the major items. In the aggregate these items may represent a small fraction of the total value of the inventory, but where the remaining items are relatively unimportant individually and are generally similar in character to the major items, there is little likelihood that the conversion index would be modified significantly by expanding the volume of the double extensions. It is not practical to specify a percentage of inventory which should be double extended because the circumstances will vary in each instance. Ordinarily an extension of as much as fifty per cent of an inventory will result in a valid conversion index provided no single material item is omitted which would obviously affect the result.

In some cases the volume of the inventory items is so great that it is not practical to compute an index by even partial double-extension. Where the items fall within a distinct class of goods for which published statistics are available, a valid index may be obtained without making any individual extensions at base-year costs. Where such an index is used, the burden is on the taxpayer to establish that the statistics are appropriate. If the index is based upon data secured from the Department of Labor or other governmental agency, the taxpayer avoids the necessity of proving the consistent use of acceptable statistical methods in the basic compilations. Occasionally the Bureau of Labor Statistics has assisted taxpayers in establishing an index to be applied to their particular inventories. This procedure can generally be used only where the character of the inventories makes it practical to obtain the relative aggregate weight of the items on hand falling within established Wholesale Price Index groupings. With this information it is possible to compute an index reflecting a weighted average of all the product classes represented in the inventory.

Where base-year costs can be used as standard costs in the

accounting records, it is possible in some cases to compile information which is significant for management purposes as well as for making LIFO computations.   Over the years, however, the number of theoretical base-year costs increases because of changes in the components of the inventory pool and the base-year cost amounts lose their utility.   For this reason the standard costs must be revised periodically—after the elapse of five, eight, or ten years, depending upon the circumstances—and the relative quantity of the goods in subsequent inventories can be measured for LIFO purposes by using these unit costs in place of the original base-year costs.   The principle underlying this type of revision of base-year costs is recognized in section 1.472–8(g) (3) of Appendix C.   For some situations it is specifically provided that a later year may be used as the base year instead of the earliest year for which LIFO was adopted for items in a pool.

The transition to the use of later unit costs as base-year costs requires the extension of at least the major portion of one inventory at both the old and the new costs.   The mechanics of developing a revised index are shown on page 294 by a simplified example in which it is assumed that the total for an inventory at December 31, 1961, was $305,500 when extended at 1949 base-year costs and $600,000 when extended at current costs.   It will be noted that the originally established LIFO cost for each segment of the inventory is carried forward unchanged so long as it remains intact.   The conversion factors are actually used only when a segment has been partially liquidated.

One of the techniques developed to cope with the ever changing character of inventories is the link-chain index.   Under this procedure the change in cost levels is measured first on an annual basis, and then the cumulative change is reflected by multiplying the annual index and the last previously determined cumulative index.   This is the procedure used in compiling the Bureau of Labor Statistics, Department Store Inventory Price Indexes approved by the Treasury Department for the computation of LIFO inventories by retail stores.

A simplified example of the mechanics of the link-chain index is set forth on pages 296–97.   For the purpose of this example the following assumptions have been made:

Mechanics for Using Current Costs as Base-Year Costs

Inventory at December 31, 1961, using original base-year costs:

	Extensions at Dec. 31, 1949, unit costs	Conversion factor	LIFO cost
1949 base	$ 30,500	100%	$ 30,500
Increments:			
1950	40,000	110	44,000
1956	200,000	180	360,000
1959	5,000	200	10,000
1960	30,000	185	55,500
Total	$305,500		$500,000

Proration of total December 31, 1961, cost:

	Extensions at Dec. 31, 1949, unit costs		Proration of extensions at Dec. 31, 1961, unit costs
	Amount	%	
1949 base	$ 30,500	10	$ 60,000
Increments:			
1950	40,000	13	78,000
1956	200,000	65	390,000
1959	5,000	2	12,000
1960	30,000	10	60,000
Total	$305,500	100	$600,000

Using revised base-year costs:

	Extensions at Dec. 31, 1961, unit costs	Conversion factor	LIFO cost
1949 base	$ 60,000	51%	$ 30,500
Increments:			
1950	78,000	56	44,000
1956	390,000	92	360,000
1959	12,000	83	10,000
1960	60,000	93	55,500
Total	$600,000		$500,000

Inventory at December 31, 1962:

	Extensions at Dec. 31, 1961, unit costs	Conversion factor	LIFO cost
1949 base	$ 60,000	51%	$ 30,500
Increments:			
1950	78,000	56	44,000
1956	390,000	92	360,000
1959	12,000	83	10,000
1960	45,000	93	41,850
Total	$585,000		$486,350

1. The inventory for the business unit consisted of just two items at the beginning of the first year for which LIFO was used—10 units of Item A and 5 units of Item B.

2. Item A was maintained at a constant level of 10 units; however, over a three-year period Item C was substituted for Item B, even though an aggregate of 5 units was constantly maintained for Items B and C.

Simplified Inventories Extended at Alternative Cost Levels for Purpose of Illustrating Mechanics of Dollar-Value LIFO Computations

	Goods on hand measured in terms of					
	Current unit costs		Base-year unit costs		Beginning-of-year unit costs	
	Per unit	Total	Per unit	Total	Per unit	Total
First year:						
Opening inventory:						
Item A—10 units.......	$50	$500				
Item B— 5 units.......	10	50				
Item C— – units.......	12	—				
		$550				
Closing inventory:						
Item A—10 units.......	$52	$520	$50	$500	$50	$500
Item B— 4 units.......	12	48	10	40	10	40
Item C— 1 unit........	14	14	12	12	12	12
		$582		$552		$552
Second year:						
Closing inventory:						
Item A—10 units.......	$55	$550	$50	$500	$52	$520
Item B— 2 units.......	13	26	10	20	12	24
Item C— 3 units.......	16	48	12	36	14	42
		$624		$556		$586
Third year:						
Closing inventory:						
Item A—10 units.......	$60	$600	$50	$500	$55	$550
Item B— – units.......	15	—	10	—	13	—
Item C— 5 units.......	16	80	12	60	16	80
		$680		$560		$630

| | Computations using base-year unit costs | | |
| | Goods on hand measured in terms of base-year unit costs | | LIFO inven- |
	Total Segments	Conversion index	tory cost
First year (closing inventory):			
Total goods on hand................	$552		
Goods included in opening inventory..	550	$550	1.00(a)	$550.0
Goods acquired during year.........	$ 2	2	1.00(b)	2.0
LIFO inventory cost................				$552.0
Second year (closing inventory):			
Total goods on hand..............	$556		
Goods included in opening inventory..	552	{ 550	1.00	$550.0
		2	1.00	2.0
				$552.0
Goods acquired during year.........	$ 4	4	1.054(c)	4.2
LIFO inventory cost................				$556.2
Third year (closing inventory):			
Total goods on hand..............	$560		
Goods included in opening inventory..	556	(550	1.00	$550.0
		2	1.00	2.0
		4	1.054	4.2
				$556.2
Goods acquired during year.........	$ 4	4	1.122(d)	4.4
LIFO inventory cost................				$560.7

Explanation of Factors Designated "Conversion Index" in Illustration Above

(a) LIFO cost of basic segment is 550/550 (or 1.00) times actual cost of openin inventory for first year.

(b) LIFO cost of first-year increment is 1.00 times the quantity measured in term of base-year unit costs because the relationship of the aggregate of the extension of the opening inventory for the first year (550/550, or 1.00) establishes acquisition cos

(c) LIFO cost of second-year increment is 1.05435 times the quantity measure in terms of base-year unit costs because the relationship of the aggregate of th extensions of the opening inventory for the second year (582/552, or 1.05435) estab lishes acquisition cost.

(d) LIFO cost of third-year increment is 1.1223 times the quantity measured i terms of base-year unit costs because the relationship of the aggregate of the exte sions of the opening inventory for the third year (624/556, or 1.1223) establishe acquisition cost.

(e) Goods on hand measured in terms of base-year unit costs at end of first yea has been determined by direct computation, giving a factor of 552/552, or 1.00.

(f) Goods on hand measured in terms of base-year costs at end of second yea is 0.94845 times the quantity measured in terms of beginning-of-year unit costs becaus the relationship of the aggregate of the extensions of the opening inventory for th

ollar-Value LIFO Computations

Computations using beginning-of-year unit costs and link-chain index

Goods on hand measured in terms of beginning-of-year unit costs	Conversion index	Goods on hand measured in terms of base-year costs		Conversion index	LIFO inventory cost
		Total	Segments		
$552	1.00(e)	$552.00			
550		550.00	$550.00	1.00(a)	$550.00
$ 2		$ 2.00	2.00	1.00(b)	2.00
					$552.00
$586	0.94845(f)	$555.79			
582		552.00	{ 550.00	1.00	$550.00
			2.00	1.00	2.00
					$552.00
$ 4		$ 3.79	3.79	1.054(h)	4.00
					$556.00
$630	0.89069(g)	$561.13			
			550.00	1.00	$550.00
624		555.79	2.00	1.00	2.00
			3.79	1.054	4.00
					$556.00
$ 6		$ 5.34	5.34	1.123(i)	6.00
					$562.00

econd year (552/582, or 0.94845) establishes the cost-level change of the first year.

(g) Goods on hand measured in terms of base-year costs at end of third year is 89069 times the quantity measured in terms of beginning-of-year unit costs because e relationship of the aggregate of the extensions of the opening inventory for the ird year at second year's beginning unit costs and at current unit costs (586/624, r 0.9391) establishes the cost-level change during the second year, and this factor ultiplied by the factor for the prior year establishes the cost-level change through e second year (0.9391 × 0.94845, or 0.89069).

(h) LIFO cost of second-year segment is 1.05435 times the quantity measured in erms of base-year costs because the relationship of the aggregate of the extensions f the opening inventory for the second year (582/552, or 1.05435) establishes the ost-level change during the first year and the acquisition cost.

(i) LIFO cost of second-year segment is 1.1227 times the quantity measured in terms f base-year costs because the relationship of the aggregate of the extensions of the pening inventory for the third year at current unit costs and at second year's beginning nit costs (624/586, or 1.06485) establishes the cost-level change during the second ear, and this factor multiplied by the factor for the prior year establishes the cost-level hange through the second year (1.06485 × 1.05435, or 1.1227) and the acquisition ost.

3. A theoretical cost for Item C as of the beginning of the first year has been computed although none was actually included in the inventory.

4. The cost of the goods in the closing inventory in excess of those in the opening inventory of the year is determined by reference to the year's acquisitions in the order thereof, and the current costs for the inventory at the close of the preceding year reflects such acquisition costs.

It will be noted that in this illustration the inventory determinations are substantially the same whether the computations use the base-year unit costs or use the beginning-of-the-year unit costs and a link-chain index. In view of the fact that larger differences could result under certain circumstances, however, consideration must be given to whether one method can be said to be more appropriate in implementing the determination of the annual income of a business.

A procedure whereby the quantity of goods in each inventory is measured by using unit costs as of the beginning of the year for which LIFO was initially adopted is comparable to the mechanics of computations which do not involve the dollar-value principle, that is, where the inventories are measured in units such as gallons, pounds, or yards rather than dollars as reflected by extensions of physical quantities at unit costs prevailing at a particular date. The procedure cannot be said to be wrong, but neither can it be said to be the only proper method of applying LIFO. It becomes increasingly difficult in application as time goes by because more theoretical costs have to be computed for new items not represented in the basic inventory, and the comparisons are between what the aggregate cost would have been had the goods included in the opening and closing inventories for the year been on hand at the basic date. The full impact of a change in inventory mix between items, for which the unit cost has fluctuated differently during the period that LIFO has been used, is reflected in the income of the year in which the change in mix occurs.

The LIFO section of the Internal Revenue Code stipulates the taxpayer shall treat those goods remaining on hand at the close of the taxable year as being: first, those included in the opening inventory of the taxable year (in the order of acquisition) to the extent thereof; and second, those acquired in the taxable year.

Under the dollar-value principle it can be argued that a better comparison of the relative quantity of goods on hand at the beginning and end of any particular year can be made by extending both inventories at beginning-of-the-year unit costs than by comparing extensions at base-year unit costs. Differences in the two comparisons as illustrated in the example on pages 296–97 are as follows:

1. There is no change in the computation of the closing inventory for the first year.

2. In the second year two units of Item C were substituted for Item B, and

   a) In the computation using base-year unit costs, the quantity of goods on hand increased $4 in terms of base-year costs. The $4 increase is attributable to the fact that the cost of Item C as of the basic date was $12—$2 per unit more than the concurrent cost of Item B. The conversion index measured by reference to the total inventory (1.054) is applied to include the additional goods in the LIFO cost at $4.22.

   b) In the computation using beginning-of-the-year unit costs and a link-chain index, the quantity of goods on hand increased $4 in terms of the beginning-of-year costs. The $4 increase is attributable to the fact that the cost of Item C as of the beginning of the second year was $14—$2 more than the concurrent cost of Item B. The conversion is made in a manner which reflects the actual additional cost of $4 in the LIFO cost.

3. In the third year two additional units of Item C were substituted for Item B, and

   a) In the computation using base-year unit costs, the quantity of goods on hand increased $4 in terms of base-year costs. The $4 increase is again attributable to the fact that the cost of Item C as of the basic date was $12—$2 per unit more than the concurrent cost of Item B. The conversion index measured by reference to the total inventory (1.122) is applied to include the additional goods in the LIFO cost at $4.49.

   b) In the computation using beginning-of-the-year unit costs and a link-chain index, the quantity of goods on hand increased $6 in terms of the beginning-of-the-year costs. The $6 increase is attributable to the fact that the cost of Item C as of the beginning of the third year was $16—$3 more than the concurrent cost of Item B. The conversion is made in a way that reflects the actual cost of $6 in the LIFO cost.

It will be noted that in the computations using beginning-of-the-year unit costs and a link-chain index, the increment in the quantity of goods is included in the LIFO costs at the actual cost of the increment. In both cases the quantity of goods in the closing inventory to the extent of the goods on hand at the beginning of the year is included in the LIFO cost at the amount attributed thereto in the prior inventory. The link-chain method conforms, therefore, with the explicit requirement of the statute.

Permitting the use of the alternative amounts for current-year costs, discussed on page 289, is recognition of the various procedures for costing inventory increments. Only in the exceptionally simple case, however, would it be practical to extend the closing inventory quantities at the cost of the first acquisitions during the year for a comparable quantity on an item-by-item basis. Similarly, it is unrealistic to contemplate establishing a current-year cost for each item by computing the average cost for the entire year's acquisitions. It seems doubtful that any company would know the total current-year cost of its closing inventory under either of these methods, and the effect upon income of using one of these procedures for costing an increment rather than more practical alternatives would not justify the expense of making an additional extension of the inventory.

There is no implication in the regulations that the use of per unit current-year costs for the inventory items is the only way in which the cost of increments can be computed. Doubtless procedures similar to those described on pages 290–91 will be generally adopted, but technically their use constitutes a variation from the complete double-extension method.

The regulations provide, "Where the use of the double-extension method is impractical, because of technological changes, the extensive variety of items, or extreme fluctuations in the variety of the items, in a dollar-value pool, the taxpayer may use an index method for computing all or part of the LIFO value of the pool. An index may be computed by double-extending a representative portion of the inventory in a pool or by the use of other sound and consistent statistical methods." A taxpayer using an index method must be able to demonstrate to the satisfaction of revenue agents in connection with the examination of his tax returns the appropriateness of the method of computing the index and the suitability of the use of the index.

The regulations further provide, "The use of any so-called 'link-chain' method will be approved for taxable years beginning after December 31, 1960, only in those cases where the taxpayer can demonstrate to the satisfaction of the district director that the use of either an index method or the double-extension method would be impractical or unsuitable in view of the nature of the pool." As with an index method, a taxpayer *may* request the Commissioner's office to approve in advance the appropriateness of the link-chain method; however, advance approval is not mandatory.

The regulations impose an additional requirement if the complete double-extension method is not used:

> . . . A taxpayer using either an index or link-chain method shall attach to his income tax return for the first taxable year beginning after December 31, 1960, for which the index or link-chain method is used, a statement describing the particular link-chain method or the method used in computing the index. The statement shall be in sufficient detail to facilitate the determination as to whether the method used meets the standards set forth in this subparagraph. In addition, a copy of the statement shall be filed with the Commissioner of Internal Revenue, Attention: T:R, Washington 25, D.C. The taxpayer shall submit such other information as may be requested with respect to such index or link-chain method. Adequate records must be maintained by the taxpayer to support the appropriateness, accuracy, and reliability of an index or link-chain method. A taxpayer may request the Commissioner to approve the appropriateness of an index or link-chain method for the first taxable year beginning after December 31, 1960, for which it is used. Such request must be submitted within 90 days after the beginning of the first taxable year beginning after December 31, 1960, in which the taxpayer desires to use the index or link-chain method, or on or before May 1, 1961, whichever is later. [Section 1.472–8(e)(1), Appendix C.]

Although decisions to elect LIFO are generally made only at the end of the year, this provision in the regulations requires that, if a complete double extension is not to be made and advance approval of the Commissioner's office is desired, a request for approval of the contemplated statistical index method be filed during the first ninety days of the initial LIFO year.

CHANGING SPECIFIC GOODS POOLS TO DOLLAR-VALUE POOLS

When a change is made to a LIFO inventory procedure based upon the dollar-value principle after some other procedure has been in use for some time, there is commonly occasion to combine a number of the previously established pools. Further, it is frequently appropriate, incidental to the change, to include in a dollar-value LIFO pool one or more classes of items for which the cost has been computed under the FIFO assumption as to flow of costs.

The primary consideration in this type of change-over is that the dollar amounts assigned to the opening inventory for the year are not to be modified or adjusted. Similarly, the cost attributable to each segment of the LIFO inventory will remain the same.

The only change which is being made as a matter of basic principle is that the quantity of goods on hand at the respective inventory dates is to be measured in terms of dollars by applying to the various items the unit costs applicable thereto as of a specific date rather than in terms of tons, gallons, yards, and so forth. The date chosen for this purpose has little significance in considering the appropriateness of the computations. It should be the date which is the most practicable in each individual case, and it will generally be either the beginning of the year LIFO was first used or the beginning of the year the change in procedure is being effected.

The computations required in making the change in inventory procedure include:

1. A recapitulation of costs assigned to the various segments of the opening inventory by years of acquisition.
2. A statement of the quantity of goods represented by the various segments of the opening inventory expressed in terms of the unit costs adopted for the purpose of comparing future inventory quantities.
3. A set of conversion factors, determined from the computations referred to in (1) and (2), required to assign to the corresponding segments of future inventories included in the dollar-value LIFO pool, the same costs as have been previously established.

The complexity of these computations will depend primarily upon the number of different items included in the previously established LIFO pools and the ability to obtain unit costs for the various items as of the selected date. The difficulties involved in obtaining accurate unit costs as of an earlier date generally make it more practical, and in some instances absolutely necessary, to use unit costs as of the beginning of the year in which the change in procedure is being effected.

A previously established LIFO pool may include items which have a range of unit costs, and it will not be possible to extend the pounds included in each inventory layer on a precise item basis. For example, where different staple lengths or grades of cotton are used at different times in the same mill to produce the same class of goods, the cotton may have been inventoried as a single LIFO pool measured in terms of pounds. As demonstrated by the following illustration, only the average cost of the goods included in such a pool as of the selected inventory date can be used under these circumstances because it is impossible to identify the individual items accounting for a specific segment of the inventory:

	Quantities in inventory at	
	Beginning of year	End of year
Grade 1.........	10x lb.	7x lb.
Grade 2.........	3x	7x
Grade 3.........	7x	11x
Total.......	20x lb.	25x lb.

The quantity of goods in this inventory pool increased $5x$ lb., but it cannot be said that the increase is attributable to Grade 2 or Grade 3, or any particular combination of the two. The inventory at the end of the year contains $4x$ lb. more of both Grade 2 and Grade 3 than did the inventory at the beginning of the year.

The federal income tax regulations (section 1.472–8(f)(2) of Appendix C) contain an example intended to illustrate the mechanics of changing to a LIFO inventory procedure based upon the dollar-value principle. This example does not, however, expressly recognize differing grades of goods within any of the previously established pools. It either assumes there are no differences between the units within a pool or is intended specifically to recognize that an average unit cost as of the date LIFO was first adopted is to be used.

One alternative to using an average unit cost for the various pools as of the date LIFO was first adopted is illustrated below by computations for ABC Company which give recognition to the existence of various grades within each pool, using unit costs as of the beginning of 1962, the year in which the dollar-value principle is first applied.

Analysis of December 31, 1961, Inventory of ABC Company

1. Recapitulation of LIFO costs by years of inventory acquisition:

	1954 base	Increments 1955	Increments 1956	Increments 1961
Item A	$ 100	$ 400	$ 400	$ 600
Item B	1,800	800		500
Item C	4,000	1,200	2,400	
	$5,900	$2,400	$2,800	$ 1,100
Total LIFO cost				$12,200

2. Statement of quantity of goods represented by LIFO layers, expressed in terms of unit costs adopted for the purpose of comparing future inventory quantities:

December 31, 1961, inventory at current costs—

	Quantity	Dec. 31, 1961, unit cost	Amount
Item A:			
Grade 1	300	$ 5.75	$ 1,725
Grade 2	200	6.10	1,220
Total	500		$ 2,945
Average		5.89	
Item B:			
Grade 1	250	10.00	$ 2,500
Grade 2	100	10.50	1,050
Grade 3	100	9.75	975
Total	450		$ 4,525
Average		10.06	

Item C:

Grade 1	700	9.00	$ 6,300
Grade 2	150	9.50	1,425
Grade 3	250	8.70	2,175
Grade 4	400	9.25	3,700
Total	1,500		$13,600
Average		9.07	
Total December 31, 1961, value			$21,070

Segments of December 31, 1961, inventory—
Quantities:

	1954 base	Increments		
		1955	1956	1961
Item A..................	100	200	100	100
Item B..................	300	100		50
Item C..................	1,000	200	300	

Extensions at average of 1961 costs:

	1954 base	Increments		
		1955	1956	1961
Item A ($ 5.89)	$ 589	$1,178	$ 589	$ 589
Item B ($10.06)	3,018	1,006		503
Item C ($ 9.07)	9,070	1,814	2,721	
	$12,677	$3,998	$3,310	$ 1,092
Total December 31, 1961, value				$21,077

3. Conversion factors for assigning to corresponding segments of future inventories the previously established LIFO costs:

	Dec. 31, 1961, values	Conversion factor	LIFO cost
Segments of 1961 inventory—			
1954 base	$12,677	46.54%	$ 5,900
Increments:			
1955	3,998	60.03	2,400
1956	3,310	84.59	2,800
1961	1,092	100.73	1,100
Total	$21,077		$12,200

On the basis of the foregoing, the LIFO cost for the inventory at December 31, 1962, would be determined as follows:

Computation of LIFO Cost for December 31, 1962, Inventory of ABC Company

	1962 inventory quantities extended at Dec. 31, 1961, unit costs		
	Quantity	Unit cost	Amount
Item A:			
Grade 1	400	$ 5.75	$ 2,300
Grade 2	250	6.10	1,525
Item B:			
Grade 1	378	10.00	3,780
Grade 2	110	10.50	1,155
Grade 3	200	9.75	1,950
Item C:			
Grade 1	500	9.00	4,500
Grade 2	10	9.50	95
Grade 3	300	8.70	2,610
Grade 4	100	9.25	925
			$18,840

	Dec. 31, 1961, values	Conversion factor	LIFO cost
Segments of 1962 inventory:			
1954 base	$12,677	46.54%	$ 5,900
Increments:			
1955	3,998	60.03	2,400
1956	2,165	84.59	1,831
Total	$18,840		$10,131

Unit costs as of the beginning of the year in which LIFO was first adopted could similarly be used, but that procedure is generally not practicable because earlier costs are seldom available for each of the individual items in the current and future inventories.

The mechanics of changing to a procedure based upon the dollar-value principle where additional items are included in the pool and where it is practicable to determine unit costs as of the beginning of the year in which LIFO was first adopted may be illustrated by the XYZ Company.

Analysis of December 31, 1961, Inventory of XYZ Company

1. Recapitulation of LIFO costs by years of inventory acquisition:

| | 1949 base | Increments | | |
		1953	1957	1961
Commodity W	$400	$10	$	$ 10
Commodity X	150		120	
Commodity Y	4	1		5
Commodity Z				400*
	$554	$11	$120	$ 415
Total LIFO cost				$1,100

* Commodity Z was not part of the LIFO inventory prior to 1962.

2. Statement of quantity of goods represented by the LIFO layers, expressed in terms of unit costs adopted for the purpose of comparing future inventory quantities:

December 31, 1961, inventory at 1949 unit costs—

	Quantity	Dec. 31, 1949, unit cost	Amount
Commodity W:			
Item A	1,075 yd.	$0.15	$161.25
Item B	1,500	.16	240.00
Total	2,575 yd.		$401.25
Average		.156	
Commodity X:			
Item C	1,400 lb.	.095	$133.00
Item D	700	.10	70.00
Item E	400	.11	44.00
Total	2,500 lb.		$247.00
Average		.099	

Commodity Y:

Item F	2 gal.	.40	$ 0.80
Item G	6	.38	2.28
Item H	5	.41	2.05
Item I	4	.39	1.56
Total	17 gal.		$ 6.69
Average		.394	

Commodity Z:

Item J	80 tons	3.00	$240.00

Segments of December 31, 1961, inventory—
Quantities:

		Increments		
	1949 base	1953	1957	1961
Commodity W	2,500 yd.	50 yd.		25 yd.
Commodity X	1,500 lb.		1,000 lb.	
Commodity Y	10 gal.	2 gal.		5 gal.
Commodity Z				80 tons

Extensions at average of 1949 costs:

	1949 base	Increments		
		1953	1957	1961
Commodity W ($0.156)	$390.00	$7.80	$	$ 3.90
Commodity X ($0.099)	148.50		99.00	
Commodity Y ($0.394)	3.94	.79		1.97
Commodity Z ($3.00)				240.00
	$542.44	$8.59	$99.00	$245.87
Total December 31, 1949, value				$895.90

3. Conversion factors for assigning to corresponding segments of future inventories the previously established LIFO costs:

	Dec. 31, 1949, values	Conversion factor	LIFO cost
Segments of 1961 inventory:			
1949 base	$542.44	102.13%	$ 554
Increments:			
1953	8.59	128.05	11
1957	99.00	121.21	120
1961	245.87	168.79	415
Total	$895.90		$1,100

On the basis of the foregoing, the LIFO cost for the inventory at December 31, 1962, would be determined as follows:

Computation of LIFO Cost for December 31, 1962, Inventory of XYZ Company

	1962 inventory quantities extended at December 31, 1949, unit costs		
	Quantity	Unit cost	Amount
Commodity W:			
Item A	1,600 yd.	$0.15	$240.00
Item B	800	0.16	128.00
Commodity X:			
Item C	1,200 lb.	0.095	114.00
Item D	750	0.10	75.00
Item E	300	0.11	33.00
Commodity Y:			
Item F	5 gal.	0.40	2.00
Item G	10	0.38	3.80
Item H	8	0.41	3.28
Item I	7	0.39	2.73
Commodity Z:			
Item J	75 tons	3.00	225.00
Total			$826.81

	Dec. 31, 1949, values	Conversion factor	LIFO cost
Segments of 1962 inventory—			
1949 base	$542.44	102.13%	$554.00
Increments:			
1953	8.59	128.05	11.00
1957	99.00	121.21	120.00
1961	176.78	168.79	298.39
Total	$826.81		$983.39

The extension of the December 31, 1961, inventory quantities at 1949 unit costs on an item-by-item basis should not be necessary. Use of the average costs previously established with respect to the 1949 inventory will produce acceptable results in most cases. Had such average costs been applied in the foregoing computations, the analysis of the 1961 inventory and the conversion factors would have been as at the top of the next page.

**Alternative Analysis of December 31, 1961,
Inventory of XYZ Company**

	1949 base	Increments		
		1953	1957	1961
Extensions at 1949 costs:				
Commodity W (16¢)	$400.00	$8.00	$	$ 4.00
Commodity X (10¢)	150.00		100.00	
Commodity Y (40¢)	4.00	.80		2.00
Commodity Z ($3.00)				240.00
	$554.00	$8.80	$100.00	$246.00
Total December 31, 1949, value				$908.80

Conversion factors:

	Dec. 31, 1949, values	Conversion factor	LIFO cost
Segments of 1961 inventory—			
1949 base	$554.00	100.00%	$ 554.00
Increments:			
1953	8.80	125.00	11.00
1957	100.00	120.00	120.00
1961	246.00	168.70	415.00
Total	$908.80		$1,100.00

The 1962 inventory will presumably be extended on a detailed basis so the aggregate 1949 value of $826.81 would be converted to a LIFO inventory cost of $961.68, as follows:

**Aternative Computation of LIFO Cost for December 31, 1962,
Inventory of XYZ Company**

	Dec. 31, 1949, values	Conversion factor	LIFO cost
Segments of 1962 inventory—			
1949 base	$554.00	100.00%	$ 554.00
Increments:			
1953	8.80	125.00	11.00
1957	100.00	120.00	120.00
1961	164.01	168.70	276.68
Total	$826.81		$ 961.68

The difference of $21.71 ($983.39 − $961.68) is not material and will not increase because all subsequent inventories will be extended on a basis comparable to the 1962 inventory.

13

Retail Method of Computing Inventories

Few customers realize the tremendous amount of paper work required to operate a retail department store of any size, or even a specialty store. Although the customers are aware that there are different departments, each of which handles a specific type of merchandise, they probably do not reflect upon the subject sufficiently to realize that the store may have thousands of individual items on display or in the reserve stock rooms, receiving departments, and warehouse concealed from view. The task of designing appropriate accounting records for these inventories is not simple; however, the retail method minimizes the effort necessary to maintain adequate control.

The basic difference between the inventory procedures commonly used by retailers and by industrial concerns is indicated by the following general statements:

1. Under the retail method, the inventory control records are maintained by departments on the basis of total retail dollars (selling prices). Markup percentages are determined for each department and used subsequently to reduce the retail value to cost. In many instances stores do maintain a unit control or perpetual inventory record, but these unit records are used primarily by buyers or for special purposes and are seldom used in computing cost for inventory purposes.

2. Industrial concerns usually maintain inventory control accounts on a cost basis. They will also maintain statistical records on a unit basis or list the units of individual items on hand periodically at the time of taking a physical inventory. The dollar amounts assigned to such inventories are computed by multiplying the quantities by the appropriate unit costs.

A difference is also sometimes found in the manner of using the inventory account in the general ledger. In the smaller department stores the general ledger inventory account may remain constant at the carrying value at the beginning of the year until the year's operations are closed. Departmental inventory controls (sometimes referred to as stock control ledgers) are maintained to reflect the changes in the inventories during the various accounting periods within the year and are the basis for interim operating statements. In an industrial concern the general ledger control accounts for inventories usually reflect the monthly changes. The closing monthly balances represent the dollar amount assigned to the inventory on hand.

DEPARTMENTAL INVENTORY CONTROLS

In the operation of the departmental control records maintained under the retail inventory method, four sets of basic figures must be available: (1) merchandise purchases at retail value and at cost, (2) inbound transportation costs, (3) adjustments in retail prices, and (4) sales of merchandise.

The accounting procedures followed in a typical store are:

1. *Purchases:* Purchases of merchandise for resale are recorded on a departmental basis. Posting information is obtained from previously approved vendor invoices which have been marked with the total retail price for the various merchandise items on the invoice. Postings are made for the retail value and the invoice cost price. At the month end, a summary of purchases at both retail value and invoice cost price is prepared. The total invoice cost price for purchases of all departments becomes the basis of an entry in the general ledger to record the merchandise purchases and vendor invoices payable with respect to merchandise received during the month.

2. *Inbound transportation costs:* The freight and express costs on inbound shipments are recorded in the expense accounts payable ledger, maintained, as in the case of the purchase ledger, by

departments. Alternatively, the inbound freight may be entered in the departmental purchase ledger. At the month end, a summary of all such inbound transportation becomes the basis of an entry in the general ledger debiting Freight and Express and crediting Accounts Payable.

3. *Adjustments in retail prices:* The retail prices originally placed on incoming merchandise may be subsequently adjusted for a variety of reasons. To determine the actual markup percentage (as well as to provide a measure of stock shortages), a record must be maintained of all such changes. These adjustments are also compiled on a departmental basis and are commonly segregated as to additional markups, markdowns, outright "adjustments," and discounts allowed.

4. *Sales:* The details surrounding the analyses and summaries of the sales transactions are not essential to a discussion of inventory control; however, information must be provided for posting to the general ledger an entry debiting Cash and Accounts Receivable and crediting Sales.

The monthly totals of (1) the retail value and invoice cost price of merchandise received, obtained from the individual departmental purchase ledgers, (2) the departmental freight and express costs, (3) the price adjustments made with reference to the merchandise in the various departments, and (4) the departmental sales, are posted to the inventory controls, a sample form of which is shown on page 314.

The departmental inventory control is a vital part of the accounting records. Normally, this inventory control computation is part of a departmental operating report which contains also the income and expenses of the department. For the present purpose, however, only the inventory control need be considered and only that portion of the operating report relative to inventory control is shown. Columns are provided for information at retail value and cost price, on a year-to-date basis and on a monthly basis. Except for the beginning inventory amounts, the information required is inserted in the monthly columns first. The year-to-date figures are obtained by adding the current month's figures to the year-to-date figures at the previous month end. The following comments explain the various lines on the form:

1. *Beginning inventory and markup %:* The amounts to be inserted on this line in the year-to-date columns are copied from

the closing inventory lines of the prior year, and the amounts in the month columns are copied from the closing inventory of the previous month. The manner in which these figures would have been determined will be revealed as the closing inventory for the current month is explained below. The total of the year-to-date beginning inventory at cost for all depart-

Departmental Inventory Control

No. _____   Month of: _____ 19___
      (Department)

		RETAIL				COST	
Line		Year to date	%	Month	%	Year to date	Month
1	Beginning inventory and markup %	$		$		$	$
	Add:						
2	Purchases.....................	$		$		$	$
3	Freight and express...........	**		**			
4	Additional markups...........					**	**
5	Retail adjustments............					**	**
6	Total: Purchases and markup %....	$		$		$	$
7	Total: Inventory plus purchases, and markup %.................	$		$		$	$
	Less:						
8	Markdowns..................	$		$			
9	Employees' discounts..........						
10	Other discounts..............						
11	Shortages...................						
12	Total reductions..............	$		$			
13		$		$			
14	Less: Sales...................						
15	Closing inventory (retail)..........	$		$			
16	Closing inventory (cost)...........					$	$

ments agrees, of course, with the general ledger inventory control amount.

2. *Purchases:* The retail value and cost price of merchandise purchased during the month are entered from the respective monthly departmental totals shown by the departmental purchase ledgers. Obviously, the total of all departmental purchases at cost must agree with the general ledger journal entry for the month.

3. *Freight and express:* Only the cost column is used to record the inbound transportation costs. The original markup made on the merchandise purchase cost has been figured sufficiently high to include the transportation costs.

4. *Additional markups:* There are instances when the retailer realizes that the retail value of merchandise should be increased. This may result, for example, from a revised appraisal of the quality of merchandise or from ascertaining that a clerical error had been made in determining the original retail value. These increases in retail value do not affect the cost of the merchandise but must be recognized as an addition to the inventory at retail.

5. *Retail adjustments:* Occasionally, the retailer may find it advantageous to adjust the retail value of certain merchandise but realizes that such adjustments may not be classified properly as either an additional markup or a markdown. These adjustments usually result in a reduction in the retail value. Markdowns, explained in detail in a later section, frequently reflect on the ability of the departmental buyer; therefore, although the adjustments are a form of markdown, they are treated separately. This line is most commonly used for markup cancellations; however, it might also be used where the retailer decides to stage a special sale, reducing the retail value of the regular merchandise. The reduction of this type could be entered as an inventory adjustment, and, in this manner, it would not be chargeable to the buyer. This adjustment does not affect the cost of the merchandise, so only the retail column is used.

6. *Total Purchases, markups, and adjustments:* The amounts on the previously described four lines are totaled and a markup percentage, sometimes referred to as markon percentage, may be computed for the month and year to date. The markup percentage is stated on the basis of the retail value, and actually represents the percentage of the retail value in excess of cost price. Assuming a retail value of $58,900 and a cost price of $34,340, the computation of the markup percentage may be made by subtracting the cost price from the retail value and

dividing the excess by the retail value, as follows:

Retail value........................	$58,900
Cost price...........................	34,340
Excess...............................	$24,560

$$\frac{\$24,560}{\$58,900} = 41.70\%, \text{ markup percentage}$$

Both the markup percentage and the complement cost percentage (100%—markup percentage) are used extensively in the retail inventory method.

7. *Total opening inventory, purchases, markups, and adjustments:* As the caption indicates, the amounts to be entered on this line represent the sum of the opening inventory and the total on the previous line. This represents the total merchandise to be accounted for. A cumulative markup percentage calculation is required at this point, for it is this cumulative markup percentage which will be used later to compute the cost price of the closing inventory. The rationale explained above also applies to this calculation; however, an alternative procedure arriving at the same result can be illustrated, assuming that the totals of opening inventory were $6,220 and $3,700, purchases, and so forth, were $58,900 and $34,340 and the sum totals were $65,120 and $38,040, each at retail value and cost price, respectively.

$$\frac{\$38,040}{\$65,120} = 58.42\%$$

$$100\% - 58.42\% = 41.58\%, \text{ markup percentage}$$

Under this procedure a direct computation of the cost percentage (58.42%) is the first step.

8. *Markdowns:* At frequent intervals, it is necessary to reduce the retail value of merchandise in an effort to move it from stock. The causes which give rise to the necessity of reducing the retail value are numerous, and only a few are given to illustrate the more common types:

   a) Seasonal goods may be still on hand, which the retailer does not desire to carry over until next year.

   b) Impending style or model changes, for example, the retailer desires to move the old items before the new ones become available.

   c) Soilage and damage, which reduce the attractiveness of the merchandise at full retail value.

   d) Odds and ends of a complete line, which the retailer desires to move.

e) Competitor's price may be less, and the retailer does not want to be undersold.

The markdowns are summarized for the month by departments, and the total is entered on this line of the control record.

The age analysis of the inventory, as hereinafter explained, is frequently used as a basis for markdowns. There is nothing to prevent a second or additional markdown from being made if the merchandise does not move after the first markdown.

There are instances when a markdown cancellation may be prepared. This may occur when a markdown is made for a short period and, after a portion of the merchandise has been disposed of at the reduced retail value, the original retail value is restored on the remaining merchandise. The markdown cancellations are used as a deduction from the markdowns, so that a net figure is taken into account.

9. *Employees' discounts:* Most department stores offer discounts to employees on merchandise purchased. The rate of discount varies between stores and frequently varies between departments. Since the sales figure will relieve inventory only at the discounted sales value, it is necessary to summarize discounts allowed employees by departments in order to remove the entire retail value from the inventory control.

10. *Other discounts:* Discounts are sometimes allowed to religious organizations and members of the clergy, and the like. The total of such discounts allowed must be recognized for the same reason as for employees' discounts.

11. *Shortages:* Shortages or shrinkage in inventories occur even though every attempt is made to reduce them to a minimum. They exist for several reasons, a few of which are errors in the preparation of the sales check, pilferage, breakage, and unreported markdowns. The amount of shortage varys between departments, depending upon the type of merchandise carried. Experience indicates what amount of shortage may be expected. In order to provide monthly for the anticipated shortage, a percentage of sales to be used as a basis of recording the monthly provision is developed.

12. *Total reductions:* The amount entered on this line, as indicated by the caption, represents the sum of the four reductions in inventory at retail just explained. These items are not entered in the cost columns and are not reflected by entries in the general ledger.

13. *Balance:* The amount to be entered on this line represents the result of subtracting the amount on line 12 from the amount

on line 7. Line 7 represents the opening inventory at retail plus purchases and certain adjustments to retail values. Line 12 represents various factors reducing the retail value. The difference between the two is the merchandise to be accounted for at retail, immediately prior to the deduction for sales made. This amount is not itself significant and could be omitted.

14. *Sales:* The net sales for the month are entered in the retail column. If an amount is entered in the cost column for the sake of completeness, it is a balancing figure determined after the closing inventory at cost (line 16) is computed.

15. *Closing inventory (retail):* Deducting the total sales should develop a figure approximating the retail value of a physical inventory if one were to be taken. Naturally the amount in the year-to-date column must agree with the monthly column figure; if the amounts differ, an error has occurred in entering one or more figures on other lines, and the error should be corrected.

16. *Closing inventory (cost):* The last operation is to reduce the inventory from retail value to cost. The markup percentage is developed on line 7. In the completed example of this Departmental Inventory Control form, shown on this page, attention is directed to the fact that the markup percentage in the year-to-date column differs from that in the month column. This is a result of monthly variations in the markup on purchases. In reducing the retail value to cost, the complement cost percentage to the cumulative markup percentage is used for both the year-to-date and month columns. Naturally, there should not be two different amounts assigned as cost for the closing inventory, and since the year-to-date markup percentage levels off monthly variations, it is used.

The Departmental Inventory Control computations are an essential, although not an integrated, part of the accounting records and also provide an important portion of the monthly operating statement required by management.

COST OR LOWER OF COST OR MARKET?

From the Departmental Inventory Control form it will be noted that three of the four items deducted in arriving at the retail value of the closing inventory (employees' discounts, other discounts, and shortages) definitely do not pertain to merchandise still on hand. Of the deduction items only the markdowns might

Departmental Inventory Control

No. 11–00   Piece Goods   Month of: March, 19—
   (Department)

Line		RETAIL Year to date	%	Month	%	COST Year to date	Month
1	Beginning inventory and markup %...........	$ 6,220	40.52	$ 5,000	41.00	$ 3,700	$ 2,950
	Add:						
2	Purchases.............	$58,795		$31,225		$34,040	$18,722
3	Freight and express.....	**		**		300	175
4	Additional markups.....	150		60		**	**
5	Retail adjustments......	(45)		—		**	**
6	Total: Purchases and markup %.................	$58,900	41.70	$31,285	39.60	$34,340	$18,897
7	Total: Inventory plus purchases, and markup %..	$65,120	41.58	$36,285	39.79	$38,040	$21,847
	Less:						
8	Markdowns............	$ 255		$ 105			
9	Employees' discounts....	75		30			
10	Other discounts........	20		—			
11	Shortages.............	150		60			
12	Total reductions........	$ 500		$ 195			
13		$64,620		$36,090			
14	Less: Sales..............	$54,620		$26,090			
15	Closing inventory (retail)...	$10,000	41.58	$10,000			
16	Closing inventory (cost)....					$ 5,842	$ 5,842

apply, at least in part, to the closing inventory. It is not generally feasible to establish the amount of the markdowns specifically applicable to the goods on hand, so the alternative recognized procedures are to assume either that a proportionate part of the total markdowns is applicable to the inventory items or that none is applicable.

If a proportionate part of the total markdown is actually applicable to merchandise on hand, the *cost* of the Piece Goods Department inventory reflected in the statement on page 321 could be determined as on the next page.

Determining Cost of Inventory by Restoring Markdowns

	Sold, etc.	Merchandise On hand	Total available
Sales....................................	$54,620		
Employees' discounts........................	75		
Other discounts............................	20		
Shortages................................	150		
	$54,865		
Sales value of merchandise on hand..........		$10,000	$64,865
Markdowns:			
54,865/64,865 × $255..................	216		
10,000/64,865 × $255..................		39	255
Retail value of beginning inventory plus purchases and markups.....................	$55,081	$10,039	$65,120
Markup %—41.58%.....................			
Cost....................................	32,175	5,865	38,040

Although the same cost figure results, it is not realistic to prepare statements like the above indicating that the markdowns are susceptible of mathematical allocation between the merchandise sold and the goods on hand. In practice the *cost* of the closing inventory is determined by taking the markdowns into account in computing the markup percentage. The amount computed in this manner as the *cost* of the merchandise on hand is reasonably accurate; but if less than a proportionate part of the total markdowns is actually applicable to the goods in the inventory, the *cost* will be overstated. Conversely, if more than a proportionate part of the total markdowns is in fact applicable to the inventory, the amount computed as the *cost* will be understated.

In most instances the procedure illustrated on page 319 is followed in order to apply the principle of assigning an amount to the inventory which represents the *lower of cost or market*. Mechanically, this procedure assumes that no part of the markdowns is applicable to the merchandise on hand; however, the objective is to avoid stating the inventory at its full cost when some of the merchandise will not be sold at its regular price. The correctness of the resulting figure depends primarily upon two

Determining Cost of Inventory by Adjusting Markup Percentage

		Retail	Markup %	Cost
Beginning inventory plus purchases...........		$65,120	41.58	$38,040
Markdowns.............................		255		
		$64,865	41.35	
Less:				
Employees' discounts...............	$ 75			
Other discounts...................	20			
Shortages........................	150	245		
		$64,620		
Less: Sales.............................		54,620		
Closing inventory (retail)..................		$10,000		
Closing inventory (cost)....................				$ 5,865

factors: establishing a retail value for the inventory which represents prices at which the merchandise is actually being offered for sale and compiling the amount of bona fide markdowns independent of markup cancellations and other retail adjustments.

The statement by the Institute of Chartered Accountants (paragraph 11(e) of Appendix B) observes that where selling prices have been reduced, the calculation will approximate cost only if appropriate allowance for price reductions is included in fixing the gross profit margin to be deducted. If no such allowance is made, the result of the calculation will tend to approximate replacement price. This difference in result is also specifically recognized in the federal income tax regulations (section 1.471–8 of Appendix C). The regulations provide that a taxpayer using the LIFO inventory method in conjunction with retail computations must adjust retail selling prices for markdowns as well as markups, in order that there may be reflected the approximate cost of the goods on hand regardless of market values.

PHYSICAL INVENTORIES

Physical inventories should be taken at least once a year either on or near to the fiscal year-end, commonly January 31. Some stores follow the practice of taking an interim physical inventory at midyear. Others take interim physical inventories for only specific departments whose shortage or overage at a previous fiscal year-end was not fully explained. The inventory control records may or may not be adjusted for these interim physical inventories. The interim physical inventory must be of major importance or the expense thereof is out of proportion to benefits obtained. Interim physical inventories are usually taken when a change in a departmental buyer occurs, in order to establish a sound inventory for the new buyer. Also certain "trouble departments" may be inventoried regularly at the end of each month or thirteen-week operating period.

Even where unit control or perpetual inventory records are maintained, it may not be practical to maintain such records for all departments. A continuous record of units on hand, however, is generally considered important for departments handling merchandise with relatively high unit value. Furthermore, the information available from perpetual inventory card records is valuable from a management viewpoint where style, model, or color are of prime significance.

Merchandise is marked when placed in stock with a ticket, tag, or sticker to indicate the retail value. When markdowns are taken, the original retail price may be crossed out by crayon and the reduced retail price marked in crayon, or the original marker may be removed entirely and a new one substituted. Stores differ as to the manner of marking merchandise, and more than one plan may be in effect in the same store.

In addition to the retail value, the marker will have sundry symbols imprinted thereon. Again, no one rule necessarily applies even within a given store; but these symbols may reveal, in code form, such information as the date the merchandise was purchased, the manufacturer or supplier, and the individual classification within a department. A buyer for the Sporting Goods Department may desire to have a recapitulation of his departmental inventory by basketball, football, baseball, golf, fishing, and similar equipment, and, by means of a coding system, this may be accomplished.

The physical inventories are generally taken under the supervision and instructions of the controller's department by sales employees of the particular department, with additional help as required. The record of the count is made on prenumbered inventory sheets appropriately identified as to department and location of merchandise. Columns are provided to record the age of merchandise, classification, description, quantity, and retail value. Like items, with the same date of purchase and same retail value, are usually counted and entered in total; however, like items with the same retail value but with different dates of purchase are listed by groups according to age of merchandise.

Upon completion of the inventory, all sheets are accounted for and turned over to the controller's department. The clerical work involved in extending, footing, and summarizing the inventories is frequently performed by outside help either with the aid of comptometers or tabulating equipment. The total retail value of each department's inventory is completed first. Next, an age analysis may be prepared, for example, 0-6 months old; 7-12 months, 13-18 months, and over 18 months. Finally, if the departmental buyer has requested it, the inventories will be summarized in classification groupings.

Aside from the grand total of the inventory, the other statistical information is not required by the controller's department for comparing with book controls; however, the age analysis is very useful in comparing the age with previous inventories. It affords management and the departmental buyer with an instrument to appraise the over-all inventory and determine policy in respect of disposing of old merchandise, and to some extent it provides the basis for an appraisal of the buyer's efforts.

The inventory, stated at retail, is then compared with the Departmental Inventory Control previously explained. To make the proper comparison, the deduction for provision for shortage is added back to the amount of inventory computed at retail. The true shortage is thus obtained. Investigation of unusual shortages or overages is required in order to establish responsibility and to provide for corrective measures.

The final physical inventory at retail is entered on the inventory control form at the fiscal year-end closing, and the difference between the actual shortage and the shortage provided for during the year is taken into account. Should the physical inventory be taken at a date other than a month end, it is essential that proper cutoffs be made of sales, purchases, markdowns, and all the other information necessary to construct an inventory as of the date of the physical count.

SELECTION OF DEPARTMENTS

The type and extent of departmentalization in a retail establishment is generally an expression of the business management and merchandising policies. Management usually controls operations by assigning responsibility to individual buyers for specific classes of merchandise, for example, women's wear, sporting goods, major appliances, and the like. The buyer is responsible for purchasing merchandise and the control of inventory quantities. Depending upon the circumstances, he may individually, or with the aid of a department manager, control the selling and operational functions of the department. This pattern of management is evident to the consumer as he visits the various departments of a large retail store. Where management reporting follows assigned responsibilities, inventory control follows the same lines.

Although a precisely uniform markup percentage is seldom used, the markup on different classes of merchandise tends to fall within a limited range. The retail method is an averaging process, and it is desirable for calculations of markup percentages to be made for groups of merchandise with similar characteristics. In general, these group classifications follow the departmental lines. If departmental responsibilities cover a class of merchandise with several price lines and varying markups, retail inventory calculations along price lines may be necessary to give proper recognition to the averaging process. In other instances, it may be possible to group certain departments that have merchandise with similar characteristics.

COMPARISON WITH OTHER METHODS

Although the retail inventory method is widely applied by retail organizations, other methods are used and may be more appropriate in certain circumstances.

The simplest of these alternative procedures is the physical inventory method whereby cost of sales is determined periodically by computation, that is, beginning inventory, plus purchases, less ending inventory. No record is made in the inventory account of current transactions as they occur. The summaries of sales and purchases and periodic physical inventories are the essentials required for the determination of income. This procedure is most effective from a management control viewpoint when physical inventories are frequently taken—monthly, weekly, or even daily—which may be practical in small or specialized businesses where the inventory is limited and can be compiled readily (e.g., cigar stands, taverns, small grocery stores and restaurants).

The specific cost method, whereby book inventory controls are established on a unit-cost basis, may be preferable for retail operations which have only a few types of merchandise with a limited number of price lines. Examples of merchandise for which this procedure may be practical include pianos, automobiles, phonograph records, and expensive furs.

Purchases, including transportation, are added to the beginning inventory, and from this total are deducted the cost of goods sold and any markdowns required by the fact that the market value of the units on hand is less than cost. There are numerous ways in which this cost method may be operated to permit a determination of the cost of the units sold. A two-part price tag with the cost indicated in code may be placed on the merchandise and removed at the time of sale. As an alternative to the coded cost, there may be a reference on the detachable portion of the price tag to the page in the unit-control record where cost information is available.

A cumulative book inventory record is maintained showing the cost of the units on hand and the amount of any markdowns recorded to recognize a lower market value. This book inventory is checked by the taking of physical inventories on a regular periodic basis or as may be practical.

Although another procedure may be appropriate in certain instances, the reasons for the popularity of the retail method include:

1. Physical inventories are taken at retail prices, which is generally much easier than obtaining cost prices.

2. The accounting system can accommodate any volume of transactions with ease.

3. The method allows for the periodic determination of inventories and profits without the necessity of taking a physical inventory.

4. Decreases in inventory values are recorded as soon as retail prices are reduced.

5. Disclosure and segregation of stock shortages by departments is simplified.

6. The effect of markdowns on departmental profits is readily ascertainable.

The retail method is recognized as an acceptable inventory procedure in each of the statements attached as appendices, even though the amount assigned to any particular inventory is merely an approximation of the amount which might be arrived at under some other method.

14

Adapting LIFO to the
Retail Method

The procedures for adapting the LIFO concept to the determination of amounts to be assigned to retail department store inventories were developed to meet a specific business need. It was necessary to superimpose the LIFO principle upon the highly specialized costing system commonly referred to as the "retail inventory method" described in Chapter 13. This is generally done by adjusting for price fluctuations through application of a series of nationwide price indexes to the total dollar value of each departmental inventory.

The LIFO problem peculiar to retailers basically arose from the fact that there is rarely a record of the specific cost for individual inventory items. Having thousands of different items in various departments, and selling them at a rapid rate of turnover for a relatively small dollar amount per item and per transaction has generally rendered impractical the maintenance of inventory accounting records on a unit-cost basis. The retail inventory method was developed many years ago to cope with just this situation.

Fundamentally, the retail method consists of accumulating the aggregate retail value of all items in a department at the inventory

date and reducing this departmental total to an allocated cost determined by applying an adjustment representing the average gross
markup for the year on that department's goods.   The LIFO calculations may be made at the end of interim accounting periods
or only once a year.   The discussion and examples which follow
are based upon methods used by a fairly large typical department
store for which the records are maintained throughout the year
on the retail method, and at the close of the year the LIFO computations are made to adjust the amount assigned to the inventory
from current cost to cost on the LIFO basis.

DETERMINING CHANGE IN QUANTITY OF GOODS
IN THE INVENTORY

The procedures usually followed by retailers on LIFO rely
upon an approximation of the extent of changes in *physical quantities* of the goods represented by inventory amounts through the
use of a retail price index.   The purpose of this index is to eliminate from inventory dollar amounts the effect of year-to-year
price changes so that inventories of different periods may be reduced to a comparable price base.   Once the price difference factor has been eliminated by the index, the differences between
dollar amounts of inventories are considered to reflect quantity
changes.

The series of price indexes approved by the Treasury Department for federal income tax purposes is based on data furnished
by the Bureau of Labor Statistics.   To January, 1954, an index
was computed for each of ten groups, two combinations of groups,
and a store total.   In January, 1954, the former groups were revised into twenty-one departmental groups, including one group
for which no index is computed.   Each of the modified groups
was identified with one of the former groups, however, to permit
continuity.   The indexes are all stated in terms of January, 1941,
equaling 100.

Generally recognized departments as established by the Controllers Congress of the National Retail Merchants Association
(formerly the National Retail Dry Goods Association) constitute
the basis for the B.L.S. groups.   On pages 330 and 331 are listed

the B.L.S. groups for which price data are obtained semiannually, with an indication of the corresponding departments recommended by the Controllers Congress. For departments included in the group for which no specific index is computed, the Treasury Department has approved the use of a storewide index. The store total index reflects data on a national basis for all departments, including some not listed separately, with the following exceptions: candy, foods, liquor, tobacco, paints, and wallpaper, as well as contract departments.

It should be noted that B.L.S. indexes are issued semiannually as of January 15 and July 15, and the mid-month figure of January 15, for example, may be used at December 31 or January 31.

Use of the B.L.S. indexes is generally considered restricted to department stores employing the retail method of inventory valuation. Department stores or departments of retail stores using some other-than-retail method of valuation may elect LIFO and find the dollar-value principle discussed in Chapter 12 provides the most convenient and practical procedure for costing the inventory for LIFO purposes. It may be easier, however, to compute the retail value of the inventory than to make extensions of inventory quantities at the unit costs prevailing at a basic LIFO date. Under such circumstances, where the cost and retail value of each year-end inventory can be determined (which will permit a computation of the gross profit percentage for each department for the year), consideration might be given to using the B.L.S. price index to determine a cost price index and the relative inventory quantities from year to year. Such possible uses of B.L.S. price indexes are discussed in the concluding sections of this chapter in connection with the comments relative to inventories of specialty and variety stores.

Since the tabulations published by the Bureau of Labor Statistics all use January 1941 as 100 per cent, taxpayers electing LIFO in subsequent years must compute their own cumulative percentage of price change from the beginning of the year in which LIFO was adopted for the respective departments. The government statistics do show the percentage of price change during the year. If LIFO was adopted for a piece goods department commencing with the fiscal year ended January 31, 1960, the cumulative price

Grouping of Controllers Congress Departments for Purposes of Inventory Price Indexes

B.L.S. Group No.	B.L.S. Group Name	Pre-1954 Controllers Congress Department No.	Pre-1954 Controllers Congress Department Name[1]	Revised Controllers Congress Department No.	Revised Controllers Congress Department Name
I.	Piece goods	11.	Silks, velvets, and synthetics (I)	11–00	Piece goods
		12.	Woolen dress goods (I)		
		13.	Wash goods and linings (I)		
		14.	Linens (I)		
II.	Domestics and draperies	15.	Domestics—muslins, sheetings, etc. (I)	15–00	Household textiles
		18.	Blankets, comfortables, and spreads (I)	64–11	Curtains, draperies, and decorator fabrics
		74.	Draperies, curtains, and upholstery (I)		
III.	Women's and children's shoes	47.	Women's and children's shoes (II)	39–00	Women's and children's shoes
IV.	Men's and boys' shoes	67.	Men's and boys' shoes (II)	53–00	Men's and boys' shoes
V.	Infants' wear	43.	Infants' wear (III)	44–12	Infants' apparel and furniture
VI.	Women's underwear	36.	Corsets and brassieres (III)	36–00	Corsets and brassieres
		38.	Knit underwear (III)	38–00	Underwear and negligees
		39.	Silk and muslin underwear and slips (III)		
		42.	Negligees and robes (III)		
VII.	Women's and girls' hosiery	37.	Women's and children's hosiery (III)	37–00	Women's and children's hosiery
VIII.	Women's and girls' accessories	31.	Neckwear and scarfs (X)	32–00	Neckwear and accessories
		33.	Handkerchiefs (X)	33–00	Handbags and small leathers
		35.	Women's and children's gloves (X)	35–00	Women's and children's gloves and mittens
		46.	Handbags and small leather goods (X)		
IX.	Women's outerwear and girls' wear	34.	Millinery (IV)	34–00	Millinery
		51.	Women's and misses' coats and suits (IV)	41–00	Coats and suits, women's, misses', and juniors'
		52.	Junior miss coats, suits, and dresses (IV)	42–00	Dresses, women's, misses', and juniors'
		53.	Women's and misses' dresses (IV)	45–00	Housedresses, aprons, and uniforms
		54.	Blouses, skirts, and sportswear (IV)	43–00	Blouses and sportswear
		55.	Girl's wear (IV)	46–00	Furs
		57.	Aprons, housedresses, and uniforms (IV)	44–11	Girls' and teen-age apparel
		59.	Furs (IV)		
X.	Men's clothing	61.	Men's clothing (V)	51–11	Men's clothing
				or { 51–14	Men's clothing
				51–26	Men's sport clothing
XI.	Men's furnishings	62.	Men's furnishings (V)	51–12	Men's furnishings
		65.	Men's hats (V)	51–15	Men's furnishings
				or { 51–27	Men's casual furnishings

XIII. Jewelry and silverware
  25S. Silverware and clocks (IX)
  25C. Costume jewelry (IX)
  25F. Fine jewelry and watches (IX)

XIV. Notions
  21. Laces, trimmings, and ribbons (IX)
  23. Notions (IX)
  26. Umbrellas (IX)
  27. Art needlework (IX)

XV. Toilet articles and drugs
  24. Toilet articles and drug sundries (IX)

XVI. Furniture and bedding
  71M. Mattresses, springs, and studio beds (VI)
  71U. Upholstered furniture (VI)
  71O. Other furniture (VI)

XVII. Floor covering
  72. Oriental rugs (VII)
  73. Domestic floor covering (VII)

XVIII. Housewares
  76. China and glassware (VII)
  78. Housewares (VII)
  79. Gift shop (VII)
  81. Pictures, frames, and mirrors (VII)

XIX. Major appliances
  75. Lamps and shades (VIII)
  77. Major appliances (VIII)

XX. Radios and television sets
  84. Radios, phonographs, and records (VIII)

XXI. No separate index computed
  28. Books and stationery (XI)
  91. Toys and games (XI)
  92S. Sporting goods (XI)
  92C. Cameras and photographic equipment (XI)
  93. Luggage (XI)

Code	Department
24-00	Jewelry and silverware
12-00	Patterns
21-00	Notions, laces, trimmings, and ribbons
25-00	Art needlework
31-00	Umbrellas
22-00	Toilet articles and drug sundries
61-00	Furniture and beds
62-00	Oriental rugs
63-00	Domestic floor covering
65-00	China, glassware, and gift shop
66-21	Housewares
67-00	Pictures, frames, and mirrors
64-12	Lamps and shades
66-12	Major appliances
68-00	Radio, television, and records
69-00	Pianos and musical instruments
26-00	Books and stationery
66-22	Wallpaper and paint
71-00	Flower shop
72-00	Automobile accessories
73-00	Pet accessories and pet shop
74-00	Toys, sporting goods, and cameras
75-00	Luggage
76-00	Candy
77-00	Foods and groceries
78-00	Fresh and smoked meats
79-00	Liquor shop
81-00	Smoke shop

¹ Roman numerals in parentheses represent pre-1954 B.L.S. group with which the department was identified.

change from 1941 to the beginning of the year of LIFO election would be read from the government tables to be 199.5 per cent, and the price change during the year ended that date would be read from the tables to be 0.5 per cent. In the computations 100 per cent will be used for the inventory at the beginning of the 1960 fiscal year. The price index at January 31, 1960, will be 100.5 (100.0% + 100.0% × 0.5%), and the cumulative price index at January 31, 1961, will be 101.5 (100.5% + 100.5% × 1.0%). The commonly used form of work sheet hereafter explained for the compilation of LIFO inventories by departments is designed to provide for the cumulative computation of the price change regardless of the year for which LIFO is first used.

In practically all instances the actual departmentalization of retail inventories is in accord with an accepted grouping for which a specific index is computed by the Bureau of Labor Statistics. In diversified goods departments, particularly in small branch stores, the selection of the index requires careful thought. Generally the index applicable to the major portion of the inventory in the department is used for LIFO computation purposes. In cases where there is no one major class of inventory in the department, the soft goods total index, the durable goods total index, or the storewide index may be appropriate.

COMPUTATION OF LIFO INVENTORIES

The steps involved in the application of LIFO to retail inventories can best be shown by an example with supporting explanations, but the following basic principles concerning the combining of LIFO computations with the retail inventory method are significant:

1. Each closing departmental inventory at *retail value* is reduced to its base-year price level (the year the department elected LIFO) by the application of the B.L.S. index number appropriate for the merchandise group within which the departmental goods may be generally classified. This process eliminates the effect of price changes from the base year to the current year and puts the base year and current year on a comparable dollar basis.

2. The closing *retail* inventory is adjusted to eliminate price changes and is compared with the previous year's closing *retail* value (also at the base-year price level and on a comparable dollar basis).

   a) If this comparison indicates an increase in inventory, such increase, for LIFO purposes, is considered an increase in physical quantity and is multiplied by the index number applicable to the current year to get the retail value of the increase.

   b) If this comparison indicates a decrease in inventory, for LIFO purposes, it is considered a decrease in physical quantity and to have come from the most recently added merchandise. Therefore, deductions to cover the decrease are made from the latest period in which there were additions to inventory and at the cost at which they were previously added to the inventory. If there have been no increases, the deductions are taken from the base year at the base cost.

3. The adjusted increase or decrease in a retail layer on a LIFO basis is then reduced to LIFO cost through the use of the applicable cost complement percentage (the complement of the departmental "net" markon) for the current year if an increase, for the year(s) of the latest offsetting addition(s) if a decrease.

4. The adjusted increase or decrease in (3) above (now reduced to LIFO cost) is applied to the closing LIFO inventory of the previous year to obtain the LIFO closing inventory of the current year.

5. The current cost of the inventory under the retail method as determined by the inventory control records is compared with the LIFO closing inventory figure obtained in (4) above. The difference is the cumulative LIFO adjustment at that year end and represents the net difference between LIFO and FIFO since the base year.

6. The cumulative LIFO adjustment at the end of the current year is compared with the cumulative LIFO adjustment at the end of the previous year, and the difference represents the annual LIFO adjustment which is the effect on income for the current year.

Several basic forms of work sheets have been developed to accumulate the LIFO calculations by departments by years. Some contain slight variations in presentation of figures, but they all produce the same answer, that is, the cost of the merchandise inventory determined by the retail method of accounting applied on the basis of LIFO. Two forms have been included herein for illustrative purposes, but the explanatory comments which follow are directed toward the first of these forms. It will be seen that the second type (page 350) is similar to the first in its application. The first form will be used to illustrate the mechanics involved. On page 336 is a blank form with explantory comments.

Since the Internal Revenue Code requires that for LIFO purposes cost be used in lieu of the lower of cost or market, a new amount must be determined, in most instances, for the closing inventory of the year prior to adoption of the LIFO basis. The normal retail method tends to provide for a computation of the lower of cost or market. The markup percentage for the prior fiscal year's closing inventory will have been determined as explained in Chapter 13. Assuming the facts given in the following table for the woolen dress goods department, the markup percentage used at the end of the preceding fiscal year for valuing the merchandise inventory would have been 41.62 per cent.

	Retail	Cost	Markup %
Beginning inventory.........	$125,500	$ 75,551	39.80%
Purchases...................	435,200	257,520	40.83%
Inbound transportation.......		3,000	
Additional markups..........	14,961		
	$575,661	$336,071	41.62%

$575,661 − $336,071 = $239,590 ÷ $575,661 = 41.62%

However, to determine the inventory cost on the basis required for the adoption of LIFO, it is necessary to recognize the effect of markdowns taken during the year. For purposes of illustration, assume the same basic figures but, in addition, assume that markdowns amounted to $31,491. The markup percentage for LIFO purposes would be computed by recognizing the markdowns, and a LIFO markup percentage of 38.24 per cent determined as follows:

	Retail	Cost	Markup %
Beginning inventory.........	$125,500	$ 75,551	39.80%
Purchases...................	435,200	257,520	40.83%
Inbound transportation.......		3,000	
Additional markups..........	14,961		
Markdowns.................	(31,491)		
	$544,170	$336,071	38.24%

$544,170 − $336,071 = $208,099 ÷ $544,170 = 38.24%

The closing inventory at retail aggregated $132,350, and this amount is multiplied by the cost markup complement percentage (100% — markup percentage). The computations under the normal retail method indicate a lower-of-cost-or-market inventory value of $77,266, while the cost for LIFO purposes is $81,739.

		Cost
Retail	%	Amount
$132,350	58.38%	$77,266 on retail basis
$132,350	61.76%	$81,739 on retail basis
		for LIFO

The cost for LIFO is $4,473 ($81,739 — $77,266) greater than the value under the normal retail method. An adjustment for this amount would be made for tax purposes retroactively to the close of the immediately preceding year, and additional taxes paid on the resulting increase in income. Frequently, no adjustment per books is made in this type of situation, being merely consolidated with the adjustment to LIFO at the end of the year in which LIFO is adopted. A literal reading of the LIFO section in the Internal Revenue Code could lead to the conclusion that a credit to surplus should be made for the amount of the increase in the opening inventory less the additional prior year's tax; but it is common practice not to show a surplus adjustment on the financial statements.

When the LIFO work sheet is completed for the opening inventory of the base year, the form will appear as shown on page 337.

Assume next that the final inventory control records have been closed for the first LIFO year, and they show that the inventory at retail value equals $195,500. It is found that the B.L.S. index figure has increased 20.3 per cent over the 100 per cent base period index, so that the cumulative index at the end of the first year is 120.3 per cent. The ending inventory must be reduced to base price (100%) for the purpose of comparing that inventory with the beginning inventory. The reduction of the ending inventory at retail value ($195,500) to the base price is accomplished by dividing $195,500 by 120.3 per cent. The resulting amount ($162,510) reflects the ending inventory in terms of the same dollar basis as the opening inventory.

Departmental LIFO Inventory Calculations

Line	Base year	First year	Second year	Third year	Fourth year	Fifth year	Sixth year
1—Physical retail inventory...........	This represents the actual physical inventory on January 31 of each year at retail.						
2—Percentage of price index change for the year........	This is the percentage of price increase for the year only. Furnished by Bureau of Labor Statistics.						
3—Price index reflecting change accumulated since basic LIFO date	This is the cumulative price increase plus 100% from base period (line 2 × line 3 of previous year plus line 3 of previous year = line 3 to date). When the basic LIFO date is January or July, 1941 (or approximately such months), the price index reflecting the cumulative percentage of price change is available directly in the tables furnished by Bureau of Labor Statistics.						
4—1 ÷ 3 Retail inventory units........	This represents actual inventory at base prices.						
5—Increase or (decrease) on base.....	Subtract line 4 from previous year figure on line 4, and result is either increase or decrease of base in units assuming that $1 equals 1 unit.						
Decrease calculation:							
A—Unit decrease.......	As any decrease will use up a full year or years plus part of a year, it is only necessary to calculate the part of the year. The amount of decrease if a whole year is depleted will show on line 8. In order to obtain the cost of the part decrease that amount must be multiplied by the cumulative price index (line 3) for the year in which the part decrease occurs and the result multiplied by 100% minus LIFO markup (line 7) (for years of decrease).						
B—Index for decrease.......							
C—A × B.............							
D—100 minus LIFO markup %......							
E—LIFO decrease...........							
F—Unit decrease...........	This space to be used only for additional decreases.						
G—Index for decrease........							
H—F × G............							
I—100 minus LIFO markup %.....							
J—LIFO decrease...........							
6—Increase at current retail...........	As increases (line 5) are at base prices, the amount of increase must be multiplied by cumulative price index (line 3) to get the retail value of the increase for the year.						
7—Cost complement to LIFO markup %	This is the purchase markup and is obtained by subtracting true markdowns from total retail purchases for the year and dividing the result into total cost purchases for the year.						
8—Increase or (decrease) over base...	For increases this is line 6 × line 7. For decreases it is line E (and line J, if applicable) plus line 8 of those years decreased for the period.						
LIFO closing inventory............	This is previous year closing plus or minus line 8.						
Cost of inventory, retail method.......	Obtained from inventory control record.						
Cumulative LIFO adjustment...........	Represents the net difference between LIFO and FIFO since base year (difference between LIFO closing inventory and cost inventory retail method).						
Annual LIFO adjustment...........	Represents the effect on income for the current year.						

The opening inventory ($132,350) subtracted from the ending inventory at the same base dollar value ($162,510) gives $30,160 as the increase in the ending inventory over the beginning inventory in units of base dollars. Since this increase is stated at 100 per cent dollars and the current index is 120.3 per cent, the 100 per cent dollars ($30,160) must be raised to the basis of 120.3 per cent dollars ($36,282) by multiplying $30,160 by 120.3 per cent. The increase of $36,282 at retail must then be reduced to cost. The markup percentage for LIFO is computed by a procedure similar to that shown for the opening inventory of the first year except that the opening inventory is not used either at retail or at cost. After making the necessary calculations a

Departmental LIFO Inventory Calculations

No. 12—Woolen Dress Goods
      (Department)

Line	Base year
1—Physical retail inventory......................................	$132,350
2—Percentage of price index change for the year...................	
3—Price index reflecting change accumulated since basic LIFO date.....	100.0%
4—1 ÷ 3 Retail inventory units...................................	$132,350
5—Increase or (decrease) on base...............................	—
Decrease calculation:	
A—Unit decrease...	
B—Index for decrease..	
C—A × B..	
D—100 minus LIFO markup %...................................	
E—LIFO decrease...	
F—Unit decrease...	
G—Index for decrease..	
H—F × G..	
I—100 minus LIFO markup %...................................	
J—LIFO decrease...	
6—Increase at current retail...................................	
7 Cost complement to LIFO markup %...........................	
8—Increase or (decrease) over base.............................	
LIFO closing inventory...	$ 81,739
Cost of inventory, retail method.................................	$ 77,266
Cumulative LIFO adjustment.....................................	(4,473)
Annual LIFO adjustment..	(4,473)

markup for LIFO purposes of 38.87 per cent is arrived at. The cost complement to this markup percentage is 61.13 per cent, and the retail value of the increase ($36,282) is multiplied by the cost complement (61.13 per cent) to arrive at an increase in inventory at cost of $22,179.

There are now two "layers" of inventory. The first "layer" represents the cost of the base stock, the second represents the cost of the increase in inventory. By adding the two together, the cost under LIFO of the ending retail value inventory of $195,500 is determined to be $103,918. This figure can be compared with the value under the normal retail method which is available from the inventory control records. It is found that under the normal retail method $115,345 would be considered as representing the lower of cost or market.

Subtracting the LIFO cost basis ($103,918) from the retail basis ($115,345), it is found that under LIFO the inventories are $11,427 less than under the retail method at the end of this first year. This requires an adjustment to the general ledger to reduce the general ledger merchandise account to cost under the LIFO basis. There are two basic ways of reducing the general ledger balance to LIFO. One method is to reduce the inventory account directly, and an entry for this purpose might be as follows:

P & L—Cost of merchandise sold—
    LIFO adjustment $11,427
        Merchandise inventory $11,427

The alternative procedure would be to provide an adjustment account which when deducted from the merchandise inventory account would equal the inventory value on the LIFO basis. Such an entry might be stated as follows:

P & L Cost of merchandise sold—
    LIFO adjustment $11,427
        LIFO inventory adjustment $11,427

It will be observed that the cumulative effect is used as the basis for this entry, and it recognizes the effect on both the opening and closing inventories. In all subsequent years the annual LIFO adjustment would be used as the basis for the entry. If two entries are made to record separately the effect of the opening and closing inventory valuation changes, the entries might be as follows:

Merchandise inventory	$ 4,473	
Surplus—LIFO adjustments		$ 4,473
P & L Cost of merchandise sold—		
LIFO adjustment	15,900	
Merchandise inventory		15,900

If the LIFO inventory adjustment account is used instead of a direct credit to the merchandise inventory account, the entries would be the same except the charge and credit to merchandise inventory of $4,473 and $15,900, respectively, would be made to the LIFO adjustment account. Theoretically a charge might also be made to surplus for the additional amount of prior year's tax attributable to the $4,473 writeup of the opening inventory; however, the modern practice in the preparation of financial statements is not to make surplus adjustments. Such items, if material, are more commonly just shown separately in the current income statement.

The application of the figures stated above, which have been entered on the form on page 341, shows how the inventory work sheet would appear at the end of the first LIFO year.

Assume that the inventory control records are closed for the second LIFO year, and the ending inventory at retail value equals $207,670. The B.L.S. index has increased 13.7 per cent over the previous year, so there is a cumulative index at the end of the second year of 136.8 per cent. Reducing the retail value to the base period retail value level, the inventory is stated at $151,806 as compared with $162,510 at the end of the first LIFO year. This represents a decrease of $10,704 at base period retail value level.

The LIFO inventory at base period retail value level had increased $30,160 during the first year, and applying the basis of last-in first-out, the decrease in inventory during the second year represents a reduction from that increase. There should be entered in the first LIFO year column under the $30,160 increase, the figure of $10,704, circled and dated second LIFO year. This indicates that $10,704 of the increase during the first LIFO year was eliminated by the amount of the inventory decrease during the second LIFO year. From this point on, all entries will be made in the second LIFO year column.

The following steps are taken in determining the cost represented by the decrease in inventory. On line A is entered the $10,704 decrease. If the decrease had been greater than the increase of the prior year, only the excess would be entered here. For an example of the procedure to be followed in this type of situation, reference can be made to the decrease in the fourth LIFO year as reflected on page 346. Since the $10,704 is at the base period retail value and the decrease represents part of an increase during the first LIFO year, the cumulative index for the first LIFO year of 120.3 per cent is entered on line B. Multiplying $10,704 by 120.3 per cent, the decrease at retail value of the first year is determined to be $12,877. The LIFO cost complement of 61.13 per cent, secured from line 7 of the first LIFO year column, multiplied by $12,877 determines the LIFO cost of the inventory liquidated in the second LIFO year.

The closing LIFO inventory at the end of the second year is $96,046, arrived at by deducting the cost of the liquidated inventory ($7,872) from the closing LIFO inventory at the end of the first year ($103,918). The lower of cost or market value reflected by the inventory control records is $124,602, and the difference of $28,556 represents the cumulative LIFO adjustment. Since $11,427 of this cumulative adjustment had been reflected at the end of the first year, the entry for the second year would be as follows:

```
P & L—Cost of merchandise sold—
    LIFO adjustment                          $17,129
        Merchandise inventory (or LIFO
            adjustment)                                    $17,129
```

Inasmuch as the general ledger merchandise inventory account prior to the entry above represents the value normally determined under the retail method less the cumulative LIFO adjustment through the first year, after the entry the general ledger merchandise inventory account will represent the merchandise inventory on the basis of LIFO at the end of the second year.

Departmental LIFO Inventory Calculations

No. 12—Woolen Dress Goods
     (Department)

Line	Base year	First year
1—Physical retail inventory..........................	$132,350	$195,500
2—Percentage of price index change for the year.......		20.3%
3—Price index reflecting change accumulated since basic LIFO date..................................	100.0%	120.3%
4—1 ÷ 3 Retail inventory units......................	$132,350	$162,510
5—Increase or (decrease) on base....................	—	30,160
Decrease calculation:		
A—Unit decrease.................................		
B—Index for decrease.............................		
C—A × B.......................................		
D—100 minus LIFO markup %........................		
E—LIFO decrease.................................		
F—Unit decrease.................................		
G—Index for decrease.............................		
H—F × G.......................................		
I—100 minus LIFO markup %........................		
J—LIFO decrease.................................		
6—Increase at current retail......................		$36,282
7—Cost complement to LIFO markup %...............		61.13%
8—Increase or (decrease) over base.................		22,179
LIFO closing inventory................................	$ 81,739	$103,918
Cost of inventory, retail method.......................	$ 77,266	$115,345
Cumulative LIFO adjustment...........................	(4,473)	11,427
Annual LIFO adjustment..............................	(4,473)	15,900

The status of the LIFO work sheet at the end of the second year is indicated on page 343.

At the end of the third year, the inventory control record showed a retail value of $236,750, and on page 344 is set forth the LIFO work sheet completed through the end of that year. It will be observed that line 4 under the third LIFO year column shows a closing inventory of $164,296 in base year retail dollars as compared with $151,806 for the previous year end, an increase of $12,490 as shown on line 5.

The cumulative effect of LIFO at the end of the third year

is $37,204, and the LIFO adjustment chargeable to the third year is $8,648. The entry would be:

```
P & L—Cost of merchandise sold—
     LIFO adjustment                          $ 8,648
          Merchandise inventory (or LIFO
               adjustment)                                    $ 8,648
```

After posting the entry to the general ledger, the merchandise inventory account balance would be $107,214.

The retail value of the closing inventory for the fourth LIFO year has been purposely assumed to reflect a reduced amount, so that the reduction, when restated in terms of the base period retail level, would not only extinguish all increases in inventories since the base year but also reduce the inventory below that of the basic date.

The starting point is again the retail value of the closing inventory, which, in this case, is shown by the inventory control records to be $196,750. This retail value is reduced by the cumulative index of 151.0 per cent to arrive at a basic price level of $130,298. Comparison with the comparable figure at the end of the third year ($164,296) reveals a reduction of $33,998 at the basic price level. The LIFO inventory layers present in the inventory at the end of the third year are analyzed in the following tabulation:

	Retail value at base-year price	LIFO cost
Base stock still consists of...........................	$132,350	$ 81,739
During the first LIFO year there was added $30,160 and $22,179, respectively, but in the second year this increase was reduced by $10,704 and $7,872, respectively, so there is a balance of.............................	19,456	14,307
During the third LIFO year there was added $12,490 and $11,168, respectively.............................	12,490	11,168
At the end of the third LIFO year the inventory consisted of	$164,296	$107,214

In practice it is not necessary to prepare a table as outlined above for the information is obtainable from the work sheet.

The first entries on the LIFO work sheet (page 346) are as follows:

1. Enter $12,490 circled in the third-year column under the $12,490 figure shown on line 5. Indicate to left of circled figure that entry was made at end of fourth year. Draw a double line under the circled figure to indicate that the increase in the third year has been completely liquidated and further reference to this increase is unnecessary.

2. Enter $19,456 circled under the $10,704 circled figure in the first-year column. In arriving at the $19,456 amount, it is recognized that the inventory during the first year increased $30,160

Departmental LIFO Inventory Calculations

No. 12—Woolen Dress Goods
          (Department)

Line	Base year	First year	Second year
1—Physical retail inventory.................	$132,350	$195,500	$207,670
2—Percentage of price index change for the year		20.3%	13.7%
3—Price index reflecting change accumulated since basic LIFO date.................	100.0%	120.3%	136.8%
4—1 ÷ 3 Retail inventory units..............	$132,350	$162,510	$151,806
5—Increase or (decrease) on base	—	30,160	(10,704)
		2d LIFO (10,704) year	
Decrease calculation:			
A—Unit decrease.........................			$ (10,704)
B—Index for decrease.....................			120.3%
C—A × B................................			$ (12,877)
D—100 minus LIFO markup %..............			61.13%
E—LIFO decrease........................			$ (7,872)
F—Unit decrease.........................			
G—Index for decrease.....................			
H—F × G................................			
I—100 minus LIFO markup %..............			
J—LIFO decrease........................			
6—Increase at current retail.................		$ 36,282	
7—Cost complement to LIFO markup %........		61.13%	
8—Increase or (decrease) over base..........		22,179	
LIFO closing inventory......................	$ 81,739	$103,918	$ 96,046
Cost of inventory, retail method..............	$ 77,266	$115,345	$124,602
Cumulative LIFO adjustment.................	(4,473)	11,427	28,556
Annual LIFO adjustment.....................	(4,473)	15,900	17,129

Departmental LIFO Inventory Calculations

No. 12—Woolen Dress Goods
(Department)

Line	Base year	First year	Second year	Third year
1—Physical retail inventory	$132,350	$195,500	$207,670	$236,750
2—Percentage of price index change for the year		20.3%	13.7%	5.3%
3—Price index reflecting change accumulated since basic LIFO date	100.0%	120.3%	136.8%	144.1%
4—1 ÷ 3 Retail inventory units	$132,350	$162,510	$151,806	$164,296
5—Increase or (decrease) on base		30,160	(10,704)	12,490
		2d year LIFO (10,704)		
Decrease calculation:				
A—Unit decrease			$(10,704)	
B—Index for decrease			120.3%	
C—A × B			(12,877)	
D—100 minus LIFO markup %			61.13%	
E—LIFO decrease			(7,872)	
6—Increase at current retail		$36,282		$17,998
7—Cost complement to LIFO markup %		61.13%		62.05%
8—Increase or (decrease) over base		$22,179		$11,168
LIFO closing inventory	$81,739	$103,918	$96,046	$107,214
Cost of inventory, retail method	$77,266	$115,345	$124,602	$144,418
Cumulative LIFO adjustment	(4,473)	11,427	28,556	37,204
Annual LIFO adjustment	(4,473)	15,900	17,129	8,648

but $10,704 of this was liquidated in the second year; therefore, only the difference between the $30,160 and $10,704, or $19,456, can be charged to this increase. Indicate that the $19,456 represents an entry made at end of fourth year, and draw a double line under the $19,456 to indicate that entire increase of $30,160 has been liquidated.

3. At this point there has been taken into account $31,946 ($12,490 + $19,456) of the total decrease of $33,998, leaving $2,052 which is now entered in the base-year column by circling and indicating the entry was made at end of the fourth year.

The next operation is to compute the LIFO cost of these liquidations. The liquidation in the fourth year covers three different layers of inventory, and each provides slightly different problems:

1. First to be considered is the portion of the liquidation applicable to the increase during the third year. Since it liquidates this addition completely and since the LIFO cost of the addition has been determined in the third-year computations, reference can be made to line 8 under the third-year column to find the LIFO cost was $11,168. This cost is then entered on line 8 in the fourth-year column and circled to indicate the reduction on the LIFO cost basis.

2. The next calculation required is to determine the LIFO cost of the portion of the liquidation attributable to the increase in inventory which occurred in the first year. During the second year inventories had been reduced $10,704 at the basic price level, and this reduction was applied against the increase in inventory during the first year. The LIFO cost of the reduction during the second year had been computed to be $7,872. The total increase during the first year amounted to $22,179 at LIFO cost, and deducting the $7,872 from $22,179 leaves $14,307, which is determined to be the LIFO cost of the portion of the fourth-year liquidation applicable to the increase in inventory during the first year. This figure ($14,307) is then entered in the fourth-year column directly under the ($11,168) previously entered.

3. The last computation needed to determine the LIFO cost of inventory liquidated applies to the $2,052 liquidation at the basic price level which reduces the base stock. The computation is shown on lines A through E in the fourth-year column, and the mechanics are similar to those previously outlined in connection with computing the LIFO cost of the inventory reduction during the second year. Since it is base stock that is now being considered, the index number is 100.0 per cent. Following the computations through, it is found that the LIFO cost of the reduction

Departmental LIFO Inventory Calculations

No. 12—Woolen Dress Goods
(Department)

Line	Base year	First year	Second year	Third year	Fourth year
1—Physical retail inventory	$132,350	$195,500	$207,670	$236,750	$196,750
2—Percentage of price index change for the year		20.3%	13.7%	5.3%	4.8%
3—Price index reflecting change accumulated since basic LIFO date	100.0%	120.3%	136.8%	144.1%	151.0%
4—1 ÷ 3 Retail inventory units	$132,350	$162,510	$151,806	$164,296	$130,298
5—Increase or (decrease) on base		30,160	(10,704)	12,490	(33,998)
	4th(2,052)	2d(10,704)		4th(12,490)	
		4th(19,456)			
Decrease calculation:					
A—Unit decrease			$ (10,704)		$ (2,052)
B—Index for decrease			120.3%		100.0%
C—A × B			$ (12,877)		$ (2,052)
D—100 minus LIFO markup %			61.13%		61.76%
E—LIFO decrease			$ (7,872)		$ (1,267)
6—Increase at current retail		$36,282		$17,998	
7—Cost complement to LIFO markup %		61.13%		62.05%	
8—Increase or (decrease) over base		$22,179		$11,168	$ (11,168)
					(14,307)
					(1,267)
LIFO closing inventory	$81,739	$103,918	$96,046	$107,214	$ 80,472
Cost of inventory, retail method	$77,266	$115,345	$124,602	$144,418	$119,034
Cumulative LIFO adjustment	(4,473)	11,427	28,556	37,204	38,562
Annual LIFO adjustment	(4,473)	15,900	17,129	8,648	1,358

in base stock is $1,267. This is entered and circled directly under ($14,307) referred to above.

The factors have now been established to determine the LIFO cost of the closing inventory. From the LIFO cost at the end of the previous year (the third year) is deducted the three decreases on the LIFO cost basis shown in the fourth-year column. When this is done, the LIFO cost of the inventory at the end of the fourth year $80,472 ($107,214 — $11,168 — $14,307 — $1,267) can be entered on the work sheet.

The inventory cost under the normal retail method, obtained from the inventory control records, is entered as $119,034, and the cumulative LIFO adjustment of $38,562 ($119,034 — $80,472) is entered on the proper line. Deducting the cumulative adjustment of $37,204 at the end of the third year from $38,562 at the end of the fourth year gives the adjustment of $1,358 required to be made at the end of the fourth year. The general ledger entry would be as follows:

```
P & L—Cost of merchandise sold—
    LIFO adjustment                        $1,358
        Merchandise inventory (or LIFO
            adjustment)                                 $1,358
```

It will be observed from an analysis of the LIFO work sheet on page 346 that at the end of fourth year there is only one "layer" of inventory, that being the base stock "layer," and it has been reduced from $132,350 at the basic price level to $130,298 on the same price level.

The appearance of the LIFO work sheet at the conclusion of the fifth year is shown on page 348. It will be noted that the inventory increased $26,703 on the base price level over the inventory at the close of the fourth year. The entry required after the computations have been completed would be:

```
P & L—Cost of merchandise sold—
    LIFO adjustment                        $10,859
        Merchandise inventory (or LIFO
            adjustment)                                 $10,859
```

Departmental LIFO Inventory Calculations

No. 12—Woolen Dress Goods
(Department)

Line	Base year	First year	Second year	Third year	Fourth year	Fifth year
1—Physical retail inventory	$132,350	$195,500	$207,670	$236,750	$196,750	$261,720
2—Percentage of price index change for the year		20.3%	13.7%	5.3%	4.8%	10.4%
3—Price index reflecting change accumulated since basic LIFO date	100.0%	120.3%	136.8%	144.1%	151.0%	166.7%
4—1 ÷ 3 Retail inventory units	$132,350	$162,510	$151,806	$164,296	$130,298	$157,001
5—Increase or (decrease) on base		30,160	(10,704)	12,490	(33,998)	26,703
	4th(2,052)	2d(10,704)		4th(12,490)		
		4th(19,456)				
Decrease calculation:						
A—Unit decrease			$(10,704)		$(2,052)	
B—Index for decrease			120.3%		100.0%	
C—A × B			$(12,877)		$(2,052)	
D—100 minus LIFO markup %			61.13%		61.76%	
E—LIFO decrease			$(7,872)		$(1,267)	
6—Increase at current retail		$36,282		$17,998		$44,514
7—Cost complement to LIFO markup %		61.13%		62.05%	61.76%	61.85%
8—Increase or (decrease) over base		$22,179		$11,168	$(11,168)	$27,532
					(14,307)	
					(1,267)	
LIFO closing inventory	$81,739	$103,918	$96,046	$107,214	$80,472	$108,004
Cost of inventory, retail method	$77,266	$115,345	$124,602	$144,418	$119,034	$157,425
Cumulative LIFO adjustment	(4,473)	11,427	28,556	37,204	38,562	49,421
Annual LIFO adjustment	(4,473)	15,900	17,129	8,648	1,358	10,859

The foregoing discussion covers the mechanics of computing the cost of inventories under the LIFO principle in most of the situations encountered. When the index decreases below that applicable to the previous year, no change in method of computation is required. The retail value is always reduced by the cumulative index to arrive at the base price level. Should the cumulative LIFO adjustment fall below the cumulative adjustment at the end of the previous year, the effect will be to increase income, or the opposite from the effect shown by the entries in the illustration.

On page 350 a second form of LIFO work sheet is shown which is quite similar to the previously discussed type in its application. This form is an adaptation of the method outlined in Treasury Department Mimeograph 6244, issued March 9, 1948. Some retailers consider this form preferable because the computation of the net result (cumulative column) may be readily checked on the form to uncover possible errors in the annual calculations.

The Treasury Department has approved for federal income tax purposes additional alternative treatments of markdowns in computing the cost complement percentage: (1) eliminate from the annual net markon computation all markdowns specifically relating to goods in the opening inventory (which may be identified by the use of seasonal letters on the markdown notices or other identification procedures) and (2) where specific segregation of markdowns is not possible, include in the computation a portion of the total markdowns in the ratio that purchases at retail for the period relate to the opening retail inventory plus purchases at retail as shown in the following formula:

$$\frac{\text{Purchases at retail}}{\text{Opening inventory} + \text{purchases}} \times \text{Total markdowns}$$

Application of the second of these alternative procedures to a computation of the markup percentages reflected by the factors in the examples on pages 319 and 321 may be illustrated as at the top of page 351.

Departmental LIFO Inventory Calculations

(Alternative Form)

No. 12—Woolen Dress Goods (Department)

Line		Base year	First year	Second year	Third year	Fourth year	Fifth year	Cumulative through fifth year
1.	Opening inventory at basic price retail level		$132,350	$162,510	$151,806	$164,296	$130,298	$130,298
2.	Opening inventory at LIFO		81,739	103,918	96,046	107,214	107,214	80,472
3.	Cost complement to LIFO markup %	61.76%	61.13%	N/A	62.05%	N/A	61.85%	
4.	Closing inventory at retail	$132,350	$195,500	$207,670	$236,750	$196,750	$261,720	$261,720
5.	Price index reflecting change accumulated since basic LIFO date	100%	120.3%	136.8%	144.1%	151.0%	166.7%	166.7%
6.	Closing inventory at basic price retail level (4 ÷ 5)	$132,350	$162,510	$151,806	$164,296	$130,298	$157,001	$157,001
7.	Increase or (decrease) attributable to:							
	Basic inventory	132,350						$130,298
	First year's increment		30,160	(10,704)		(2,052)		—
	Second year's increment					(19,456)		—
	Third year's increment				12,490	(12,490)		
	Fourth year's increment							
	Fifth year's increment						$ 26,703	$ 26,703
						$(33,998)		$157,001
8.	Increase or (decrease) at prices existing when acquired	(100%) $132,350 (120.3%)	36,282 (120.3%)	(12,877) (144.1%)	17,998 (144.1%) (120.3%) (100%)	(17,998) (166.7%) (23,405) (120.3%) (2,052) (100%)	44,514 (166.7%) (100%)	$ 44,514 (166.7%) 130,298 (100%)
9.	Cost of increases or (decreases)	(7,872) (62.05%) (61.76%)	81,739 (61.76%)	22,179 (61.13%)	11,168 (62.05%) (61.13%) (61.76%)	(11,168) (62.05%) (14,307) (61.13%) (1,267) (61.76%)	27,532 (61.85%) (61.76%)	27,532 (61.85%) 80,472 (61.76%)
10.	LIFO closing inventory	$ 81,739	$103,918	$ 96,046	$107,214	$ 80,472	$108,004	$108,004
11.	Cost of inventory, retail method	77,266	115,345	124,602	144,418	119,034	157,425	157,425
12.	Cumulative LIFO adjustment	$(4,473)	$11,427	$28,556	$37,204	$38,562	$49,421	$49,421
13.	Annual LIFO adjustment	(4,473)	15,900	17,129	8,648	1,358	10,859	49,421

Determining Markup Percentage by Adjusting Markups
for Proportion of Markdowns

	Retail	Markup %	Cost
Beginning inventory..............	$ 6,220	40.52	$ 3,700
Purchases......................	$58,795		$34,040
Freight and express..............	—		300
Additional markups..............	150		—
Retail adjustments...............	(45)		—
	$58,900		
Markdowns—			
$\frac{58,900}{65,120} \times \$255$..............	231		—
Current-year purchases..........	$58,669	41.47	$34,340

On the basis of the foregoing, the cost complement percentage for the year 58.53 per cent. As stated on page 337, the markup percentage for LIFO purposes is computed without the use of the opening inventory.

The procedures described in this chapter and commonly used by retailers have the effect of pricing LIFO inventory increments at the average cost for the year during which the increment occurred. The general provisions of the federal income tax regulations are to the effect that taxpayers have a right of election to cost inventory increments by reference to earliest or latest purchases in the year, as alternatives to the average cost. The available statistics lend themselves to developing such alternative procedures, and they should receive careful consideration.

IN-TRANSIT AND WAREHOUSE INVENTORIES

Inventory in transit and in warehouses at the end of each year will ordinarily be treated under the LIFO method the same as all other merchandise owned by the taxpayer. The usual practice is to record such goods as a part of each department's inventory and include it in the computation of the markon percentage. The data used in determining in-transit inventory at the year end are frequently obtained by an analysis of the departmental purchase ledgers and unposted invoices in the following month, and a journal entry made to set up the amount of the inventory and the liability for its cost. This year-end entry may be reversed in the month following closing, since the shipments will be included in the regularly compiled total purchases. The in-transit and warehouse inventories are used in the departmental LIFO work sheets but do not appear as a separate item.

The inclusion of the in-transit inventory increases the departmental merchandise pools and provides a larger base. In some instances, however, retailers have chosen to ignore in-transit goods for LIFO purposes and merely show the total in-transit inventory cost as an addition to inventory in a manner similar to stores not on LIFO. If a consistent practice is followed, the Treasury Department representatives should have no objection regardless of which procedure is followed. The same latitude is not generally recognized, however, as regards warehouse stock. Even though a consistent practice is followed, the facility with which goods could be transferred from the warehouse inventory (if it is carried at specific invoice cost) to the store inventory (where it enters into the retail computation) places the control of the inventory in the hands of the retailer almost as a matter of compilation of figures rather than as a result of the exercise of business judgment in the timing of merchandise purchases.

Regardless of the benefits which may flow from including the in-transit inventory in the LIFO base, situations have arisen in practice where, at the time it was decided that the LIFO method would be adopted (generally near or after the end of the year), there was no practical procedure by which the cost of the goods in transit at the beginning of the year could be classified by departments. Wherever the possibility of adopting LIFO can be anticipated, it may be advisable currently to analyze the in-transit inventory on a departmental basis even though there would be no advantage therefrom if the ultimate decision is against adoption of LIFO. If this is not practicable, there is no reason why LIFO cannot be extended to cover the in-transit inventory at the end of the year. The result would merely be to have the in-transit merchandise reflected in the LIFO inventory as a factor determining an increase or decrease for the year rather than as part of the LIFO base. Procedurally, an additional election on Treasury Department Form 970 should be filed with the federal income tax return covering the year for which in-transit merchandise is first included in the LIFO computations of both the beginning and ending inventories.   The LIFO method can thus be extended to cover the in-transit inventory at any time at the retailer's election, but if the election is once made a consistent practice must be subsequently followed.

In many cases the retail value of the in-transit inventory is not specifically computed, but the amount to be used in the LIFO computations as the retail value is determined by applying to the cost the markon percentage for the month following the close of the year.   There are also circumstances where this procedure can appropriately be followed with respect to the warehouse stock.

RESERVE FOR CASH DISCOUNTS

Fundamentally, the reserve for cash discounts represents a valuation account which reduces inventory to the cost after discounts have been taken into account.   Department stores normally post their purchase invoices before discount, the effect of which overstates the true cost.   The conventional method is to maintain a reserve for discount for each department on the basis of experience, and the actual discount is taken up when earned.

The treatment of cash discount reserves for LIFO purposes varies with retailers and is not too significant in relation to other LIFO factors.   A good theoretical, but generally impractical, treatment is to include in each departmental inventory layer a portion of the discount reserve applicable to that year.   This, of course, involves additional calculations and record-keeping. Among alternative practical procedures is to deduct the discount reserve (at retail) from the closing retail inventories *before* application of the LIFO computation.   The effect of this procedure is to take into consideration a logical reduction in the inventory for cash discounts without getting involved in computations that would produce immaterial adjustments.   Another practice is to ignore the effect of the reserve for cash discounts for LIFO purposes and compute LIFO on the "gross" cost.   In the departmental operating statements for some stores, however, the discount earned is offset against the cost of sales to determine the gross margin.

LIFO GROUPINGS ON DEPARTMENTAL BASIS

As previously noted, department stores are required generally to make separate LIFO computations for each department even though the same price index will be applied to several of the departments. For LIFO purposes, a department is commonly regarded as being comprised of any group of merchandise items for which a separate stock ledger is maintained under the retail inventory method. As with other accounting and tax questions, however, recognition must be given to the circumstances of each individual case, and a sounder application of the LIFO principle may result from the combining of several departments into a single LIFO group. Approximately ninety departments in one store were found to be susceptible of classification into less than forty groups for which the LIFO computations were made. Combining of inventories with from one to five other departments was appropriate for approximately 80 per cent of the total number. The prime consideration in combining the departments was the interchangeability of merchandise for sale, although such factors as price range, homogeneity of buying or merchandising control, and department location afforded some support for certain combinations. Examples of groupings include the combining of basement departments with regular store departments selling like goods and the pooling of summer furniture with regular furniture. Generally, in the case of retailers operating several stores in different locations, the similar departments should be combined for LIFO purposes in order to preserve, through offsets, the base inventory volume of layers which might be lost in yearly fluctuations of individual departments.

A retailer need not place all his departmental inventories on LIFO; but once the LIFO method is elected for a particular department, it may not be changed without permission from the Commissioner of Internal Revenue. Certain "cost" and "contract" departments (e.g., alteration and wholesale departments) usually do not determine their inventories under the retail method nor use LIFO, but the great majority of other departments are suitable for LIFO.

Based on forecasts of price movements in particular lines of goods and the extent of turnovers and resultant inventory changes, management must decide which departments will apply the LIFO principle. Some retailers who adopted LIFO in 1941 excluded from their election such departments as electrical appliances, hosiery, and toys because of the uncertainty of war restrictions and government allocations. The greatest tax benefit from LIFO is secured if the election is made when faced with increasing prices and taxes; however, an actual tax detriment may be sustained if income deferred by reason of applying LIFO must be recognized because of an inventory liquidation in a higher tax-rate year.

Continuity of departments is a problem that arises frequently with retailers. In the usual department store there are frequent changes in departmental structure, due to establishing new departments, discontinuing old departments, and combining or subdividing existing departments. Continuity may also be affected by leasing a department or otherwise placing its operations in the hands of a concessionaire. Conversely, a retailer may take over a department which has been operated by a concessionaire.

The problem created by lack of continuity is especially significant since, under the retail method, there is no specific identity of goods and dollar units only are used.

If the election is made to put a new department on LIFO, the base is established by using the year-end figures for the inventory and price level of the initial LIFO year, and subsequent quantity and price-level changes are determined from this base. The discontinuance of a department results in reflecting in the income statement the departmental cumulative LIFO adjustment.

Combining two or more existing departments after a period of operation of LIFO can be achieved by combining the corresponding dollar figures to date for each departmental retail layer. Each retail layer making up the total remains intact on the combined basis; but it is necessary to recompute the LIFO markon complement percentage, using the combined figures. In most cases the departments being combined will be similar, at least to the extent that they have been within the same B.L.S. price index grouping; however, the same procedure can be used in the case of two departments in different price index groups. The index covering the greater portion of the merchandise would be used for the department after the consolidation.[2]

Continuing to record the data on a combined basis after a previously existing department has been split may be the only practical procedure. This is a logical exception to the general rule that each departmental computation should be carried out separately. If separate computations are to be made, however, each of the LIFO inventory layers may be apportioned on the basis of the relative volume of the inventories of the split departments at the time of the separation.[3]

SPECIALTY STORES

Every retail store does not automatically qualify as a department store under the rulings which have been issued by the Treasury Department with respect to the use of the B.L.S. price indexes. Generally, a retail store may use the B.L.S. indexes for federal income tax purposes if it has a reasonable number and variety of departments and if the goods carried in the various departments are reasonably similar to those carried in the corresponding departments by a typical department store in the particular locality. It is not necessary that all the departments of the most elaborate store be represented.

The Treasury Department has not yet conceded that an extremely specialized store carrying a single line of goods, such as a shoe store, a radio and television store, or an electrical appliance store, could elect LIFO and use a single B.L.S. index. In such a situation the burden would be upon the retailer to show that the B.L.S. index is adequately representative of its whole inventory. On the other hand, a retail establishment known in the trade as a *specialty store*, may use the appropriate B.L.S. index if it employs the retail inventory method and its departmental inventories are reasonably similar to those carried by department stores. Types of recognized specialty stores include establish-

[2] The procedure for combining dollar-value LIFO pools is commented upon in section 1.472–8(g)(2) of the regulations, Appendix C.
[3] This procedure for separating a dollar-value LIFO pool is illustrated in section 1.472–8(g)(2)(ii) of the regulations.

ments carrying a variety of ladies' wear and accessories or men's clothing and furnishings, or a reasonably full line of furniture and home furnishings.

There have been cases where specialty stores chose to use the B.L.S. indexes even though the inventory records are kept on the basis of cost, rather than the retail method. For this purpose cost price indexes may be computed from the department store inventory (retail) price indexes. The theory is that the difference between the movements of wholesale (or cost) and retail prices for any given year will be reflected in a change in the markon percentage. If the markon is uniform within any particular department or line of merchandise, the cost and retail prices for the goods handled will necessarily change in the same relative amount.

The computed cost indexes for various inventory dates will be equal to the retail price indexes multiplied by the fraction representing the ratio of the cost percentages. A good merchandiser will know his average net markon and cost percentages even though he does not use the retail method. The LIFO inventory computations in this situation may be illustrated as follows:

	Base year	First year	Second year
Cost indexes:			
1. Retail price index....................	100	105	115
2. Net markon %......................	40.5%	42.0%	39.1%
3. Cost %...........................	59.5%	58.0%	60.9%
4. Ratio of cost %....................	59.5/59.5	58.0/59.5	60.9/59.5
5. Cost index (1 × 4)..................	100	102.3	117.7
LIFO inventories:			
6. Inventory at cost (FIFO).............	$50,000	$70,000	$55,000
7. Inventory at base-year cost			
(6 ÷ 5 × 100)..................	$50,000	$68,426	$46,729
8. LIFO inventories—			
$50,000 × 100 =	$50,000		
	————		
$50,000 × 100 =		$50,000	
18,426 × 102.3 =		18,850	
$68,426 =		$68,850	
————		————	
$46,729 × 100 =			$46,729

The net markon and cost percentages (lines 2 and 3 above) are determined for each department on the basis of the retailer's own average for the year. These percentages will be based upon the year's sales (rather than being based upon purchases as under the retail inventory method), but any differences will tend to average out over a few years.[4]

VARIETY STORES

For June and December, 1953, the Treasury Department published special price indexes for use by *variety stores*. These establishments are those engaged primarily in selling at retail a variety of merchandise in the low and popular price ranges, such as stationery, gift items, women's accessories, toilet articles, light hardware, toys, housewares, confectionery, and so forth. They are commonly known as *5 and 10 cent stores* and *5 cents to a dollar stores*, although higher-priced merchandise is usually carried.

Twenty-seven departments were grouped for the purpose of establishing eleven B.L.S. indexes in a manner somewhat similar to the indexes for retail department stores. The use of the indexes was not mandatory; and for federal income tax purposes stores were permitted to prepare their own indexes provided sound statistical methods were used. When the Bureau of Labor Statistics discontinued publication of variety store inventory price indexes, retailers were permitted to use indexes prepared from their own data.[5]

[4] The application of B.L.S. indexes to specialty stores is discussed in Rev. Rul. 23, 1953–1 C.B. 34; and Rev. Rul. 54–49, 1954–1 C.B. 32.
[5] The development of price indexes for variety stores is discussed in Rev. Rul. 54–63, 1954–1 C.B. 33; and Rev. Rul. 55–220, 1955–1 C.B. 247.

Appendix A

"Inventory Pricing" by the Committee on Accounting Procedure of the American Institute of Certified Public Accountants*

(Chapter 4 of Accounting Research Bulletin No. 43)

Periodic inventories are necessary.   1. Whenever the operation of a business includes the ownership of a stock of goods, it is necessary for adequate financial accounting purposes that inventories be properly compiled periodically and recorded in the accounts.[1] Such inventories are required both for the statement of financial position and for the periodic measurement of income.

Conclusions directed to merchandisers and manufacturers.   2. This chapter sets forth the general principles applicable to the pricing of inventories of mercantile and manufacturing enterprises. Its conclusions are not directed to or necessarily applicable to noncommercial businesses or to regulated utilities.

STATEMENT 1

The term *inventory* is used herein to designate the aggregate of those items of tangible personal property which (1)

---

* Quoted by permission of the American Institute of Certified Public Accountants. The marginal notations are the author's.
[1] Prudent reliance upon perpetual inventory records is not precluded.

are held for sale in the ordinary course of business, (2) are in process of production for such sale, or (3) are to be currently consumed in the production of goods or services to be available for sale.

Discussion

Scope of the term "inventory." 3. The term *inventory* embraces goods awaiting sale (the merchandise of a trading concern and the finished goods of a manufacturer), goods in the course of production (work in process), and goods to be consumed directly or indirectly in production (raw materials and supplies). This definition of inventories excludes long-term assets subject to depreciation accounting, or goods which, when into use, will be so classified. The fact that a depreciable asset is retired from regular use and held for sale does not indicate that the item should be classified as part of the inventory. Raw materials and supplies purchased for production may be used or consumed for the construction of long-term assets or other purposes not related to production, but the fact that inventory items representing a small portion of the total may not be absorbed ultimately in the production process does not require separate classification. By trade practice, operating materials and supplies of certain types of companies such as oil producers are usually treated as inventory.

STATEMENT 2

A major objective of accounting for inventories is the proper determination of income through the process of matching appropriate costs against revenues.

Discussion

Major objective of an inventory is determination of realized income. 4. An inventory has financial significance because revenues may be obtained from its sale, or from the sale of the goods or services in whose production it is used. Normally such revenues arise in a continuous repetitive process or cycle of operations by which goods are acquired and sold, and further goods are acquired for additional sales. In accounting for the goods in the inventory at any point of time, the major objective is the matching of appropriate costs against revenues in order that there may be a proper determination of the realized income. Thus, the inventory at any given date is the balance of costs applicable to goods on hand remaining after the matching of absorbed costs with concurrent revenues. This balance is appropriately carried to future periods provided it does not exceed an amount properly chargeable against the revenues expected to be obtained from ultimate disposition of the goods carried forward. In practice, this balance is determined by the process of pricing the articles comprised in the inventory.

STATEMENT 3

The primary basis of accounting for inventories is cost, which has been defined generally as the price paid or consideration given to acquire an asset. As applied to inventories, cost means in principle the sum of the applicable expenditures and charges directly or indirectly incurred in bringing an article to its existing condition and location.

Discussion

Definition of "cost" as applied to inventories. 5. In keeping with the principle that accounting is primarily based on cost, there is a presumption that inventories should be stated at cost. The definition of cost as applied to inventories is understood to mean acquisition and production cost,[2] and its determination involves many problems. Although principles for the determination of inventory costs may be easily stated, their application, particularly to such inventory items as work in process and finished goods, is difficult because of the variety of problems encountered in the allocation of costs and charges. For example, under some circumstances, items such as idle facility expense, excessive spoilage, double freight, and rehandling costs may be so abnormal as to require treatment as current period charges rather than as a portion of the inventory cost. Also, general and administrative expenses should be included as period charges, except for the portion of such expenses that may be clearly related to production and thus constitute a part of inventory costs (product charges). Selling expenses constitute no part of inventory costs. It should also be recognized that the exclusion of all overheads from inventory costs does not constitute an accepted accounting procedure. The exercise of judgment in an individual situation involves a consideration of the adequacy of the procedures of the cost accounting system in use, the soundness of the principles thereof, and their consistent application.

STATEMENT 4

Cost for inventory purposes may be determined under any one of several assumptions as to the flow of cost factors (such as first-in first-out, average, and last-in first-out); the major objective in selecting a method should be to choose the one which, under the circumstances, most clearly reflects periodic income.

[2] In the case of goods which have been written down below cost at the close of a fiscal period, such reduced amount is to be considered the cost for subsequent accounting purposes.

Discussion

Use of identi-
fied cost for
items sold may
not most clearly
reflect income.

6. The cost to be matched against revenue from a sale may not be the identified cost of the specific item which is sold, especially in cases in which similar goods are purchased at different times and at different prices. While in some lines of business specific lots are clearly identified from the time of purchase through the time of sale and are costed on this basis, ordinarily the identity of goods is lost between the time of acquisition and the time of sale. In any event, if the materials purchased in various lots are identical and interchangeable, the use of identified cost of the various lots may not produce the most useful financial statements. This fact has resulted in the development of general acceptance of several assumptions with respect to the flow of cost factors (such as *first-in first-out*, *average*, and *last-in first-out*) to provide practical bases for the measurement of periodic income.[3] In some situations a reversed mark-up procedure of inventory pricing, such as the retail inventory method, may be both practical and appropriate. The business operations in some cases may be such as to make it desirable to apply one of the acceptable methods of determining cost to one portion of the inventory or components thereof and another of the acceptable methods to other portions of the inventory.

Benefit of
uniformity
within an
industry.

7. Although selection of the method should be made on the basis of the individual circumstances, it is obvious that financial statements will be more useful if uniform methods of inventory pricing are adopted by all companies within a given industry.

STATEMENT 5

A departure from the cost basis of pricing the inventory is required when the utility of the goods is no longer as great as its cost. Where there is evidence that the utility of goods, in their disposal in the ordinary course of business, will be less than cost, whether due to physical deterioration, obsolescence, changes in price levels, or other causes, the difference should be recognized as a loss of the current period. This is generally accomplished by stating such goods at a lower level commonly designated as *market*.

---

[3] Standard costs are acceptable if adjusted at reasonable intervals to reflect current conditions so that at the balance-sheet date standard costs reasonably approximate costs computed under one of the recognized bases. In such cases descriptive language should be used which will express this relationship, as, for instance, "approximate costs determined on the first-in first-out basis," or, if it is desired to mention standard costs, "at standard costs, approximating average costs."

Discussion

Where the utility of goods is less than cost, a loss should be recognized.

8. Although the cost basis ordinarily achieves the objective of a proper matching of costs and revenues, under certain circumstances cost may not be the amount properly chargeable against the revenues of future periods. A departure from cost is required in these circumstances because cost is satisfactory only if the utility of the goods has not diminished since their acquisition; a loss of utility is to be reflected as a charge against the revenues of the period in which it occurs. Thus, in accounting for inventories, a loss should be recognized whenever the utility of goods is impaired by damage, deterioration, obsolescence, changes in price levels, or other causes. The measurement of such losses is accomplished by applying the rule of pricing inventories at *cost or market, whichever is lower.* This provides a practical means of measuring utility and thereby determining the amount of the loss to be recognized and accounted for in the current period.

STATEMENT 6

As used in the phrase *lower of cost or market*[4] the term *market* means current replacement cost (by purchase or by reproduction, as the case may be) except that:

(1) Market should not exceed the net realizable value (i.e., estimated selling price in the ordinary course of business less reasonably predictable costs of completion and disposal); and (2) Market should not be less than net realizable value reduced by an allowance for an approximately normal profit margin.

Discussion

Definition of "market" as applied to inventories.

9. The rule of *cost or market, whichever is lower* is intended to provide a means of measuring the residual usefulness of an inventory expenditure. The term *market* is therefore to be interpreted as indicating utility on the inventory date and may be thought of in terms of the equivalent expenditure which would have to be made in the ordinary course at that date to procure corresponding utility. As a general guide, utility is indicated primarily by the current cost of replacement of the goods as they would be obtained by purchase or reproduction. In applying the rule, however, judgment must always be exercised and no loss should be recognized unless the evidence indicates

[4] The terms *cost or market, whichever is lower* and *lower of cost or market* are used synonymously in general practice and in this chapter. The committee does not express any preference for either of the two alternatives.

clearly that a loss has been sustained. There are therefore exceptions to such a standard. Replacement or reproduction prices would not be appropriate as a measure of utility when the estimated sales value, reduced by the costs of completion and disposal, is lower, in which case the realizable value so determined more appropriately measures utility. Furthermore, where the evidence indicates that cost will be recovered with an approximately normal profit upon sale in the ordinary course of business, no loss should be recognized even though replacement or reproduction costs are lower. This might be true, for example, in the case of production under firm sales contracts at fixed prices, or when a reasonable volume of future orders is assured at stable selling prices.

Definition of "market" is not a literal rule.   10. Because of the many variations of circumstances encountered in inventory pricing, Statement 6 is intended as a guide rather than a literal rule. It should be applied realistically in the light of the objectives expressed in this chapter and with due regard to the form, content, and composition of the inventory. The committee considers, for example, that the retail inventory method, if adequate markdowns are currently taken, accomplishes the objectives described herein. It also recognizes that, if a business is expected to lose money for a sustained period, the inventory should not be written down to offset a loss inherent in the subsequent operations.

STATEMENT 7

Depending on the character and composition of the inventory, the rule of *cost or market, whichever is lower* may properly be applied either directly to each item or to the total of the inventory (or, in some cases, to the total of the components of each major category). The method should be that which most clearly reflects periodic income.

Discussion

No absolute basis for cost/market comparison.   11. The purpose of reducing inventory to *market* is to reflect fairly the income of the period. The most common practice is to apply the *lower of cost or market* rule separately to each item of the inventory. However, if there is only one end-product category the cost utility of the total stock—the inventory in its entirety—may have the greatest significance for accounting purposes. Accordingly, the reduction of individual items to *market* may not always lead to the most useful result if the utility of the total inventory to the business is not below its cost. This might be the case if selling prices are not affected by temporary or small fluctuations in current costs of purchase or manufacture. Similarly, where more than one major product or operational category exists, the application of the *cost or market, whichever is lower* rule to the total of the items included in such major categories may result in the most useful determination of income.

Significance of balanced inventories. 12. When no loss of income is expected to take place as a result of a reduction of cost prices of certain goods because others forming components of the same general categories of finished products have a market equally in excess of cost, such components need not be adjusted to market to the extent that they are in balanced quantities. Thus, in such cases, the rule of *cost or market, whichever is lower* may be applied directly to the totals of the entire inventory, rather than to the individual inventory items, if they enter into the same category of finished product and if they are in balanced quantities, provided the procedure is applied consistently from year to year.

Cost/market comparison on item basis for excessive quantities. 13. To the extent, however, that the stocks of particular materials or components are excessive in relation to others, the more widely recognized procedure of applying the *lower of cost or market* to the individual items constituting the excess should be followed. This would also apply in cases in which the items enter into the production of unrelated products or products having a material variation in the rate of turnover. Unless an effective method of classifying categories is practicable, the rule should be applied to each item in the inventory.

Specific reporting of unusual losses. 14. When substantial and unusual losses result from the application of this rule it will frequently be desirable to disclose the amount of the loss in the income statement as a charge separately identified from the consumed inventory costs described as *cost of goods sold.*

STATEMENT 8

The basis of stating inventories must be consistently applied and should be disclosed in the financial statements; whenever a significant change is made therein, there should be disclosure of the nature of the change and, if material, the effect on income.

Discussion

Inconsistency in basis for inventories may improperly affect income statements. 15. While the basis of stating inventories does not affect the overall gain or loss on the ultimate disposition of inventory items, any inconsistency in the selection or employment of a basis may improperly affect the periodic amounts of income or loss. Because of the common use and importance of periodic statements, a procedure adopted for the treatment of inventory items should be consistently applied in order that the results reported may be fairly allocated as between years.

A change of such basis may have an important effect upon the interpretation of the financial statements both before and after that change, and hence, in the event of a change, a full disclosure of its nature and of its effect, if material, upon income should be made.

STATEMENT 9

Only in exceptional cases may inventories properly be stated above cost. For example, precious metals having a fixed monetary value with no substantial cost of marketing may be stated at such monetary value; any other exceptions must be justifiable by inability to determine appropriate approximate costs, immediate marketability at quoted market price, and the characteristic of unit interchangeability. Where goods are stated above cost this fact should be fully disclosed.

Discussion

Some inventories may be based on sales prices. 16. It is generally recognized that income accrues only at the time of sale, and that gains may not be anticipated by reflecting assets at their current sales prices. For certain articles, however, exceptions are permissible. Inventories of gold and silver, when there is an effective government-controlled market at a fixed monetary value, are ordinarily reflected at selling prices. A similar treatment is not uncommon for inventories representing agricultural, mineral, and other products, units of which are interchangeable and have an immediate marketability at quoted prices and for which appropriate costs may be difficult to obtain. Where such inventories are stated at sales prices, they should of course be reduced by expenditures to be incurred in disposal, and the use of such basis should be fully disclosed in the financial statements.

STATEMENT 10

Accrued net losses on firm purchase commitments for goods for inventory, measured in the same way as are inventory losses, should, if material, be recognized in the accounts and the amounts thereof separately disclosed in the income statement.

Discussion

Recognition of commitment losses. 17. The recognition in a current period of losses arising from the decline in the utility of cost expenditures is equally applicable to similar losses which are expected to arise from firm, uncancelable, and unhedged commitments for the future purchase of inventory items. The net loss on such commitments should be measured in the same way as are inventory losses and, if material, should be recognized in the accounts and separately disclosed in the income statement. The utility of such commitments is not impaired, and hence there is no loss, when the amounts to be realized from the disposition of the future inventory items are adequately protected by firm sales contracts or when there are other circumstances which reasonably assure continuing sales without price decline.

One member of the committee, Mr. Wellington, assented with qualification, and two members, Messrs. Mason and Peloubet, dissented to adoption of chapter 4.

Points of qualification or dissent by committee members. Mr. Wellington objects to footnote (2) to statement 3. He believes that an exception should be made for goods costed on the *last-in first-out* (LIFO) basis. In the case of goods costed on all bases other than LIFO the reduced amount (market below cost) is cleared from the accounts through the regular accounting entries of the subsequent period, and if the market price rises to or above the original cost there will be an increased profit in the subsequent period. Accounts kept under the LIFO method should also show a similar increased profit in the subsequent period, which will be shown if the LIFO inventory is restored to its original cost. To do otherwise, as required by footnote (2), is to carry the LIFO inventory, not at the lower of cost or current market, but at the lowest market ever known since the LIFO method was adopted by the company.

Mr. Mason dissents from this chapter because of its acceptance of the inconsistencies inherent in *cost or market, whichever is lower*. In his opinion a drop in selling price below cost is no more of a realized loss than a rise above cost is a realized gain under a consistent criterion of realization.

Mr. Peloubet believes it is ordinarily preferable to carry inventory at not less than recoverable cost, and particularly in the case of manufactured or partially manufactured goods which can be sold only in finished form. He recognizes that application of the *cost or market* valuation basis necessitates the shifting of income from one period to another, but objects to unnecessarily accentuating this shift by the use, even limited as it is in this chapter, of reproduction or replacement cost as *market* when such cost is less than net selling price.

Appendix B

"Treatment of Stock-in-Trade and Work in Progress in Financial Accounts" Issued November 16, 1960, as Statement 22 by The Institute of Chartered Accountants in England and Wales*

The Council of The Institute of Chartered Accountants in England and Wales makes the following Recommendation to members of the Institute on the treatment of stock-in-trade and work in progress in the financial accounts of industrial and commercial enterprises. The Recommendation replaces Recommendation 10 and it is hoped that it will be helpful to members in advising, in appropriate cases, as to the best practice.

Appropriate-ness of basis and consist-ency are essential. 1. In the financial accounts of industrial and commercial undertakings few matters require more careful consideration than the amount to be attributed to stock-in-trade and work in progress. Circumstances vary so widely that no one basis of arriving at the amount is suitable for all types of business nor even for all undertakings within a particular trade or industry. Unless the basis adopted is appropriate to the circumstances of the particular undertaking and used consistently from period to period, the accounts will not give a true and fair view either of the state

---

* Quoted by permission of The Institute of Chartered Accountants in England and Wales. The marginal notations are the author's.

368

of affairs of the undertaking as on the balance sheet date or of the trend of its trading results from period to period.   The need to give a true and fair view is the overriding consideration applicable in all circumstances.

Periodic   2. In order to arrive at the amount to be carried forward, as
inventories   on the balance sheet date, for stock-in-trade and work in
are neces-   progress it is necessary to ascertain (from stocktaking at
sary.   the end of the period or from stock records maintained and
verified during the period) the quantities on hand and to make a proper calculation of the amount.   It cannot be emphasized too strongly that all stocks belonging to the business should be taken into account, whatever their location or nature.   This Recommendation does not deal with the methods of ascertaining the quantities on hand but is confined to an examination of the factors to be considered when computing the amount.   The word "stock" is used hereafter to embrace stock-in-trade and work in progress.

NORMAL BASIS

Normally   3. The basis normally used for the determination of the
at cost   amount to be carried forward for stock is its cost less any
or less.   part thereof which properly needs to be written off at the
balance sheet date.   It is in computing cost and the amount, if any, to be written off that practical difficulties arise.

Cost

Elements of cost

Elements   4. The elements making up the cost of stock are:
of "cost."

(*a*) direct expenditure on the purchase of goods bought for resale, and of materials and components used in the manufacture of finished goods

(*b*) other direct expenditure which can be identified specifically as having been incurred in acquiring the stock or bringing it to its existing condition and location; examples are direct labour, transport, processing and packaging

(*c*) such part, if any, of the overhead expenditure as is properly carried forward in the circumstances of the business instead of being charged against the revenue of the period in which it was incurred.

Treatment of overhead expenditure

Consider-   5. Before deciding upon the method by which to compute
ation of   "cost" it is necessary to consider to what extent, if at all,
overhead.   the inclusion of overhead expenditure is appropriate to
the particular business.

Elements of   6. Overhead expenditure may be divided into (*a*) produc-
"overhead."   tion expenses such as factory rent, rates, depreciation,
insurance and supervision, and other indirect expenses of acquiring and
producing stock; (*b*) administration expenses not attributable directly to
the acquisition or production of stock or the bringing of it to a saleable
condition and location; (*c*) selling expenses; (*d*) finance charges. Another
classification (which can be applied also to each of the foregoing divisions)
is to distinguish between "fixed overheads," that is to say standing charges
such as rent and rates which accrue and expire wholly or largely on a time
basis, and "variable overheads," which vary in a greater or lesser degree
with the level of activity of the undertaking or of the department concerned
but are not so closely associated with production or the volume of production as to be classed as direct expenditure.

Differing   7. Opinions differ on the extent to which overhead expen-
views of   diture should be included in computing the cost of stock,
overhead.   though it is generally agreed that it cannot properly include
selling and finance and other expenses which do not relate to the bringing of
stock to its existing condition and location. The following are some practices which reflect the differing views on this matter:

(*a*) in some businesses no overhead expenditure is included as an element
in determining the cost of stock which is to be carried forward

(*b*) in others only the "marginal" cost of unsold stock is included,
that is to say that part of the cost of production of the period which
has been incurred only because the stock remaining on hand was
acquired or produced; all other expenses, including depreciation, are
dealt with as revenue charges of the period for which they are
incurred, the ground being that they arise irrespective of the quantity
of stock which remains on hand at the end of the period and therefore
are not an element in its cost

(*c*) in other businesses an appropriate proportion of the overhead
expenditure relevant to the period of production is included on the
ground that for the purpose of financial accounting any expense,
whatever its characteristics, which is related even though indirectly
to the acquisition or production of goods ought to be included in the
cost of those goods and ought not to be charged against revenue
until they are sold; an "appropriate proportion" is determined by
reference to a normal level of activity.

Method   8. These differing views about the inclusion of overhead
should be   expenditure may be very important in their effect upon
changed only   the amounts carried forward for stock and upon the
with circum-   profits disclosed in the accounts. No one method of
stances.   dealing with overhead expenditure is suitable for all businesses. The method selected by the management needs to be clearly
defined and must have regard to the nature and circumstances of the business

so as to ensure that the trend of the trading results will be shown fairly. Once the method has been selected it needs to be used consistently from period to period regardless of the amount of profits available or losses sustained. A change of method is appropriate only if there is a change in the relevant circumstances of the business. If material, the effect of a change of method would need to be disclosed in the accounts.

Consider- 9. In selecting a method of dealing with overhead expendi-
ations in ture the following are among the considerations which
selecting a arise:
method.

(a) *The nature of the business*
    In deciding whether to include a proportion of the overheads as expenditure on stock and also in deciding which elements of expense may properly be included for that purpose, it is necessary to have regard to the nature and the stage of development of the business, particularly factors such as the length of the production period, the probability of fluctuations in the level of production or the volume of sales, the risk of selling campaigns by competitors at reduced prices and the extent to which production is undertaken only to a customer's order or "for stock" in expectation of sales. At one extreme a business may operate at widely differing levels of production and produce goods in quantity in a highly competitive and sensitive market; at the other extreme, a business may be engaged on a long-term single project contract such as building a ship, a bridge, a road or a heavy engineering installation.

(b) *The levels of production and sales*
    Where the levels of production and sales are relatively stable and production and sales are kept in balance the inclusion of overhead expenditure in the amount attributed to stock may have little impact upon the incidence of profits as between the accounts of one period and those of another. Where however the levels are subject to material fluctuation and are not kept in balance it may be decided to exclude these expenses from stock on the ground that as they would be incurred whatever the levels of production or sales their inclusion in stock has the effect of relieving the profit and loss account in the period when they are incurred of expenses which it should fairly bear and of charging these expenses in a later period to which they do not properly relate.

(c) *Interruption or other exceptional curtailment of production*
    If overhead expenditure is included in the amount attributed to stock an adjustment will be necessary in the event of disruption in production by events such as a strike, a fire, an abnormal falling off in orders, or temporary difficulties in obtaining materials, with the result that the volume of production is abnormally or unexpectedly low. In such circumstances the amount included in respect of over-

head expenditure ought not to exceed an appropriate proportion on the basis of normal activity (see paragraph 7 (c)), the excess being treated as a charge against revenue in the period in which the expenditure was incurred. If the overhead expenditure is not related in this way to the normal, instead of the actual, level of production the effect may be to carry forward an excessive part of the expenditure of the period in which the disruption occurred. The profit and loss account of that period would thereby be relieved of charges which it ought to include and it would fail to reflect the adverse effects of the disruption during that period.

(d) *The risks of realisation at a loss*

In businesses which are highly competitive or have a sensitive market for their products, overhead expenditure may properly be omitted in order to avoid carrying forward expenditure which may prove irrecoverable. Examples are businesses dealing in "fashion" goods or those of a speciality character where the public taste may change quickly with the result that stocks can be realised only at a loss; businesses whose competitors may launch selling campaigns at short notice to get rid of stocks at reduced prices, sometimes at no more than the cost of the material and direct manufacturing expenditure; and businesses where new methods of production or improved designs may render existing stocks obsolete.

(e) *Maturing stocks*

In businesses which mature large stocks over long periods (for example, whisky, wine, timber) it is usual to exclude fixed overheads in order to avoid carrying forward large and increasing amounts of time-expired expenditure the recovery of which in the ultimate selling price is uncertain.

(f) *Long-term contracts*

In businesses which undertake contracts extending over a period of years the normal tendency is to include overhead expenditure in work in progress except where it is considered to be irrecoverable. If overheads are not included in work in progress on such contracts the accounts for the early years may indicate losses, followed by unduly large profits in the years when the contracts are completed. This would be a wholly unrealistic presentation in relation to a contract showing a normal profit. The distinction between businesses of this type and those referred to in (e) above is that in a business with firm contracts the prices are normally known or can be calculated whereas in a business with maturing stocks the ultimate price at which unsold stocks will be realised in the ordinary course of business is unknown and uncertain.

(g) *The extent of the variation in fixed or standing charges*

The less the fixed or standing charges vary in amount with variations in the volume of output, and the more they accrue on a purely time basis, the greater is the justification for their exclusion.

Allocation of expense question.   10. After weighing all relevant considerations it is necessary to decide whether and if so to what extent overhead expenditure should be included.   In this connection members are reminded of the Council publication entitled NOTES ON THE ALLOCATION OF EXPENSE.*

Methods of computation of cost

Methods of computing cost.   11. Apart from the variations which occur in calculating the amount to be attributed to each of the elements of cost there are various methods of computing cost.   In a small business one method only will normally be used but in a large composite business carrying on a variety of activities different methods may be used for different activities; once selected however the methods should be applied consistently to those activities from period to period.   The following are the principal methods:

(a) *"Unit" cost*

The total cost of stock is computed by aggregating the individual costs of each article, batch, parcel or other unit.   The method is not always capable of application, either because the individual units lose their identity (notably where stocks are bulked or pass through a number of processes) or because it would involve undue expense or complexity to keep individual records of cost particularly where these necessitate allocations of expense.

(b) *"First in, first out"*

Cost is computed on the assumption that goods sold or consumed are those which have been longest on hand and that those remaining in stock represent the latest purchases or production.

(c) *"Average" cost*

Cost is computed by averaging the amount at which stock is brought forward at the beginning of a period with the cost of stock acquired during the period; consumption in the period is then deducted at the average cost thus ascertained.   The periodical rests for calculating the average are as frequent as the circumstances and nature of the business require and permit.   In times of rising price levels this method tends to give a lower amount than the cost of unsold stock ascertained on a "first in, first out" basis and in times of falling prices a higher amount.

(d) *"Standard" cost*

A predetermined or budgeted cost per unit is used.   The method is particularly convenient where goods pass through a number of processes or are manufactured on mass production lines; but it will not result in a fair approximation to actual cost unless there is a regular review of the standards with appropriate adjustment and revision where necessary.

* A discussion of the relevant paragraphs from this publication commences on page 116.

(e) "*Adjusted selling price*"

This method is used widely in retail businesses. The cost of stock is estimated by calculating it in the first instance at selling prices and then deducting an amount equal to the normal margin of gross profit on such stocks. It should be appreciated that where the selling prices have been reduced the calculation will bring out cost only if appropriate allowance for price reductions is included in fixing the margin to be deducted; if no such allowance is made it may bring out amounts which approximate to replacement price as defined in paragraph 18. The calculations under this method may be made for individual items or groups of items or by departments.

Reduction to Net Realisable Value

Recognizing irrecoverable portion of cost.
12. When the cost of the stock has been determined it is then necessary to establish whether any portion of the outlay on stock is irrecoverable; to that extent a provision for the loss needs to be made. This calculation may be made either (i) by considering each article separately or (ii) by grouping articles in categories having regard to their similarity or inter-changeability or (iii) by considering the aggregate cost of the total stock in relation to its aggregate net realisable value. The third method involves setting foreseeable losses against expected but unrealised profits and would not normally be used in businesses which carry stocks which are large in relation to turnover.

Compare cost with "net realizable value."
13. The irrecoverable portion of the cost of the stock is the excess of its cost, as computed by the method of cost ascertainment which is deemed appropriate for the business, over the net realisable value of the stock. "Net realisable value" means the amount which it is estimated, as on the balance sheet date, will be realised from disposal of the stock in the ordinary course of business, either in its existing condition or as incorporated in the product normally sold, after allowing for all expenditure to be incurred on or before disposal.

Definition of "net realizable value."
14. "Net realisable value" is estimated by taking account of all available information, including changes in selling prices since the balance sheet date, so far as the information is of assistance in determining, as on the balance sheet date, the net realisable value of the stock in the ordinary course of business. This involves consideration of the prospects of disposal, having regard to the quantity and condition of the stock in relation to the expected demand (particular attention being given to obsolete or excessive stock) and to the expected effect, if any, on selling prices of any change which has taken place in buying prices of materials or goods.

Alternative comparison. 15. In some circumstances the replacement price of stock (as defined in paragraph 18) may be considered to be the best available guide to its net realisable value.

Reduction to Replacement Price

When is replacement price used? 16. In many businesses it is important to have regard to the price at which stock can be replaced if such price is less than cost. The considerations which lead to the use of replacement price include the following:

(a) *Uncertainty as to net realisable value*

Where the volume of stock carried is large in relation to turnover or there is a long period between the purchase of raw material and its conversion into and disposal as finished goods, selling prices current at the balance sheet date for the volume of orders then available may afford an unreliable guide to the prospective net realisable value of the stock as a whole. Replacement price may be considered to be the best available guide for this purpose.

(b) *Selling prices based on current replacement prices*

In some businesses where selling prices are based on or reflect current replacement prices it may be considered that the trading results of a subsequent period will be prejudiced if they are burdened with any amount for stock which exceeds its replacement price; where this view is taken it is regarded as important in reporting the results of the activities of a period, as compared with those of its successor or predecessor, that the period in which a reduction in buying prices occurs should bear the diminution in profit rather than the period of disposal whose realisations will be adversely affected by the events of the previous period.

(c) *Recognition of uneconomic buying or production*

Skill in buying or efficiency in production are most important matters in many businesses; the inclusion of stock in the accounts on a replacement price basis (where lower than net realisable value and cost) may be considered to reflect inefficiency in these respects on the ground that it involves the writing down of stock by an amount which represents approximately the result of misjudged buying or inefficient production.

Net realizable value also significant. 17. Where the replacement price basis is adopted the stock is stated at the lowest of (a) cost, (b) net realisable value, (c) replacement price, with the effect that the profit and loss account is charged with any reductions necessitated by an excess of (a) over (b) or (c) as the case may be.

Definition of "replacement price." 18. "Replacement price" for this purpose means an estimate of the amount for which, in the ordinary course of business, the stock could have been acquired or produced either at the balance sheet date or during the latest period up to and including that date.   In a manufacturing business this estimate would be based on the replacement price of the raw material content plus other costs of the under-taking which are relevant to the condition of the stock on the balance sheet date.   In all cases the prices used should be a fair reflection of the ordinary course of business; a depression which has passed before the accounts are completed would generally be disregarded.

Consistency in use of replacement price.   19. In the same way as it is necessary (as pointed out in paragraph 10) to decide whether and if so to what extent overhead expenditure should be included in calculating cost, it is necessary in each business to determine whether replacement price shall be taken into account in computing the amount carried forward for stock.   The basis selected by the management should be clearly defined and applied consistently from period to period regardless of the amount of profits available or the losses sustained, so as to enable the accounts to show a true and fair view of the trading results and the financial position.   If the basis is changed, the effect on the accounts would need to be disclosed if material.

SPECIAL BASES USED IN SOME BUSINESSES

Stocks at Selling Prices

Use of selling prices in some busi-nesses.   20. In some types of businesses, such as tea and rubber producing companies and some mining companies, it is a recognised practice to bring stocks of products into account at the prices realised subsequent to the balance sheet date, less only selling costs.   By this means the whole of the profit is shown in the period in which the crop is reaped or the minerals won.   This basis has come to be accepted as customary in the industries concerned.

Use of selling prices for by-products.   21. In manufacturing businesses which carry stocks of by-products the separate cost of which is not ascertainable these stocks are normally included at current selling price (or contract sale price where applicable) less any expenses to be incurred before disposal; the cost of the main product is reduced accordingly.

Long-term Contracts

Partially completed long-term contracts.   22. In businesses which involve the acceptance and comple-tion of long-term contracts it is often appropriate to spread over the period of the contracts, on a properly determined basis, the profits which are expected to be earned when the contracts are completed.   This procedure takes up in each period during the performance of the contract a reasonable amount as representing the contribution of that period towards the eventual profit; it thus recognises to a prudent extent the value of the work done in each period and restricts the distortion which would result from bringing in the whole of the profit in the period of completion. The principles which determine whether an element of profit is to be included are:

(a) profit should not be included until it is reasonably clear from the state of the work that a profit will ultimately be earned; it is therefore inappropriate to include any profit element where at the balance sheet date the contract has been in progress for a comparatively short time or to include an amount in excess of the profit element properly attributable to the work actually done

(b) provision should be made for foreseeable losses and allowance should be made as far as practicable for penalties, guarantees and other contingencies

(c) a clear basis for including a profit element should be established and adhered to consistently.

"Base Stock"

"Base stock" method. 23. In some businesses the minimum quantity of raw materials or other goods, without which they cannot operate their plant or conduct their operations, is treated as being a fixed asset which is under constant renewal by charges to revenue; that part of their stock (the base stock) is therefore carried forward not at its cost at the date of the accounts but at the cost of the original quantity of stock with which the business commenced operation. In old established businesses the amount will be based on prices paid for stocks acquired many years previously and many times replaced.

"Last in, First out"

LIFO method. 24. The "last in, first out" basis, which is in use in some overseas countries, assumes that the stocks sold or consumed in any period are those which were most recently acquired or made and therefore that the stocks whose cost is to be carried forward are those which were acquired, or made, earliest. The result is to charge consumption at prices approximating to current replacement prices and to carry forward stocks held at the close of the period at prices at which goods were purchased, or made, in earlier periods. When prices are falling this basis may result in showing the stock at an amount in excess of current prices in which event provision is made for the excess. During periods of rising prices, except in those instances where the physical movement of goods corresponds with the assumption that "last in" is "first out," the effect is to state the stock at less than its cost. The amount carried forward for stock may represent prices at which goods were acquired or produced several years earlier.

DESCRIPTION IN THE ANNUAL ACCOUNTS

Descriptions of method in financial statements. 25. In most businesses the amounts carried forward for stock from one period to another are material in their effect upon the presentation of the trading results and financial position. The differences which exist among the methods which are recognised as proper for the computation of those amounts are also so important that, unless an indication is given of the way in which the amounts are computed, the significance of the results and of the financial position shown by the accounts may be obscured. The following are illustrations of how such an indication might be given concisely where the circumstances make this appropriate:

(a) *Normal basis*
"at cost"
"at the lower of cost and net realisable value"
"at the lowest of cost, net realisable value and replacement price"
"at cost less provision to reduce to net realisable value (or 'to the lower of net realisable value and replacement price')"
The expression "market value" does not indicate whether it implies net realisable value or replacement price and is therefore not regarded as an appropriate description. Such terms as "at or under cost" or "as valued by the company's officials" are also not regarded as suitable.

(b) *Special bases*
If one of the special bases mentioned in paragraphs 20 to 24 is used an appropriate description would be required.

Adequacy of word "cost." 26. Whether a concise indication on the lines of the illustrations given above will be adequate for an appreciation of the significance of the accounts will depend upon the circumstances of the undertaking. The use of the word "cost" may be inadequate unless it is accompanied by an explanation of the extent to which overhead expenditure is included as cost; in that event the explanation might be as follows:

"Cost is confined to materials, direct wages and direct expenses, no addition having been made for overhead expenditure"
"Cost includes an appropriate proportion of variable overhead expenditure but excludes fixed overhead expenditure"
"Cost includes an appropriate proportion of all production and administrative overhead expenditure"

Minimum is assurance as to appropriateness and consistency. 27. In some businesses the complex nature of the stock and the use of different bases and methods of computation for determining the amounts of the various sections of the stock, particularly in a large composite undertaking or a holding company with subsidiaries of different types, may mean that no concise indication is feasible. In such circumstances it is however important that those to whom the accounts are submitted should have a specific assurance that the amount included for stock has been determined for the whole of the stock at the balance sheet date on bases and by methods of computation which are considered appropriate in the circumstances of the business and have been applied consistently.

Effect of change. 28. The effect of any change of basis or method of computation should be disclosed if the effect of the change is material.

Recommendations

Having regard to the foregoing considerations, it is recommended that the following principles be applied by every industrial and commercial enterprise.

All stock should be appropriately recognized. 29. Appropriate amounts for all stock-in-trade (including raw materials and partly finished or finished stocks) and all work in progress, wherever situated and whatever their nature, should be included in the financial accounts and should be computed in accordance with the recommendations below. There is no justification for the omission of stock nor for stating stock at an amount which is higher or lower than the amount so computed; to use a higher amount would be to overstate profits (or understate losses) of the period and reduce the profits (or increase the losses) of the next period, whilst to use a lower amount would be to create a reserve which should be so described and disclosed and should not be treated as a charge against revenue.

Anticipating profits. 30. A profit should not be anticipated unless this is justified by the special bases used in some businesses but provision should be made to the full extent of expected losses.

Basis should give "true and fair" results. 31. The amount carried forward for stock and work in progress should be computed on a basis which, having regard to the nature and circumstances of the business, will enable the accounts to show a true and fair view of the trading results and the financial position. In most businesses the basis should be the cost of the stock held, less any part thereof which properly needs to be written off at the balance sheet date.

Basis should be appropriate to each business. 32. The circumstances of each business should determine the basis which is appropriate and the method of computation which should be adopted in determining cost and the part thereof, if any, which should be written off. In most businesses the choice lies between writing off any excess of cost over either (*a*) the net realisable value of the stock or (*b*) the lower of net realisable value and replacement price, these terms having the meanings attributed to them below. In some businesses it may be appropriate to use special bases, including some which depart from the rule that profit should not be anticipated.

Basis should be used consistently.   33. The basis adopted and the methods of computation should be used consistently from period to period. A change of basis or method should not normally be made unless the circumstances have changed in such a way that its continued use would prevent the accounts from showing a true and fair view of the position and results. When a change is made the effect, if material, should be disclosed as an exceptional item in the profit and loss account or by way of note.

Definitions.   34. The following are the meanings attributed to "cost," "net realisable value" and "replacement price" in this Recommendation:

(a) "cost" means all expenditure incurred directly in the purchase or manufacture of the stock and the bringing of it to its existing condition and location, together with such part, if any, of the overhead expenditure as is appropriately carried forward in the circumstances of the business instead of being charged against the revenue of the period in which it was incurred

(b) "net realisable value" means the amount which it is estimated, as on the balance sheet date, will be realised from disposal of the stock in the ordinary course of business, either in its existing condition or as incorporated in the product normally sold, after allowing for all expenditure to be incurred on or before disposal

(c) "replacement price" means an estimate of the amount for which in the ordinary course of business the stock could have been acquired or produced either at the balance sheet date or in the latest period up to and including that date. In a manufacturing business this estimate would be based on the replacement price of the raw material content plus other costs of the undertaking which are relevant to the condition of the stock on the balance sheet date.

Providing for forseeable losses.   35. The comparison between cost and net realisable value or replacement price may be made by considering each article separately, or by grouping articles in categories having regard to their similarity or interchangeability, or by considering the aggregate cost of the total stock in relation to its aggregate net realisable value or, as the case may be, aggregate replacement price. The aggregate method involves setting foreseeable losses against unrealised profits on stock and may not be suitable for businesses which carry stocks which are large in relation to turnover.

Disclosure of method.   36. Where the amount carried forward for stock is material in relation to either the trading results or the financial position, the accounts should indicate concisely the manner in which the amount has been computed. If this is not practicable the accounts should contain a note to the effect that a concise statement of the bases and methods used is not practicable but that the amount has been determined for the whole of the stock at the balance sheet date on bases and by methods of computation which are considered appropriate in the circumstances of the business and have been used consistently. The use of the term "market value" should be discontinued.

Recognition of commitment losses. 37. Goods purchased forward do not form part of the stock-in-trade or work in progress on the balance sheet date but where they are not covered by forward sales provision should be made in the accounts for the excess, if any, of the purchase price over the net realisable value (or over replacement price, where lower than net realisable value, if stock is stated at the lowest of cost, net realisable value, and replacement price). Similarly, where goods have been sold forward and are not covered by stocks and forward purchases, provision should be made in the accounts for the excess, if any, of the expected cost over their net realisable value. Such provisions should not be deducted from the amount at which stock is stated.

Appendix C

United States Internal Revenue Code Provisions with Respect to "Inventories" and Related Regulations

§ 1.471   Statutory provisions; general rule for inventories.

General statutory provision. SEC. 471. *General rule for inventories.* Whenever in the opinion of the Secretary or his delegate the use of inventories is necessary in order clearly to determine the income of any taxpayer, inventories shall be taken by such taxpayer on such basis as the Secretary or his delegate may prescribe as conforming as nearly as may be to the best accounting practice in the trade or business and as most clearly reflecting the income.

§ 1.471–1   Need for inventories.

Inventories needed where goods are produced or purchased for sale. In order to reflect taxable income correctly, inventories at the beginning and end of each taxable year are necessary in every case in which the production, purchase, or sale of merchandise is an income-producing factor. The inventory should include all finished or partly finished goods and, in the case of raw materials and supplies, only those which have been acquired for sale or which will physically become a part of merchandise intended for sale, in which class fall containers, such as kegs, bottles, and cases, whether returnable or not, if title thereto will pass to

*The marginal notations are the author's.

382

the purchaser of the product to be sold therein. Merchandise should be included in the inventory only if title thereto is vested in the taxpayer. Accordingly, the seller should include in his inventory goods under contract for sale but not yet segregated and applied to the contract and goods out upon consignment, but should exclude from inventory goods sold (including containers), title to which has passed to the purchaser. A purchaser should include in inventory merchandise purchased (including containers), title to which has passed to him, although such merchandise is in transit or for other reasons has not been reduced to physical possession, but should not include goods ordered for future delivery, transfer of title to which has not yet been effected. (But see § 1.472–1.)

§ 1.471–2 Valuation of inventories.

Inventory rules recognize industry accounting practices.
(a) Section 471 provides two tests to which each inventory must conform:

(1) It must conform as nearly as may be to the best accounting practice in the trade or business, and

(2) It must clearly reflect the income.

(b) It follows, therefore, that inventory rules cannot be uniform but must give effect to trade customs which come within the scope of the best accounting practice in the particular trade or business. In order clearly to reflect income, the inventory practice of a taxpayer should be consistent from year to year, and greater weight is to be given to consistency than to any particular method of inventorying or basis of valuation so long as the method or basis used is substantially in accord with §§ 1.471–1 through 1.471–9. An inventory that can be used under the best accounting practice in a balance sheet showing the financial position of the taxpayer can, as a general rule, be regarded as clearly reflecting his income.

Inventories may be written down to net realizable values.
(c) The bases of valuation most commonly used by business concerns and which meet the requirements of section 471 are (1) cost and (2) cost or market, whichever is lower. (For inventories by dealers in securities, see § 1.471–5.) Any goods in an inventory which are unsalable at normal prices or unusable in the normal way because of damage, imperfections, shop wear, changes of style, odd or broken lots, or other similar causes, including second-hand goods taken in exchange, should be valued at bona fide selling prices less direct cost of disposition, whether subparagraph (1) or (2) of this paragraph is used, or if such goods consist of raw materials or partly finished goods held for use or consumption, they shall be valued upon a reasonable basis, taking into consideration the usability and the condition of the goods, but in no case shall such value be less than the scrap value. Bona fide selling price means actual offering of goods during a period ending not later than 30 days after inventory date. The burden of proof will rest upon the taxpayer to show that such excep-

tional goods as are valued upon such selling basis come within the classifications indicated above, and he shall maintain such records of the disposition of the goods as will enable a verification of the inventory to be made.

Method adopted to be used consistently. (d) In respect of normal goods, whichever method is adopted must be applied with reasonable consistency to the entire inventory of the taxpayer's trade or business except as to those goods inventoried under the last-in, first-out method authorized by section 472 or to animals inventoried under the elective unit-livestock-price-method authorized by §1.471–6. See paragraph (d) of § 1.446–1 for rules permitting the use of different methods of accounting if the taxpayer has more than one trade or business. Where the taxpayer is engaged in more than one trade or business the Commissioner may require that the method of valuing inventories with respect to goods in one trade or business also be used with respect to similar goods in other trades or businesses if, in the opinion of the Commissioner, the use of such method with respect to such other goods is essential to a clear reflection of income. Taxpayers were given an option to adopt the basis of either (1) cost or (2) cost or market, whichever is lower, for their 1920 inventories. The basis properly adopted for that year or any subsequent year is controlling, and a change can now be made only after permission is secured from the Commissioner. Application for permission to change the basis of valuing inventories shall be made in writing and filed with the Commissioner as provided in paragraph (e) of § 1.446–1. Goods taken in the inventory which have been so intermingled that they cannot be identified with specific invoices will be deemed to be the goods most recently purchased or produced, and the cost thereof will be the actual cost of the goods purchased or produced during the period in which the quantity of goods in the inventory has been acquired. But see section 472 as to last-in, first-out inventories. Where the taxpayer maintains book inventories in accordance with a sound accounting system in which the respective inventory accounts are charged with the actual cost of the goods purchased or produced and credited with the value of goods used, transferred, or sold, calculated upon the basis of the actual cost of the goods acquired during the taxable year (including the inventory at the beginning of the year), the net value as shown by such inventory accounts will be deemed to be the cost of the goods on hand. The balances shown by such book inventories should be verified by physical inventories at reasonable intervals and adjusted to conform therewith.

Records to be preserved for investigation. (e) Inventories should be recorded in a legible manner, properly computed and summarized, and should be preserved as a part of the accounting records of the taxpayer. The inventories of taxpayers on whatever basis taken will be subject to investigation by the district director, and the taxpayer must satisfy the district director of the correctness of the prices adopted.

Examples of unapproved methods. (f) The following methods, among others, are sometimes used in taking or valuing inventories, but are not in accord with the regulations in this part:

(1) Deducting from the inventory a reserve for price changes, or an estimated depreciation in the value thereof.

(2) Taking work in process, or other parts of the inventory, at a nominal price or at less than its proper value.

(3) Omitting portions of the stock on hand.

(4) Using a constant price or nominal value for so-called normal quantity of materials or goods in stock.

(5) Including stock in transit, shipped either to or from the taxpayer, the title to which is not vested in the taxpayer.

§ 1.471–3 Inventories at cost.

Cost means:

Meaning of "cost." (a) In the case of merchandise on hand at the beginning of the taxable year, the inventory price of such goods.

(b) In the case of merchandise purchased since the beginning of the taxable year, the invoice price less trade or other discounts, except strictly cash discounts approximating a fair interest rate, which may be deducted or not at the option of the taxpayer, provided a consistent course is followed. To this net invoice price should be added transportation or other necessary charges incurred in acquiring possession of the goods.

(c) In the case of merchandise produced by the taxpayer since the beginning of the taxable year, (1) the cost of raw materials and supplies entering into or consumed in connection with the product, (2) expenditures for direct labor, (3) indirect expenses incident to and necessary for the production of the particular article, including in such indirect expenses a reasonable proportion of management expenses, but not including any cost of selling or return on capital, whether by way of interest or profit.

(d) In any industry in which the usual rules for computation of cost of production are inapplicable, costs may be approximated upon such basis as may be reasonable and in conformity with established trade practice in the particular industry. Among such cases are: (1) Farmers and raisers of livestock (see § 1.471–6); (2) miners and manufacturers who by a single process or uniform series of processes derive a product of two or more kinds, sizes, or grades, the unit cost of which is substantially alike (see § 1.471–7); and (3) retail merchants who use what is known as the "retail method" in ascertaining approximate cost (see § 1.471–8).

§ 1.471–4 Inventories at cost or market, whichever is lower.

Meaning of "market." (a) Under ordinary circumstances and for normal goods in an inventory, "market" means the current bid price prevailing at the date of the inventory for the particular merchandise in the volume in which usually purchased by the taxpayer, and is applicable in the cases—

(1) Of goods purchased and on hand, and

(2) Of basic elements of cost (materials, labor, and burden) in goods in process of manufacture and in finished goods on hand; exclusive, however, of goods on hand or in process of manufacture for delivery upon firm sales contracts (i.e., those not legally subject to cancellation by either party) at fixed prices entered into before the date of the inventory, under which the taxpayer is protected against actual loss, which goods must be inventoried at cost.

(b) Where no open market exists or where quotations are nominal, due to inactive market conditions, the taxpayer must use such evidence of a fair market price at the date or dates nearest the inventory as may be available, such as specific purchases or sales by the taxpayer or others in reasonable volume and made in good faith, or compensation paid for cancellation of contracts for purchase commitments. Where the taxpayer in the regular course of business has offered for sale such merchandise at prices lower than the current price as above defined, the inventory may be valued at such prices less direct cost of disposition, and the correctness of such prices will be determined by reference to the actual sales of the taxpayer for a reasonable period before and after the date of the inventory. Prices which vary materially from the actual prices so ascertained will not be accepted as reflecting the market.

Cost/market comparison for each article. (c) Where the inventory is valued upon the basis of cost or market, whichever is lower, the market value of each article on hand at the inventory date shall be compared with the cost of the article, and the lower of such values shall be taken as the inventory value of the article.

§ 1.471–5   Inventories by dealers in securities.

Dealers in securities may use market value. A dealer in securities who in his books of account regularly inventories unsold securities on hand either—

(a) At cost,

(b) At cost or market, whichever is lower, or

(c) At market value,

may make his return upon the basis upon which his accounts are kept, provided that a description of the method employed is included in or attached to the return, that all the securities are inventoried by the same method, and that such method is adhered to in subsequent years, unless another method is authorized by the Commissioner pursuant to a written application therefor filed as provided in paragraph (e) of § 1.446–1. A dealer in securities in whose books of account separate computations of the gain or loss from the sale of the various lots of securities sold are made on the basis of the cost of each lot shall be regarded, for the purposes of this section, as regularly inventorying his securities at cost. For the purposes of this section, a dealer in securities is a merchant of securities, whether an individual, partnership, or corporation, with an established place of business, regularly engaged in the purchase of securities and their resale to customers; that is, one who as a merchant buys securities and sells them to customers with a view to the gains and profits that may be derived therefrom. If such business is simply a branch of the activities carried on by such person, the securities inventoried as provided in this section may include only those held for purposes of resale and not for investment. Taxpayers who buy and sell or hold securities for investment or speculation, irrespective of whether such buying or selling constitutes the carrying on of a trade or business, and officers of corporations and members of partnerships who in their individual capacities buy and sell securities, are not dealers in securities within the meaning of this section.

§1.471—6 Inventories of livestock raisers and other farmers.

Use of an inventory method is optional for farmers.
(a) A farmer may make his return upon an inventory method instead of the cash receipts and disbursements method. It is optional with the taxpayer which of these methods of accounting is used but, having elected one method, the option so exercised will be binding upon the taxpayer for the year for which the option is exercised and for subsequent years unless another method is authorized by the Commissioner as provided in paragraph (e) of § 1.446–1.

(b) In any change of accounting method from the cash receipts and disbursements method to an inventory method, adjustments shall be made as provided in section 481 (relating to adjustments required by change in method of accounting) and the regulations thereunder.

Special alternative methods.
(c) Because of the difficulty of ascertaining actual cost of livestock and other farm products, farmers who render their returns upon an inventory method may value their inventories according to the "farm-price method," and farmers raising livestock may value their inventories of animals according to either the "farm-price method" or the "unit-livestock-price method."

"Farm-price method."
(d) The "farm-price method" provides for the valuation of inventories at market price less direct cost of disposition. If this method of valuing inventories is used, it must be applied to the entire inventory except as to livestock inventoried, at the taxpayer's election, under the "unit-livestock-price method." If the use of the "farm-price method" of valuing inventories for any taxable year involves a change in method of valuing inventories from that employed in prior years, permission for such change shall first be secured from the Commissioner as provided in paragraph (e) of § 1.446–1.

"Unit-livestock-price method."   (e) The "unit-livestock-price method" provides for the valuation of the different classes of animals in the inventory at a standard unit price for each animal within a class. A livestock raiser electing this method of valuing his animals must adopt a reasonable classification of the animals in his inventory with respect to the age and kind included so that the unit prices assigned to the several classes will reasonably account for the normal costs incurred in producing the animals within such classes. Thus, if a cattle raiser determines that it costs approximately $15 to produce a calf, and $7.50 each year to raise the calf to maturity, his classifications and unit prices would be as follows: Calves, $15; yearlings, $22.50; 2-year olds, $30; mature animals, $37.50. The classification selected by the livestock raiser, and the unit prices assigned to the several classes are subject to approval by the district director upon examination of the taxpayer's return.

(f) A taxpayer who elects to use the "unit-livestock-price method" must apply it to all livestock raised, whether for sale or for draft, breeding, or dairy purposes. Once established, the unit prices and classifications selected by the taxpayer must be consistently applied in all subsequent taxable years in the valuation of livestock inventories. No changes in the classification of animals or unit prices will be made without the approval of the Commissioner.

Purchased animals to be inventoried at cost.   (g) A livestock raiser who uses the "unit-livestock-price method" must include in his inventory at cost any livestock purchased, except that animals purchased for draft, breeding, or dairy purposes can, at the election of the livestock raiser, be included in inventory or be treated as capital assets subject to depreciation after maturity. If the animals purchased are not mature at the time of purchase, the cost should be increased at the end of each taxable year in accordance with the established unit prices, except that no increase is to be made in the taxable year of purchase if the animal is acquired during the last six months of that year. If the records maintained permit identification of a purchased animal, the cost of such animal will be eliminated from the closing inventory in the event of its sale or loss. Otherwise, the first-in, first-out method of valuing inventories must be applied.

Rules for changing inventory method.   (h) If a taxpayer using the "farm-price method" desires to adopt the "unit-livestock-price method" in valuing his inventories of livestock, permission for the change shall first be secured from the Commissioner as provided in paragraph (e) of § 1.446–1. However, a taxpayer who has filed returns on the basis of inventories at cost, or cost or market whichever is lower, may adopt the "unit-livestock-price method" for valuing his inventories of livestock without formal application for permission, but the classifications and unit prices selected are subject to approval by the district director upon examination of the taxpayer's return. A livestock raiser who has adopted a constant unit-price method of valuing livestock inventories and filed returns on that basis will be considered as having elected the "unit-livestock-price method."

Correction of incomplete inventories. (i) If returns have been made in which the taxable income has been computed upon incomplete inventories, the abnormality should be corrected by submitting with the return for the current taxable year a statement for the preceding taxable year. In this statement such adjustments shall be made as are necessary to bring the closing inventory for the preceding taxable year into agreement with the opening complete inventory for the current taxable year. If necessary clearly to reflect income, similar adjustments may be made as at the beginning of the preceding year or years, and the tax, if any be due, shall be assessed and paid at the rate of tax in effect for such year or years.

§ 1.471–7 Inventories of miners and manufacturers.

Allocation of costs among products. A taxpayer engaged in mining or manufacturing who by a single process or uniform series of processes derives a product of two or more kinds, sizes, or grades, the unit cost of which is substantially alike, and who in conformity to a recognized trade practice allocates an amount of cost to each kind, size, or grade of product, which in the aggregate will absorb the total cost of production, may, with the consent of the Commissioner, use such allocated cost as a basis for pricing inventories, provided such allocation bears a reasonable relation to the respective selling values of the different kinds, sizes, or grades of product. See section 472 as to last-in, first-out inventories.

§ 1.471–8 Inventories of retail merchants.

"Retail method." (a) Retail merchants who employ what is known as the "retail method" of pricing inventories may make their returns upon that method, provided that the use of such method is designated upon the return, that accurate accounts are kept, and that such method is consistently adhered to unless a change is authorized by the Commissioner as provided in paragraph (e) of § 1.446–1. Under the retail method the total of the retail selling prices of the goods on hand at the end of the year in each department or of each class of goods is reduced to approximate cost by deducting therefrom an amount which bears the same ratio to such total as—

(1) The total of the retail selling prices of the goods included in the opening inventory plus the retail selling prices of the goods purchased during the year, with proper adjustment to such selling prices for the mark-ups and mark-downs, less

(2) The cost of the goods included in the opening inventory plus the cost of the goods purchased during the year, bears to (1).

The result should represent as accurately as may be the amounts added to the cost price of the goods to cover selling and other expenses of doing business and for the margin of profit.

(b) For further adjustments to be made in the case of a retail merchant using the last-in, first-out inventory method authorized by section 472, see paragraph (k) of § 1.472–1.

Profit percentages applied by departments. (c) A taxpayer maintaining more than one department in his store or dealing in classes of goods carrying different percentages of gross profit should not use a percentage of profit based upon an average of his entire business but should compute and use in valuing his inventory the proper percentages for the respective departments or classes of goods.

Ignoring markdowns to approximate lower of cost or market. (d) A taxpayer (other than one using the last-in, first-out inventory method) who previously has determined inventories in accordance with the retail method, except that, to obtain a basis of approximate cost or market, whichever is lower, has consistently and uniformly followed the practice of adjusting the retail selling prices of the goods included in the opening inventory and purchased during the taxable year for mark-ups but not for mark-downs, may continue such practice subject to the conditions prescribed in this section. The adjustments must be bona fide and consistent and uniform. Where mark-downs are not included in the adjustments, mark-ups made to cancel or correct mark-downs shall not be included; and the mark-ups included must be reduced by the mark-downs made to cancel or correct such mark-ups.

Computation to reflect goods on hand at selling prices. (e) In no event shall mark-downs not based on actual reduction of retail sale prices, such as mark-downs based on depreciation and obsolescence, be recognized in determining the retail selling prices of the goods on hand at the end of the taxable year.

(f) A taxpayer (other than one using the last-in, first-out inventory method) who previously has determined inventories without following the practice of eliminating mark-downs in making adjustments to retail selling prices may adopt such practice, provided permission to do so is obtained in accordance with, and subject to the terms provided by, paragraph (e) of § 1.446–1. A taxpayer filing a first return of income may adopt such practice subject to approval by the district director upon examination of the return.

LIFO users must adjust for markdowns. (g) A taxpayer using the last-in, first-out inventory method in conjunction with retail computations must adjust retail selling prices for mark-downs as well as mark-ups, in order that there may be reflected the approximate cost of the goods on hand at the end of the taxable year regardless of market values.

§ 1.471–9 Inventories of acquiring corporations.

For additional rules in the case of certain corporate acquisitions specified in section 381 (a), see section 381 (c) (5) and the regulations thereunder.

§ 1.472 Statutory provisions; last-in, first-out inventories.

LIFO statutory provisions. SEC. 472. *Last-in, first-out inventories—*(a) *Authorization.* A taxpayer may use the method provided in subsection (b) (whether or not such method has been prescribed under section 471) in inventorying goods specified in an application to use such method filed at such time and in such manner as the Secretary or his delegate may prescribe. The change to, and the use of, such method shall be in accordance with such regulations as the Secretary or his delegate may prescribe as necessary in order that the use of such method may clearly reflect income.

(b) *Method applicable.* In inventorying goods specified in the application described in subsection (a), the taxpayer shall:

(1) Treat those remaining on hand at the close of the taxable year as being: First, those included in the opening inventory of the taxable year (in the order of acquisition) to the extent thereof; and second, those acquired in the taxable year;

(2) Inventory them at cost; and

(3) Treat those included in the opening inventory of the taxable year in which such method is first used as having been acquired at the same time and determine their cost by the average cost method.

(c) *Condition.* Subsection (a) shall apply only if the taxpayer establishes to the satisfaction of the Secretary or his delegate that the taxpayer has used no procedure other than that specified in paragraphs (1) and (3) of subsection (b) in inventorying such goods to ascertain the income, profit, or loss of the first taxable year for which the method described in subsection (b) is to be used, for the purpose of a report or statement covering such taxable year—

(1) To shareholders, partners, or other proprietors, or to beneficiaries or

(2) For credit purposes.

(d) *Preceding closing inventory.* In determining income for the taxable year preceding the taxable year for which the method described in subsection (b) is first used, the closing inventory of such preceding year of the goods specified in the application referred to in subsection (a) shall be at cost.

(e) *Subsequent inventories.* If a taxpayer, having complied with subsection (a) uses the method described in subsection (b) for any taxable year, then such method shall be used in all subsequent taxable years unless—

(1) With the approval of the Secretary or his delegate a change to a different method is authorized; or,

(2) The Secretary or his delegate determines that the taxpayer has used for any such subsequent taxable year some procedure other than that specified in paragraph (1) of subsection (b) in inventorying the goods specified in the application to ascertain the income, profit, or loss of such subsequent taxable year for the purpose of a report or statement covering such taxable year (A) to shareholders, partners, or other proprietors, or beneficiaries, or (B) for credit purposes; and requires a change to a method different from that prescribed in subsection (b) beginning with such subsequent taxable year or any taxable year thereafter.

If paragraph (1) or (2) of this subsection applies, the change to, and the use of, the different method shall be in accordance with such regulations as the Secretary or his delegate may prescribe as necessary in order that the use of such method may clearly reflect income.

(f) *Cross reference.* For provisions relating to involuntary liquidation and replacement of LIFO inventories, see section 1321.

§ 1.472–1   Last-in, first-out inventories.

Any taxpayer may elect LIFO as of close of any year. (a) Any taxpayer permitted or required to take inventories pursuant to the provisions of section 471, and pursuant to the provisions of §§ 1.471–1 to 1.471–9, inclusive, may elect with respect to those goods specified in his application and properly subject to inventory to compute his opening and closing inventories in accordance with the method provided by section 472, this section, and § 1.472–2. Under this last-in, first-out (LIFO) inventory method, the taxpayer is permitted to treat those goods remaining on hand at the close of the taxable year as being:

(1) Those included in the opening inventory of the taxable year, in the order of acquisition and to the extent thereof, and

(2) Those acquired during the taxable year.

The LIFO inventory method is not dependent upon the character of the business in which the taxpayer is engaged, or upon the identity or want of identity through commingling of any of the goods on hand, and may be adopted by the taxpayer as of the close of any taxable year.

Matched purchases and sales for future delivery may be treated as completed transactions. (b) If the LIFO inventory method is used by a taxpayer who regularly and consistently, in a manner similar to hedging on a futures market, matches purchases with sales, then firm purchases and sales contracts (i.e., those not legally subject to cancellation by either party) entered into at fixed prices on or before the date of the inventory may be included in purchases or sales as the case may be, for the purpose of determining the costs of goods sold and the resulting profit or loss, provided that this practice is regularly and consistently adhered to by the taxpayer and provided that, in the opinion of the Commissioner, income is clearly reflected thereby.

LIFO may be applied to only material in inventory costs. (c) A manufacturer or processor who has adopted the LIFO inventory method as to a class of goods may elect to have such method apply to the raw materials only (including those included in goods in process and in finished goods) expressed in terms of appropriate units. If such method is adopted, the adjustments are confined to costs of the raw material in the inventory and the cost of the raw material in goods in process and in finished goods produced by such manufacturer or processor and reflected in the inventory. The provisions of this paragraph may be illustrated by the following examples:

Example (1). Assume that the opening inventory had 10 units of raw material, 10 units of goods in process, and 10 units of finished goods, and that the raw material cost was 6 cents a unit, the processing cost 2 cents a unit, and overhead cost 1 cent a unit. For the purposes of this example, it is assumed that the entire amount of goods in process was 50 per cent processed.

Opening Inventory

	Raw material	Goods in process	Finished goods
Raw material..........	$0.60	$0.60	$0.60
Processing cost........	—	.10	.20
Overhead............	—	.05	.10

In the closing inventory there are 20 units of raw material, 6 units of goods in process, and 8 units of finished goods and the costs were: Raw material 10 cents, processing cost 4 cents, and overhead 1 cent.

Closing Inventory

[Based on cost and prior to adjustment]

	Raw material	Goods in process	Finished goods
Raw material..........	$2.00	$0.60	$0.80
Processing costs........	—	.12	.32
Overhead............	—	.03	.08
Total.............	2.00	.75	1.20

There were 30 units of raw material in the opening inventory and 34 units in the closing inventory. The adjustment to the closing inventory would be as follows:

Closing Inventory As Adjusted

	Raw material	Goods in process	Finished goods
Raw material:			
20 at 6 cents.........	$1.20	—	—
6 at 6 cents.........	—	$0.36	—
4 at 6 cents.........	—	—	$0.24
4 at 10 cents[1].......	—	—	.40
Processing costs........	—	.12	.32
Overhead.............	—	.03	.08
Total.............	1.20	.51	1.04

[1] This excess is subject to determination of price under section 472 (b) (1) and § 1.472–2. If the excess falls in goods in process, the same adjustment is applicable.

The only adjustment to the closing inventory is the cost of the raw material; the processing costs and overhead cost are not changed.

Example (2). Assume that the opening inventory had 5 units of raw material, 10 units of goods in process, and 20 units of finished goods, with the same prices as in example (1), and that the closing inventory had 20 units of raw material, 20 units of goods in process, and 10 units of finished goods, with raw material costs as in the closing inventory in example (1). The adjusted closing inventory would be as follows in so far as the raw material is concerned:

Raw material, 20 at 6 cents............. $1.20
Goods in process:
   15 at 6 cents....................... .90
   5 at 10 cents[1]...................... .50
Finished goods:
   None at 6 cents..................... .00
   10 at 10 cents[1].................... 1.00

[1] This excess is subject to determination of price under section 472 (b) (1) and § 1.472–2.

The 20 units of raw material in the raw state plus 15 units of raw material in goods in process make up the 35 units of raw material that were contained in the opening inventory.

LIFO com-
parisons to
be by similar
types of
materials.

    (d) For the purposes of this section, raw material in the opening inventory must be compared with similar raw material in the closing inventory. There may be several types of raw materials, depending upon the character, quality, or price, and each type of raw material in the opening inventory must be compared with a similar type in the closing inventory.

Groupings
in cotton
textile
industry.

    (e) In the cotton textile industry there may be different raw materials depending upon marked differences in length of staple, in color or grade of the cotton. But where different staple lengths or grades of cotton are being used at different times in the same mill to produce the same class of goods, such differences would not necessarily require the classification into different raw materials.

Primal cuts
from hogs may
be grouped.

    (f) As to the pork packing industry a live hog is considered as being composed of various raw materials, different cuts of a hog varying markedly in price and use. Generally a hog is processed into approximately 10 primal cuts and several miscellaneous articles. However, due to similarity in price and use, these may be grouped into fewer classifications, each group being classed as one raw material.

Each raw
material
must be
identified.

    (g) When the finished product contains two or more different raw materials as in the case of cotton and rayon mixtures, each raw material is treated separately and adjustments made accordingly.

Material-content
method can
be elected at
any time.

    (h) Upon written notice addressed to the Commisner of Internal Revenue, Attention T:R, Washington 25, D.C. by the taxpayer, a taxpayer who has heretofore adopted the LIFO inventory method in respect of any goods may adopt the method authorized in this section and limit the election to the raw material including raw materials entering into goods in process and in finished foods. If this method is adopted as to any specific goods, it must be used exclusively for such goods for any prior taxable year (not closed by agreement) to which the prior election applies and for all subsequent taxable years, unless permission to change is granted by the Commissioner.

Material-
content method
can be limited
to basic
processing.

    (i) The election may also be limited to that phase in the manufacturing process where a product is produced that is recognized generally as a salable product as, for example, in the textile industry where one phase of the process is the production of yarn. Since yarn is generally recognized as a salable product, the election may be limited to that portion of the process when yarn is produced. In the case of copper and brass processors, the election may be limited to the production of bars, plates, sheets, etc., although these may be further processed into other products.

All materials need not be on LIFO.   (j) The election may also apply to any one raw material, when two or more raw materials enter into the composition of the finished product; for example, in the case of cotton and rayon yarn, the taxpayer may elect to inventory the cotton of section only.   However, a taxpayer who has previously made an election to use the LIFO inventory method may not later elect to exclude any raw materials that were covered by such previous election.

LIFO may be used with the retail method.   (k) If a taxpayer using the retail method of pricing inventories, authorized by § 1.471–8, elects to use in connection therewith the LIFO inventory method authorized by section 472 and this section, the apparent cost of the goods on hand at the end of the year, determined pursuant to § 1.471–8, shall be adjusted to the extent of price changes therein taking place after the close of the preceding taxable year.   The amount of any apparent inventory increase or decrease to be eliminated in this adjustment shall be determined by reference to acceptable price indexes established to the satisfaction of the Commissioner.   Price indexes prepared by the United States Bureau of Labor Statistics which are applicable to the goods in question will be considered acceptable to the Commissioner.   Price indexes which are based upon inadequate records, or which are not subject to complete and detailed audit within the Internal Revenue Service, will not be approved.

LIFO may be used with the dollar-value method.   (1) If a taxpayer uses consistently the so-called "dollar-value" method of pricing inventories, or any other method of computation established to the satisfaction of the Commissioner as reasonably adaptable to the purpose and intent of section 472 and this section, and if such taxpayer elects under section 472 to use the LIFO inventory method authorized by such section, the taxpayer's opening and closing inventories shall be determined under section 472 by the use of the appropriate adaptation.   See § 1.472–8 for rules relating to the use of the dollar-value method.

§ 1.472–2   Requirements incident to adoption and use of LIFO inventory method.

General requirements for adoption of LIFO.   Except as otherwise provided in § 1.472–1 with respect to raw material computations, with respect to retail inventory computations, and with respect to other methods of computation established to the satisfaction of the Commissioner as reasonably adapted to the purpose and intent of section 472, and in § 1.472–8 with respect to the "dollar-value" method, the adoption and use of the LIFO inventory method is subject to the following requirements:

(a) The taxpayer shall file an application to use such method specifying with particularity the goods to which it is to be applied.

(b) The inventory shall be taken at cost regardless of market value.

(c) Goods of the specified type included in the opening inventory of the taxable year for which the method is first used shall be considered as having been acquired at the same time and at a unit cost equal to the actual cost of the aggregate divided by the number of units on hand. The actual cost of the aggregate shall be determined pursuant to the inventory method employed by the taxpayer under the regulations applicable to the prior taxable year with the exception that restoration shall be made with respect to any writedown to market values resulting from the pricing of former inventories.

(d) Goods of the specified type on hand as of the close of the taxable year in excess of what were on hand as of the beginning of the taxable year shall be included in the closing inventory, regardless of identification with specific invoices and regardless of specific cost accounting records, at costs determined pursuant to the provisions of subparagraph (1) or (2) of this paragraph, dependent upon the character of the transactions in which the taxpayer is engaged:

(1) (i) In the case of a taxpayer engaged in the purchase and sale of merchandise, such as a retail grocer or druggist, or engaged in the initial production of merchandise and its sale without processing, such as a miner selling his ore output without smelting or refining, such costs shall be determined—

(*a*) By reference to the actual cost of the goods most recently purchased or produced;

(*b*) By reference to the actual cost of the goods purchased or produced during the taxable year in the order of acquisition;

(*c*) By application of an average unit cost equal to the aggregate cost of all of the goods purchased or produced throughout the taxable year divided by the total number of units so purchased or produced, the goods reflected in such inventory increase being considered for the purposes of section 472 as having been acquired all at the same time; or

(*d*) Pursuant to any other proper method which, in the opinion of the Commissioner, clearly reflects income.

(ii) Whichever of the several methods of valuing the inventory increase is adopted by the taxpayer and approved by the Commissioner shall be consistently adhered to in all subsequent taxable years so long as the LIFO inventory method is used by the taxpayer.

(iii) The application of subdivisions (i) and (ii) of this subparagraph may be illustrated by the following examples:

Example (*1*). Suppose that the taxpayer adopts the LIFO inventory method for the taxable year 1957 with an opening inventory of 10 units at 10 cents per unit, that it makes 1957 purchases of 10 units as follows:

January............	1 at $0.11 =		$0.11
April.............	2 at	.12 =	.24
July..............	3 at	.13 =	.39
October...........	4 at	.14 =	.56
Totals..........	10		1.30

and that it has a 1957 closing inventory of 15 units. This closing inventory, depending upon the taxpayer's method of valuing inventory increases, will be computed as follows:

(*a*) Most recent purchases—

	10 at $0.10............	$1.00
	4 at	.14 (October)....	.56
	1 at	.13 (July).......	.13
Totals...........	15		1.69

or

(*b*) In order of acquisition—

	10 at $0.10............	$1.00
	1 at	.11 (January)....	.11
	2 at	.12 (April)......	.24
	2 at	.13 (July).......	.26
Totals...........	15		1.61

or

(*c*) At an annual average—

	10 at $0.10............	$1.00
	5 at	.13 (130/10)....	.65
Totals...........	15		1.65

Example (2). Suppose that the taxpayer's closing inventory for 1958, the year following that involved in example (1) of this subdivision, reflects an inventory decrease for the year, and not an increase; suppose that there is, accordingly, a 1958 closing inventory of 13 units. Inasmuch as the decreased closing inventory will be determined wholly by reference to the 15 units reflected in the opening inventory for the year, and will be taken "in the order of acquisition" pursuant to section 472 (b) (1), and inasmuch as the character of the taxpayer's opening inventory for 1958 will be dependent upon its method of valuing its 5-unit inventory increase for 1957, the closing inventory for 1958 will be computed as follows:

(*a*) In case the increase for 1957 was taken by reference to the most recent purchases—

	10 at $0.10 (from 1956)..............	$1.00
	1 at	.13 (July 1957)..............	.13
	2 at	.14 (October 1957)..........	.28
Totals...........	13		1.41

or

(*b*) In case the increase for 1957 was taken in the order of acquisition—

	10 at $0.10 (from 1956)..............	$1.00
	1 at	.11 (January 1957)...........	.11
	2 at	.12 (April 1957)..............	.24
Totals...........	13		1.35

or

(*c*) In case the increase for 1957 was taken on the basis of an average—

	10 at $0.10 (from 1956)..............	$1.00
	3 at .13 (from 1957)..............	.39
Totals............ 13		1.39

(2) In the case of a taxpayer engaged in manufacturing, fabricating, processing, or otherwise producing merchandise, such costs shall be determined:

(i) In the case of raw materials purchased or initially produced by the taxpayer, in the manner elected by the taxpayer under subparagraph (1) of this paragraph to the same extent as if the taxpayer were engaged in purchase and sale transactions; and

(ii) In the case of goods in process, regardless of the stage to which the manufacture, fabricating, or processing may have advanced, and in the case of finished goods, pursuant to any proper method which, in the opinion of the Commissioner, clearly reflects income.

Interim statements need not reflect LIFO, and market values may be used in annual statements. (e) The taxpayer shall establish to the satisfaction of the Commissioner that the taxpayer, in ascertaining income, profit, or loss for the taxable year for which the LIFO inventory method is first used or for any subsequent taxable year, for credit purposes or for the purpose of reports to shareholders, partners, or other proprietors, or to beneficiaries, has not used any inventory method other than that referred to in § 1.472–1 or at variance with the requirement referred to in paragraph (c) of this section. The taxpayer's use of market value in lieu of cost or his issuance of reports or credit statements covering a period of operations less than the whole of the taxable year is not considered at variance with this requirement.

Starting inventory to be at cost. (f) Goods of the specified type on hand as of the close of the taxable year preceding the taxable year for which this inventory method is first used shall be included in the taxpayer's closing inventory for such preceding taxable year at cost determined in the manner prescribed in paragraph (c) of this section.

Conditions for change from LIFO. (g) The LIFO inventory method, once adopted by the taxpayer with the approval of the Commissioner, shall be adhered to in all subsequent taxable years unless—

(1) A change to a different method is approved by the Commissioner; or

(2) The Commissioner determines that the taxpayer, in ascertaining income, profit, or loss for the whole of any taxable year subsequent to his adoption of the LIFO inventory method, for credit purposes or for the purpose of reports to shareholders, partners, or other proprietors, or to beneficiaries, has used any inventory method at variance with that

referred to in § 1.472–1 and requires of the taxpayer a change to a different method for such subsequent taxable year or any taxable year thereafter.

Records to be preserved for verification. (h) The records and accounts employed by the taxpayer in keeping his books shall be maintained in conformity with the inventory method referred to in § 1.472–1; and such supplemental and detailed inventory records shall be maintained as will enable the district director readily to verify the taxpayer's inventory computations as well as his compliance with the requirements of section 472 and §§ 1.472–1 through 1.472–7.

Use of LIFO may be required for all similar goods. (i) Where the taxpayer is engaged in more than one trade or business, the Commissioner may require that if the LIFO method of valuing inventories is used with respect to goods in one trade or business the same method shall also be used with respect to similar goods in the other trades or businesses if, in the opinion of the Commissioner, the use of such method with respect to such other goods is essential to a clear reflection of income.

§1.472–3   Time and manner of making election.

LIFO election and supporting data to be filed with tax return. (a) The LIFO inventory method may be adopted and used only if the taxpayer files with his income tax return for the taxable year as of the close of which the method is first to be used, in triplicate on Form 970, and pursuant to the instructions printed thereon and to the requirements of this section, a statement of his election to use such inventory method. Such statement shall be accompanied by an analysis of all inventories of the taxpayer as of the beginning and as of the end of the taxable year for which the LIFO inventory method is proposed first to be used, and also as of the beginning of the prior taxable year. In the case of a manufacturer, this analysis shall show in detail the manner in which costs are computed with respect to raw materials, goods in process, and finished goods, segregating the products (whether in process or finished goods) into natural groups on the basis of either (1) similarity in factory processes through which they pass, or (2) similarity of raw materials used, or (3) similarity in style, shape, or use of finished products. Each group of products shall be clearly described.

Other data may be requested. (b) The taxpayer shall submit for the consideration of the Commissioner in connection with the taxpayer's adoption or use of the LIFO inventory method such other detailed information with respect to his business or accounting system as may be at any time requested by the Commissioner.

Use of LIFO may be required for other goods. (c) As a condition to the taxpayer's use of the LIFO inventory method, the Commissioner may require that the method be used with respect to goods other than those specified in the taxpayer's statement of election if, in the opinion of the Commissioner, the use of such method with respect to such other goods is essential to a clear reflection of income.

LIFO proce-
dures subject
to review.
(d) Whether or not the taxpayer's application for the adoption and use of the LIFO inventory method should be approved, and whether or not such method, once adopted, may be continued, and the propriety of all computations incidental to the use of such method, will be determined by the Commissioner in connection with the examination of the taxpayer's income tax returns.

§1.472–4   Adjustments to be made by taxpayer.

Objective is to
reflect true
income.
A taxpayer may not change to the LIFO method of taking inventories unless, at the time he files his application for the adoption of such method, he agrees to such adjustments incident to the change to or from such method, or incident to the use of such method, in the inventories of prior taxable years or otherwise, as the district director upon the examination of the taxpayer's returns may deem necessary in order that the true income of the taxpayer will be clearly reflected for the years involved.

§1.472–5   Revocation of election.

Election is
irrevocable.
An election made to adopt and use the LIFO inventory method is irrevocable, and the method once adopted shall be used in all subsequent taxable years, unless the use of another method is required by the Commissioner, or authorized by him pursuant to a written application therefor filed as provided in paragraph (e) of § 1.446–1.

§1.472–6   Change from LIFO inventory method.

Procedure
for changing
from LIFO.
If the taxpayer is granted permission by the Commissioner to discontinue the use of LIFO method of taking inventories, and thereafter to use some other method, or if the taxpayer is required by the Commissioner to discontinue the use of the LIFO method by reason of the taxpayer's failure to conform to the requirements detailed in § 1.472–2, the inventory of the specified goods for the first taxable year affected by the change and for each taxable year thereafter shall be taken—

(a) In conformity with the method used by the taxpayer under section 471 in inventorying goods not included in his LIFO inventory computations; or

(b) If the LIFO inventory method was used by the taxpayer with respect to all of his goods subject to inventory, then in conformity with the inventory method used by the taxpayer prior to his adoption of the LIFO inventory method; or

(c) If the taxpayer had not used inventories prior to his adoption of the LIFO inventory method and had no goods currently subject to inventory .

by a method other than the LIFO inventory method, then in conformity
with such inventory method as may be selected by the taxpayer and approved
by the Commissioner as resulting in a clear reflection of income; or

(d) In any event, in conformity with any inventory method to which the
taxpayer may change pursuant to application approved by the Commissioner.

§1.472–7   Inventories of acquiring corporations.

For additional rules in the case of certain corporate acquisitions specified
in section 381(a), see section 381 (c) (5) and the regulations thereunder.

§ 1.472–8   Dollar-value method of pricing LIFO inventories.

Mechanics of   (a) *Election to use dollar-value method.* Any taxpayer
"dollar-value"   may elect to determine the cost of his LIFO inventories
method.   under the so-called "dollar-value" LIFO method, provided
such method is used consistently and clearly reflects the income of the
taxpayer in accordance with the rules of this section.   The dollar-value
method of valuing LIFO inventories is a method of determining cost by
using "base-year" cost expressed in terms of total dollars rather than the
quantity and price of specific goods as the unit of measurement.   Under
such method the goods contained in the inventory are grouped into a pool
or pools as described in paragraphs (b) and (c) of this section.   The term
"base-year cost" is the aggregate of the cost (determined as of the beginning
of the taxable year for which the LIFO method is first adopted, i.e., the base
date) of all items in a pool.   The taxable year for which the LIFO method
is first adopted with respect to any item in the pool is the "base year" for
that pool, except as provided in paragraph (g) (3) of this section.   Liquidations and increments of items contained in the pool shall be reflected only
in terms of a net liquidation or increment for the pool as a whole.   Fluctuations may occur in quantities of various items within the pool, new items
which properly fall within the pool may be added, and old items may dis-
appear from the pool, all without necessarily effecting a change in the
dollar value of the pool as a whole.   An increment in the LIFO inventory
occurs when the end of the year inventory for any pool expressed in terms
of base-year cost is in excess of the beginning of the year inventory for that
pool expressed in terms of base-year cost.   In determining the inventory
value for a pool, the increment, if any, is adjusted for changing unit costs or
values by reference to a percentage, relative to base-year cost, determined
for the pool as a whole. See paragraph (e) of this section.   See also
paragraph (f) of this section for rules relating to the change to the dollar-
value LIFO method from another LIFO method.

Manufacturers   (b) *Principles for establishing pools of manufacturers*
and processors   *and processors*—(1) *Natural business unit pools.*   A pool
may use one   shall consist of all items entering into the entire inventory
LIFO pool for   investment for a natural business unit of a business enter-
each natural   prise, unless the taxpayer elects to use the multiple pooling
business unit.   method provided in subparagraph (3) of this paragraph.

Thus, if a business enterprise is composed of only one natural business unit, one pool shall be used for all of its inventories, including raw materials, goods in process, and finished goods. If, however, a business enterprise is actually composed of more than one natural business unit, more than one pool is required. Where similar types of goods are inventoried in two or more natural business units of the taxpayer, the Commissioner may apportion or allocate such goods among the various natural business units, if he determines that such apportionment or allocation is necessary in order to clearly reflect the income of such taxpayer. Where a manufacturer or processor is also engaged in the wholesaling or retailing of goods purchased from others, any pooling of the LIFO inventory of such purchased goods for the wholesaling or retailing operations shall be determined in accordance with the rules of paragraph (c) of this section.

Considerations in establishing natural business units.   (2) *Definition of natural business unit.* (i) Whether an enterprise is composed of more than one natural business unit is a matter of fact to be determined from all the circumstances. The natural business divisions adopted by the taxpayer for internal management purposes, the existence of separate and distinct production facilities and processes, and the maintenance of separate profit and loss records with respect to separate operations are important considerations in determining what is a business unit, unless such divisions, facilities, or accounting records are set up merely because of differences in geographical location. In the case of a manufacturer or processor, a natural business unit ordinarily consists of the entire productive activity of the enterprise within one product line or within two or more related product lines including (to the extent engaged in by the enterprise) the obtaining of materials, the processing of materials, and the selling of manufactured or processed goods. Thus, in the case of a manufacturer or processor, the maintenance and operation of a raw material warehouse does not generally constitute, of itself, a natural business unit. If the taxpayer maintains and operates a supplier unit the production of which is both sold to others and transferred to a different unit of the taxpayer to be used as a component part of another product, the supplier unit will ordinarily constitute a separate and distinct natural business unit. Ordinarily, a processing plant would not in itself be considered a natural business unit if the production of the plant, although saleable at this stage, is not sold to others, but is transferred to another plant of the enterprise, not operated as a separate division, for further processing or incorporation into another product. On the other hand, if the production of a manufacturing or processing plant is transferred to a separate and distinct division of the taxpayer, which constitutes a natural business unit, the supplier unit itself will ordinarily be considered a natural business unit. However, the mere fact that a portion of the production of a manufacturing or processing plant may be sold to others at a certain stage of processing with the remainder of the production being further processed or incorporated into another product will not of itself be determinative that the activities devoted to the production of the portion sold constitute a separate business unit.   Where a manufacturer or processor is also engaged in the wholesaling or retailing of goods purchased from others, the wholesaling or retailing operations with respect to such purchased goods shall not be considered a part of any manufacturing or processing unit.

Examples of natural business units.   (ii) The rules of this subparagraph may be illustrated by the following examples:

Example (1).   A corporation manufactures, in one division, automatic clothes washers and driers of both commercial and domestic grade as well as electric ranges, mangles, and dishwashers.   The corporation manufactures, in another division, radios and television sets.   The manufacturing facilities and processes used in manufacturing the radios and television sets are distinct from those used in manufacturing the automatic clothes washers, etc.   Under these circumstances, the enterprise would consist of two business units and two pools would be appropriate, one consisting of all of the LIFO inventories entering into the manufacture of clothes washers and driers, electric ranges, mangles, and dishwashers and the other consisting of all of the LIFO inventories entering into the production of radio and television sets.

Example (2).   A taxpayer produces plastics in one of its plants.   Substantial amounts of the production are sold as plastics.   The remainder of the production is shipped to a second plant of the taxpayer for the production of plastic toys which are sold to customers.   The taxpayer operates his plastics plant and toy plant as separate divisions.   Because of the different product lines and the separate divisions the taxpayer has two natural business units.

Example (3).   A taxpayer is engaged in the manufacture of paper.   At one stage of processing, uncoated paper is produced.   Substantial amounts of uncoated paper are sold at this stage of processing.   The remainder of the uncoated paper is transferred to the taxpayer's finishing mill where coated paper is produced and sold.   This taxpayer has only one natural business unit since coated and uncoated paper are within the same product line.

Multiple pools may be used.   (3) *Multiple pools*—(i) *Principles for establishing multiple pools.*   (*a*) A taxpayer may elect to establish multiple pools for inventory items which are not within a natural business unit as to which the taxpayer has adopted the natural business unit method of pooling as provided in subparagraph (1) of this paragraph.   Each such pool shall ordinarily consist of a group of inventory items which are substantially similar.   In determining whether such similarity exists, consideration shall be given to all the facts and circumstances.   The formulation of detailed rules for selection of pools applicable to all taxpayers is not feasible.   Important considerations to be taken into account include, for example, whether there is substantial similarity in the types of raw materials used or in the processing operations applied; whether the raw materials used are readily interchangeable; whether there is similarity in the use of the products; whether the groupings are consistently followed for purposes of internal accounting and management; and whether the groupings follow customary business practice in the taxpayer's industry.   The selection of pools in each case must also take into consideration such factors as the nature of the inventory items subject to the dollar-value LIFO method and the significance of such items to the taxpayer's business operations. Where similar types of goods are inventoried in natural business units and multiple pools of the taxpayer, the Commissioner may apportion or allocate such goods among the natural business units and the multiple pools, if he determines that such apportionment or allocation is necessary in order to clearly reflect the income of the taxpayer.

Pooling of raw materials. (*b*) Raw materials which are substantially similar shall be pooled together in accordance with the principles of this subparagraph. However, inventories of raw or unprocessed materials of an unlike nature may not be placed into one pool, even though such materials become part of otherwise identical finished products.

Pooling of finished and in-process inventories. (*c*) Finished goods and goods-in-process in the inventory shall be placed into pools classified by major classes or types of goods. The same class or type of finished goods and goods-in-process shall ordinarily be included in the same pool. Where the material content of a class of finished goods and goods-in-process included in a pool has been changed, for example, to conform with current trends in an industry, a separate pool of finished goods and goods-in-process will not ordinarily be required unless the change in material content results in a substantial change in the finished goods.

Pool for miscellaneous items. (*d*) The requirement that pools be established by major types of materials or major classes of goods is not to be construed so as to preclude the establishment of a miscellaneous pool. Since a taxpayer may elect the dollar-value LIFO method with respect to all or any designated goods in his inventory, there may be a number of such inventory items covered in the election. A miscellaneous pool shall consist only of items which are relatively insignificant in dollar value by comparison with other inventory items in the particular trade or business and which are not properly includible as part of another pool.

Raw materials and material-content pool. (ii) *Raw materials content pools.* The dollar-value method of pricing LIFO inventories may be used in conjunction with the raw materials content method authorized in § 1.472–1. Raw materials (including the raw material content of finished goods and goods-in-process) which are substantially similar shall be pooled together in accordance with the principles of subdivision (i) of this subparagraph. However, inventories of materials of an unlike nature may not be placed into one pool, even though such materials become part of otherwise identical finished products.

Pools for wholesalers, retailers, etc. (c) *Principles for establishing pools for wholesalers, retailers, etc.* Items of inventory in the hands of wholesalers, retailers, jobbers, and distributors shall be placed into pools by major lines, types, or classes of goods. In determining such groupings, customary business classifications of the particular trade in which the taxpayer is engaged is an important consideration. An example of such customary business classification is the department in the department store. In such case, practices are relatively uniform throughout the trade, and departmental grouping is peculiarly adapted to the customs and needs of the business. However, in appropriate cases, the principles set forth in paragraphs (b) (1) and (2) of this section, relating to pooling by natural business units, may be used, with permission of the Commissioner, by wholesalers, retailers, jobbers, or distributors. Where a wholesaler or retailer is also engaged in the manufacturing or processing of goods, the pooling of the LIFO inventory for the manufacturing or processing operations shall be determined in accordance with the rules of paragraph (b) of this section.

If found appropriate, pooling may not be changed.   (d) *Determination of appropriateness of pools.* Whether the number and the composition of the pools used by the taxpayer is appropriate, as well as the propriety of all computations incidental to the use of such pools, will be determined in connection with the examination of the taxpayer's income tax returns. Adequate records must be maintained to support the base-year unit cost as well as the current-year unit cost for all items priced on the dollar-value LIFO inventory method, regardless of the method authorized by paragraph (e) of this section which is used in computing the LIFO value of the dollar-value pool. The pool or pools selected must be used for the year of adoption and for all subsequent taxable years unless a change is required by the Commissioner in order to clearly reflect income, or unless permission to change is granted by the Commissioner as provided in paragraph (e) of § 1.446–1. However, see paragraph (h) of this section for authorization to change the method of pooling in certain specified cases.

Alternatives to "double-extension" method of computation.   (e) *Methods of computation of the LIFO value of a dollar-value pool*—(1) *Methods authorized.* A taxpayer may ordinarily use only the so-called "double-extension" method for computing the base-year and current-year cost of a dollar-value inventory pool. Where the use of the double-extension method is impractical, because of technological changes, the extensive variety of items, or extreme fluctuations in the variety of the items, in a dollar-value pool, the taxpayer may use an index method for computing all or part of the LIFO value of the pool. An index may be computed by double-extending a representative portion of the inventory in a pool or by the use of other sound and consistent statistical methods. The index used must be appropriate to the inventory pool to which it is to be applied. The appropriateness of the method of computing the index and the accuracy, reliability, and suitability of the use of such index must be demonstrated to the satisfaction of the district director in connection with the examination of the taxpayer's income tax returns. The use of any so-called "link-chain" method will be approved for taxable years beginning after December 31, 1960, only in those cases where the taxpayer can demonstrate to the satisfaction of the district director that the use of either an index method or the double-extension method would be impractical or unsuitable in view of the nature of the pool. A taxpayer using either an index or link-chain method shall attach to his income tax return for the first taxable year beginning after December 31, 1960, for which the index or link-chain method is used, a statement describing the particular link-chain method or the method used in computing the index. The statement shall be in sufficient detail to facilitate the determination as to whether the method used meets the standards set forth in this subparagraph. In addition, a copy of the statement shall be filed with the Commissioner of Internal Revenue, Attention: T:R, Washington 25, D.C. The taxpayer shall submit such other information as may be requested with respect to such index or link-chain method. Adequate records must be maintained by the taxpayer to support the appropriateness, accuracy, and reliability of an index or link-chain method. A taxpayer may request the Commissioner to approve the appropriateness of an index or link-chain method for the first taxable year beginning after December 31, 1960, for which it is used. Such request must be submitted within 90 days after the beginning of the first taxable year beginning after December 31, 1960, in which the taxpayer desires to use the index or link-chain method, or on or before May 1, 1961, whichever is later. A taxpayer entitled to use the retail method of pricing LIFO inventories authorized by paragraph (k) of § 1.472–1 may use retail price indexes prepared by the United States Bureau of Labor Statistics. Any method of computing the LIFO value of a dollar-value pool must be used for the year of adoption and all subsequent taxable years, unless the taxpayer obtains the consent of the Commissioner in accordance with paragraph (e) of § 1.446–1 to use a different method.

Mechanics of double-extension method. (2) *Double-extension method.* (i) Under the double-extension method the quantity of each item in the inventory pool at the close of the taxable year is extended at both base-year unit cost and current-year unit cost. The respective extensions at the two costs are then each totaled. The first total gives the amount of the current inventory in terms of base-year cost and the second total gives the amount of such inventory in terms of current-year cost.

(ii) The total current-year cost of items making up a pool may be determined—

(*a*) By reference to the actual cost of the goods most recently purchased or produced;

(*b*) By reference to the actual cost of the goods purchased or produced during the taxable year in the order of acquisition;

(*c*) By application of an average unit cost equal to the aggregate cost of all of the goods purchased or produced throughout the taxable year divided by the total number of units so purchased or produced; or

(*d*) Pursuant to any other proper method which, in the opinion of the Commissioner, clearly reflects income.

(iii) Under the double-extension method a base-year unit cost must be ascertained for each item entering a pool for the first time subsequent to the beginning of the base year. In such a case, the base-year unit cost of the entering item shall be the current-year cost of that item unless the taxpayer is able to reconstruct or otherwise establish a different cost. If the entering item is a product or raw material not in existence on the base date, its cost may be reconstructed, that is, the taxpayer using reasonable means may determine what the cost of the item would have been had it been in existence in the base year. If the item was in existence on the base date but not stocked by the taxpayer, he may establish, by using available data or records, what the cost of the item would have been to the taxpayer had he stocked the item. If the base-year unit cost of the entering item is either reconstructed or otherwise established to the satisfaction of the Commissioner, such cost may be used as the base-year unit cost in applying the double-extension method. If the taxpayer does not reconstruct or establish to the satisfaction of the Commissioner a base-year unit cost, but does reconstruct or establish to the satisfaction of the Commissioner the cost of the item at some year subsequent to the base year, he may use the earliest cost which he does reconstruct or establish as the base-year unit cost.

(iv) To determine whether there is an increment or liquidation in a pool for a particular taxable year, the end of the year inventory of the pool expressed in terms of base-year cost is compared with the beginning of the year inventory of the pool expressed in terms of base-year cost. When the end of the year inventory of the pool is in excess of the beginning of the year inventory of the pool, an increment occurs in the pool for that year. If there is an increment for the taxable year, the ratio of the total current-year cost of the pool to the total base-year cost of the pool must be computed. This ratio when multiplied by the amount of the increment measured in terms of base-year cost gives the LIFO value of such increment. The LIFO value of each such increment is hereinafter referred to in this section as the "layer of increment" and must be separately accounted for and a record thereof maintained as a separate layer of the pool, and may not be combined with a layer of increment occurring in a different year. On the other hand, when the end of the year inventory of the pool is less than the beginning of the year inventory of the pool, a liquidation occurs in the pool for that year. Such liquidation is to be reflected by reducing the most recent layer of increment by the excess of the beginning of the year inventory over the end of the year inventory of the pool. However, if the amount of the liquidation exceeds the amount of the most recent layer of increment, the preceding layers of increment in reverse chronological order are to be successively reduced by the amount of such excess until all the excess is absorbed. The base-year inventory is to be reduced by liquidation only to the extent that the aggregate of all liquidation exceeds the aggregate of all layers of increment.

Examples of double-extension method.   (v) The following examples illustrate the computation of the LIFO value of inventories under the double-extension method.

Example (1).   (*a*) A taxpayer elects, beginning with the calendar year 1961, to compute his inventories by use of the LIFO inventory method under section 472 and further elects to use the dollar-value method in pricing such inventories as provided in paragraph (a) of this section. He creates Pool No. 1 for items A, B, and C. The composition of the inventory for Pool No. 1 at the base date, January 1, 1961, is as follows:

Items	Units	Unit cost	Total cost
A........................	1,000	$5	$5,000
B........................	2,000	4	8,000
C........................	500	2	1,000
Total base-year cost at Jan. 1, 1961........			14,000

(*b*) The closing inventory of Pool No. 1 at December 31, 1961, contains 3,000 units of A, 1,000 units of B, and 500 units of C. The taxpayer computes the current-year cost of the items making up the pool by reference to the actual cost of goods most recently purchased. The most recent purchases of items A, B, and C are as follows:

Item	Purchase date	Quantity purchased	Unit cost
A..............	Dec. 15, 1961	3,500	$6.00
B..............	Dec. 10, 1961	2,000	5.00
C..............	Nov. 1, 1961	500	2.50

(c) The inventory of Pool No. 1 at December 31, 1961, shown at base-year and current-year cost is as follows:

Item	Quantity	Dec. 31, 1961, inventory at Jan. 1, 1961, base-year cost		Dec. 31, 1961, inventory at current-year cost	
		Unit cost	Amount	Unit cost	Amount
A....................	3,000	$5.00	$15,000	$6.00	$18,000
B....................	1,000	4.00	4,000	5.00	5,000
C....................	500	2.00	1,000	2.50	1,250
Total.............			$20,000		$24,250

(d) If the amount of the December 31, 1961, inventory at base-year cost were equal to, or less than, the base-year cost of $14,000 at January 1, 1961, such amount would be the closing LIFO inventory at December 31, 1961. However, since the base-year cost of the closing LIFO inventory at December 31, 1961, amounts to $20,000, and is in excess of the $14,000 base-year cost of the opening inventory for that year, there is a $6,000 increment in Pool No. 1 during the year. This increment must be valued at current-year cost, i.e., the ratio of 24,250/20,000, or 121.25 per cent. The LIFO value of the inventory at December 31, 1961, is $21,275, computed as follows:

Pool No. 1

	Dec. 31, 1961, inventory at Jan. 1, 1961, base-year cost	Ratio of total current-year cost to total base-year cost	Dec. 31, 1961, inventory at LIFO value
		Per cent	
Jan 1, 1961, base cost............	14,000	100.00	$14,000
Dec. 31, 1961, increment............	6,000	121.25	7,275
Total......................	20,000		21,275

Example (2). (*a*) Assume the taxpayer in example (1) during the year 1962 completely disposes of item C and purchases item D. Assume further that item D is properly includible in Pool No. 1 under the provisions of this section. The closing inventory on December 31, 1962, consists of quantities at current-year unit cost, as follows:

Items	Units	Current-year unit cost Dec. 31, 1962
A............	2,000	$6.50
B............	1,500	6.00
D............	1,000	5.00

(*b*) The taxpayer establishes that the cost of item D, had he acquired it on January 1, 1961, would have been $2.00 per unit. Such cost shall be used as the base-year unit cost for item D, and the LIFO computations at December 31, 1962, are made as follows:

Item	Quantity	Dec. 31, 1962, inventory at Jan. 1, 1961, base-year cost		Dec. 31, 1962, inventory at current-year cost	
		Unit cost	Amount	Unit cost	Amount
A....................	2,000	$5.00	$10,000	$6.50	$13,000
B....................	1,500	4.00	6,000	6.00	9,000
D....................	1,000	2.00	2,000	5.00	5,000
Total.............			18,000		27,000

(*c*) Since the closing inventory at base-year cost, $18,000, is less than the 1962 opening inventory at base-year cost, $20,000, a liquidation of $2,000 has occurred during 1962. This liquidation is to be reflected by reducing the most recent layer of increment. The LIFO value of the inventory at December 31, 1962, is $18,850, and is summarized as follows:

Pool No. 1

	Dec. 31, 1962, inventory at Jan. 1, 1961, base-year cost	Ratio of total current-year cost to total base-year cost	Dec. 31, 1962, inventory at LIFO value
		Per cent	
Jan. 1, 1961, base cost.............	14,000	100.00	$14,000
Dec. 31, 1961, increment............	4,000	121.25	4,850
Total.....................	18,000		18,850

Change from another LIFO procedure to dollar-value method requires advance permission if pools are changed.

(f) *Change to dollar-value method from another method of pricing LIFO inventories—*(1) *Consent required.* Except as provided in § 1.472–3 in the case of a taxpayer electing to use a LIFO inventory method for the first time, or in the case of a taxpayer changing to the dollar-value method and continuing to use the same pools as were used under another LIFO method, a taxpayer using another LIFO method of pricing inventories may not change to the dollar-value method of pricing such inventories unless he first secures the consent of the Commissioner in accordance with paragraph (e) of § 1.446–1.

Mechanics of change to dollar-value method.

(2) *Method of converting inventory.* Where the taxpayer changes from one method of pricing LIFO inventories to the dollar-value method, the ending LIFO inventory for the taxable year immediately preceding the year of change shall be converted to the dollar-value LIFO method. This is done to establish the base-year cost for subsequent calculations. Thus, if the taxpayer was previously valuing LIFO inventories on the specific goods method, these separate values shall be combined into appropriate pools. For this purpose, the base year for the pool shall be the earliest taxable year for which the LIFO inventory method had been adopted for any item in that pool. No change will be made in the overall LIFO value of the opening inventory for the year of change as a result of the conversion, and that inventory will merely be restated in the manner used under the dollar-value method. All layers of increment for such inventory must be retained, except that all layers of increment which occurred in the same taxable year must be combined. The following examples illustrate the provisions of this subparagraph:

Example (1). (i) Assume that the taxpayer has used another LIFO method for finished goods since 1954 and has complied with all the requirements prerequisite for a change to the dollar-value method. Items A, B, and C, which have previously been inventoried under the specific goods LIFO method, may properly be included in a single dollar-value LIFO pool. The LIFO inventory value of items A, B, and C at December 31, 1960, is $12,200 computed as follows:

Year	Base quantity and yearly increments	Unit cost	Dec. 31, 1960, inventory at LIFO value
Item A			
1954 (base year)........................	100	$1	$100
1955..................................	200	2	400
1956..................................	100	4	400
1960..................................	100	6	600
Total..............................	500		1,500
Item B			
1954 (base year)........................	300	6	1,800
1955..................................	100	8	800
1960..................................	50	10	500
Total..............................	450		3,100
Item C			
1954 (base year)........................	1,000	4	4,000
1955..................................	200	6	1,200
1956..................................	300	8	2,400
Total..............................	1,500		7,600
LIFO value of items A, B, and C at Dec. 31, 1960......................			12,200

There were no increments in the years 1957, 1958, or 1959.

(ii) The computation of the ratio of the total current-year cost to the total base-year cost for the base year and each layer of increment in Pool No. 1 is shown as follows:

Item	1954 base-year unit cost	Year 1954	Increments		
			1955	1956	1960
A					
Base-year cost............	$1.00	$100	$200	$100	$100
LIFO value...............		100	400	400	600
B					
Base-year cost............	6.00	1,800	600	—	300
LIFO value...............		1,800	800	—	500
C					
Base-year cost............	4.00	4,000	800	1,200	—
LIFO value...............		4,000	1,200	2,400	—
Total—base-year cost....		5,900	1,600	1,300	400
Total—LIFO value.......		5,900	2,400	2,800	1,100
Ratio of total current-year cost to total base-year cost (per cent).........		100.00	150.00	215.38	275.00

(iii) On the basis of the foregoing computations, the LIFO inventory of Pool No. 1, at December 31, 1960, is restated as follows:

	Dec. 31, 1960, inventory at base-year cost	Ratio of total current-year cost to total base-year cost	Dec. 31, 1960, inventory at LIFO value
		Per cent	
1954 base cost....................	5,900	100.00	$5,900
1955 increment....................	1,600	150.00	2,400
1956 increment....................	1,300	215.38	2,800
1960 increment....................	400	275.00	1,100
Total.......................	9,200		12,200

Example (2). Assume the same facts as in example (1) and assume further that the base-year cost of Pool No. 1 at December 31, 1961, is $8,350. Since the closing inventory for the taxable year 1961 at base-year cost is less than the opening inventory for that year at base-year cost, a liquidation has occurred during 1961. This liquidation absorbs all of the 1960 layer of increment and part of the 1956 layer of increment. The December 31, 1961, inventory is $10,131, computed as follows:

	Dec. 31, 1961, inventory at base-year cost	Ratio of total current-year cost to total base-year cost	Dec. 31, 1961 inventory at LIFO value
		Per cent	
1954 base cost....................	5,900	100.00	$5,900
1955 increment....................	1,600	150.00	2,400
1956 increment....................	850	215.38	1,831
Total.......................	8,350		10,131

Pooling treated as a method of accounting. (g) *Transitional rules*—(1) *Change in method of pooling.* Any method of pooling authorized by this section and used by the taxpayer in computing his LIFO inventories under the dollar-value method shall be treated as a method of accounting. Any method of pooling which is authorized by this section shall be used for the year of adoption and for all subsequent taxable years unless a change is required by the Commissioner in order to clearly reflect income, or unless permission to change is granted by the Commissioner as provided in paragraph (e) of § 1.446–1. Where the taxpayer changes from one method of pooling to another method of pooling permitted by this section, the ending LIFO inventory for the taxable year preceding the year of change shall be restated under the new method of pooling.

Changing pools will not change previously established costs. (2) *Manner of combining or separating dollar-value pools.* (i) A taxpayer who has been using the dollar-value LIFO method and who is permitted or required to change his method of pooling, shall combine or separate the LIFO value of his inventory for the base year and each yearly layer of increment in order to conform to the new pool or pools. Each yearly layer of increment in the new pool or pools must be separately accounted for and a record thereof maintained, and any liquidation occurring in the new pool or pools subsequent to the formation thereof shall be treated in the same manner as if the new pool or pools had existed from the date the taxpayer first adopted the LIFO inventory method. The combination or separation of the LIFO value of his inventory for the base year and each yearly layer of increment shall be made in accordance with the appropriate method set forth in this subparagraph, unless the use of a different method is approved by the Commissioner.

Mechanics of separating pools. (ii) Where the taxpayer is permitted or required to separate a pool into more than one pool, the separation shall be made in the following manner: First, each item in the former pool shall be placed in an appropriate new pool. Every item in each new pool is then extended at its base-year unit cost and the extensions are totaled. Each total is the amount of inventory for each new pool expressed in terms of base-year cost. Then a ratio of the total base-year cost of each new pool to the base-year cost of the former pool is computed. The resulting ratio is applied to the amount of inventory for the base year and each yearly layer of increment of the former pool to obtain an allocation to each new pool of the base-year inventory of the former pool and subsequent layers of increment thereof. The foregoing may be illustrated by the following example of a change for the taxable year 1961:

Example. (a) Assume that items A, B, C, and D are all grouped together in one pool prior to December 31, 1960. The LIFO inventory value at December 31, 1960, is computed as follows:

	Pool ABCD		
	Dec. 31, 1960, inventory at Jan. 1, 1956, base-year cost	Ratio of total current-year cost to total base-year cost	Dec. 31, 1960, inventory at LIFO value
		Per cent	
Jan. 1, 1956, base cost............	10,000	100	$10,000
Dec. 31, 1956, increment...........	1,000	110	1,100
Dec. 31, 1958, increment...........	5,000	120	6,000
Dec. 31, 1960, increment...........	4,000	125	5,000
Total......................	20,000		22,100

(*b*) The extension of the quantity of items A, B, C, and D at respective base-year unit costs is as follows:

Item	Quantity	Base-year unit cost	Amount
A.................	2,000	$2	$4,000
B................	1,000	3	3,000
C.................	1,000	5	5,000
D................	4,000	2	8,000
Total..........			20,000

(*c*) Under the provisions of this section the taxpayer separates former Pool ABCD into two pools, Pool AB and Pool CD. The computation of the ratio of total base-year cost for each of the new pools to the base-year cost of the former pool is as follows:

Item	Total base-year cost	Ratio
Pool AB:		
A.....................	$4,000	
B.....................	3,000	
	7,000	7,000/20,000
Pool CD:		
C.....................	5,000	
D....................	8,000	
	13,000	13,000/20,000
Total for pool ABCD....	20,000	

(*d*) The ratio of the base-year cost of new Pools AB and CD to the base-year cost of former Pool ABCD is 7,000/20,000 and 13,000/20,000, respectively. The allocation of the January 1, 1956 base cost and subsequent yearly layers of increment of former Pool ABCD to new Pools AB and CD is as follows:

	Base-year cost to be allocated	Pool	
		AB	CD
Jan. 1, 1956, base cost............	$10,000	$3,500	$6,500
Dec. 31, 1956, increment..........	1,000	350	650
Dec. 31, 1958, increment..........	5,000	1,750	3,250
Dec. 31, 1960, increment..........	4,000	1,400	2,600
Total.....................	20,000	7,000	13,000

(*e*) The LIFO value of new Pools AB and CD at December 31, 1960, as allocated, is as follows:

	Dec. 31, 1960, inventory at Jan. 1, 1956, base-year cost	Ratio of total current-year cost to total base-year cost	Dec. 31, 1960, inventory at LIFO value
Pool AB			
		Per cent	
Jan. 1, 1956, base cost............	3,500	100	$3,500
Dec. 31, 1956, increment...........	350	110	385
Dec. 31, 1958, increment...........	1,750	120	2,100
Dec. 31, 1960, increment...........	1,400	125	1,750
Total.....................	7,000		7,735
Pool CD			
Jan. 1, 1956, base cost............	6,500	100	6,500
Dec. 31, 1956, increment...........	650	110	715
Dec. 31, 1958, increment...........	3,250	120	3,900
Dec. 31, 1960, increment...........	2,600	125	3,250
Total.....................	13,000		14,365

Mechanics of combining pools.   (iii) Where the taxpayer is permitted or required to combine two or more pools having the same base year, they shall be combined into one pool in the following manner: The LIFO value of the base-year inventory of each of the former pools is combined to obtain a LIFO value of the base-year inventory for the new pool. Then, any layers of increment in the various pools which occurred in the same taxable year are combined into one total layer of increment for that taxable year. However, layers of increment which occurred in different taxable years may not be combined. In combining the layers of increment a new ratio of current-year cost to base-year cost is computed for each of the combined layers of increment. The foregoing may be illustrated by the following example:

Example. (*a*) Assume the taxpayer has two pools at December 31, 1960. Under the provisions of this section the taxpayer combines these pools into a single pool as of January 1, 1961. The LIFO inventory value of each pool at December 31, 1960, is shown as follows:

	Dec. 31, 1960, inventory at Jan. 1, 1957, base-year cost	Ratio of total current-year cost to total base-year cost	Dec. 31, 1960, inventory at LIFO value
Pool No. 1			
		Per cent	
Jan. 1, 1957, base cost.............	10,000	100	$10,000
Dec. 31, 1957, increment............	2,000	110	2,200
Dec. 31, 1960, increment...........	1,000	120	1,200
Total......................	13,000		13,400

	Dec. 31, 1960, inventory at Jan. 1, 1957, base-year cost	Ratio of total current-year cost to total base-year cost	Dec. 31, 1960, inventory at LIFO value
Pool No. 2			
Jan. 1, 1957, base cost.............	5,000	100	5,000
Dec. 31, 1960, increment...........	3,000	140	4,200
Total......................	8,000		9,200

(*b*) The computation of the ratio of the total current-year cost to the total base-year cost for the base year and each yearly layer of increment in the new pool is as follows:

| | | Increments | |
Pool	Base year 1957	Dec. 31, 1957	Dec. 31, 1960
No. 1:			
Base-year cost.........................	$10,000	$2,000	$1,000
LIFO value.............................	10,000	2,200	1,200
No. 2:			
Base-year cost.........................	5,000	—	3,000
LIFO value.............................	5,000	—	4,200
Total, base-year cost....................	15,000	2,000	4,000
Total, LIFO value.......................	15,000	2,200	5,400
Ratio of total current-year cost to total base-year cost (per cent)	100	110	135

(c) On the basis of the foregoing computations, the LIFO inventory of the new pool at December 31, 1960, is restated as follows:

	Dec. 31, 1960, inventory at Jan. 1, 1957, base-year cost	Ratio of total current-year cost to total base-year cost	Dec. 31, 1960, inventory at LIFO value
		Per cent	
Jan. 1, 1957, base cost.............	15,000	100	$15,000
Dec. 31, 1957, increment............	2,000	110	2,200
Dec. 31, 1960, increment............	4,000	135	5,400
Total......................	21,000		22,600

(iv) In combining pools having different base years, the principles set forth in subdivision (iii) of this subparagraph are to be applied, except that all base years subsequent to the earliest base year shall be treated as increments, and the base-year costs for all pools having a base year subsequent to the earliest base year of any pool shall be redetermined in terms of the base cost for the earliest base year. The foregoing may be illustrated by the following example:

Example. (*a*) Assume that the taxpayer has two pools at December 31, 1960. Under the provisions of this section the taxpayer combines these pools into a single pool as of January 1, 1961. The LIFO inventory value of each pool at December 31, 1960, is shown as follows:

	Dec. 31, 1960, inventory at Jan. 1, 1956, base-year cost	Ratio of total current-year cost to total base-year cost	Dec. 31, 1960, inventory at LIFO value
Pool No. 1			
		Per cent	
Jan. 1, 1956, base cost............	7,000	100	$7,000
Dec. 31, 1956, increment...........	1,000	105	1,050
Dec. 31, 1957, increment...........	500	110	550
Dec. 31, 1958, increment...........	500	110	550
Dec. 31, 1960, increment...........	1,000	120	1,200
Total......................	10,000		10,350

	Dec. 31, 1960, inventory at Jan. 1, 1958, base-year cost		
Pool No. 2			
Jan. 1, 1958, base cost............	3,500	100	$3,500
Dec. 31, 1958, increment...........	1,000	110	1,100
Dec. 31, 1959, increment...........	500	115	575
Total......................	5,000		5,175

(*b*) The next step is to redetermine the 1958 base-year cost for Pool No. 2 in terms of 1956 base-year cost. January 1, 1956, base-year unit cost must be reconstructed or established in accordance with paragraph (e) (2) of this section for each item in Pool No. 2. Such costs are assumed to be $9.00 for item A, $20.00 for item B, and $1.80 for item C. A ratio of the 1958 total base-year cost to the 1956 total base-year cost for Pool No. 2 is computed as follows:

Item	Quantity	Jan. 1, 1956, base-year unit cost	Jan. 1, 1956, base-year cost
A....................	250	$9.00	$2,250
B....................	75	20.00	1,500
C....................	500	1.80	900
Total............			4,650

Item	Quantity	Jan. 1, 1958, base-year unit cost	Jan. 1, 1958, base-year cost
A...................	250	$10.00	$2,500
B...................	75	20.00	1,500
C...................	500	2.00	1,000
Total.............			5,000

(c) The ratio of the 1956 total base-year cost to the 1958 total base-year cost for Pool No. 2 is 4,650/5,000 or 93 per cent. The January 1, 1958, base cost and each yearly layer of increment at 1958 base-year cost is multiplied by this ratio. Such compution is as follows:

	Dec. 31, 1960, inventory at Jan. 1, 1958, base-year cost	Ratio	Dec. 31, 1960, inventory restated at Jan. 1, 1956, base-year cost
		Percent	
Jan. 1, 1958, base cost..................	3,500	93	$3,255
Dec. 31, 1958, increment.................	1,000	93	930
Dec. 31, 1959, increment.................	500	93	465
Total.............................			4,650

(d) The computation of the ratio of the total current-year cost to the total base-year cost for the base year(1956) and each yearly layer of increment in the new pool is as follows:

Pool	Base year 1956	Increments				
		Dec. 31, 1956	Dec. 31, 1957	Dec. 31, 1958	Dec. 31, 1959	Dec. 31, 1960
No. 1:						
Base-year cost........	$7,000	$1,000	$500	$500	—	$1,000
LIFO value...........	7,000	1,050	550	550	—	1,200
No. 2:						
Base-year cost as restated...........	—	—	3,255	930	$465	—
LIFO value...........	—	—	3,500	1,100	575	—
Total, base-year cost...	7,000	1,000	3,755	1,430	465	1,000
Total, LIFO value......	7,000	1,050	4,050	1,650	575	1,200
Ratio of total current-year cost to total base-year cost (percent).........	100.00	105.00	107.86	115.38	123.66	120.00

(e) On the basis of the foregoing computation, the LIFO inventory of the new pool at December 31, 1960, is restated as follows:

	Dec. 31, 1960, inventory at Jan. 1, 1956, base-year cost	Ratio of total current-year cost to total base-year cost	Dec. 31, 1960, inventory at LIFO value
		Percent	
Jan. 1, 1956, base cost.............	7,000	100.00	$7,000
Dec. 31, 1956, increment............	1,000	105.00	1,050
Dec. 31, 1957, increment............	3,755	107.86	4,050
Dec. 31, 1958, increment............	1,430	115.38	1,650
Dec. 31, 1959, increment............	465	123.66	575
Dec. 31, 1960, increment............	1,000	120.00	1,200
Total.......................	14,650		15,525

An authorized dollar-value computation method must be used for years beginning after Dec. 31, 1960.

(3) *Change in methods of computation of the LIFO value of a dollar-value pool.* For the first taxable year beginning after December 31, 1960, the taxpayer must use a method authorized by paragraph (e) (1) of this section in computing the base-year cost and current-year cost of a dollar-value inventory pool for the end of such year. If the taxpayer had previously used any methods other than one authorized by paragraph (e) (1) of this section, he shall not be required to recompute his LIFO inventories for taxable years beginning on or before December 31, 1960, under a method authorized by such paragraph. The base cost and layers of increment previously computed by such other method shall be retained and treated as if such base cost and layers of increment had been computed under a method authorized by paragraph (e) (1) of this section. The taxpayer shall use the year of change as the base year in applying the double-extension method or other method approved by the Commissioner, instead of the earliest year for which he adopted the LIFO method for any items in the pool.

Right to change pooling in first year ending after April 15, 1961.

(h) *Change without consent in method of pooling—* (1) *Authorization.* Notwithstanding the provisions of paragraph (g) of this section, a taxpayer, for his first taxable year ending after April 15, 1961, may change from one method of pooling authorized by this section to any other method of pooling authorized by this section provided the requirements of subparagraph (2) of this paragraph are met. Also, for such year, if a taxpayer is currently using only a method of pooling authorized by this section, or a method of pooling which would be authorized by this section if additional items were included in the pool, and could change to the natural business unit method, except for the fact he has not inventoried all items entering into the inventory investment for such natural business unit on the LIFO method, he may change to the natural business unit method if he elects under the provisions of § 1.472–3 to extend the LIFO election to all items entering into the entire inventory investment for such natural business unit, provided the requirements of subparagraph (2) of this paragraph are met.   The method of pooling adopted shall be used for the year of change and for all subsequent taxable years unless a change is required by the Commissioner in order to clearly reflect income, or unless permission to change is granted by the Commissioner as provided in paragraph (e) of § 1.446–1.

(2) *Requirements.*   A statement shall be attached to the income tax return for the year of change referred to in subparagraph (1) of this paragraph setting forth, in summary form, the following information:

(i) A description of the new pool or pools,

(ii) The basis for selection of the new pool or pools,

(iii) A schedule showing the computation of the LIFO value of the former pool or pools, and,

(iv) A schedule showing the transition from the former pool or pools to the new pool or pools.

In addition, a copy of the statement shall be filed with the Commissioner of Internal Revenue, Attention: T: R, Washington 25, D.C.   The taxpayer shall submit such other information with respect to the change in method of pooling as may be requested.

Appendix D

"Certification of Income Statements" Issued by the Securities and Exchange Commission

(Accounting Series Release No. 90)

It has come to the attention of the Commission that wide variations have developed in certificates of independent accountants contained in registration statements filed under the Securities Act of 1933 with respect to representations concerning the verification of inventories of prior years in first audits. This development has been noted particularly in situations involving the offering of securities of closely held corporations which have failed to maintain and preserve accounting records and data necessary to permit verification of financial statements. In some cases a question arises whether the certifying accountant intended to limit his opinion as to the fairness of presentation of the income statements.

The following is the pertinent part of an example of this type of certificate:

. . . Except as noted in the succeeding paragraph, our examination was made in accordance with generally accepted auditing standards and accordingly included such tests of the accounting records and such other auditing procedures as we considered necessary in the circumstances.

Since this was our initial examination of the Financial Statements of the Company, September 30, 1961, was the only date at which we observed the taking of physical inventories. However, based on other tests we applied, including tests of gross profits and review of physical inventory records, we have no reason to believe that inventories at September 30, 1958, 1959, and 1960, were not also fairly stated.

In our opinion, with the foregoing comment regarding inventories. . . .

In view of the large number of companies which are now offering securities to the public for the first time and which have this problem, the Commission deems it advisable to remind the financial community that the Securities Act requires that registration statements contain a certificate of an independent accountant based on an audit conducted in accordance with generally accepted auditing standards and meeting the reporting requirements of the Commission.

After testimony was taken from twelve expert witnesses called by the Commission in the investigation of McKesson & Robbins, Inc.,[1] the membership of the American Institute of Accountants at the 1939 annual meeting approved the extension of auditing procedures to require observation of inventory taking.

In January 1942 the Commission, to avoid any possible interruption in the production and delivery of war material, announced a liberalized policy with respect to physical inventory verification by independent public accountants. (Accounting Series Release No. 30.) After specifying information to be furnished in the certificate the release said:

In many cases, it is probable that by means of their alternative and extended procedures the independent public accountants will have satisfied themselves as to the substantial fairness of the amounts at which inventories are stated, and in such case a positive statement to that effect should be made. In some cases it may be that, while the scope of procedures followed will not be such as to have so satisfied the accountants, they will be able to take the position that on the basis of the work done they have no reason to believe that the inventories reflected in the statements are unfairly stated.

Of course, if the scope of the work done or the results obtained from the procedures followed or the data on which to base an opinion are so unsatisfactory to the accountants as to preclude any expression of opinion, or to require an adverse opinion, that situation must be disclosed not only by an exception running to the scope of the audit, but also by means of an exception in the opinion paragraph as to the fairness of the presentation made by the financial statements. . . .

In the Drayer-Hanson matter (Accounting Series Release No. 64, March 15, 1948) the accountants' opinion included a now-familiar sentence: "On the basis of the examinations and tests made by us,

---

[1] See Report on Investigation and Testimony of Expert Witnesses, Government Printing Office, 1940 and 1939.

we have no reason to believe that the inventories as set forth in the accompanying statements are unfairly stated." The Commission found in this case that in addition to the work done on the inventories, other effective procedures could have been applied and hence that the representation cited was entirely without justification.

The first-time audit situation was considered in Accounting Series Release No. 62 which dealt with the circumstances under which independent public accountants may properly express an opinion with respect to summaries of earnings. Concluding that the accountant can express an opinion on completion of a first audit, the release said "It is recognized that some auditing procedures commonly applicable in the examination of financial statements for the latest year for which a certified profit and loss statement is filed, such as the independent confirmation of accounts receivable or the observation of inventory-taking, are either impracticable or impossible to perform with respect to the financial statements of the earlier years and, hence, would not be considered applicable in the circumstances."

This statement in the Commission's release is consistent with interpretations of "extensions of auditing procedure" approved by the membership of the Institute at the 1939 annual meeting. Such extension of auditing procedures to require observation of inventories and confirmation of receivables applies where either of these assets represents a significant proportion of the current assets or of the total assets of a concern. As to inventories, Codification of Statements on Auditing Procedure says "The procedures, it will be noted, must be *both* practicable and reasonable. In the province of auditing, *practicable* means 'capable of being done with the available means' or ' . . .with reason or prudence'; *reasonable* means 'sensible in the light of the surrounding circumstances.' For example, the observation of physical inventories at the beginning of the period or year under examination would seldom, if ever, be practicable or reasonable in initial or 'first' audits. However, the independent accountant must satisfy himself as to such inventories by appropriate methods."

It seems clear from the discussion above that if an accountant reports that his examination was made in accordance with generally accepted auditing standards, and accordingly included such tests of the accounting records and such other auditing procedures as he considered necessary in the circumstances, an exception as to failure to observe beginning inventories is contradictory and should be omitted. A middle paragraph explaining that the certificate covers a first audit is informative and in some cases is essential to describe the alternative procedures applied. A negative type conclusion to this paragraph appears to be a carry-over from wartime usage and is not acceptable. Lost and inadequate records may give rise to questions as to the reliability of the results shown in the financial statements and may make it impracticable to apply alternative audit procedures. Alternative procedures must be adequate to support an unqualified opinion as to the fairness of presentation of the income statements by years.

If, as a result of the examination and the conclusions reached, the accountant is not in a position to express an affirmative opinion as to the fairness of the presentation of earnings year by year, the registration statement is defective because the certificate does not meet the requirements of Rule 2-02 of Regulation S-X. If the accountant is not satisfied with the results of his examination he should not issue an affirmative opinion. If he is satisfied, any reference from the opinion paragraph to an explanatory paragraph devoted solely to the scope of the audit is inconsistent and unnecessary. Accordingly, phrases such as "with the foregoing explanation as to inventories" raise questions as to whether the certifying accountant intended to limit his opinion as to the fairness of the presentation of the results shown and should be omitted.

A "subject to" or "expect for" opinion paragraph in which these phrases refer to the scope of the audit, indicating that the accountant has not been able to satisfy himself on some significant element in the financial statements, is not acceptable in certificates filed with the Commission in connection with the public offering of securities. The "subject to" qualification is appropriate when the reference is to a middle paragraph or to footnotes explaining the status of matters which cannot be resolved at statement date.

Appendix E

Summary of Practices Relative to Use of LIFO in Determining Income for State Tax Purposes

A review of the practices in the District of Columbia and in the states imposing corporate taxes on or measured by income, discloses none that purports not to allow the use of LIFO in income determinations under present policy. The courts in the State of New Jersey have held that the Director of the Division of Taxation acted within the discretionary powers accorded by the statute in requiring a taxpayer to price LIFO inventories on a FIFO basis for purposes of determining the portion of the franchise tax measured by *net worth*. The decision does not affect the use of LIFO in determining the portion of the tax measured by *income*. The questions involved in corporate taxes of this type are similar to personal property tax determinations by the various local governments.

The practices followed where income is the base for the tax vary in many respects. Some states have requirements covering the adoption of LIFO which are similar to the federal requirements. Others require the filing of an application for permission to use LIFO in advance of the end of the year. In some instances

	Federal use a pre-requisite	Application for permission to use	
		Should be filed	Time prescribed for filing
Alabama............	x	x	
Alaska..............	x		
Arizona.............	x	x	
Arkansas...........	x	x	At least 60 days prior to end of year
California...........		x	With return
Colorado...........	x		
Connecticut..........	x		
Delaware...........	x		
District of Columbia....	x	x	
Georgia.............	x		
Hawaii..............	x	x	Within 90 days from beginning of year
Idaho...............	x		
Illinois..............	x		
Indiana.............	x		
Iowa................	x		
Kansas..............	x		
Kentucky............	x		
Louisiana...........		x	
Maine...............	x		
Maryland...........	x		
Massachusetts........	x		
Michigan............	x		
Minnesota...........	x	x	Within 90 days from beginning of year
Mississippi..........			
Missouri............	x		
Montana............	x		
Nebraska...........	x		
New Jersey..........	x		
New Mexico..........	x	x	
New York............	x		
North Carolina.......	x		
North Dakota........	x		
Oklahoma...........	x	x	Within 90 days from beginning of year
Oregon.............	x	x	Within 90 days from beginning of year
Pennsylvania.........	x		
Rhode Island.........	x		
South Carolina.......	x		
Tennessee...........			
Utah...............	x	x	With return
Vermont............	x		
Virginia............	x		
West Virginia........	x	x	Within 90 days from beginning of year
Wisconsin...........	x	x	With return

it is only necessary to indicate in the state return that the federal procedure has been adopted.

In the majority of cases costing inventories on a LIFO basis for federal purposes is a prerequisite to reporting on that basis in the state return. In others, if the LIFO basis is used for federal purposes, it is the mandatory basis in the state returns. In a few states LIFO could be allowed even though not used in reporting income to the federal government.

The principal factors in state tax practice are summarized in tabular form on page 429 and are discussed generally in the following paragraphs. Particularly for the states whose laws, regulations, or rulings do not mention the LIFO method but which acquiesce in its use under a general provision regarding inventories, current inquiries should be made as to local practice when LIFO is being adopted. Practices not formalized in published rulings are always subject to change.

ALABAMA statute provides that inventory is to be taken as prescribed by the Department of Revenue and conforming as far as may be to the methods prescribed by the United States Commissioner of Internal Revenue under the acts of Congress and any other additional regulations pursuant thereto. In this connection Alabama permits the use of LIFO where used for federal purposes.

ALASKA has adopted, by reference, the accounting and inventory provisions of the Internal Revenue Code; therefore, use of LIFO is permitted in the same manner as used for federal purposes.

ARIZONA has a LIFO section similar to the Internal Revenue Code and requires a statement, similar to that filed with the federal return, to be filed with the state return for the first LIFO year.

ARKANSAS statute makes no reference to LIFO but has an inventory provision broad enough to encompass its use. Application for permission to change inventory basis must be filed at least sixty days prior to end of first LIFO year.

CALIFORINA has LIFO provisions similar to the Internal Revenue Code and the federal regulations. A statement comparable to Form 970 must be filed with the return for the first LIFO year.

COLORADO has adopted legislation substantially conforming its income tax act to the Internal Revenue Code. There are no specific modifications of federal provisions regarding inventories;

therefore, the use of LIFO is permitted in the same manner as used for federal purposes.

CONNECTICUT requires the filing of the state return on the same basis as the federal return. Accordingly where LIFO has been elected for federal purposes it must be used in the Connecticut return.

DELAWARE statute provides for the computation of tax on the basis of federal net income with certain enumerated adjustments which have no effect on inventories; therefore, if LIFO is used for federal purposes it must be used for state purposes.

DISTRICT OF COLUMBIA statute provides for the taking of inventories upon such basis as the tax authorities "may prescribe as conforming to the best accounting practice in the trade or business and as most clearly reflecting income." Taxpayers are permitted to use LIFO when it is used in the federal return; however, an inventory method, once adopted, is controlling until permission to change has been obtained from the Finance Officer.

GEORGIA requires that taxable income be the same as federal taxable income (with few exceptions) for years beginning on or after January 1, 1969. Thus, where LIFO is used for federal purposes, it must be used in Georgia returns.

HAWAII has adopted, by reference, the inventory provisions of the Internal Revenue Code, but it appears that permission for a change in accounting method should be obtained in order to adopt LIFO. An application for permission would be filed within ninety days from the beginning of the first LIFO year; however, a taxpayer following the required federal procedure in electing to adopt the last-in, first-out method of reporting inventories by filing Form 970 with the income tax return on or before the due date of the return, may make a similar election for purposes of the Hawaii return.

IDAHO permits the use of LIFO where used for federal purposes. Taxable income computed under federal laws is the basic starting point for determining Idaho taxable income.

ILLINOIS statute provides that taxable income for state tax purposes is federal taxable income with certain adjustments which do not affect inventories. If LIFO is used for federal purposes, its use is required for Illinois purposes.

INDIANA statute provides taxable income for state tax purposes is federal taxable income with certain adjustments which do not affect inventories. If LIFO is used for federal purposes, its use would apparently be required for Indiana purposes.

IOWA permits the use of LIFO provided it has been allowed for federal income tax purposes. A copy of the federal election should be filed with the State Tax Commission.

KANSAS has a statutory inventory section and regulations broad enough in scope to permit the use of LIFO. Prior to 1968, where a taxpayer changed to LIFO from another method, permission was required from the Department of Revenue. After 1967, tax is based on federal taxable income with state modifications, both determined under the provisions of the federal Code. Hence, if a taxpayer uses the LIFO inventory method for federal income tax purposes, it will be necessary to also use the same method for Kansas income tax purposes.

KENTUCKY has a policy of permitting any method of valuing inventories provided such method is permitted by the federal authorities.

LOUISIANNA has a policy of permitting LIFO upon the filing of an application to make a change to use such method. The State prefers to receive a copy of whatever application is filed with the Internal Revenue Service for federal income tax purposes at the same time that the federal application is made, together with a statement from the taxpayer that he desires to use LIFO in determining his Louisiana net income.

MAINE statute provides that taxable income for state tax purposes is federal taxable income with certain adjustments which do not affect inventories. If LIFO is used for federal purposes, its use is required for Maine purposes.

MARYLAND requires that inventories be determined consistent with the method adopted in the federal return; therefore, the use of LIFO is mandatory if used for federal purposes, and no permission is required for its adoption.

MASSACHUSETTS, in computing net income for state purposes, uses as a base gross income from all sources minus deductions permitted under the federal law applicable to the taxable year. While the statute does not specifically provide that the gross income for state purposes shall be determined by using the same inventory method as is used for federal purposes, the State Tax Commission has required the use of the federal method of valuing inventories as an administrative practice. Accordingly, the use of LIFO is required for state purposes once it has been elected for federal purposes.

MICHIGAN statute provides that taxable income for state tax purposes is federal taxable income with certain adjustments which do not affect inventories. If LIFO is used for federal purposes, its use is required for Michigan purposes.

MINNESOTA has an inventory regulation which provides for acceptance of any method consistent with good accounting practice and used in preparing the taxpayer's financial reports. Adoption of LIFO is treated as a change in accounting method for which permission must be obtained from the State Tax Commissioner. An application for permission must be filed within ninety days from the beginning of the year in which the change to LIFO occurs.

MISSISSIPPI statute states net income shall be computed in accordance with the method of accounting regularly employed in keeping the books, with adjustments made, if necessary, to conform to the provisions of the act. With respect to inventories the statute provides they shall be upon such basis as the Commissioner may prescribe in order to conform as nearly as may be to the best accounting practice and in order to clearly reflect income. General acceptance implies LIFO meets the accounting-practice and clear-reflection-of-income tests; consequently, the only requirement appears to be that the amounts shown on the state tax return be those on the books of account, that is, those used in preparing financial statements published for shareholders, and others.

MISSOURI has no formal provisions relating to inventories, and the only accounting provision pertains to the use of the over-all cash or accrual method. Inasmuch as the return forms do not require disclosure of the inventory method used in computing income and the law has a provision with respect to the adoption of the federal rules for the assessment and collection of taxes, it appears that Missouri does not have any policy against the use of LIFO.

MONTANA permits the use of LIFO provided its use has been

approved by federal authorities and the method is used for federal purposes.

NEBRASKA statute provides that taxable income for state tax purposes is federal taxable income with certain adjustments which do not affect inventories. If LIFO is used for federal purposes, its use is required for Nebraska purposes.

NEW JERSEY statute provides "entire net income shall be deemed prima facie to be equal to the federal taxable income"; therefore, LIFO must be used in a state return where it is used for federal purposes.

NEW MEXICO has adopted federal taxable income as a base for computing its tax. The statute provides for the taking of inventories on the same basis as prescribed by the Internal Revenue Code and regulations. An election similar to that required by the federal regulations should be filed with the state.

NEW YORK statutes provide net income for state purposes is presumably federal net income with certain adjustments which do not affect inventories; accordingly, if LIFO is elected for federal purposes, its use is mandatory in New York State. No application for permission to use such method need be made. The same rule applies for the New York City general corporation tax.

NORTH CAROLINA has announced a policy of making the use of LIFO mandatory when used for federal purposes.

NORTH DAKOTA requires the use of LIFO when such method is used for federal purposes.

OKLAHOMA has inventory provisions broad enough to encompass the use of LIFO. Its adoption constitutes a change of accounting method for which an application for permission should be filed with the Tax Commission within ninety days from the beginning of the first LIFO year.

OREGON authorities have issued rulings indicating that the use of LIFO is permissible; however, it appears that a change to LIFO is treated as a change of accounting method for which permission must be obtained. Application for permission to change to LIFO must be filed within ninety days after the beginning of the year.

PENNSYLVANIA defines net income as that reported to the federal government. Election of LIFO for federal purposes makes its use mandatory for state purposes.

RHODE ISLAND provides that the net income base for state purposes is the same as net income for federal purposes. The net income schedule in the state's return is a copy of the federal; accordingly, where LIFO is elected in the federal return its use follows automatically.

SOUTH CAROLINA has announced a policy of making the use of LIFO mandatory when used for federal purposes.

TENNESSEE requires only that income be computed in accordance with generally accepted accounting procedures. If LIFO is not being used for federal purposes, however, its use for state purposes may be questioned. The state generally follows the provisions of the Internal Revenue Code and has allowed the use of LIFO pursuant to this policy.

UTAH permits a change to LIFO under the same conditions as required by the federal authorities. Use in the federal return is a prerequisite for use in the state return, and a LIFO election should be included in the return.

VERMONT defines net income as net income, with certain adjustments, under the Internal Revenue Code in effect on June 1, 1947. Election of the LIFO method for federal purposes, therefore, determines its use for state purposes. The LIFO provisions of the current Code correspond to those of 1947.

VIRGINIA generally follows the federal regulations with respect to inventories and permits the use of LIFO if it is also used for federal purposes. The adopted method is controlling until permission to change is obtained from the Department of Taxation.

WEST VIRGINIA statute provides that taxable income for state tax purposes is federal taxable income with certain adjustments which do not affect inventories. If LIFO is used for federal purposes, its use is required for West Virginia purposes.

WISCONSIN has authorized the use of LIFO if used for federal purposes. An application to use LIFO should be filed with the Wisconsin Department of Taxation in substantially the same form as required by the federal tax authorities, and a copy of the application should be filed with the return for the first LIFO year. Under the Wisconsin rule, however, the opening inventory of the first LIFO year does not have to be adjusted upward from market to cost.

Index

437

RAYMOND A. HOFFMAN, Partner, Price Waterhouse & Co., is a C.P.A. of Illinois and several other states, and has had extensive practical experience with the subject of inventories. This has led to his frequent appearance as a speaker before leading professional groups and to his contribution of many articles to accounting, tax, and business periodicals. A graduate of the University of Illinois and the De Paul University College of Law, he is the author of *LIFO: A Review of Its Application in Valuing Inventories*, published by Price Waterhouse & Co.

HENRY GUNDERS, Partner, Price Waterhouse & Co., is a C.P.A. of New York and several other states. Mr. Gunders received his academic degrees at Boston University and the New York University Graduate School of Business Administration, and has for many years had direct experience in dealing with systems, procedures, and inventory controls in many industries. His writings have appeared in various professional journals and books.